Making Monitoring and Evaluation Systems Work

Making Monitoring and Evaluation Systems Work

A Capacity Development Toolkit

Marelize Görgens and Jody Zall Kusek

 THE WORLD BANK

ISBN: 978-0-8213-8186-1
eISBN: 978-0-8213-8187-8
DOI: 10.1596/978-0-8213-8186-1

Cover design: Naylor Design, Inc.

Library of Congress Cataloging-in-Publication Data

Görgens, Marelize.

Making monitoring and evaluation systems work : a capacity development tool kit / Marelize Görgens and Jody Zall Kusek.

p. cm.

Includes bibliographical references.

   ISBN 978-0-8213-8186-1 (alk. paper) – ISBN 978-0-8213-8187-8

1. Government productivity—Developing countries—Evaluation. 2. Performance standards—Developing countries—Evaluation. 3. Total quality management in government—Developing countries—Evaluation. 4. Public administration—Developing countries—Evaluation. I. Kusek, Jody Zall, 1952- II. World Bank. III. Title.

JF1525.P67G87 2010

352.3'57091724 – dc22

2009043703

Contents

Introduction

List of Figures

Introduction

Chapter 1

Chapter 2

Chapter 3

Chapter 4

Chapter 7

Chapter 8

Chapter 9

Chapter 10

Chapter 11

Chapter 12

List of Tables

List of Annexes

Chapter 12

Acknowledgments

The authors thank Masauso Nzima (Joint United Nations Programme on AIDS) for his partnership in building M&E systems and co-creating the "11 component concept" (which formed the basis of the 12 Components M&E framework); Wendy Heard (World Bank consultant), John Chipeta (Malawi National AIDS Commission), Verne Kemerer (MEASURE Evaluation), Julie Tumbo (World Bank consultant), Peter Badcock-Walters and Donald Whitson (World Bank consultant), who peer reviewed the 12-component resource library; David Wilson (The World Bank) for his ideas on succinctness and keeping it client-focused; Robert Oelrichs (The World Bank) for advice on some of the chapters; members of the East and Southern Africa M&E curriculum development team for their insights [Win Brown (United States Agency for International Development), Claude Cheta (International HIV/AIDS Alliance), James Guwani (Joint United Nations Programme on AIDS), Michiko Tajima (Japan International Cooperation Agency), Christa vd Bergh (John Snow International consultant)]; Andy Beke (University of Pretoria), Yasuo Sumita (Japan International Cooperation Agency) and Hitesh Hurckchand (John Snow International)] for sharing ideas about M&E capacity building and helping to keep the passion going; participants in a workshop in Tanzania in March 2009 for their constructive and practical feedback as users; Rosalia Rodriguez-Garcia (The World Bank) for sharing her thinking about strategic planning; Sue Bawale (World Bank consultant) for her skill with editing; Karien Ingenkamp (World Bank consultant) for the graphics; Carmen Bibby for the final MS Word formatting; Theo Hawkins (World Bank consultant) for typesetting and copy-editing; Ronnie Miller (World Bank consultant) for the final proofreading of the contents, and Joy de Beyer (The World Bank) for her excellent technical edits, eye for details, and introducing us to Tufte's work. We also would like to thank Laura Rawlings and Benjamin Loevinsohn (The World Bank) for the time they took to review and comment on the final manuscript.

Special and heartfelt thanks go to all the National AIDS Coordinating Authorities with which The World Bank's Global HIV/AIDS Program has worked over the years, learning together and sharing ideas about how to build functioning M&E systems.

Abbreviations and Glossary of Terms

ABC   Activity Based Costing

Advocacy   The act of arguing on behalf of something, such as a cause, idea, or policy. Advocacy is intended to educate, sensitize, influence and change opinion

AfriCASO   African Council of AIDS Service Organizations

AfrEA   African Evaluation Association

AIDS   Acquired Immune Deficiency Syndrome

Bias   A bias is a "feature of the study which makes a particular result more likely – like a football pitch which slopes from one end to the other" (Leung, 2001a)

Capacity   The ability to perform appropriate tasks effectively, efficiently, and sustainably

Capacity assessment   A structured and analytical process whereby the various dimensions of capacity are measured and evaluated within the broader environmental or systems context, as well as specific entities and individuals within the system. (BPPS/MDGD and FMP International, 1997)

Capacity development   Improvement of human resources and operational capabilities of systems, institutions/organizations and individuals so they can perform better (Lamptey et al., 2001)

CBO   Community-Based Organization

CCA   Conventional Cost Accounting

CDC   Centers for Disease Control and Prevention

CF   Conceptual Framework

CHAT   Country Harmonization Alignment Tool

Communication   A process of exchanging information using various means or media

Costed M&E work plan   A costed, multi-year, multi-sectoral and multi-level M&E work plan including budgets for all M&E activities that M&E stakeholders aim to undertake in a defined time period

CRIS   Country Response Information System (UNAIDS database management system)

DAC   Development Assistance Committee

Data auditing   Process of verifying the completeness and accuracy of one or more data management processes

Data quality	Extent to which data adheres to the six dimensions of quality – which are accuracy, reliability, completeness, precision, timeliness and integrity (USAID, 2007)
Data quality assurance	Set of internal and external mechanisms and processes to ensure that data meets the six dimensions of quality
Database	An organized set of records – usually in columns and tables.
Database management system	Computer program used to manage and query a database
Database requirements	All the functions the database will perform
DBMS	Database Management System
DevInfo	Development Information (UNDP database)
DFID	Department For International Development
DHS	Demographic and Health Survey
Economic evaluation	Economic evaluation looks at costs and funding associated with development interventions, to assess value for money, i.e., how efficient the interventions are
Epi Info	Epidemiological Information (CDC's database for managing epidemiological data)
Evaluation	The systematic and objective assessment of an on-going or completed project, program or policy, its design, implementation and results
ERL	Electronic Resource Library
FHI	Family Health International
Formative evaluation	Designed to assess the strengths and weaknesses of program design, materials or campaign strategies before implementation
GAMET	Global AIDS Monitoring and Evaluation Team
GAO	Government Accountability Office
GF	The Global Fund to Fight AIDS, Tuberculosis and Malaria
GIS	Geographic Information System
GRIPP	Getting Research Results into Policy and Practice
HCD	Human Capacity Development
HIV	Human Immunodeficiency Virus
HMIS:	Health Management Information System

HR	Human Resources
HTML	Hypertext Mark-up Language
ICASO	International Council of AIDS Service Organizations
Impact evaluation	Systematic identification of the long-term effects (positive or negative, intended or not) on individuals, households, institutions and/or the environment, caused by a given activity such as a program or project
IEG	Independent Evaluation Group
IRB	Institutional Review Board
IT	Information Technology
LGA	Local Government Authority
M&E	Monitoring and Evaluation
M&E plan	An M&E plan is a comprehensive narrative document on all M&E activities. It addresses key M&E questions; what indicators to measure; sources, frequency and method of indicator data collection; baselines, targets and assumptions; how to analyze or interprete data; frequency and method for report development and distribution of the indicators, and how the 12 components of the M&E system will function (Rugg, Peersman and Carael, 2004)
MERG	Global HIV Monitoring and Evaluation Reference Group
MOE	Ministry of Education
MOH	Ministry of Health
MS Access	Microsoft Access
MSC	Most Significant Changes
MTEF	Medium-Term Expenditure Framework
NACA:	National AIDS Coordinating Authority
National M&E plan	Special type of M&E plan that focuses on how a national M&E system (for example HIV, the education sector, health sector, non-governmental sector, or others) would work
NCA	National Coordinating Authority
NDP	Ninth Development Plan
NGO	Non-Governmental Organization
NSP	National Strategic Plan
OECD	Organisation for Economic Cooperation and Development

OECD-DAC	Organization for Economic Cooperation and Development – Development Assistance Committee
OR	Operations Research
Organization's authority	An organization's authority to carry out M&E functions usually will come from the need to assess progress towards it's strategy
Organization's mandate	An organization's mandate for M&E is the specific order given to an organization to execute M&E functions
Organization's responsibility	An organization's responsibility to carry out M&E functions can be defined as its obligation to perform assigned functions (Robbins and Decenzo, 2001)
Organizational culture	The set of shared beliefs, assumptions, and values that operate in organizations
Organizational structure	Describes the hierarchy, reporting lines, and systematic arrangement of work in an organization
Outcome evaluation	Used to obtain descriptive data on a project and to document short-term results
OVC	Orphans and Other Vulnerable Children
Partnership	A partnership is an agreement between two or more parties to work together to achieve common aims
PLHIV	Persons living with HIV (includes people living with AIDS)
PPP	Policy, Program or Project
Process evaluation	Examination of procedures and tasks involved in implementing a program
RDBMS	Relational Database Management System
Research	Systematic investigation designed to develop or contribute to a generalized knowledge; includes developing, testing and evaluating the research
Respondent	The person who answers questions during an interview
	Sample size The sample size is the number of units that will be selected from the sample frame, to produce statistically reliable results
Sampling	Sampling is the process of selecting respondents for the survey
Sampling frame	A list of all members of the population being studied so that each has an equal chance of being included in the sample (Scheuren, 2004)

Sampling methodology	The method applied to select respondents for the survey sample
Sampling unit	The unit that is selected during the process of sampling
Six routine data management processes	Data sourcing, data collection, data collation, data analysis, data reporting, and data use
SPSS	Statistical Package for Social Sciences
SQL	Structured Query Language
Supervision	Directing and overseeing the performance of others while transmitting skills, knowledge and attitudes
Surveillance	Surveillance includes biological and behavioral surveillance. Biological surveillance involves collecting specific biological data through repeated cross-sectional surveys in a representative population. Behavioral surveillance refers to repeat cross-sectional surveys of behavior in a representative population (UNAIDS and WHO, 2000)
Survey	A method of collecting information from respondents – who can be either a sample of the population or selected, targeted organizations (or facilities).
SWOT	Strengths, Weaknesses, Opportunities and Threats
TWG	Technical Working Group
TOR	Terms of Reference
UN	United Nations
UNAIDS	Joint United Nations Programme on AIDS
UNDP	United Nations Development Programme
WHO	World Health Organisation

Preface

Now more than ever, development programs are expected to deliver results. For everyone involved in development, the value of their ideas, advice, and action produced is increasingly being gauged by whether it improves lives. Moreover, the global economic crisis has doubled the importance of getting the maximum impact from every program, as countries are facing painful tradeoffs. Consequently, every program needs the information to answer two vital questions: "What would constitute success in addressing this problem?" and "How will we know success when we achieve it"? The answers to these questions will help everyone understand which programs are working, which are not, which can be scaled up, and which should be phased out.

It is obvious that achieving results starts with a good design, including a well-crafted implementation strategy. However, ensuring that knowledge learned along the way is put to use is equally important. This knowledge can be learned both through periodic detailed analyses of a problem, as well as through the everyday, incremental learning that comes with implementation. Good monitoring and evaluation systems capture both forms of knowledge. This is why the World Bank continues to invest in strengthening the capacity of countries to build and use monitoring and evaluation systems to regularly assess the progress of policies and programs.

No one, including the World Bank, thinks enough is being done to capture and share this vital knowledge. Development partners have learned the hard way that it is not enough merely to ensure that each individual project has a framework for measuring results. Too often, countries still lack the capacity or incentives to sustain real monitoring and evaluation systems once external investments have closed. This handbook provides a road map of the components to a sustainable monitoring and evaluation system: it defines all the pieces of an M&E system jigsaw puzzle. The use of this new 12 Component model can help answer questions about how to ensure the sustainability of investments in monitoring and evaluation systems.

Ngozi N. Okonjo-Iweala
Managing Director, World Bank

Making Monitoring and Evaluation Systems Work is available as an interactive textbook at **http://www.worldbank.org/pdt**

This tool enables students and teachers to share notes and related materials for an enhanced, multimedia learning experience.

1. M&E Systems Make Managing for Results Possible[1]

There are constant and growing pressures on governments and organizations around the world to be more responsive to demands from internal and external stakeholders for good governance, accountability and transparency, greater development effectiveness and delivery of tangible results. Governments, parliaments, citizens, the private sector, non-governmental organizations (NGOs), civil society, international organizations and donors are all among stakeholders interested in better performance. As demands for greater accountability and results have grown, there is an accompanying need for useful and useable results-based monitoring and evaluation systems to support the management of policies, programs, and projects.

Monitoring and Evaluation (M&E) is a powerful public management tool that can be used to improve the way governments and organizations achieve results. Just as governments need financial, human resource, and accountability systems, they also need good performance feedback systems. M&E helps answer the *So what?* questions: *So what that a government invested in 50 new hospitals? So what that 2000 km of roads were built in the country and so what that 100 teachers were hired?* How do these actions result in the achievement of a country's key national or ministerial goals? Credible answers to *So what?* questions address accountability concerns of stakeholders, give government managers information on progress towards achieving stated targets and goals, and provide substantial evidence on what is working and what is not.

---

[1] This introductory module is adapted from *Ten Steps to a Results-Based M&E System* by Jody Zall Kusek and Ray C. Rist, World Bank 2004. See Annex B for a more detailed explanation of the Ten Steps.

The Organisation for Economic Cooperation and Development (OECD) defines monitoring and evaluation as follows:

> **Monitoring** is a continuous function that uses the systematic collection of data on specified indicators, to provide management and the main stakeholders of an ongoing development intervention with indications of the extent of progress and achievement of objectives and progress in the use of allocated funds.

> **Evaluation** is the systematic and objective assessment of an ongoing or completed project, program, or policy, including its design, implementation, and results. The aim is to determine the relevance and fulfillment of objectives, development efficiency, effectiveness, impact, and sustainability. An evaluation should provide information that is credible and useful, enabling the incorporation of lessons learned into the decision-making process of both recipients and donors.

It is immediately evident that monitoring and evaluation are distinct yet complementary. Monitoring gives information on where a policy, program, or project is at any given time (and over an extended period) relative to its targets and outcome goals. It is descriptive. Evaluation gives evidence about why targets and outcomes are, or are not, being achieved. It explores causality.

Monitoring and evaluation systems are not new to governments. The ancient Egyptians regularly monitored grain and livestock production more than 5,000 years ago. Today, modern governments all do some monitoring and evaluation. Most track their expenditures, revenues, staffing levels, resources, program and project activities, goods and services produced, and so forth.

Governments and other organizations have many different kinds of tracking systems as part of their management toolkits: good human resource systems, financial systems, and accountability systems. They also need good feedback systems. A results-based M&E system is essentially such a feedback system; it is a management tool to measure and evaluate outcomes, providing information for governance and decision making.

Many management systems have been missing a feedback component to enable them to track the consequences of actions. Building an M&E system gives decision-makers an additional management tool by providing feedback on performance as a basis for future improvement.

1.1. How can results-based M&E systems support better governance?

Project, Program, and Policy Applications: Results-based M&E systems have been successfully designed to monitor and evaluate at all levels of project, program, and policy. Information and data can be collected and analyzed at any stage to provide regular feedback. The information can be used to better inform key decision-makers, the general public and other stakeholders.

Monitoring and evaluation can and should be conducted throughout the life cycle of a project, program, or policy, including after completion. Continuing streams of M&E data and feedback add value at every stage, from design through implementation and close-out. "The specific information will also be different at each level, the complexity of collecting data may change, and the uses of the information may change from one level to another" (Kusek and Rist, 2001:17).

Internal and external use of results-based M&E systems: M&E can be conducted at local, regional and national level. A functioning M&E system, at any level, provides a continuous flow of information that is useful internally and externally. Internal use of information from the M&E system is a crucial management tool that helps managers ensure that specific targets are met. Information on progress, problems, and performance are all vital to managers who are striving to achieve results. Likewise, the information from an M&E system is important to those outside the public sector (or other organization) who are expecting results and wanting to see demonstrable impacts. The information can build trust in a government or any other organization striving to better the life of its citizens or clients.

M&E systems can help identify promising programs or practices. They can also identify unintended, but perhaps useful, project, program and policy results. M&E systems can help managers identify program weaknesses and take action to correct them. M&E can be used to diminish fear within organizations and governments and to foster an open atmosphere in which people learn from mistakes, make improvements, and develop skills along the way.

Transparency and accountability: M&E systems can promote transparency and accountability within organizations and governments. Beneficial spillover effects may also occur from shining a light on results. External and internal stakeholders will have a clear sense of the status of projects, programs, and policies. The ability to demonstrate positive results can increase popular and political support. There are organizational and political costs, and risks associated with implementing results-based M&E systems. However, there are also crucial costs and risks in not implementing such systems.

Poverty reduction: Results-based M&E systems can help strengthen governments and other organizations by reinforcing the emphasis on demonstrable outcomes. Getting a better handle on the working and outcomes of economic and other government programs and policies can contribute to poverty reduction, economic growth and the achievement of goals.

Political dynamics — the political side of M&E: Implementing results-based M&E systems can pose political challenges in both developed and developing countries. It takes strong and consistent political leadership (usually by a political champion). Making results-based information available to the public can change the dynamics of institutional relations, budgeting and resource allocation, personal political agendas, and public perceptions of government. Strong, vested interests may feel threatened. There may be counter-reformers within and outside the government/organization who actively oppose M&E efforts. This makes the role of a strong champion key to ensuring the institutionalization and sustainability of a results-based M&E system.

Results-based M&E systems are essential components of governance structures and, thus, are fundamentally related to political and power systems. They provide critical information and empower policy-makers to make better-informed decisions. At the same time, the information may limit the options that can be justified, constraining decision-makers' room to maneuver.

1.2. How does one build a results-based M&E system?

Kusek and Rist (2004) suggest that building an M&E system that responds to the results in an organization's strategy is a 10-step process, as summarized below. For a more detailed summary, see the book *Ten Steps to a Results-based M&E System.*

Step One: Conducting a Readiness Assessment to determine the capacity and willingness of the government/organization and its development partners to construct a results-based M&E system. This assessment addresses such issues as the presence or absence of champions, the barriers to building a system, who will own it, and who will oppose the M&E system.

Step Two: Agreeing on Outcomes to Monitor and Evaluate addresses the key requirement of developing strategic outcomes that then focus and drive resource allocation and activities. These outcomes should be derived from the strategic priorities (goals).

Step Three: Developing Key Indicators to Monitor Outcomes, so the degree to which the outcomes are being achieved can be assessed. Developing indicators is a core activity in building an M&E system and drives all subsequent data collection, analysis, and reporting. Both the political and methodological issues in creating credible and appropriate indicators are not to be underestimated.

Step Four: Gathering Baseline Data on Indicators involves describing and measuring the initial conditions being addressed by the outcomes. It is the first measurement of the indicators and defines the starting point.

Step Five: Planning for Improvements requires setting realistic targets and recognizes that most outcomes are long-term, complex, and not quickly achieved. It is helpful to establish interim targets that specify how much progress towards an outcome is to be achieved each year (or other time period) and the resources needed. Measuring results against targets can involve both direct and proxy indicators and use of both quantitative and qualitative data.

Step Six: Monitoring for Results is the administrative and institutional task of establishing data collection, analysis and reporting guidelines; designating who will be responsible for activities; establishing quality control processes; establishing timelines and costs; working through roles and responsibilities; and establishing guidelines on transparency and dissemination of the information and analysis. It is emphasized that, in constructing an M&E system, the challenges of ownership, management, maintenance, and credibility need to be addressed clearly.

Step Seven: Evaluative Information to Support Decision Making focuses on the contributions that evaluation studies and analyses can make throughout this process to assess results and move towards outcomes. Analysis of program theory, evaluability assessments, process evaluations, outcome and impact evaluations, and evaluation syntheses are among the strategies discussed that can be employed in evaluating a results-based M&E system.

Step Eight: Analyzing and Reporting Findings is a crucial step, as it determines what findings are reported to whom, in what format, and at what intervals. This step has to address the existing capacity for producing the information, and focuses on the methodologies for accumulating and assessing information, and preparing analyses and reports.

Step Nine: Using the Findings emphasizes that the crux of the system is not simply generating results-based information, but getting the information to the appropriate users in a timely fashion so that they can take the information into account in making decisions. This step also addresses the roles of development partners and civil society in using the information to strengthen accountability, transparency, and resource allocation procedures.

Step Ten: Sustaining the M&E System recognizes the long-term process involved in ensuring the longevity and utility of an M&E system. Six criteria are seen as crucial to the sustainability of an M&E system: demand, structure, trustworthy and credible information, accountability, incentives, and capacity. Each dimension needs constant attention over time to ensure the viability of the system. As noted earlier, building an M&E system does not have to be done according to these 10 steps. One could define a more detailed number of steps, or fewer. The issue is to ensure that key strategies and activities are recognized, clustered together in a logical manner, and then completed in an appropriate sequence.

What does a sustainable results-based M&E system look like? How can we make and keep such a system functioning? To answer these questions, it is necessary to understand the components of a results-based M&E system and then to build each component.

2. The Technical Side of M&E: The 12 Components of a Functional M&E System

"It is a capital mistake to theorize before one has data. Insensibly, one begins to twist facts to suit theories, instead of theories to suit facts."
Sherlock Holmes

Sustaining an M&E system that can produce trustworthy, timely, and relevant information on the performance of government, civil society, or private sector projects, programs, and policies requires that one overcome many M&E system challenges and approach the implementation of such a system with experience, skill, and real institutional capacity. The *12 Components of a Functional M&E System* offers a framework for what a strong M&E system that works, looks like and is the focus of this book.

2.1. Challenges in setting up M&E systems

As a professional field, M&E is comparatively new, as are M&E systems and the experience of the personnel and institutions that support them. The recent introduction of the field and the concept of drawing data from a single M&E system pose a challenge for development partners, as does the pressure to deliver results.

There is a great demand for skilled professionals and capacity in building M&E systems. However, there is a dearth of skilled M&E professionals and a lack of harmonized training courses and technical advice. There is demand for M&E systems in all sectors at the same time as national cross-sectoral systems are being developed.

Decentralization of government structures and programs requires decentralization of M&E systems requiring sub-national and national systems to be developed simultaneously. The power inherent in making data widely available poses a political challenge and emphasizes the need for greater accountability.

Prevailing misconceptions about the purpose of M&E, suspicions about its *policing* function, and lack of integration into traditional reporting systems must be addressed and debunked.

2.2. Addressing the challenges: the 12 Components of a functional M&E system

2.2.1. History and application of the 12 Components

Addressing these challenges will take time and professional application. One approach is to create a standard or common definition of what constitutes a functional M&E system.

A "system" is defined as a group of interacting, interrelated, or interdependent elements forming a complex whole (The Free Dictionary, 2007), and "systems thinking" is about gaining insight into the whole by understanding the linkages and interactions between the elements that comprise the whole system (Senge, 1990). Applying such a systems approach to M&E systems building, it requires

- Identifying the **components** of the system (understanding that they are interrelated) as a means to describe the system; and

- Ensuring that **each component is functional** to ensure that the system is functional.

Applying this thinking, the World Bank identified eleven components of a working monitoring and evaluation system. After international peer review a 12th component was recommended. This 12 Component approach was adopted for world-wide use by UNAIDS and partners to support the measurement and management of the HIV/AIDS epidemic. While any program can apply the 12 Components, the authors are pleased that UNAIDS formally adopted this approach for their M&E capacity building efforts in 2007. The 12 Components are illustrated in Figure 1 as interlocking and interdependent parts of a larger whole.

The 12 Components of a functional M&E system[2]

Components relating to "people, partnerships and planning"

1. Structure and organizational alignment for M&E systems

2. Human capacity for M&E systems

3. M&E partnerships

---

[2] Source: Adapted from the graphic in the publication *Organizing Framework for a Functional National HIV Monitoring and Evaluation System*. Geneva, UNAIDS, 2008 (http://siteresources.worldbank.org/INTHIVAIDS/Resources/375798 – 1132695455908/GROrganizingFrameworkforHIVMESystem.pdf, accessed 15 Sept 08).

Figure 1: The 12 Components of a functional M&E system

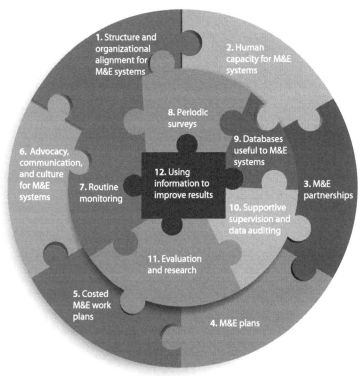

4. M&E plans[3]
5. Costed M&E work plans
6. Advocacy, communication, and culture for M&E systems

Components relating to "collecting, capturing and verifying data"

7. Routine monitoring
8. Periodic surveys
9. Databases useful to M&E systems
10. Supportive supervision and data auditing
11. Evaluation and research

Final component about "using data for decision-making"

12. Using information to improve results

2.2.2. Characteristics of the 12 Components[4]

Figure 1 indicates several important characteristics of the 12 Components:

a) **Some components link strongly together to form a sub-set:** It is possible to group related components together, as done in Figure 2:

    Sub-set 1: Components in the outer ring: 6 linked components related to people, partnerships, and planning that support data production and data use constitute the enabling environment for M&E to function. To sum up the components in this ring: People (Component 1) who are skilled (Component 2) and work together (Component 3) to plan (Component 4), budget and cost (Component 5), motivate for and maintain a functional

[3] Although the concepts were developed with a national, cross-sectoral system in mind, they also apply to any other M&E system, such as a ministry system or other organization-specific systems.

[4] Source: *Organizing framework for a functional national HIV monitoring and evaluation system.* Geneva, UNAIDS, 2008 (http://siteresources.worldbank.org/INTHIVAIDS/Resources/375798 – 1132695455908/GROrganizingFrameworkforHIVMESystem.pdf, accessed 15 September 2008).

M&E system
(Component 6).

**Sub-set 2:
Components in the
middle ring:** 5 linked
components related
to data management
processes that involve
collection, capture, and
verification of all types
of M&E data. This
ring of components
generates the data
that are essential to
the M&E system
just as fuel is for an
engine. Even with the
most perfect enabling
environment (the outer
ring of components),
M&E systems cannot
be operational or
used to *manage for
results* unless data are
generated.

Figure 2: How the 12 Components are grouped

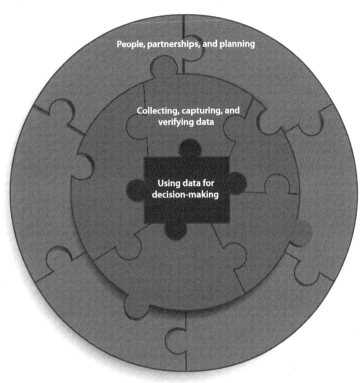

People, partnerships, and planning

Collecting, capturing, and
verifying data

Using data for
decision-making

Sub-set 3: The inner component: This component captures the system's
central purpose – to analyze data in order to create information that is
disseminated as a means to inform and empower decision making at all levels.
This final component of the M&E system is red (see front cover of the
book for a full color version of the 12 Components graphic) as it represents
the *bull's eye* in making and keeping an M&E system functional. If we are
not using data and information from M&E systems, we are not using these
systems in the way they were designed. The *raison d'être* of M&E systems
is to provide information and use it to improve our projects, policies, and
programs.

b) **Individual components are linked and therefore inter-dependent
(within and across the three "rings"):** The graphic above illustrates
the different components and rings as intersecting and interlocking parts
of an integral whole, reflecting the inter-dependence of the 12 individual
components and the three rings. Without aligned organizational structures,
for example, collecting routine data or getting people to work together
would be difficult. Although we need to make each component functional,
we also need to remember that the components depend on each other.

Completely ignoring one component could affect the extent to which the other components and, therefore, the entire M&E system, works.

c) **Components, not implementation steps:** These 12 Components are not implementation steps, and are not necessarily sequential. Different organizations may focus on or prioritize different sets of components, depending on the status of each organization's M&E system. Assessing the status of your organization's M&E system from time to time is, therefore, important in order to provide an overview of how the M&E system is working and to help you decide which components need to be prioritized over the next 12 months. Section 2.2.4 provides more information about how you can use the 12 Components framework to assess the overall status of your organization's M&E system.

d) **Applicable to M&E systems of different programs:** These 12 Components were initially designed to measure the status of a national health program. The examples we provide in this book make it clear that the approach has general applicability. It can be used for M&E systems in education, agriculture, tourism, finance, civil society, the private sector, and so forth.

e) **Component use by level and sector:** These 12 Components could equally be applied to a national M&E system or to a sub-national (decentralized), local government authority's M&E system or to the M&E system of an individual organization. An individual organization may not implement all the components (e.g., Component 7 — Periodic surveys), but may draw data from a national survey of, for example, education sector employees to inform the organization's program. When developing plans for strengthening an M&E system, stakeholders can focus on any of the 12 Components at any level of the M&E system. In practice, however, improving system performance in one component or at one level may require concurrent intervention at another level. In other words, a systems approach is needed when using these components to improve system performance. For example, health managers and workers, no matter how skilled, are unlikely to perform essential M&E functions without adequate supplies and equipment, proper motivation and support, and technical guidance.

2.2.3. Practical uses of the 12 Components

The 12 Components are an organizing framework for an M&E system and address the challenges of M&E systems in the following ways:

a) As an organizing framework for thinking about staff, resources, support, and funding required for the M&E system

b) As the basis for conducting assessments of the national M&E system in which the status of each component can be assessed

c)   As a way to develop joint M&E reports or updates on the status of an M&E system, in which each of the components can be reported on

d)   As a way to establish a clear division of labor at country level and a framework within which all partners can work together

e)   As a means to develop indicators to measure levels of M&E system operationalization, and the extent to which each component within the system is operational

f)   As the basis for job descriptions and building the capacity of staff in the organization's M&E unit, to ensure that staff members collectively have the capacity and competence to focus on all 12 Components of their organization's M&E system

g)   As the basis for a checklist identifying the information requirements which need to be met by the national information system

2.2.4. Using the 12 Components to diagnose the strengths and weaknesses of M&E systems

You can use the framework of the 12 Components to assess the status of your organization's M&E system by assessing in a systematic way, the status of each of the 12 Components of your organization's M&E system. The assessment process could be formal or informal. The *formal way* uses a diagnostic tool that asks a series of questions about each of the 12 Components. Such a diagnostic tool has been developed, and can be found on www.worldbank.org/12components. The *informal way* is still diagnostic in nature, and involves assessing in a more qualitative way the achievement of the short-, medium- and long-term results that you identified for your M&E system's components.

Small group participation can be encouraged by asking them to list the strengths and weaknesses of each component, and then to circulate the results so that each small group can assess and record their views about each of the 12 Components. Annex A has a list of all the short-, medium-, and long-term results for the 12 Components which you can use as a basis for your discussion.

After assessing the 12 Components of your M&E system, you may use the assessment to decide which parts of this Toolkit would be most useful to use in making your M&E system work.

3. Introduction to the Capacity Development Toolkit for Making M&E Systems Work

"The beautiful thing about learning is that no one can take it away from you."

B.B King

This section focuses on how to use the Toolkit: the purpose and objectives; how the Toolkit and each chapter is structured; what you can expect to learn working through the Toolkit; and how you can use the information contained in each chapter of the Toolkit. There is a final section for facilitators or trainers who may want to use the Toolkit for capacity development purposes.

3.1. Purpose of the Toolkit

The purpose of the Toolkit is to provide resources, tools and recipes that can be used to develop the capacity of government, civil society and other organization program managers and M&E staff to build M&E systems that work well and are results-driven. As such, the Toolkit provides both theoretical and practical information, step-by-step instructions on how to make M&E systems work, and examples to demonstrate how others have accomplished it.

3.2. Target audiences

This Toolkit will be useful to *monitoring and evaluation technicians and development practitioners*: people who need to design, operationalize, review and *make M&E systems work*. Its goal is to help those who work (mostly fulltime) with M&E systems to build M&E systems that work.

How this Toolkit relates to the *Ten Steps to a Results-Based M&E System* course: *The Ten Steps to a Results-Based M&E System* course is aimed at policy and decision-makers who need to be involved in strategic discussions around "What does success look like for this organization and how will we know it when we see it?" This audience is likely to interact closely with other parts of the organization, particularly finance and planning and external funders. The Ten Steps approach helps to organize thinking around strategy and planning while recognizing the need to measure and monitor the success of what is planned. This Toolkit provides information about what a functional M&E system looks like and how to make it functional. By teaching M&E professionals how to design and implement an M&E system that will provide the data to decision-makers, at the right time, in order to measure results.

3.3. Toolkit structure, aims and learning objectives

We first introduce the 12 Components and the Toolkit. The Toolkit has a separate chapter for each component (e.g., Component 1 in Chapter 1,

Component 2 in Chapter 2, etc.). Each chapter of the Toolkit conveys specific knowledge and skills about the respective component. Table 1 summarizes the aim, knowledge and skills that are conveyed in each chapter and component.

Table 1:   **Aims, Knowledge and Skills of Each Chapter of the Toolkit**

Chapter	Chapter aim	Knowledge and skills about the component conveyed in the chapter
Component 1. Structure and organizational alignment for M&E systems	The aim of this chapter is to enable you to understand the importance of organizational structure and its relation to organizational alignment, when designing and making M&E systems work and to help you to plan the human resources needed for your M&E system.	a) Explain to others the key concepts relating to organizational structures and organizational alignment for M&E (in other words, explain where M&E "fits" within an organizational structure and its alignment with other key functions of the organization). b) Design an M&E organizational structure of appropriate size with appropriate responsibilities for your organization. c) Know the pitfalls to avoid when designing the M&E part of an organization.
Component 2. Human capacity for M&E systems	The aim of this chapter is to enable you to build the skills that people need to fulfill their M&E responsibilities (develop human capacity), so that the M&E system works well.	a) Explain the most important human capacity development terminology and definitions. b) Identify the key implementation issues concerning human capacity development. c) Manage and undertake a human capacity assessment for the M&E system. d) Manage the development of a human capacity development strategy and plan.
Component 3. M&E partnerships	The aim of this chapter is to enable you to understand the importance of establishing and maintaining strong M&E partnerships and bring diverse people from different organizations together, to work towards similar objectives and goals. M&E partnerships are especially important given that many of the people involved do not necessarily work in the same institutions or sectors.	a) Explain to others the different types of partnerships, the benefits and different partnership mechanisms. b) Recognize the implementation issues in establishing and maintaining partnerships. c) Establish and maintain a national M&E technical working group as an M&E partnership mechanism. d) Organize a joint mission/trip with other development partners.

Chapter	Chapter aim	Knowledge and skills about the component conveyed in the chapter
Component 4. M&E plans	The aim of this chapter is to enable you to develop or review your organization's M&E plan. This plan, together with a costed M&E work plan, is at the heart of an M&E system. It describes the purpose of the system, the data the system will collect, and how the system will operate.	a) Know what an M&E plan and a national M&E plan are, and how these differ from M&E frameworks and M&E work plans. b) Understand the linkage between a national M&E plan and the M&E plans of individual organizations. c) Be able to explain to others what to include in an M&E plan. d) Develop or review an M&E plan — at the national level or at the organizational level. e) Develop a sub-national or sector M&E plan linked to a national M&E plan.
Component 5. Costed M&E work plans	The aim of this chapter is to enable you to develop, cost, and prioritize an M&E work plan and mobilize resources for it. The M&E work plan is an action plan that includes activities, responsibilities, time frames, and costs that make each of the 12 Components of an M&E system work.	a) Know about various costing methods. b) Develop an M&E work plan. c) Cost an M&E work plan (using the activity-based costing method). d) Use the M&E work plan for management purposes.
Component 6. Advocacy, communications and culture for M&E systems	The aim of this chapter is to enable you to plan, develop and manage an advocacy and communication strategy for your organization's or country's M&E system. The purpose of an advocacy and communication strategy is to help ensure knowledge of, and commitment to, M&E and the M&E system among policy-makers, program managers, program staff and other stakeholders.	a) Explain the difference between advocacy and communications. b) Know why advocacy and communications for M&E are important. c) Know how advocacy and communications can contribute greatly toward creating a positive culture for M&E in your organization. d) Plan and manage the advocacy and communication plan for your country's M&E system. e) Be familiar with different communication strategies and channels.

Chapter	Chapter aim	Knowledge and skills about the component conveyed in the chapter
Component 7. Routine monitoring	The aim of this chapter is to enable you to manage the different types of routine monitoring data that your organization needs to collect, report on and use effectively.	a) Understand the benefits of routine monitoring for interpreting program outcomes and impacts. b) Explain and implement the six routine data management processes. c) Include attention to quality in every data management step. d) Know how to link your organization's routine data management efforts to that of the national government ministry or other main system of your organization, and how to build national reporting requirements into your organization's routine monitoring system. e) Know how to link program monitoring and financial data in your organization. f) Design and develop a new routine monitoring system for your organization. g) Write routine monitoring guidelines for your organization.
Component 8. Periodic surveys	The aim of this chapter is to enable you to decide whether you need a survey to collect the data you need and, if required, how to design and implement a good quality survey.	a) Decide whether or not a survey is useful for the type of data you need to collect. b) Know the steps involved in planning, designing and implementing a survey. c) Design each step of the survey. d) Implement a survey with as little bias as possible. e) Know the process steps involved in calculating a sample size.

Chapter	Chapter aim	Knowledge and skills about the component conveyed in the chapter
Component 9. Databases useful for M&E systems	The aim of this chapter is to enable you to know the basics of how to develop an electronic database to hold all your organization's monitoring and evaluation data. This knowledge can help you to oversee a database development process.	a) Explain the terminology and functions of databases. b) Recognize the various issues involved in choosing a database and the process of developing one. c) Develop a national, sub-national or sectoral database (this HowTo guide is for in-country technicians responsible for database design and implementation or for managers interested in this field). d) Manage the process of developing a national, sub-national or sectoral database (this HowTo guide is for managers of M&E systems at all levels).
Component 10. Supportive supervision and data auditing	The aim of this chapter is to enable you to improve the quality of data and build the capacity of staff involved in M&E, by implementing routine supportive supervision and data auditing processes in your organization.	a) Recognize the need for supportive supervision and data auditing as part of the M&E system. b) Explain the difference between data auditing and supportive supervision. c) Distinguish between M&E supervision and implementation supervision. d) Identify all the levels in your organization where supportive supervision and data auditing should take place. e) Develop guidelines for supportive supervision and data auditing. f) Access global resources about supportive supervision and data auditing. g) Prepare and plan to follow up after supportive supervision and/or data auditing processes.

Chapter	Chapter aim	Knowledge and skills about the component conveyed in the chapter
Component 11. Evaluation and research	The aim of this chapter is to enable you to improve your program by conducting targeted evaluations and research when needed.	a) Explain why evaluation is important and useful to help programs achieve results. b) Be familiar with definitions of evaluation and research, and the different types of each. c) Develop a national evaluation and research strategy. d) Ensure that research and evaluations are done in an ethical way. e) Develop and/or update a national evaluation and research agenda. f) Manage and oversee a program evaluation.
Component 12. Using information to improve results	The aim of this chapter is to show how you can use information to improve the results your organization achieves. The aim is to teach you strategies you can use to increase the extent to which information from the M&E system is used to inform decisions that improve results.	a) Explain the concepts relating to data, information, how decisions are made, and how data are analyzed and displayed. b) Analyze and synthesize routine, survey, research and evaluation data generated by the M&E system. c) Produce effective reports (information products), including effective displays of information, that help managers and decision-makers take action. d) Implement innovative and diverse strategies to maximize use of the information.

Every chapter includes "HowTo" Guides. These are step-by-step *recipes*, with specific deliverables on different parts of the components. All the "HowTo" guides have been listed here.

Component 1: Structure and Organizational Alignment for M&E Systems

HowTo Guide 1.1.   **How to design and align an organizational structure for M&E:** This guide provides the logical steps to follow when designing an organizational structure for an M&E unit, and when an M&E unit needs to be incorporated into the larger organizational structure such as a national Ministry of Education. The principles mentioned here can be used for any organizational design.

Component 2: Human Capacity for M&E Systems

HowTo Guide 2.1. **How to undertake a human capacity development assessment for the M&E system:** This provides step-by-step instructions on how to assess the technical and managerial skills and competencies that need to be developed in an organization, for a well-functioning M&E system. Example assessment tools and guidelines are referenced.

HowTo Guide 2.2. **How to develop a human capacity development strategy and plan:** After undertaking a human capacity development assessment (or once human capacity needs are known), the next step is to design appropriate strategies to address human capacity needs. This HowTo Guide explains how to develop such a strategy.

Component 3: M&E Partnerships

HowTo Guide 3.1. **How to establish and manage a national M&E Technical Working Group (TWG):** M&E TWGs are important partnership mechanisms and their functionality often impacts on the quality of the M&E partnership in a country. Given their importance, this HowTo Guide provides information about how to establish an M&E TWG.

HowTo Guide 3.2. **How to plan for and undertake a joint M&E mission/ trip:** This HowTo Guide is meant for development partner representatives, especially those who are not based in the country. It describes how to organize and undertake a joint visit to the country as a mechanism to improve coordination of M&E technical support.

Component 4: M&E Plans

HowTo Guide 4.1. **How to develop or review a national M&E plan:** An M&E plan is a *recipe book* for a national M&E system. This HowTo Guide provides step-by-step instructions on how to develop a national M&E plan and describes the critical elements that the plan should contain.

HowTo Guide 4.2. **How to develop a sub-national or sectoral M&E plan linked to the national M&E plan:** If a national or sectoral M&E plan already exists, it is important to link a sector, local government authority or project M&E plan to the national M&E plan. This HowTo Guide explains how to do this and what is possible.

Component 5: Costed M&E Work Plans

HowTo Guide 5.1. **How to develop or update a multi-year, multi-sectoral and multi-level M&E work plan:** Work plans are the basis for practical coordination and collaboration among partners. They enable the government (or organization whose M&E system is being built) to drive and control the plan and help prevent duplication of effort and gaps. GAMET's many years of practical experience in developing these work plans are shared in this HowTo Guide.

HowTo Guide 5.2. **How to cost and mobilize resources for an M&E work plan:** Once developed, the work plan needs to be costed and resources mobilized. This HowTo Guide describes how to cost and mobilize resources for M&E work plans.

HowTo Guide 5.3. **How to use a work plan for management:** The primary function of a work plan is to manage all the planned M&E activities. This HowTo Guide explains how to use the work plan to do this.

Component 6: Advocacy, Communication, and Culture for M&E Systems

HowTo Guide 6.1. **How to develop a supportive organizational culture and leadership for M&E:** This HowTo Guide suggests ways to assess the organizational culture and readiness to *manage for results*, identify M&E champions and resistors, and help make the organizational culture positive and supportive of M&E. This will foster employee support, strengthen and keep the M&E system functional, add value and make it more likely that data from the M&E system are used to plan, manage, and perform better.

HowTo Guide 6.2. **How to develop and implement a national M&E advocacy and communications strategy:** The steps to a results-based approach for M&E-related advocacy and communications include: understanding the advocacy and communication challenges, defining objectives and target audiences, developing messages, approaches, communication channels, materials and budgets, implementing, then monitoring and evaluating the results.

Component 7: Routine Monitoring

HowTo Guide 7.1. **Designing a new program monitoring system for routine monitoring data:** This HowTo Guide explains all the procedures that you need to follow when designing a new routine monitoring system.

Component 8: Periodic Surveys

HowTo Guide 8.1. **How to undertake a periodic survey:** This HowTo Guide sets out the process for undertaking surveys which may be needed for your organization's M&E system.

HowTo Guide 8.2. **How to calculate a sample size:** The survey size needed to yield reliable results depends on the survey purpose, precision needed, how common the main dependent variables are in the sample population, and the extent of variation in factors of interest. This HowTo Guide takes you through the necessary decisions and calculations.

Component 9: Databases Useful to M&E Systems

HowTo Guide 9.1. **How to develop a national, sub-national or sectoral database:** This is a technical HowTo Guide for database developers and details a standard database development process.

HowTo Guide 9.2. **How to manage a national database development process:** This HowTo Guide complements HowTo Guide 9.1. It provides information for the person who needs to manage a database development process.

Component 10: Supportive Supervision and Data Auditing

HowTo Guide 10.1. **How to undertake a supportive supervision visit:** Supportive supervision can improve routine data collection and help ensure the quality, reliability and regularity of routine data. This HowTo Guide provides details around how to undertake a supportive supervision visit.

Component 11: Evaluation and Research

HowTo Guide 11.1. **How to develop a national research and evaluation strategy:** Research and evaluation require a strategic approach. For this purpose, this HowTo Guide focuses on the process steps required to develop a national research and evaluation strategy.

HowTo Guide 11.2. **How to develop or update a national research and evaluation agenda:** Once a national research and evaluation strategy has been developed, the next step is to develop a national research and evaluation agenda. The process of developing such an agenda (a set of prioritized research and evaluation questions that need to be answered) is described here.

HowTo Guide 11.3. **How to undertake a program evaluation:** This HowTo Guide provides links to other sections and resources that describe the process of undertaking a program evaluation. (The process steps for a program evaluation are described in other guidelines.)

Component 12: Using Information to Improve Results

HowTo Guide 12.1. **How to analyze quantitative data:** This HowTo Guide provides a brief overview of the steps required for quantitative analysis (descriptive and inferential statistics). For methods as to how to do the actual calculations, links to online resources are provided.

HowTo Guide 12.2. **How to analyze qualitative data:** Steps are outlined for analyzing qualitative data to ensure rigor and objectivity in the analysis of non-numerical data.

HowTo Guide 12.3. **How to improve the visual presentation of data:** This HowTo Guide provides practical guidance in what to do and what not to do when presenting visual data. It also shows what can go wrong if data are presented inappropriately or in misleading ways.

4. How the Toolkit Can Be Used for Teaching and Learning

The chapters and each of the 12 Components in this Toolkit can be used for self-study or in a formal teaching environment, workshop, or classroom with groups of people.

Using the Toolkit for self-study: Each chapter is self-contained. Therefore, if you use the chapters for self-study, we suggest that you first determine and select which are most applicable for your work needs. As you read through each chapter, take the time to answer the questions "For reflection" that are interspersed throughout the chapter.

There are learning activities at the end of each chapter. We suggest that when you have read the chapter, you complete these activities as these will help you master the content.

An electronic Answer Book with detailed answers for all the Learning Activities that provide practice in skills and reinforce the knowledge in each chapter can be downloaded at the following website: www.worldbank.org/12components.

Using the Toolkit for in-service or pre-service training: Here is some information that may be useful in planning a training course using this book as a resource in a formal teaching environment.

How long should the training be? It is very useful to understand your audience's learning needs as the the focus and duration of the course depends on this. To determine the learning needs of your audience, ask them how their M&E systems are performing, the problems/challenges they are experiencing, or provide them with a list of the chapters and learning objectives and asking them how much they want to know and learn about each chapter. Alternatively, you could also send them the list of HowTo Guides and ask them which ones they would like to know more about. You may also want to base the selection of chapters to be covered in the capacity building program on the status of the M&E system in the country (Chapter 4 provides more information on how M&E system assessments can be done and on a formal assessment of M&E skills of the individuals whose capacity will be built). An example of such a formal M&E skills assessment can be found at www.unaids.org (search for "M&E capacity building standards"). After completing the assessment, aspects of the M&E system that need to be strengthened can be determined and skills can be developed.

The Toolkit can be used in training courses for an overview of the 12 Components that can be as short as 2 hours to one day per chapter. Alternatively, it is possible to provide an overview of the 12 Components and then focus on only one or two relevant chapters. Annex C contains an example of a program for a 4-day 12 Components training course and Annex D contains an example of a similar, but longer and more in-depth 8-day training course.

Does it matter in what order the 12 Components are taught? First, as described above, determine which of the chapters should be taught. Then focus your attention on those chapters where the training needs assessment has revealed that skills are needed. If you teach all 12 Components, it is important that you do not teach the chapters in sequential order (i.e., from Chapter 1 to 12, one after the other).

If you are teaching all (or most of) the components, then Components 4 and 5 should always be taught at the end, as the 8-day training program in Annex D illustrates. The reason is that Componentr 4 (M&E Plans) and Component 5

(M&E Work Plans) require that participants be familiar with each of the other components. Because an M&E plan contains a description of each of the 12 Components (see Chapter 4 of this course for more details), it works best for participants to develop a draft M&E plan, based on what they have learned about (or their knowledge of) each of the 12 Components, at the end of the training course. It is also a practical way of cementing the learning and ensuring that not only knowledge but also skills are transferred.

The same applies for Component 5. Since this component is about costing an M&E work plan, which needs to happen for each of the 12 Components in an M&E work plan (depending on the M&E system priorities), Component 5 should only be taught after Component 4; and Component 4 should preferably be taught after participants have gained an understanding of how each of the 12 Components work..

How many students in the class? Small classes are better, so that you can give more individual attention to each student. We recommend a class of not more than 20 students.

Classroom set-up: A group setting which enables interaction and discussion is preferable to a lecture theater or classroom arrangement, which does not facilitate learning.

Teaching modalities: As far as possible, use participatory adult learning techniques. Overwhelming students with didactic (lecture-style) teaching will not encourage them to learn and discover for themselves and, therefore, to really explore and remember the material. You can download additional resources about the 12 Components at http://gametlibrary.worldbank.org.

Evaluating students' performance: Giving students a sense of completion at the end of the training session is important. Therefore, you may wish to assess their performance either informally or as part of a formal assessment. You can use the Learning Activities as evaluation activities, group work or exercises. You could also assess participants' understanding at the end of each chapter by asking them (or giving them an exercise to check) what skills and knowledge from the Component they have mastered.

5. Learning Activities

LEARNING ACTIVITY 1:   USING THE 12 COMPONENTS IN DIFFERENT ORGANIZATIONS

1.1. Can the concept of the 12 Components be used for building a national M&E system (a) by an education ministry; (b) at a local government level (i.e. municipality, regional, provincial or local government office); and (c) by a civil society organization?

1.2. What are the potential challenges to using the 12-component framework?

LEARNING ACTIVITY 2:   USING THE 12 COMPONENTS TO DESIGN AN M&E PLAN AND WORK PLAN

2.1. How can the concept of the 12 Components be used when designing (a) an education sector's M&E plan or (b) an M&E plan for measuring progress toward food security?

2.2. How can the 12 Components be used to assess progress in implementing an M&E system?

LEARNING ACTIVITY 3:   12 COMPONENTS AND JOB DESCRIPTIONS

3.1 How can the 12 Components be used to develop the job descriptions of staff members of a national health statistics unit in a Ministry of Health?

3.2 Suggest a job profile for a manager of a health statistics unit at a Ministry of Health.

Annex A: Suggested Results Checklist for the 12 Components

Component	Component's long-term result	Component's medium-term results
1. Structure and Organizational Alignment for M&E Systems	The staff in the organization are clear on the organization's overall goals and the strategies it has chosen to achieve its goals, understand the role of M&E in helping the organization meet its goals, are motivated to fulfill their M&E responsibilities, and are able to execute their M&E responsibilities without hindrance.	• Clear and relevant job descriptions for M&E staff • Adequate number of skilled M&E staff • Effective leadership for M&E and commitment to ensuring M&E system performance • Incentives for individuals to be involved in ensuring M&E system performance • Defined career path in M&E for M&E professionals
2. Human Capacity for M&E Systems	There are adequately skilled M&E staff who can effectively and efficiently complete all activities defined in the M&E work plan.	• Defined skill set for individuals responsible for M&E functions • Human capacity assessment, including career paths for M&E • Human capacity development plan • Standard curricula for M&E capacity building • Local and/or regional training institutions that offer good quality M&E training courses • Supervision, in-service training, and mentoring as mechanisms for continuous capacity building
3. M&E Partnerships	Internal and external partnerships to strengthen the M&E system are established and maintained.	• Inventory of all M&E stakeholders • Mechanism to coordinate and communicate with all M&E stakeholders • Participation in a National M&E Technical Working Group • Local leadership and capacity for stakeholder coordination

Component	Component's long-term result	Component's medium-term results
4. M&E Plans	An M&E plan is developed and updated periodically for your organization. The plan addresses: data needs; national standardized indicators; data collection tools and procedures; and roles and responsibilities in order to implement a functional M&E system.	• Participation of all relevant stakeholders in developing the M&E plan • The M&E plan meets these requirements: (a) indicators are derived from and linked to the strategic/program objectives that the indicators are intended to measure; (b) the plan describes the implementation of all 12 Components of an M&E system; and (c) adheres to international and national technical standards for M&E • The M&E plan and its revisions are based on the findings of periodic M&E system assessments • Sector-specific, sub-national and organizational M&E plans are linked to the national M&E plan
5. M&E Work Plans	A multi-partner and multi-year M&E work plan is used as the basis for planning, prioritizing, and costing; mobilizing resources and funding all M&E activities.	• The M&E work plan contains activities, responsible implementers, time frames, activity costs calculated using a unit cost table, and identified funding • The M&E work plan links to the program work plans and (where relevant) to the government's medium-term expenditure framework and annual budgets • Resources (human, physical, and financial) are committed to implement the M&E work plan • All relevant stakeholders are committed to implementing and contributing to the national M&E work plan • The M&E work plan is developed/updated annually, based on performance monitoring

Component	Component's long-term result	Component's medium-term results
6. **Advocacy, Communications and Culture for M&E Systems**	Knowledge of, and commitment to, M&E and the M&E system among policy-makers, program managers, program staff, and other stakeholders.	• An M&E communication and advocacy plan is part of the national communication strategy (if it exists). The plan should identify the objectives of the advocacy and communications efforts, the target audiences, key messages to be communicated, and the communication and advocacy channels. • M&E is reflected in the planning and policies of the program being monitored. • There are M&E champions among high-level officials who endorse M&E actions. An M&E champion is usually a senior decision-maker or person of influence who is positive about and fully values and understands the benefits of using information for decision making. An M&E champion would speak, act and write on behalf of those responsible for managing the program's M&E, to promote, protect and defend the creation of a functional M&E system. • Targeted, structured, and planned M&E advocacy activities • M&E materials for different audiences to communicate key M&E messages as defined in the M&E advocacy and communications plan
7. **Routine Monitoring**	Timely and high quality routine data are used for routinely assessing program implementation and taking decisions and actions to improve programs.	• Routine monitoring forms, data flow, and manual • Defined data management processes for routine data (sourcing, collection, collation, analysis, reporting, and use) • Routine procedures for data transfer from sub-national to national levels
8. **Periodic Surveys**	Surveys that answer relevant questions and that are unbiased and accurate, generalized, ethical and economical are undertaken, or existing survey results are used, as required by the program data needs.	• Inventory of relevant surveys that have already been conducted • Specified schedule for future surveys (either to be conducted by the organization or from where the organization should draw its data) • Protocols for all surveys based on international or national standards (if in existence)

Component	Component's long-term result	Component's medium-term results
9. Databases useful for M&E systems	Databases are developed and maintained that enable stakeholders to access relevant data for policy formulation, program management and improvement.	• Database(s) requirements respond to the decision-making and reporting needs of stakeholders • Well-defined and managed database(s) for collating, verifying, cleaning, analyzing and presenting program monitoring data from all levels and sectors • If applicable, linkages among different relevant databases to ensure consistency and avoid duplication
10. Supportive Supervision and data auditing	Data quality (valid, reliable, comprehensive, and timely) and the thoroughness of all six data management processes are externally verified on a periodic basis, and actions implemented to address obstacles to producing high quality data.	• Guidelines for supportive supervision are developed • Data auditing protocols are followed • Supportive supervision visits, including data assessments and feedback, take place • Data audit visits take place periodically • Supervision reports and data audit reports are produced
11. Evaluation and Research	Research and evaluation results are used to inform policy, programming and intervention selection.	• Inventory of completed and ongoing program evaluation and research studies • Inventory of local program evaluation and research capacity, including major research institutions and their areas of work • Program evaluation and research agenda • Ethical approval procedures and standards in place • Guidelines on evaluation and research standards and methods • Program research and evaluation findings are disseminated and discussed • Evidence of use of evaluation/research findings (e.g. research results referenced in planning documents)

Component	Component's long-term result	Component's medium-term results
12. **Using information to improve results**	Stakeholders involved in the program have learned from the data presented, gained knowledge about the program, and are, therefore, able to make better decisions about how to achieve the program results.	• Analysis of information needs and users • Standard formats for reporting and tabulations • Timetable for reporting • Information products tailored to different audiences • Evidence of information use (e.g., improvement decisions based on information, programs have improved, etc.)

Annex B: Summary of the "Ten Steps to a Results-Based Monitoring and Evaluation System"

Ten Steps to a Results-Based Monitoring and Evaluation System

Jody Zall Kusek[5]
The World Bank
Washington, DC

Ray C. Rist[6]
Advisor
Washington, DC

Summary

An effective state is essential to achieving sustainable socioeconomic development. With the advent of globalization, there are significant pressures on governments and organizations around the world to be more responsive to the demands of internal and external stakeholders for good governance, accountability, and transparency; greater development effectiveness and delivery of tangible results. Government, parliaments, citizens, the private sector, non-governmental organizations (NGOs), civil society, international organizations, and donors are among the stakeholders interested in ensuring that funds used achieve desired results. As the demands for greater accountability have increased there is an attendant need for enhanced results-based monitoring and evaluation of policies, programs and projects.

Monitoring and evaluation (M&E) is a powerful public management tool that can be used to improve the way governments and organizations achieve results. Just as governments need financial, human resource, and audit systems, governments also need good performance feedback systems. Over the last several years, there has been an evolution in the field of monitoring and evaluation involving a movement away from traditional implementation-based approaches toward new results-based approaches. The latter helps answer the *so what* question. In other words, governments and organizations may successfully implement programs or policies but have they produced the actual, intended results? Have government and organizations delivered on promises made to their stakeholders?

For example, it is not enough simply to implement health programs and assume that successful implementation is equivalent to actual improvements in public

---

[5] The views expressed here are solely those of this author and no endorsement by the World Bank Group is intended or should be inferred.

[6] Ray C. Rist is an independent advisor to governments and organizations throughout the world.

health. One must also examine if outcomes and impacts were achieved. The introduction of a results-based M&E system takes decision-makers one step further in assessing whether, and how, goals are being achieved over time. These systems help to answer the all important *so what* questions, and respond to stakeholders growing demands for results.

This annex provides a summary of the book *Ten Steps to a Results–Based Monitoring and Evaluation System* by Jody Zall Kusek and Ray C. Rist. This book, published in 2004, is currently in its fourth printing and has been translated into six languages. It is being used in government offices, NGOs, and universities across the world to introduce concepts and principles of results-based monitoring and evaluation. We, the authors, have agreed to summarize its contents to support this book introducing the 12 Components.

The Ten Steps model addresses the challenge of how governments in general, but those in developing countries in particular, can begin to build results-based monitoring and evaluation systems to provide credible and trustworthy information for their own use, and to share with their citizens. The reality is that putting in place even a rudimentary system of monitoring, evaluating, and reporting on government performance is not easy in the best of circumstances. The obstacles for developing countries are even greater and more formidable, even as they build experience in constructing more traditional M&E systems. These traditional systems typically are used to assess the progress and track the implementation of government projects, programs, and policies.

It should also be acknowledged that it is not a new phenomenon that governments monitor and evaluate their own performance. For this reason, a theoretical distinction needs to be drawn between traditional M&E and results-based M&E. Traditional M&E focuses on the monitoring and evaluation of inputs, activities, and outputs, i.e., project or program implementation. Governments have over time tracked their expenditures and revenues, staffing levels and resources, program and project activities, numbers of participants, goods and services produced, and so forth.

Indeed, traditional efforts at M&E have been a function of many governments for many decades or longer. In fact, there is evidence that the ancient Egyptians (3000 BC) regularly employed traditional monitoring as they tracked their government's outputs in grain and livestock production (Egyptian Museum, Cairo, Egypt). Results-based M&E, however, combines the traditional approach of monitoring implementation with the assessment of results (Mayne and Zapico-Goni, 1999.) It is this linking of both implementation progress with progress in achieving the desired objectives or goals (results) of government policies and programs that make results-based M&E most useful as a tool for public management. Implementing this type of M&E system allows the organization to modify and make adjustments to its theories of change and logic models as well as its implementation processes in order more directly to support the achievement of desired objectives and outcomes

Why Build a Results-Based M&E System Anyway?

A results-based M&E system can help policy-makers answer the fundamental questions of whether promises were kept and outcomes achieved. If governments are promising to achieve improvements in policy areas such as in health care or education, there needs to be some means of demonstrating that such improvements have or have not occurred, i.e., there is a need for measurement. But the issue is not measurement as such. There is a general need, both to document and demonstrate government's own performance to its stakeholders as well as use the performance information to continually improve. As Binnendijk (1999:3) observed: One key use is to ensure transparent reporting on performance and results achieved to external stakeholder audiences. In many cases, government-wide legislation or executive orders have recently mandated such reporting. Moreover, such reporting can be useful in the competition for funds by convincing a skeptical public or legislature that the agency's programs produce significant results and provide *value for money*. Annual performance reports are often directed to ministers, parliament, stakeholders, customers, and the general public. Performance or results information should also be used for internal purposes, such as for management decision making and identifying areas of improvement. This requires that results information be integrated into key management systems and processes of the organization; such as in policy formulation, in project/program planning and management, and in budget allocation processes.

If Information on Results Achieved Is the Key, Then Where Does It Come From?

Results information can come, essentially, from two essential sources, a monitoring system and an evaluation system. Both are needed, but they are not the same. The distinction between monitoring and evaluation is made here both for conceptual and practical purposes. Monitoring can be viewed as periodically measuring progress toward explicit short-, intermediate-, and long-term results. It also can provide feedback on the progress made (or not) to decision-makers who can use the information in various ways to improve the effectiveness of government. Monitoring involves measurement — and what is measured is the progress toward achieving an objective or outcome (result). However, the outcome cannot be measured directly. It must first be translated into a set of indicators that, when regularly measured, will provide information whether or not the outcome is being achieved.

For example: If country X selects the outcome of improving the health of children by reducing childhood morbidity from diarrheal disease by 30% over the next five years, it must now identify a set of indicators that translate childhood morbidity into more specific measurements. Indicators that can help assess the changes in childhood morbidity may include: 1) access to clean water; 2) the level of maternal education; and 3) the degree to which children have access to health clinics. Measuring a disaggregated set of indicators provides important information about how well government programs and policies are working to support the overall outcome.

Understanding the importance of information about whether one's government is keeping promises made or achieving results that are important for various users, is a central reason for building a monitoring system in the first place. Key users in many societies who are often left out of the information flow are citizens, NGO groups, and the private sector, the point being that monitoring data have both internal (governmental) and external uses (societal). It is important to emphasize that information obtained from a monitoring system only reveals information about what is being measured at that time, although it can be compared against both past performance and some planned present level or anticipated performance. Monitoring data do not reveal why a level of performance occurred or provide the likely cause of changes in performance from one reporting period to another. This information comes from an evaluation system. An evaluation system serves as a complementary but distinct function from that of a monitoring system within a results management framework.

Building an evaluation system allows for a more in-depth study of why results (outcomes and impacts) were achieved, or not. It can draw on data sources other than extant indicators; can address factors that are too difficult or expensive to continuously monitor; and, perhaps most important, can tackle the issue of why and how the trends being tracked with monitoring data are moving in the directions they are. Impact data and causal attribution are not to be taken lightly and can play an important role in an organization when making strategic resource allocations. Some performance issues, such as long-term impacts, attribution, cost-effectiveness and sustainability, are better addressed by evaluation than by routine performance monitoring reports.

An additional point is that an M&E system can be designed for, and be applicable to, the project level, the program level, the sector level, and the country level. The specific indicators may be different (as the stakeholders' needs for information will also be different at each level), the complexity of collecting the data will be different, the political sensitivity on collecting the data may change, and the uses of the information may vary from one level to another. But, in the end, it is the creation of a system that is aligned from level to level that is most critical because in this way information can flow up and down in a governmental system rather than being collected only at one level or another, stored and used at that level, but never being shared across levels. Blocking the information from being shared ensures that the linkages between policies, programs, and projects stay disconnected and uncoordinated. At each level, performance information is necessary and there should be the means to collect it. While levels will have different requirements that need to be understood and respected, the creation of an M&E system requires interdependency, alignment, and coordination across all levels.

Usually statistical systems in developed countries can provide precise figures on the numbers of children in rural areas, the number of new swine flu cases in the past 12 months, or the number of disabled adults. However, in developing countries, such information may or may not be available and with widely varying degrees of precision.

Moreover, many developing countries lack the skill base available in government agencies to make this possible. One significant hurdle is the likely certainty that few developing countries will have capacity in the workforce to develop, support, and sustain these systems. Typically, few government officials will have been trained in modern data collection and monitoring methods. Further, still fewer will have been trained in how to interpret different modalities of data analysis. The challenge for development agencies, international NGOs interested in governance issues, and for in-country universities and research institutes, is to provide the needed technical support and training; to accommodate the rapid turnover in staff, the competing priorities, and the need to rebuild political support and commitment as each new political administration comes into office.

This challenge has been particularly noted in many of the most heavily indebted countries, for whom borrowing from the international community is crucial and subsequent relief from this debt essential. The World Bank and the International Monetary Fund (IMF) do allow for debt relief if these countries can demonstrate a serious commitment toward reform, particularly reforms that promote poverty reduction as outlined in a country's national development strategy.

A second challenge for developing countries is that the governments themselves are often only loosely inter-connected, lack strong administrative cultures, and function without the discipline of transparent financial systems. This has resulted in the government being uncertain of the actual levels of resource allocation, whether the allocation in question is applied where it is intended and when it arrives, and if it is used as intended to achieve the desired results. In such an environment, measuring if governments have achieved desired results can be an approximation at best. In some countries, the budget process is one where final budget approval into law does not occur until mid-way through, or near the end of, the budget year. Agencies, thus, can spend well into the budget year without an actual approved budget. This makes it very difficult to introduce fiscal discipline that includes any concern about whether programs are achieving their intended results.

Third, and based on the above two noted constraints, the construction of a results-based system is hindered when there is no means to link results achieved to a public expenditure framework or strategy. Keeping results information separate from the resource allocation process ensures that budget allocation decisions do not consider past results achieved by line agencies. Linking the budget process to knowledge from the M&E system initiates the allocation process of aligning resources to strategic objectives and targets. If no such link is made, then the budget process can be at risk of supporting project and program failures just as readily as it funds those that are successful.

Back to the Beginning – First Things First

We turn now in this last section to the very beginning of building an M&E system by conducting a readiness assessment. This first step is often overlooked by system designers and, we believe, merits special emphasis here. Understanding the complexities and subtleties of the country or sector context is critical to the ultimate success or failure in introducing and using an M&E system (cf. Kusek and Rist, 2001). Furthermore, the needs of the end users are often only somewhat understood by those ready to start the system-building process. For all the good intentions to advance the use of M&E information in the public sector, there has been, from our vantage, too little attention given to organizational, political, and cultural factors. The obvious question is "Why?" The answer lies with insufficient attention given to understanding the influence of these factors on whether the country is *ready* to commit to measuring the performance of government programs and policies. Thus we believe that the first step in the design of a results-based M&E system should be to determine the *readiness* of a government to design and use such a system. If one reads through the literature on building such a system, regardless of the number of steps, the presumption, time and again, is that, like a runner getting ready to begin a race, the designer comes up to the starting line, hears the gun, and then starts building the system.

Why Is it Important to Begin with a Readiness Assessment?[7]

Our experiences in conducting readiness assessments prior to assisting in the building of an M&E system point to one fundamental fact: conducting the readiness assessment is like constructing the foundation for a building. It is below ground, not seen, but critical. A readiness assessment allows those building an M&E system to assess a wide range of contextual factors before any design work begins. The published literature in this area is rather sparse but there are several key sources available that emphasize the importance of studying current organizational capacity in designing an M&E system (Boyle and Lemaire, 1999; Guerrero, 1999; and Mayne, 1997). In this same arena, there are also

---

[7] The use of the term "readiness assessment" here is deliberately used in contrast to the term "needs assessment." We are of the view that it is no longer a question of whether a government ought to collect and report information on its own performance (i.e., does it need such information), but rather only when it has sufficient institutional capacity and political will to do so (is it ready to initiate such a system?).

several diagnostic guides or checklists related to the construction of a strategy for evaluation capacity development (Mackay, 1999).

These guides and checklists are often, appropriately, rather technical in nature as they have to provide information on the quality and quantity of available statistical data, on capacity for data analysis and reporting, and on the capacity of the government to generate new data collection procedures. These guides tend to focus more on the nature of the *supply* of information and data than on the *demand* side. Assessing such supply-side capacity is a necessary part of the design process but it is not enough. The key question we continually emphasize in this regard is "Why collect the information in the first place?"[8] Supplying information should be the response to a need and not an end it itself. Thus, the demand for information to monitor and evaluate public policy and programs comes as the answer to whether desired outcomes and results are or are not being achieved. Building an M&E system that provides such information is a profoundly political event. It is not simply a set of technical procedures. A number of other factors must also be studied when building the foundation for a sustainable M&E system.

From our experience, addressing the following seven questions is critical in ensuring that the key organizational, political, and social dimensions are directly addressed before any M&E system construction begins.

What Is Driving the Need for a Monitoring and Evaluation System within the Public Sector?

Where and why the demand for such a system originates are essential factors in creating a successful and sustainable system. There are internal political and organizational pressures, as well as potential external factors, for building an M&E system that need to be acknowledged and addressed if the response is to be appropriate to the demand. Internal demand can come from efforts to push reform in the public sector, e.g., fighting corruption, strengthening the role of the parliament, and expanding the authority of the Auditor General. It can also come internally from political parties in opposition to the sitting government. External pressures from the international aid community which has been pressing for stronger tracking of the consequences and impacts of its development interventions, can also add to demands. They may also come from such international organizations as the European Union and the criteria it is setting for the accession countries, or from Transparency International, a

---

[8] We are also framing the issue differently to proposing an "evaluability assessment" (cf. Smith, 1987; Wholey, 1987). The issue here is not to see if the logic and specification of a project or program is sufficiently clear to construct an evaluation design prior to the initiation of the project or program, but to inquire whether the particular level or levels of government are in a position to begin collecting, analyzing, and reporting on performance-based M&E data in a continuous fashion in order to inform the decision-making process. In this sense, the emphasis here is less on the program theory of a policy or program than on the operational capacity of a government to initiate such a new function.

global NGO that addresses issues of public sector corruption (cf. Furubo, Rist, and Snadahl, 2002). Other pressures, including new rules of the game that are emerging with globalization, where financial capital and the private sector want a stable investment climate, the rule of law, and the protection of their property and patents before they will commit to investing in a country. The role that external organizations can play in generating pressures for a country to move towards an M&E system should not be underestimated.

Box 1: The case of Egypt — slow, systematic moves toward M&E

One of the most important components of assessing a country's readiness to introduce results-based M&E is whether a champion can be found who is willing to take on ownership of the system. In Egypt, conducting a readiness assessment uncovered significant interest on the part of many senior government officials for moving toward a climate of assessing whether or not results were being achieved. The President himself had called for better information to support economic decision making.

The Minister of Finance was found to be a key champion for the government of Egypt's move to a results focus. This minister was well versed in the international experience of other countries, such as Malaysia and OECD member countries. The minister underscored the importance of giving increased attention to improving the management of public expenditures by moving forward with a set of pilots to demonstrate how results-based M&E could be used to better manage budgetary allocation.

The Minister of Finance will play a key leadership role in any effort to introduce results-based M&E in Egypt.

It was also established that a number of other senior officials were identified who could play important leadership roles. The First Lady of Egypt, who chairs the National Council for Women, is developing a system to monitor and evaluate efforts across many ministries to enhance the status and condition of women. However, for an M&E effort to be successful and sustainable, there must be a *buy-in* (or a sense of ownership) from line ministers who are responsible for resource expenditures and overseeing the implementation of specific programs. The team found interest in monitoring and evaluation for results on the part of several line ministers, including the Minister of Electricity and Energy, and the Minister of Health.

The readiness assessment also revealed a high level of capacity in Egypt to support the move toward a results-based strategy. A number of individuals with evaluation training were identified at the University of Cairo, the American University

---

of Cairo, and private research organizations. In addition, the Central Agency for Public Mobilization and Statistics, and the Cabinet Information Decision Support Center were identified as having key roles in collecting, analyzing, and disseminating data to be used by both government and non-government researchers and policy-makers.

A key criterion for a successful shift toward results is the development of a well-communicated and executable strategy. The diagnostic results identified a fragmented strategy for moving the effort forward. A set of pilots had tentatively been identified, yet there were few, if any, criteria for establishing these as performance pilots. Nor was there a management structure set up within the government to effectively manage the overall effort. The Minister of Finance, however, had begun to define an approach that, if implemented, would provide the necessary leadership to move the effort forward. The minister was determined to move slowly and nurture the pilots, learning along the way.

The results of this readiness assessment suggest that the government of Egypt is prepared to take ownership of the effort and to systematically and slowly begin to introduce the concepts of results management. Visible capacity exists that can be drawn upon to sustain the effort. Significantly, there is strong political support to provide the necessary leadership. (The complete Egypt Readiness Assessment can be found in Annex II of the *Ten Steps* book).

There is no consensus on how many steps are necessary for building an M&E system. Holzer (1999) proposes seven steps; an American NGO (The United Way, 1996) proposes eight steps; and Sharp (2001) proposes a model with four areas for measuring performance to provide the data for monitoring and evaluation.

We have described elsewhere (Kusek and Rist, 2004) a 10-step approach that we have been using in working with a number of developing countries as they each design and construct their M&E system. We have opted for 10 steps (rather than fewer) for the reason that it is important when building such a system that there is sufficient differentiation among tasks. There are so many challenges in building a system that reducing the ambiguity regarding the sequence and activities required at each step can only help.

It is not the intent here to discuss in detail the 10 steps as a more thorough discussion of this is done within the book itself. Suffice it to say, although we have labeled each of the following as a *step*, we are not implying that there is a rigid sequencing here that allows for no concurrent activities. There are a number of areas where there is the need for concurrent activity that can span over steps and over time. The selection of the word *steps* is more to suggest a focus on discrete components in building an M&E system, some of which are sequential and essential before you move on to others.

Step One: Conducting a Readiness Assessment is the means of determining the capacity and willingness of the government and its development partners to construct a results-based M&E system. This assessment addresses such issues as the presence or absence of champions in the government, the barriers to building a system, who will own the system, and who will be the resistors to the system.

Step Two: Agreeing on Outcomes to Monitor and Evaluate addresses the key requirement of developing strategic outcomes that then focus and drive the resource allocation and activities of the government and its development partners. These outcomes should be derived from the strategic priorities (goals) of the country.

Step Three: Developing Key Indicators to Monitor Outcomes is the means of assessing the degree to which the outcomes are being achieved. Indicator development is a core activity in building an M&E system, and drives all subsequent data collection, analysis, and reporting. Both the political and methodological issues in creating credible and appropriate indicators should not be underestimated.

Step Four: Gathering Baseline Data on Indicators emphasizes that the measurement of progress towards outcomes begins with the description and measurement of initial conditions being addressed. Collecting baseline data means essentially to take the first measurements of the indicators.

Step Five: Planning for Improvements and Setting Realistic Targets recognizes that most outcomes are long-term, complex, and not quickly achieved. Thus there is a need to establish interim targets that specify how much progress toward an outcome is to be achieved, in what time frame, and with what level of resource allocation. Measuring results against these targets can involve both direct and proxy indicators as well as the use of both quantitative and qualitative data.

Step Six: Monitoring for Results becomes the administrative and institutional task of establishing data collection, analysis, and reporting guidelines; designating who will be responsible for which activities; establishing means of quality control; establishing timelines and costs; working through the roles and responsibilities of the government, the other development partners, and civil society; and establishing guidelines on the transparency and dissemination of the information and analysis. It is emphasized that the construction of an M&E system needs to address clearly the challenges of ownership, management, maintenance, and credibility.

Step Seven: Evaluative Information to Support Decision Making focuses on the contributions that evaluation studies and analyses can make throughout this process to assessing results and the movement toward outcomes. Analysis of program theory, evaluability assessments, process evaluations, outcome and impact evaluations, and evaluation syntheses are but five of the strategies discussed that can be employed in evaluating a results-based M&E system.

Step Eight: Analyzing and Reporting Findings is a crucial step in this process as it determines what findings are reported to whom, in what format, and at what intervals. This step has to address the existing capacity for producing such information as it focuses on the methodological dimensions of accumulating, assessing, and preparing analyses and reports.

Step Nine: Using the Findings emphasizes that the crux of the system is not in simply generating results-based information but in getting that information to the appropriate users in the system in a timely fashion so that they can take the information into account (as they choose) in the management of the government or organization. This step also addresses the roles of the development partners and civil society in using the information to strengthen accountability, transparency, and resource allocation procedures.

Step Ten: Sustaining the M&E System within Government recognizes the long-term process involved in ensuring longevity and utility. There are six key criteria that are seen to be crucial in the construction of a sustainable system: demand, structure, trustworthy and credible information, accountability, incentives, and capacity. Each of these dimensions needs constant attention over time to ensure the viability of the system. As noted earlier, there is no orthodoxy required that the building of an M&E system has to be done according to these 10 steps. One can posit strategies that are more detailed in the number of steps as well as those with fewer steps (four of which we cited earlier.) The issue is one of ensuring that key strategies and activities are recognized, clustered together in a logical manner, and then done in an appropriate sequence.

Developing Countries Have Notable Challenges

The challenges for developing countries in following the Ten-Step model or any other model are many. First, in Step Two, it is assumed that governments are likely to undertake a process whereby there will be an agreement on national or sector-wide outcomes. Although developed countries typically undertake a strategic (usually 5-10 years) or a medium-term (3-5 years) plan to guide their government priorities, developing countries can find it difficult to do so. This difficulty may stem from a lack of political will, a weak central agency (such as the Ministry of Planning or Ministry of Finance), or a lack of capacity in planning and analysis.

Thus, we continue to emphasize in Step Six that it is important to make sure that traditional implementation-focused M&E is achieved by tracking budget and resource expenditures, making sure that funded activities and programs actually occur, and that promised outputs (number of wells dug, miles of road constructed, youth competing a vocational program, etc.) all exist. The People's

Republic of China represents an interesting example where efforts are being made in this area, especially with its large infrastructure projects (Rist, 2000.)

There is no way to move to a results-based M&E system without the foundation of a basic traditional M&E system. To paraphrase from Louis Carroll's *Alice in Wonderland*: "It is hard to know where to go if you do not know where you are." Thus, in Step Four, we describe how the absence of information on the current conditions (baselines) directly hinders policy and resource planning for how to essentially address what is missing.

1. **Who is driving the need for an M&E system within the organization?** Champions in government are critical to the success and stability of an M&E system. A champion who is highly placed in the government can give a strong voice to the need for better-informed decision making and can help diffuse the attacks of counter-reformers who have vested interests in not seeing such a system implemented. However, if the champion is removed from the center of policy making and has little influence with key decision-makers, it will be more difficult for an M&E system in these circumstances to take hold. Box 1 above provides a summary of the readiness assessment undertaken in Egypt and the location of a champion (Minister of Finance) to carry the effort forward. It also should be noted that, while the presence of a champion is so important, it is also important to work toward the institutionalization of the M&E system with legislation, regulation, or decree. The need in the end is not to have a system that is personalized or based on charisma, but on the structured requirements in the government to produce quality information.

2. **What is motivating the champion?** To build an M&E system is to take a real political risk. Producing information in a government on performance and strengthening the basis for accountability are not neutral activities. Consequently, the question has to be posed of the political benefits for the champion and for his/her institution in order to be willing to take these risks. One cluster of benefits can come from responding to the pressures so that doing something is better than doing nothing and letting the pressures mount still further. Another set of benefits can come from being perceived as a reformer in the government and, hence, as a source of political capital. Third, there are benefits in being on the right side of the issue with the international aid community. The calls for reform, for accountability, and demonstrated evidence of impacts are all being made by the aid community. Showing responsiveness to these pressures is not without its benefits. Finally, the champion may be one who is instilled with a sense of public responsibility, and taking on this challenge is important and not to be walked away from.

3. **Who will own the system? Who will benefit?** And how much information is really required? For an M&E system to be used, it should

be accessible, understandable, and relevant. These criteria drive a need for a careful readiness assessment prior to designing the system regarding ownership of, benefits to, and utility for the relevant stakeholders. Further, while these issues are on the demand side, there is a whole spectrum of issues on the supply side to be addressed, as well such as the capacity to collect and analyze data, capacity to produce reports, capacity to manage and maintain the M&E system, capacity to use the information that is produced, and so forth. The implications for those who will design the system is the risk of building too much complexity or to over-design. There will be constant erosion in the system that has to be addressed, stakeholders may want to pull the system in too many different directions at once and the political arena will not stay the same for long. Such an assessment will also provide important information and baseline data against which necessary capacity building activities can be incorporated into the system. Having said all this, there is still the absolute requirement to collect no more information than is essential. We have found time and again that M&E systems are designed that suffer from immediate overload with too much data being collected and all too often with not enough thought on how to or whether they will be used.

4. **How will the system directly support better resource allocation and the achievement of program goals?** M&E is not an end in itself. It is a tool to promote modern management practices and better accountability. The idea in creating such a system is to support innovation, reform, and better governance. This is done by producing useful information that is also transparent, trustworthy, and relevant. It is also our view that treating the creation of an M&E system as a discrete event that is unconnected to other public sector and public administration reform efforts, or to efforts at creating a medium-term public expenditure framework, or to a restructuring of the administrative culture of the government, is not sustainable. In fact, it is quite the contrary. Linking the creation of the M&E system to precisely such initiatives creates inter-dependencies and reinforcements that can be crucial to the sustainability of the system. The issue for the readiness assessment is whether such linkages are both structurally and politically possible.

5. **How will the organization, the champions, and the staff all react to negative or potentially detrimental information generated by the M&E system?** It is hard for an M&E system to function in an organization or political climate where there is a great deal of fear and corruption. For it is inevitable that an M&E system will at some point (even infrequently) produce data that can be embarrassing, politically sensitive, or detrimental to those who exercise power. The information can also be detrimental to units and individuals in the organization that have produced the information, and going after the messenger is not an unknown event

in organizations. If it is clear from the readiness assessment that only politically popular and *correct* information will be allowed to come from the system, then the system is compromised from the beginning. It will not be seen to be credible by those who are outside the system or by others inside the system. Rather, it will be understood to be a hollow exercise. In such a setting, building the system carefully, starting slowly and trying to find units that will risk the generation of potentially detrimental information about their own performance is, perhaps, the best that can be achieved. Consequently, it is good to understand the barriers and obstacles that exist in the organization, whether these are cultural, structural, political, or individual. Not all barriers can be addressed simultaneously in the design of the system. But not recognizing their presence, not picking the most critical and strategic ones to tackle first, and not taking some initiative to address them is to ensure a level of resistance greater, longer, and more tenacious than would have been necessary otherwise.

6. **How will the M&E system link, even in a rudimentary fashion, the project outcomes to the program outcomes and to sector and national outcomes?** It is a key task of the readiness assessment to learn of the opportunities for and barriers against linking information in a vertical and aligned fashion inside the government. In an ideal situation, the project-level performance data would feed into and be linked to assessment of programs which, in turn, would be linked to assessments of sectoral, regional, and eventually national outcomes and targets. Results-based information at any level that is not linked vertically to the information needs at the next level is not useful beyond the restricted information needs at that same level. Choking off the flow of information between levels is to ensure that performance-based decisions cannot be made where one level informs decisions to the next. It is also relevant in this context to ascertain if there is a commitment in the collection and analysis of data to ensure that where data is collected at a level that it is shared or used with persons at that same level. Stated differently, can the system address the need at every level to be both producers and consumers of results-based information. Building a system that allows relevant questions to be asked and answered at the appropriate levels even as some components of that information feeds needs at other levels is the objective. Breaks in that system (much as a chain where links are missing) renders the entire initiative less useful.

Postscript

Building an M&E system is easier said than done; otherwise, we would see these systems as an integral part of good public management practices in governments without the need to consider this issue. But the reality is otherwise. There are few such systems (in whole or in part) fully integrated into the public management strategies of developed countries and still fewer in developing countries. It is not that governments are not trying, because many are. It is just that creating such a system takes time, resources, stability in the political environment, and champions who are not faint-of-heart. This brings us to the significant challenge of sustainability. Indeed, governments willing to use results-based information to assist in the governance of the political system and frame public policies, give evidence of some level of democracy and openness. But even in these countries, there is often a reluctance to measure and monitor for fear that the process will present bad news to the leadership and other stakeholders. Presenting one's performance shortfalls to others is not typical bureaucratic behavior. Thus, the efforts to build such a system should recognize the inherent and real political limitations and should start with a simple approach, working with stakeholders to help them recognize that it is their right to be regularly informed on the performance of their government and continue to emphasize, time and again, that information can help improve policy making and public management. To achieve these modest goals should then be reason for longer-term optimism.

Annex C: Example of a 4-Day 12-Component Training Program

Training curriculum for 4-day training chapter on:

(a)   Managing to HIV Results and

(b)   Building HIV M&E Systems to Measure Results

Learning Objectives

There are three main learning objectives for this curriculum: First, to enable participants to understand the importance of managing to results; second, to equip participants to manage to results; and third, to enable participants to build HIV M&E systems to measure results.

Course Schedule

	08:00 – 10:00	10:30 – 13:00	14:00 – 15:00	15:30 – 17:00
Day 1	Introduction to concepts in relation to Managing to Results	The need for "knowing Your Epidemic," Making Strategies Results-Focused, Selecting Outcomes and Indicators	Group work	Group work
Day 2	From Planning for Results to Measuring Results: Key concepts on building HIV M&E systems	**Component 1:** Organizational Structures **Group work** for Component 1	**Component 2:** Human capacity	**Component 3:** M&E partnerships Group work for Component 3
Day 3	**Components 4 and 5:** M&E frameworks & developing a costed M&E work plan Group work for Component 5	**Component 6:** Advocacy and Communications	**Component 7:** Surveys and Surveillance	**Component 8:** Routine Program Monitoring
Day 4	**Component 9:** Data auditing and supervision	**Component 10:** HIV information systems **Group work** for Component 10	**Component 11:** HIV Research and Evaluation	**Component 12:** Data dissemination and data use **Group work:** Component 12

Day 1

Session name and times	Session learning objectives	Knowledge areas covered	Methodology	Evaluation of session
DAY 1: 08:00 – 10:00 Introduction to concepts in relation to managing to results	a) To introduce concepts of results-based monitoring and evaluation b) To show how these concepts can be applied to strategy planning and system development	a) Strategic planning b) Management principles c) Principles of results management	Plenary and small-group work	Understanding logic sequencing
DAY 1: 10:30 – 13:00 Knowing your epidemic and selecting outcomes and indicators	a) To introduce concepts on epidemiological analysis, and use of this data for learning b) Introduce logic frameworks and their use in management and planning c) To help students choose appropriate outcomes and indicators for good planning	a) Knowledge use b) Monitoring and evaluation principles c) Use of logic diagrams	Plenary and small-group work	Developing results frameworks
DAY 1: 14:00 – 16:30 Group work	Students will review a " pretend" country epidemiological profile and develop a results framework for a national HIV/AIDS National Response	Same knowledge areas covered throughout the day	Group work	Ability to use data to help develop a national response

Making Monitoring and Evaluation Systems Work

Day 2

Session name and times	Session learning objectives	Knowledge areas covered	Methodology	Evaluation of session
DAY 2: 08:00 – 10:00 **From Planning for Results to Measuring Results:** Key concepts on building HIV M&E systems	a) To confirm that all learners understand key M&E terms b) To introduce learners to the concept of the 12 Components c) To help learners understand that all M&E learning in this course will be focused on either one of the 12 Components — i.e., that the 12 Components provide an organizing framework for the course d) To introduce learners to the Resource Library	• Short refresher: key M&E terms • Goal and objectives of M&E systems • History of the 12 Components • Introduction to the 12 Components and the Resource Library	• **Plenary:** Five questions with key M&E terms • **Plenary brainstorm:** Goals and objectives of M&E systems • **PowerPoint:** 12 Components • **Small group brainstorm:** Assign sessions of the training course to one of the 12 Components • **On-screen demonstration** of the Resource Library • **Individual exercise** to identify 12 Components	**Individual exercise** to identify the 12 Components within their own organizations

Day 2

Session name and times	Session learning objectives	Knowledge areas covered	Methodology	Evaluation of session
DAY 2: **10:30 – 13:00** **Component 1:** Organizational structures with HIV M&E	To enable learners to: a) design organizational structures across sectors with HIV M&E functions embedded in them b) develop job descriptions for full-time M&E staff	• Principles of organizational design • Impact of decentralization on M&E organizational design • Examples of organizational structures with M&E functions embedded in them • Writing job descriptions for M&E posts in NAC organogram	• **PowerPoint:** Design principles in organizational design • **Plenary discussion:** People involved in HIV M&E in a country — at all levels — are they in full-time posts or part-time assignments • **PowerPoint:** Impact of decentralization on M&E organizational design • **Plenary discussion:** Identify challenges with organizational structures presented • **PowerPoint:** Designing job descriptions — technical aspects, authority and power • **Group exercise:** Designing job descriptions	**Group work exercise:** Customize the job descriptions of officers of an M&E unit of a National AIDS Commission to ensure that they are comprehensive (different groups, different posts)
DAY 2: **14:00 – 15:00** **Component 2:** Human capacity for HIV M&E	To make learners aware of: a) the types of capacity that are required to operationalize HIV M&E systems b) the stakeholders whose capacity need to be built c) the different capacity building mechanisms	• Range of human capacity requirements for M&E systems • Stakeholders involved in HIV M&E • Types of capacity building mechanisms	• **PowerPoint:** Types of capacity building mechanisms and examples of capacity development assessments • **Plenary discussion:** Types of human capacity for M&E systems	Plenary discussion

Day 2

Session name and times	Session learning objectives	Knowledge areas covered	Methodology	Evaluation of session
DAY 2: 15:30 – 17:00 **Component 3:** M&E partnerships	To enable learners to: a) articulate the importance of partnerships b) distinguish between internal and external partnerships c) identify stakeholders with whom partnerships should be built d) write the TOR for a partnership structure	• Reasons why partnerships are important • Types of partnerships (internal and external) • Mechanisms for establishing partnerships • Creating a partnership forum • Mechanisms to maintain partnerships	• **Class brainstorm:** Write on flip charts the existing M&E partnerships — formal or informal — in your country; and how these partnerships have been useful • **PowerPoint:** Establishing the counterfactual — what if there were no partnerships; listing types of partnerships, and mechanisms for creating and maintaining partnerships • **Individual exercise:** Improve the TOR of an existing partnership forum	**Individual exercise:** Improve a Terms of Reference of an existing partnership forum

Day 3

Session name and times	Session learning objectives	Knowledge areas covered	Methodology	Evaluation of session
DAY 3: 08:00 – 10:00 **Component 4:** (M&E framework) and **Component 5:** (Costed M&E work plan)	To enable learners to a) evaluate the quality of an M&E framework b) lead the development of a national costed M&E work plan	• Purpose of M&E frameworks • Types of M&E frameworks and how they link to the 12 Components • Purpose of developing national HIV M&E plans • Process of developing national HIV M&E plans • Challenges in developing M&E frameworks and national costed M&E plans	• **Plenary discussion:** Brainstorm terminology, and distinguish between them • **PowerPoint:** Typical process of development and typical contents of a national HIC M&E framework • **Plenary exercise:** Identify which of the 12 Components have been covered in the example M&E framework provided to the group • **PowerPoint:** Steps in costing a national HIV M&E work plan; and key principles to take into account when costing a national HIV M&E work plan • Group exercise: Develop a unit cost table and cost a national HIV M&E work plan	**Group work exercises:** (a) Link Tables of contents of M&E frameworks to 12 Components (b) identify possible challenges during the development of a national HIV M&E work plan
DAY 3: 10:30 – 13:00 **Component 6:** Advocacy, culture and communications for HIV M&E	To enable learners to: a) understand types of communications and advocacy for HIV M&E	• Target groups for communications and advocacy • Process of developing communication strategies • Types of communications — above the line, below the line and through the line • Types of communication channels	• **Plenary discussion:** Target groups for HIV M&E communications and advocacy • **PowerPoint:** Process of developing a communications and advocacy strategy; types of communications and types of communication channels	**Plenary discussion** about target groups for HIV M&E communications and advocacy

Day 3

Session name and times	Session learning objectives	Knowledge areas covered	Methodology	Evaluation of session
DAY 3: **14:00 – 15:00** **Component 7:** Routine Program Monitoring	To enable learners to: a) Recognize types of routine program monitoring b) Understand the processes involved in managing routine data	• Types of routine program data in HIV and sources of data • Mechanisms for collecting routine program monitoring data • Challenges for routine program monitoring	• **Plenary discussion:** Types of routine monitoring for HIV, their sources, and experience in collecting such data • **PowerPoint:** Case studies from 5 countries in Africa: operationalizing routine program monitoring systems • **Individual exercise:** List the individuals involved in routine program monitoring systems and their functions	**Plenary discussion**
DAY 3: **15:30 – 17:00** **Component 8:** Data auditing and supervision	To enable learners to: a) distinguish between mentoring, support, data auditing and supervision b) design data auditing and supervision processes taking key principles into account To make learners aware of issues to consider when conducting data auditing and supervision visits	• Definitions of supervision and data auditing • Principles of supervision and data auditing • Supervision and data auditing processes • Example data auditing and supervision guidelines • Experiences in executing data auditing or supervision visits	• **PowerPoint:** Supervision and Data Auditing definitions; Principles of Data Auditing and Supervision • **Plenary:** Points to be included in data auditing and Supervision Guidelines • **PowerPoint:** Example Data Auditing and Supervision Guidelines • **Group exercise:** Conduct a 5-minute role play of a good/bad supervision and data audit visit	**Group work exercise:** Conduct a 5- minute role play of a good/bad supervision and data audit visit

Day 4

Session name and times	Session learning objectives	Knowledge areas covered	Methodology	Evaluation of session
DAY 4: 08:00 – 10:00 **Component 9:** Surveys and surveillance	To enable learners to distinguish between types of surveys and surveillance relating to HIV	• Purpose and types of epidemiological surveillance • Other surveys relating to HIV/AIDS • Typical surveillance or survey process	• **Plenary:** Brainstorm types of surveys relating to HIV that you are aware of • **PowerPoint:** Types of surveys and surveillance relating to HIV/AIDS; using surveillance data to estimate HIV prevalence • **Group exercise:** Difference between surveys, surveillance, research and routine program monitoring data • **PowerPoint:** Typical survey or surveillance implementation process	**Group work exercise:** Describe the difference between surveys, surveillance, research and routine program monitoring data
DAY 4: 10:30 – 13:00 **Component 10:** HIV information systems	To give learners an overall awareness of issues to consider in terms of HIV database design	• Principles of relational database design • Mechanisms for data capture into system • Steps in database / information system design • Key products from information system design processes • Example concept proposals and technical specifications	• **Plenary:** Familiarity with relational databases • **PowerPoint:** Introduction to relational databases; mechanisms for data capture into database • **PowerPoint:** Models of information system design and key deliverables	Plenary discussion

Day 4

Session name and times	Session learning objectives	Knowledge areas covered	Methodology	Evaluation of session
DAY 4: 14:00 – 15:00 **Component 11:** HIV research and learning	To enable learners to: a) conduct an inventory of HIV research b) lead the development of a national HIV research strategy and research agenda	• Types of HIV research • Linkages with national research councils • Ethical approvals • Inventories of HIV research • Process steps in developing a national HIV research strategy	• **PowerPoint:** Types of HIV research; ethical approval processes and considerations; Example HIV research inventories • **Group exercise:** Write down the steps of developing an HIV research strategy	**Group exercise:** Write down the steps of developing an HIV research strategy
DAY 4: 15:30 – 17:00 **Component 12:** Data dissemination and data use	To enable learners to: a) use data for decision making	• Data analysis — descriptive statistics • Types of information products • Developing an information product matrix • Developing a dissemination matrix • Data use	• **PowerPoint:** Strategies for Data Use • **Plenary:** Example descriptive statistics • **Group exercise:** Use data provided	**Group exercise:** Use data provided

Annex D: Example of an 8-Day 12-Component Training Program

Designing and Implementing Sustainable Results-based Monitoring and Evaluation Systems in the Public Sector in Turkey

Learning Outcomes

- Participants should have developed sector outcomes that are linked to the ninth development plan (NDP) outcomes.

- Participants should have developed indicators for their sector outcomes.

- Participants should be able to assess, design and revise their sector's M&E system to measure the achievement of their sector outcomes.

- Participants should be able to design or revise their sector's M&E plan based on assessment results.

- Participants should be able to develop a prioritized work plan for their M&E system, and cost it.

Course Schedule

	09:30 – 10:45	11:00 – 12:30	13:30 – 15:00	15:15 – 17:30
Day 1	What does it mean to "manage to results" and what do we need to do different?	Understanding the issues in your sector and linking the issues in your sector to the outcomes that your sector needs to achieve	Group work on developing sector outcomes that are linked to national NDP outcomes	Group work on developing sector outcomes that are linked to national NDP outcomes
Day 2	Using information to improve your sector's NDP outcomes	Introduction to M&E concepts	Selecting key indicators to monitor the sector outcomes	Group work on indicators for each sector's outcomes
Day 3	Group work on indicators for each sector's outcomes	Group work on indicators for each sector's outcomes	Baseline data and setting targets: how do I do it?	Practical on baseline data and setting targets for the sector's indicators
Day 4	What does my sector's M&E system need to look like to be sustainable? Introduction to the 12 Components of a sustainable sector-wide M&E system	Practical on understanding each of the 12 Components and how these contribute to a sustainable results-based M&E system for your sector	Design M&E system components and plan for their improvement: Overview	Design M&E system components and plan for their improvement: Data collecting, processing and quality control (Components 7, 8, 9, 10 and 11)

	09:30 – 10:45	11:00 – 12:30	13:30 – 15:00	15:15 – 17:30
Day 5	Practical on designing M&E system components and plan for their improvement: **Data collecting, processing and quality control**	Design M&E system components and plan for their improvement: **Enabling environment for M&E system (Components 1, 2, 3, and 6)**	Practical on design M&E system components and plan for their improvement: **Enabling environment for M&E system**	Practical on designing M&E system components and plan for their improvement: **Enabling environment for M&E system**
Day 6	Assessing the status of the M&E system/s in your sector	Practical on M&E system status assessments	Using M&E system assessment results to prioritize M&E system improvements: how to and how not to do it	Developing an M&E plan for the M&E system for your sector
Day 7	Practical on developing an M&E plan for your sector's M&E system (Component 4)	Practical on developing an M&E plan for your sector's M&E system (continued)	Practical on developing an M&E plan for your sector's M&E system (continued)	Introduction to costing an M&E system (Component 5)
Day 8	Practical on costing an M&E plan for your sector (Component 5)	Practical on costing an M&E plan for your sector (continued)	Putting it all together: Using information from the M&E system to improve your sector's contribution to overall NDP results (Component 12)	Practical on using information from the M&E system to improve your sector's contribution to overall NDP results

Chapter 1
Structure and Organizational Alignment for Monitoring and Evaluation Systems

Chapter Aim

The aim of this chapter is to enable you to understand the importance of organizational structure and its relation to organizational alignment when designing and making M&E systems work and to help you plan the human resources needed for your M&E system.

Chapter Knowledge and Skills

By the end of this chapter, you should be able to:

a) Explain to others the key concepts relating to organizational structures and organizational alignment for M&E (in other words, explain where M&E "fits" within an organizational structure and its alignment with other key functions of the organization).

b) Design an M&E organizational structure of appropriate size and responsibilities for your organization.

c) Know the pitfalls to avoid when designing the M&E part of an organization.

Before You Begin…

Take a few minutes to read through the questions below. You may find it helpful to write down your answers. As you work through the chapter, compare your answers to the views of the authors.

- Are your organization's mission and goals written down?
- Does everyone in the organization understand how their job contributes to the organization's goals (alignment)?
- Are there incentives for successfully achieving the goals of the organization?
- Does your organization have the mandate and authority to carry out monitoring and evaluation tasks?
- Is everybody clear on their monitoring and evaluation responsibilities?
- Do the parts of the organization involved in M&E have relevant job descriptions that include adequately defined M&E functions, and are these posts filled?
- Do the organization and its staff feel responsible for monitoring and evaluation functions just as they do for other aspects of the work?
- Are staff supported by their managers in carrying out their M&E tasks?
- How is technical support for M&E managed in your organization?

These questions remind us that, without people, an organization's M&E system cannot work. People need to be motivated to complete their M&E tasks, they must be clear on what their tasks are and must be rewarded if they complete their tasks well. This chapter will teach you how to design organizational structures with embedded M&E functions and how to design job descriptions for staff with M&E functions.

Component 1: Structure and Organizational Alignment for M&E Systems

1. Introduction

> *"Individually, we are one drop. Together, we are an ocean."*
>
> Ryunosuke Satoro

Skilled personnel are vital for an M&E system and this component is about the people involved in the M&E system, the first component in the trio of *people, partnerships, and planning* in the M&E system (see introductory chapter).

How this chapter is organized: The chapter begins with selected background information and definitions that provide context and theory on organizational structure, processes and management (Section 2), followed by a suggested results goal for this part of an M&E system (Section 3). Section 4 raises relevant implementation issues. Section 5 goes through the steps for ensuring a strong role for M&E in the organization, to codify it in an organogram in order to define the role of M&E in the organization and plan the visible, *hard* aspects, including the people required to make the M&E system work. The chapter closes with a summary of skills and knowledge gained (Section 6) and a practical exercise to cement what you have learned (Section 7).

2. Background Information and Definitions

Organizational structure: Organizational structure describes the hierarchy, reporting lines, and systematic arrangement of work in an organization. It is depicted in an organizational chart or organogram, showing how the various parts of the organization relate to each other.

Types of Organizational Structures:[1] An organization should choose the type of structure that best suits its needs. This will depend on a variety of things; for example, the structure can be based on geographical regions, products or hierarchy.

- **Traditional Structure:** Traditional structures are based on functional divisions and departments. These kinds of structures tend to have clear rules and procedures with precise authority lines for all levels. Sub-types of traditional organizational structures include:

  i. *Line structure:* This kind of structure has a very specific line of command. Approvals and orders originate from top to bottom in a

---

[1] This section is adapted from Irani, K, 2007.

line, hence, the name *line structure*. This kind of structure is suitable for smaller organizations. Decision making tends to be easy and informal. There are usually relatively few departments.

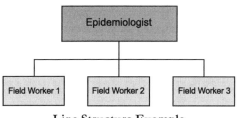

Line Structure Example

ii. *Line and staff structure:* Though line structure is suitable for most organizations, especially small ones, it is not effective for larger companies. This is where the line and staff organizational structure comes into play. This combines line structure, where information and approvals originate from top to bottom, with staff departments for support and specialization. Line and staff organizational structures are more centralized. Managers of line and staff have authority over their subordinates but staff managers have no authority over line managers and their subordinates. Decision making tends to be slower because there are typically several layers and guidelines and more formality.

iii. *Functional structure:* This kind of organizational structure classifies people or parts of the organization according to the functions they perform. The organization chart for a functionally based organization may, for example, consist of the Minister and the

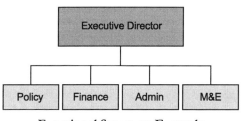

Functional Structure Example

departments for Research, Partnerships, Planning, Accounting, and Administration.

- **Divisional Structure:** This kind of structure is based on divisions in the organization, which may be defined by products, services or location.

  i. *Product/service structure:* A product structure

Service Structure Example

organizes employees and work on the basis of different types of products or services. If the company produces three different types of products, it will have three different divisions for these products.

ii. *Geographic structure:*
Large organizations
have offices in
different places. For
example, there could
be north, south, west,
and east regions.
The organizational
structure could
follow a regional structure.

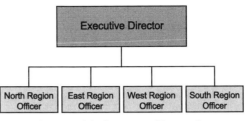

Geographic Structure Example

- **Team Structure:** Many organizations with divisional structures adopt a team-based approach which is different from the organizational structures described above because *structure* is not permanent. When a new project or intervention is created, a team is formed to achieve the outcomes. Teams often have to deal with internal conflict issues and difficulties can arise when team members belong to other unrelated teams at the same time. Teams may be formed by people from different departments. Teams tend to be self-directed working groups organized around work processes, with very flat spans of control and little formalization.

- **Matrix Structure:** This combines functional and product structures and aims to achieve the best of both worlds and to produce an efficient organizational structure. This is the most complex organizational structure. It is important to find a structure that works best for the organization because the wrong set up could hamper proper functioning in the organization. A matrix "has two axes, rather than a pyramid shape. The vertical hierarchy is overlaid by some lateral authority, influence or

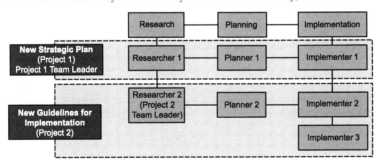

Matrix Structure Example

communication, and there are dual lines line of responsibility, authority and accountability that violate the traditional 'one-boss,' principle of management" (Manage 2008: 12).

- **Hybrid Structure:** An organization can also have a hybrid structure where more than one type of organizational structure is used.

The example shown here is a hybrid of the functional and geographic organizational structures.

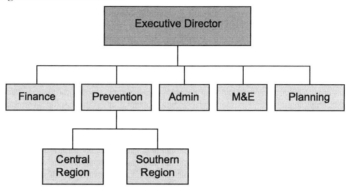

Hybrid Structure Example

Span of control: This concept in organizational design refers to the number of subordinates that a manager can direct efficiently and effectively manage (Robbins and Decenzo, 2001).

Principle of organizational design [adapted for M&E context from Ad Esse (2005)] Structure should follow strategy and processes: organizational structure is only determined after the organization's strategy (in this case, for M&E) and processes (to execute the M&E strategy) have been defined.

Mandate, authority, and responsibility: The specific requirements placed on each organization to execute M&E functions and the organization's response to these can be described in terms of the organization's mandate, authority and responsibility to carry out M&E functions. Different organizations may be given different mandates, areas of authority, and authority levels to execute M&E functions.

- An organization's **mandate** for M&E is the specific order given to an organization to execute M&E functions. A mandate could be provided verbally or established in writing, for example, in a national policy, national strategic plan or national monitoring and evaluation plan. For example, at a meeting of civil society organizations, one organization may be given the mandate to represent the other organizations in a national M&E technical working group.

- An organization's **authority** to carry out M&E functions usually will come from the need to assess progress toward the organization's strategy. This function is undertaken by units within an organization that are capable of measuring, analyzing, and reporting on a core set of indicators that, when tracked regularly, will help assess progress towards the organization's goals. As with all organizational functions, the authority to carry out M&E functions should be documented in writing.

- An organization's **responsibility** to carry out M&E functions can be defined as its obligation to perform assigned functions (Robbins and Decenzo, 2001). If an organization has been given the mandate and authority to perform specific M&E functions, then it is the organization's responsibility to ensure that it is able to execute its M&E functions. Evidence that an organization is executing its M&E responsibilities (or is preparing to do so), could include: M&E posts created and filled, relevant and specific M&E functions included in the job descriptions of M&E staff, and M&E functions being completed (and, thus, the M&E system becoming or remaining functional).

Organizational culture: One of the most important building blocks for a highly successful organization and workplace is *organizational culture*. We define organizational culture as the set of shared beliefs, assumptions, and values that operate in organizations. Organizational culture has been described as "...how people behave when no one is looking."

3. Results to Be Achieved When Implementing this Component

Long-term result: The staff in the organization are clear on the organization's overall goals and the strategies it has chosen to achieve its goals, understand the role of M&E in helping the organization meet its goals, are motivated to fulfil their M&E responsibilities, and are able to execute their M&E responsibilities without hindrance.

Short- and medium-term results:

- Clear and relevant job descriptions for M&E staff
- Adequate number of skilled M&E staff
- Effective leadership for M&E and commitment to ensuring M&E system performance
- Incentives for individuals to be involved in ensuring M&E system performance
- Defined career path in M&E for M&E professionals

For reflection 1:

Reflect on the organizational goals and strategy of your organization. Is there a codified role for M&E and is the M&E structure easily found on the overall organization's organogram? Does your organization have M&E functions? Are M&E functions executed? Are M&E formally assigned to one or more posts or units in the organization? How many of the short- and medium-term results listed here are visible in your organization?

4. Implementation Issues Regarding Organizational Alignment and Structure for M&E Systems

4.1. Where should M&E units be located?

The literature varies in its views on the correct placement of an M&E unit within the organization. Certainly, the M&E function must work collaboratively with the planning and budget functions. Some organizations give the M&E function separate and equal placement within the organization, others co-locate the M&E function with the budget or planning function.

If M&E is mandated primarily for accountability (did the organization spend its funds wisely in pursuit of organizational goals?) then the best place for the M&E function may be outside the primary organization — such as the United States Government Accountability Office (GAO) or the World Bank's Independent Evaluation Group (IEG), or DFID's Department of Evaluation (see Annex A). These M&E units provide an independent review function of an organization's programs.

Likewise, there may be a need to create a separate evaluation office or function for operations research and/or program evaluation. This *Evaluation Unit* would focus on evaluation only, and not on implementing an entire 12-component M&E system (as presented in this course).

The alternatives of locating M&E units independently or as part of a planning or programming division both have advantages and disadvantages (see Table C1-1).

There is not one *correct* option. It is necessary to strike a balance, and all factors that could influence the dynamics within the organization are taken into account before a decision is made where to place the unit. What has worked in some contexts is to place the M&E unit within the policy and planning unit and to create a senior post, e.g., deputy director, to lead the M&E unit. This gives the M&E unit sufficient authority and some autonomy to initiate new actions, get budgets approved, and so forth.

The following questions may help you decide where to place an M&E unit in your organization:

- What have been previous experiences with M&E units within the organization?

- What are your organization's culture and leadership styles (dramatic, suspicious, detached, depressive, compulsive; see De Vries, 2001)?

- Which people are currently employed to fulfill M&E positions?

- How does your organization view its information-sharing role and what priority does it give to M&E?

- What are the major challenges facing the M&E unit internally?
- What are the major decisions that the M&E unit needs to make?
- What are the future intentions of the organization on M&E and information sharing?

Table C1-1: Advantages and Disadvantages of Locating M&E Units Within a Planning Unit, as a Stand-Alone Unit, or Sub-Contracted Out

	Advantages	Disadvantages
M&E unit within the planning unit	• M&E functions better linked to policy and planning processes • M&E unit likely to play stronger role in Joint Annual Program Reviews • Better opportunities for M&E to be mainstreamed	• Less authority, autonomy and power • More bureaucratic processes • Managed by a person who may not be technically proficient in M&E • M&E spokesperson may not be an advocate
M&E unit as a stand-alone unit	• More autonomy, authority and power • Quicker decision making • Less bureaucratic procedures	• M&E not mainstreamed within organization or within planning processes • M&E may be seen by staff as a policing function • M&E results and processes may not be well understood by staff • Distinction or complement between M&E and program management/coordination not well understood or implemented
M&E sub-contracted out	• M&E activities can have strong results focus: no performance, no pay • Salary scales not bound by public service; can contract higher expertise • Performance-based contract should generate high level of performance	• Changes in direction in M&E may affect the contractual relationship between the organization and M&E contractor • M&E is seen as practically an outsourced function • Higher cost of M&E • M&E not mainstreamed in organization's functions • Contractor cannot officially represent the organization in meetings or make decisions on its behalf

4.2. M&E responsibilities need to be formally assigned to individual posts in the organizational structure

Employees are more likely to fulfill tasks that are officially assigned to them and for which their performance is explicitly rewarded. This makes it critical that each organization involved in M&E be given specific M&E functions, so that these M&E functions can be assigned to relevant posts. Unless the organization's M&E functions are assigned to specific posts in the organization, it is unlikely that people in the organization will execute M&E functions on their own initiative.

4.3. Embedding M&E into an organization does not require full-time staff in all cases

Responsibility for M&E and M&E functions in an organizational structure does not necessarily require new staff appointments. Although in some cases, posts may be needed with full-time staff dedicated to M&E tasks (i.e., M&E officers, data clerks, and statisticians in an M&E unit), existing staff could also have M&E responsibilities assigned to them, in addition to their regular responsibilities.

4.4. Human resource planning and management is paramount in retaining good quality staff

Once organizations with M&E functions have identified and defined the positions required to execute them, the posts must be filled with appropriately skilled individuals (see Component 2). These individuals (human resources) need to be managed well. This requires responsive human resource (HR) policies, systems, and strategies and sound HR practices to retain good quality staff.

4.5. Technical support for M&E needs to be managed

Given the importance of results for development partners and the recent emergence of M&E systems, levels of M&E technical support made available to governments have increased exponentially. This support needs to be managed. It is important to understand the types of consultancy arrangements as they will affect the way the M&E system is managed. Each type of consultancy arrangement has its own advantages and disadvantages (see Figure C1-1).

- **Who issues the contract and pays?** The client may issue the contract and pay for some consultancies, or the development partner may do so.
- **Consultants may be hired as individuals, or through a firm:** Some consultants are appointed in their individual capacity while other consultants are appointed through a consulting company or agency that employs full-time or short-term staff who are deployed to countries as needed.
- **Other variables:** Consultants may be local or international, based within

the country or travel to the country specifically to perform the consultancy services. All of these factors will determine the scope of technical support that the client will have to manage. Irrespective of the type of consultancy agreement, it is necessary to agree on how M&E technical support will be managed.

Figure C1–1: Advantages and Disadvantages of Consultancy Arrangements

Consultant appointed by client
(i.e., contract between consultant and client)

Freelance consultant (contract is with individual consultant)

ADVANTAGES:	ADVANTAGES:
- Highly flexible — scope of work can be adjusted as consultancy proceeds - Lower cost — no organization overheads - Usually, quicker procurement procedures - Fewer politics in the recommendations that are accepted — seen as client recommendations, not influenced by development partner agenda **DISADVANTAGES:** - Selection of consultant is paramount - If consultant selection is wrong, funding for consultancy is wasted	- Highest level of quality assurance possible - Client is in direct control of contract - Client can hold company responsible for quality of deliverables - Less politics in the recommendations — seen as client recommendations, not influenced by development partner agenda **DISADVANTAGES:** - Less flexibility in terms of the contract
ADVANTAGES: - Client can hold development partner accountable - Development partner can allow for some flexibility **DISADVANTAGES:** - Development partner reputation is dependent on quality of consultant - Client is dependent on selection procedures of development partner	**ADVANTAGES:** - More quality assurance — development partner can hold company responsible for performance standards - Client does not need to deal with contract administration **DISADVANTAGES:** - Client is dependent on development partner selection procedures - Client does not manage consultancy — so less influence over outputs

Consultant is employee of organization (contract is with organization)

Consultant appointed by development partner (i.e., contract between consultant and development partner, and written agreement between development partner and client for support that will be provided)

4.6. Organizational culture plays an important role

Organizational culture is subtle and seldom made explicit. A negative organizational culture with respect to data management and information dissemination will make it difficult for the M&E system to be functional and effective. Organizational culture is part of the *hidden* and informal forces that drive an organization (i.e., submerged part of the iceberg that cannot be seen; see Figure C1-2 below) (Ketz De Vries, 2001). It plays a strong role in the organization's effectiveness and should be taken into account. Organizational culture is strongly influenced by the leadership of the organization.

Component 6 provides more information about how to create an organizational culture that is strongly supportive of M&E.

Figure C1-2:   Visible and Hidden Organizational Processes

What's visible
Vision   Goals
Mission   Strategies
Structure   Operating policies
Job descriptions

Formal organization:
Rational forces

What's hidden   Power and influence patterns
Informal organization: Group dynamics
Irrational forces   Conformity forces
                          Impulsiveness
                          Feelings
                          Interpersonal; relations
                          Organizational culture
                          Individual needs

Source: Ketz De Vries, 2001

5. HowTo Guide C1-1: How to Design and Align an Organizational Structure for M&E

When designing how an organization should work, the following organizational design principles should be understood and considered: structure should follow strategy at all times, ensure an appropriate span of control, and establish a clear chain of command. However, it is **not** simply the structure of an organization that makes it function appropriately. The organizational processes, and their alignment, help ensure that appropriate information will flow (refer back to section 2 for more details). There are a number of different steps to ensure that an organization's design and function support its strategy. Remember, the purpose of an M&E function/unit is to ensure that the organization is able to generate and feed back information to allow the decision-makers of the organization to use evidence when making decisions.

The following nine steps, found in the organizational design literature, are often used to design organizations' M&E unit/functions. They are not the only ones, and depending on why an organization has decided to ensure that M&E functions are carried out, there may be others.

Step 1:   Agree on the top five reasons why M&E is necessary for your organization (ministry, functional group, and so forth)

Step 2:   Identify the M&E champions and counter-reformers

Step 3:   Define the M&E functions for which the organization is responsible

Step 4:   Group the M&E functions logically together and assign post/s to each logical grouping

Step 5:   Develop an organizational structure

Step 6:   Develop a job description for each post with M&E functions in the organization

Step 7:   Plan for the implementation of the new organizational structure

Step 8:   Gain approval for the organizational structure for M&E

Step 9:   Implement the change management plan and the new organizational structure

Step 1:   Agree on the top five reasons why M&E is necessary for your organization

Unless an organization knows why M&E is necessary and useful to the organization and its success, neither management nor the organization staff will be motivated to amend the organizational structure to include M&E functions. Write down the reasons why M&E are useful and find examples or case studies from similar organizations where M&E has worked and worked well.

Deliverable: A clear understanding of the role of M&E for the organization.

Step 2:   Identify the M&E champions and counter-reformers

Ensuring political and management buy-in is a very important but neglected step. Ask "Who are the champions?" to find those who will use information to make better decisions. Hold close to these individuals. Also ensure you have asked the question, "Who are the counter-reformers who would prefer that evidence-based decision making does not occur in the organization?" These individuals will have to be managed carefully.

Although designing an organizational structure is primarily a technical process, political and management buy-in is needed for three reasons:

a)   The results of the process will need to be approved and implemented by the management of the organization and they will be more inclined to do so if they are aware of the process.

b)   Employees of the organization are more likely to participate in and be positive about organizational design processes that have been seen to be initiated and endorsed by senior management.

c)   Senior management needs to lead the change-management process, if organizational design changes are to be effectively implemented.

Obtaining political buy-in requires that management be presented with the following:

*   The objectives of the organizational design change

*   Reasons why it is necessary (i.e., the reasons why M&E will be useful to the organization)

*   The persons involved in the process

*   The expected time frame

*   Anticipated costs

*   Process steps to be followed (briefly, from start to approval)

*   Likely organizational benefits

Deliverable: A clear mandate from the organization's leadership to revise the organization's structure and a commitment to follow through on the results of the organizational restructuring process.

Step 3:   Define the M&E functions for which the organization is responsible

The organization's M&E functions can be derived from the mandate and authority that the organization has been given or from some other organizational documents such as:

*   The national M&E work plan

*   The organizations' own vision and mission statement

*   The national monitoring and evaluation plan

*   The organization's M&E plan

*   The program monitoring guidelines

*   A relevant national policy

If a national M&E work plan has been developed, this should be the first document that is consulted. This work plan (see Component 5) contains, or should contain, specific responsibilities for M&E activities, for each of the 12 Components (if the work plan has been developed based on the 12 Components of a functional M&E system). It is, therefore, possible to extract M&E functions from the national M&E work plan and use these as a basis to define the organization's M&E functions.

If M&E functions have not yet been defined, the following questions may help one to do so:

- What is the organization's vision and mission? Does it include any reference to quality, outcomes, or achieving specific results?

- What does the organization want to achieve in terms of M&E (long-term M&E results)?

- What M&E functions must be executed in order to meet these M&E results?

When developing a list of the organization's M&E functions, it is important to keep in mind that:

a) An organization's M&E functions should fall within its overall vision, mission, and objectives. This will ensure that M&E functions support the broader roles and responsibilities of the organization. M&E will help an organization to achieve its vision, mission and objectives by tracking progress achieving these results.

b) M&E functions should be worded as high-level activities, and not as a detailed list of tasks (e.g., an M&E function would be to "manage routine program monitoring data," and **not** the detailed level tasks such as "capture data onto computer, archive forms, clean data, and analyze data").

Deliverable: A list of the M&E functions for which the organization is responsible — sometimes referred to as an M&E job analysis (by HR professionals), or as a work breakdown structure (by project management professionals).

Step 4: Group the M&E functions logically together and assign post/s to each logical grouping

First, determine the current number of persons responsible for M&E (full-time or part-time), usually through an assessment. The assessment can be done in different ways, either through a questionnaire that each stakeholder has to complete or through commissioned data gathering at different sites. We call this a Human Resource Inventory Report.

With the organization's M&E functions established, the next step is to logically group the functions, keeping the organization's specific circumstances and M&E performance goals in mind when doing so. Once the functions have been logically grouped together, the next step is to determine the number and type of posts required for each logical grouping of functions. These tips (adapted from www.ad-esse.com) may help to define the number and types of posts.

Organize functions so that they form logically arranged, manageable blocks of work/output ("whole tasks"). Whole tasks are sets of process steps that, when carried out together, deliver a recognizable, complete output. Whole tasks are almost the opposite of the *Taylorist*, assembly-line approach to tasks, in which each individual carries out a very narrow range of often highly repetitive tasks. Examples of whole tasks include managing monthly reporting processes, undertaking evaluations, or managing capacity building in M&E. Eventually, personnel responsible for executing these functions should be able to identify clearly outputs, customers, effectiveness and results.

- Each post should have control loops and feedback mechanisms to enable the *right first-time* output; in other words, making sure that an individual post is supported throughout a process to achieve good quality outputs the first time around.

- Each post should promote self-sufficiency and self-checking mechanisms for employees to evaluate their own performance on their M&E tasks.

- Each post should have a level of flexibility and capability to cope with fluctuating M&E demands.

- Not all posts need to be full-time. For example, a data entry clerk may also be the organization's receptionist. It is important to identify each post (even posts that will only do M&E work as part of a bigger job function) so that comprehensive M&E job descriptions can be written.

- The apparent need for a new M&E post (i.e., full-time M&E post) should be carefully weighed against the possibility that the tasks could be done within an existing post in the organization (i.e., a part-time M&E post). If M&E functions are to be linked to an existing post, ensure that this is indicated in the job description.

Deliverables: (a) A Human Resource Inventory Report that lists the name, education, training, prior employment, languages spoken and professional experience of employees currently in the organization (Robbins and Decenzo, 2001); and (b) a functional diagram that shows the logical grouping of functions, as illustrated in Figure C1-3, as well as a list of all the posts required in an organization.

Step 5.   Develop an organizational structure

An organizational structure is a visual depiction of how the different posts in the organization work together. It shows the chain of command (who reports to whom), as well as the different line authorities and staff authorities. Tips for designing effective organizational structures are as follows:

a)   Start with *standard* types of organization designs (see Figure C1-1) and then make a custom design that will address the logical grouping of M&E functions.

b)   It is possible to create a hybrid organizational structure by using different types of organizational designs in one structure (e.g., partly functional and partly geographical, as Figure C1-1 illustrates).

c) Keep the organization's broader structure in mind and link the M&E organizational structure to the broader structure of the organization.

d) Every person must only have one manager (the chain of command principle). Keep chains of command as short as possible. Make sure that an M&E task is the responsibility of one post. If an M&E task seems to be a shared responsibility, try to distinguish the parts of the task that belong to each post.

e) One person can only effectively manage a limited number of subordinates, but the more subordinates per manager, the lower the organization's management costs. The span of control must be balanaced with management and cost-effectiveness. Span of control can increase with process clarity and automation. In other words, in well-defined processes with high degrees of automation, fewer managers are required. Changes in span cause changes in job specifications.

f) In a mature organizational structure, the rule of thumb is usually that "the flatter the structure, the better," as it involves less supervision with more self-reliance and teamwork (i.e., avoid one-to-one manager-subordinate relationships).

Figure C1-3: **Example of functional diagram to show the logical grouping of organization's M&E functions**

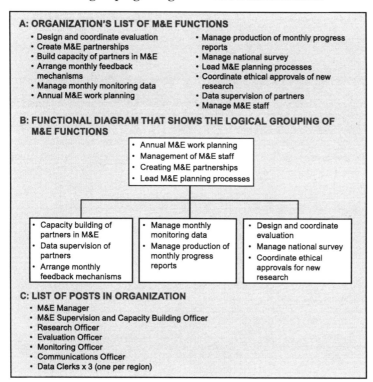

A: ORGANIZATION'S LIST OF M&E FUNCTIONS
- Design and coordinate evaluation
- Create M&E partnerships
- Build capacity of partners in M&E
- Arrange monthly feedback mechanisms
- Manage monthly monitoring data
- Annual M&E work planning
- Manage production of monthly progress reports
- Manage national survey
- Lead M&E planning processes
- Coordinate ethical approvals of new research
- Data supervision of partners
- Manage M&E staff

B: FUNCTIONAL DIAGRAM THAT SHOWS THE LOGICAL GROUPING OF M&E FUNCTIONS

- Annual M&E work planning
- Management of M&E staff
- Creating M&E partnerships
- Lead M&E planning processes

- Capacity building of partners in M&E
- Data supervision of partners
- Arrange monthly feedback mechanisms

- Manage monthly monitoring data
- Manage production of monthly progress reports

- Design and coordinate evaluation
- Manage national survey
- Coordinate ethical approvals for new research

C: LIST OF POSTS IN ORGANIZATION
- M&E Manager
- M&E Supervision and Capacity Building Officer
- Research Officer
- Evaluation Officer
- Monitoring Officer
- Communications Officer
- Data Clerks x 3 (one per region)

Organizational design is an iterative process. Once the organizational structure has been designed, the appropriateness of the design should be assessed and changes made, if necessary.

Deliverable: An *organizational structure* for M&E, also known as an organogram (see Figure C1-4).

Figure C1-4: Example of organization organogram for M&E based on the functional diagram

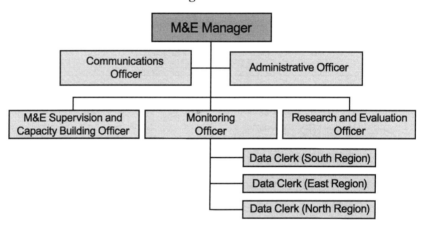

Step 6: Develop a job description for each post with M&E functions in the organization

After the posts and the relationships between posts have been defined (depicted in organogram, Step 5), the next step is to develop *post profiles* for each post. A post profile consists of a job description and a job specification (usually merged). A job description is a written statement of what a job holder is required to do, how it is to be done, and why it is to be done. A job specification is a statement of the minimum acceptable qualifications that an incumbent must possess to perform a given job successfully. Using a standard format for post profiles throughout the organization will help to integrate M&E functions within the organization.

Deliverable: Post profile (job description and job specification) for each post with M&E tasks in the organization.

Table C1-2: Post Profile Explanation and Example

Aspect of post profile	Explanation	Example for M&E manager in Figure C1-4
Job title	The name of the post that will be written on the office door.	M&E Manager
Location	Where the post will be located.	Gaberone, Botswana
Reporting line	The name of the post to whom the person will report.	Director of Programs
Primary purpose of this position	A statement of the primary purpose of the post. What is the main outcome that the post will be expected to achieve?	To ensure that the organization uses accurate, up-to-date and relevant information to inform its strategic and operational decisions
Key performance areas	This is a description of the main M&E functions that the person would need to undertake (use results from Step 3). If the person also has other functions, create two sub-sections: one for other responsibilities and one for M&E responsibilities. Include both sets of functions in this section. The person's performance appraisal is usually linked to the areas listed here, so make sure that person's M&E functions are included in the list of key performance areas.	1. Create and maintain M&E partnerships 2. Lead annual M&E work planning 3. Manage M&E staff 4. Lead M&E planning processes
Job description	This is a detailed account of how the person will fulfill his/her functions. It defines the M&E functions in more detail by breaking every M&E function into individual tasks.	(Example of one of the Key Performance Areas expanded) 1. Create and maintain M&E partnerships • Maintain an inventory of M&E partners • Set up and establish relationships with partners • Organize and chair quarterly M&E partners meetings
Job specification	This is a list of the academic qualifications that the person must have obtained in order to fulfil the post, as well as work experience and any professional skills required or specified. Academic qualifications are usually post-graduate; undergraduate; certificates; diplomas; and/or short courses (e.g., training workshops).	First degree in social sciences Master's degree in international development or social sciences in a related field Five years' experience in management of at least 5 staff Five years' experience in monitoring and evaluation Excellent systems building and communication skills

Step 7: Plan for the implementation of the new organizational structure

Why think about how to implement a new organizational structure? People fear and, therefore, tend to resist change. Because a change in organizational structure could bring about changes in the organization as a whole, it is important to design a change management plan once the technical team has agreed upon the organizational structure. In this context, change is defined as an alteration of an organization's environment, structure, technology or people (Robbins and Decenzo, 2001).

Why do people resist change? Individual resistance is a result of at least three factors: fear of the unknown, fear of losing something of value, and the belief that change is not good for the organization (Robbins and Decenzo, 2001).

How can one manage an organizational change? Ketz De Vries (2001:197) suggests a number of actions to help manage change in organizational structures (or other changes) within an organization. The organization's leadership must lead these actions if the implementation of the new structure is to be successful, as follows:

a)   Create a shared mindset, which is characterized by a sense of urgency, genuine dialogue; collective ambition; controlled anxiety, commitment and motivation; and openness about the need for organizational change. This can be achieved by briefing all employees on the need for change, the purpose and scope of the change (i.e., not everything is being changed, only the parts that are not working well), and the benefits that it will bring.

b)   Focus employees' attention on the value to the entire organization and the improvements that change will bring to the organization's performance.

c)   Manage employees' expectations about what the change process will and will not involve.

d)   Brief employees on the progress of the change design process.

e)   Allow employees the opportunity to provide input into the process and to express their concerns and frustrations in a *safe* environment where they can speak their minds.

f)   Make firm decisions once the process has been completed.

g)   Communicate the decisions that have been made.

h)   Create opportunities for team building and inter-group development.

Deliverables: An implementation plan of how the new organizational structure will be realized, with clear activities, responsibilities and time frames.

Step 8:   Approve the organizational structure for M&E

Once the new organizational structure has been agreed upon and the change management plan developed, the new structure and change management plan needs to be submitted for approval. A rationale for the new organizational structure will need to be prepared. This document will need to detail the organizational structure changes; the benefits to the organization; the actual changes to be made; the long-term cost implications of the changes; and any related expenses such as additional office space. Approval procedures will depend on the organization and the scope of the organizational design.

If the organizational design change is for a public sector organization, such as a central ministry or agency of government, then it usually needs approval from the Public Service Commission (or equivalent). In addition, there may also be a Board that will have to approve any change and resultant cost implications.

Deliverables: A written rationale for the proposed changes and written approval to go ahead and implement the changes from the organization's management.

Step 9:   Implement the new organizational structure

Once approved, the new organizational structure needs to be implemented. This is done through HR management processes, including recruitment, training, motivation and development of employees in the organization.

Deliverables: Plan to implement the new organizational structure that includes the elements listed in Step 9.

For reflection 2:

Reflect on your organization's M&E organizational structure. Which of these steps have been followed and at what stage? Was management informed of the changes? What are some of the pitfalls in following these steps? Will these steps address all the concerns that you may have? What would your reaction be if you were involved in an activity of this nature? How would you go about managing the change in your own organization?

6. Summary of Chapter 1 Knowledge and Skills

In this chapter, you learned about the theory and technical process steps that are required to design an organizational structure with M&E functions embedded in it. You learned about the importance of aligning your organization's M&E

structure with other management processes in the organization and of finding and working with M&E champions while keeping possible counter-reformers at bay.

You learned that M&E needs to be part of your organization's mandate and that it is essential to enable your organization to track progress towards its objectives. You learned that it is important to decide where to locate M&E functions, to include M&E as a specific part of staff's job descriptions, and to manage technical support well. You also learned about the need to manage the staff within your organization in order to keep them positive and motivated about their M&E responsibilities and to give them incentives to do their M&E work well.

7. Learning Activity

a)   Read HowTo Guide C1-1 in detail (How To Align and Design an Organizational Structure for M&E).

b)   On pp. 91 – 93, the current organizational structure and organizational culture of the Ministry of Education of Goldstar State are summarized.

c)   There is a list of M&E functions of a Ministry of Education head office below. Assume these functions are the outputs of Step 3 of the steps in HowTo Guide C1-1.

d)   There is also a human resource inventory below. Consider this as the first deliverable of Step 4.

e)   Complete the second deliverable of Step 4, Step 5 and Step 6 in the HowTo Guide
C1-1. When executing Step 6, only develop one job description.

Output 1.   A functional diagram for the organization (deliverable (b) from Step 4)

Output 2.   An organizational structure for the M&E unit (with clearly defined functions for each sub-unit within the M&E unit) (deliverable from Step 5).

Output 3.   A job description for one of the posts in the organization (deliverable from Step 6).

A: Goldstar State Current Organizational Structure and Organizational Culture

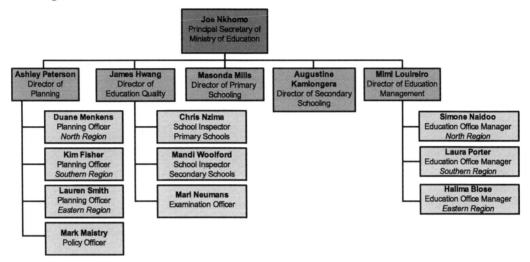

Source: Authors

a) **Planning Directorate:** This directorate is responsible for setting education policies and strategies at the national level, for supporting all regions in developing their own annual education sector work plans, for compiling a national education sector work plan and budget for submission to the Ministry of Finance on a three-year budgeting cycle, and for preparing materials for the annual joint review of the education sector strategy implementation progress.

b) **Education Quality Directorate:** This directorate is responsible for making sure that education is up to standard. The unit sets exam and curriculum standards, develops standard curricula, moderates the external exams at the end of the primary and secondary school years, and conducts school inspections to assess the quality of teaching and learning on an ongoing basis.

c) **Primary Schooling Directorate:** This directorate oversees all aspects of primary education including the setting up of new schools, hiring of teachers for schools, primary school teacher training, construction of new schools, provision of textbooks to schools, and managing enrollment in the primary school sector.

d) **Secondary Schooling Directorate:** This directorate oversees all aspects of secondary education including the setting up of new schools, hiring of teachers for schools, secondary school teacher training, construction of new schools, provision of textbooks to schools, and managing enrollment in the secondary school sector.

e) **Education Management Directorate:** This directorate provides managers for the education sector at the regional, local government level. These managers are supposed to ensure that education sector policies are coordinated and implemented in each region and that other sectors integrate their work well with the education sector work. They are also responsible for acting as a liaison with civil society organizations working in schools and with parents and teachers to improve the quality of and access to education.

In terms of the **organizational culture** in Goldstar State's Ministry of Education, a recent institutional assessment revealed that:

a) Each of the directorates works in isolation and there is, therefore, some level of overlap between what the different units are doing. The regional managers, for example, implement projects and oversee civil society's work in the education sector which is not always aligned to, or follows education sector qualities.

b) The education quality directorate does not give feedback about education quality to the planning department, so the quality of education (as a measure of the strength of the education sector) is not known.

c) Directorates do not easily share information with each other and the annual joint review of the education sector consists of individual presentations by different units without the units agreeing beforehand on presenting a coherent picture of the status of the education sector.

d) The civil society organizations working in the education sector do not report to the Ministry of Education officials. The data that these organizations collect are only about the number of schools, students and teachers that they support.

B: M&E Functions of the Organization

1. Coordinate the development and update of the national M&E framework for the education sector.

2. Support the regions to develop M&E plans to track regional progress.

3. Prepare quarterly education statistical bulletins.

4. Train everyone in education-related monitoring and evaluation.

5. Coordinate the development and update of a national M&E integrated work plan.

6. Implement the Annual Education Census for 2007, 2008 and 2009.

7. Improve the quality of education data.

8. Coordinate dissemination at the annual education sector joint review.

9. Check the quality of teacher training programs.

10. Support non-governmental organizations to develop M&E work plans.

11. Set up and maintain a national M&E committee for the education sector.

12. Set up and maintain the education monitoring system for the regions, and a database to capture all education sector data.

13. Manage the education management information system.

14. Support education-related research being undertaken, as per research agenda.

15. Support the inclusion of your program in a national research strategy and agenda for prioritized research.

16. Analyze trends in teacher absenteeism.

17. Undertake research to determine the effectiveness of the curriculum.

18. Check the quality of education through more supervision visits to schools.

19. Participate in government forums and committees where M&E issues are discussed.

20. Respond to specific requests for education data from the Minister.

21. Suggest improvements to education sector strategies to improve the pass rates.

22. Develop an annual education strategy implementation progress report and have it approved each year.

23. Develop training programs in M&E for the education sector.

C: Human Resource Inventory of the Organization

Name of employee (alphabetical, by first name)	Post name and level	Education qualifications	Professional experience and career results before joining the Ministry	Career path in the Ministry
Ashley Peterson	Director of Planning (P2)	B.Sc.	Started career with education ministry Led the development of the latest education sector strategy Team leader for the 2008 annual education sector review	**1995 — 2003:** Science teacher at 3 primary schools in Goldstar State **2003 — 2005:** Regional Education Manager **2005 — current:** Director of Planning
Augustine Kamlongera	Director of Secondary Schooling (P2)	B.Ed.	Taught for 10 years at Goldstar National University Initiated a new curriculum at Goldstar National University	**1998 — 2001:** Head teacher of largest secondary school in Goldstar State **2002 — current:** Director of Secondary Schooling
Chris Nizima	School Inspector: Primary Schools (P4)	B.Ed.	Initiated a private sector education program for communities in northern region of country Developed curricula in basic finance and budgeting	**2005 — 2007:** Head teacher of Gillford Secondary School **2008 — current:** School Inspector
Duane Menkens	Planning Officer: North Region	Statistics	Started career with Ministry of Education	**1991 — 1993:** Math teacher at Gillfrod Secondary School **1993 — 1994:** Head of Department in math at Maison's Secondary School **1994 — 1998:** **1998 — current:** Planning Officer

Name of employee (alphabetical, by first name)	Post name and level	Education qualifications	Professional experience and career results before joining the Ministry	Career path in the Ministry
Halima Blose	Education Office Manager: Southern Region	Statistics	Statistician for the National Bureau of Statistics Team leader for the national census in 1997 and 2007	**2007 — current:** Education Office Manager
James Hwang	Director of Education Quality	B.Ed.	Public relations manager for national chain of supermarkets Copy editor for the National Education Council Head of the NGO, Inguluma, that works to support teachers Produced the last 2 independent evaluations of the status of the education sector for civil society	**1995 — 2000:** Taught English and French at 4 secondary schools. **2000 — 2001:** Head teacher of Dynamite Secondary School **2001 — 2004:** School inspector in all 3 regions **2005 — current:** Director of Education Quality
Joe Nkhomo	Principal Secretary	M.B.A.	Started career with Ministry of Agriculture Led the modernization of the Agriculture Extension Program	**1990 — 1991:** Agriculture Extension Officer **1992 — 2000:** Director of Planning at Ministry of Agriculture **2000 — current:** Principal Secretary
Kim Fisher	Planning Officer: Southern Region	B.Sc.	Laboratory assistant at Phizzer Laboratories Editor for all reports at Phizzer Laboratories Produced 4 annual progress reports for the Phizzer board of directors at annual general meeting	**1992 — 2000:** Science teacher at Dinkum Secondary school **2000 — current:** Planning Officer

Name of employee (alphabetical, by first name)	Post name and level	Education qualifications	Professional experience and career results before joining the Ministry	Career path in the Ministry
Laura Porter	Education Office Manager	Final year, secondary school certificate	Started career with Ministry of Education	**1990 — 2000:** Assistant teacher at 2 primary schools and teacher education in-service training program participant **2000 — 2005:** Taught history and life sciences at 3 primary schools. **2005 — 2006:** Head teacher **2007 — current:** Education Office Manager
Lauren Smith	Planning Officer	Final year, secondary school certificate	Started career with Ministry of Education	**1990 — 2000:** Assistant teacher at 2 primary schools and teacher education in-service training program participant **2000 — 2005:** Taught history and life sciences at 3 primary schools **2005 — 2006:** Head teacher **2007 — current:** Planning Officer
Mandi Woolford	School Inspector: Secondary Schools	M.B.A.	Project manager for construction company Proposal manager and fund raiser for national council for the Blind Started a new company specialising in imported fabrics	**2005 — 2006:** School inspector training program participant **2006 — current:** School inspector

Name of employee (alphabetical, by first name)	Post name and level	Education qualifications	Professional experience and career results before joining the Ministry	Career path in the Ministry
Mari Neumans	Examinations Officer	Statistics	Town planner of the national capital city council Head of marketing department at pharmaceutical company Led a process of improving the stock levels in pharmacies around the county	**1998 — 2000:** Math teacher on a locum basis on Saturdays at 5 secondary schools that did not have math teachers (schools had a remedial math program to catch up in math) **2000 — 2006:** Head of department of Kinshaga Secondary School and managed to increase math pass rate from 15% to 94% in 4 years. Won award for best math teacher for 4 years. **2006 — current:** Examinations Officer
Mark Maistry	Policy Officer	M.B.A.	Office administrator Office manager (ran an office of 30 persons — payroll, human resources, etc.)	**1992 — 2000:** Planning Officer **2000 — current:** Policy Officer
Masonda Mills	Director of Primary Schooling	Final year, secondary school certificate	Started career with Ministry of Education	**1988 — 1990:** Assistant teacher at 3 secondary Schools and teacher education in-service training program participant **1991 — 2005:** Taught history, geography, maths, and life sciences at 11 secondary schools; 2005 – 2007: Head teacher of St Mary's secondary school **2008 — current:** Director of Primary Schooling
Mimi Louireiro	Director of Education Management	B.Ed.	Started career with Ministry of Education	**2000 — 2003:** Regional Education Manager for Southern region **2003 — current:** Director of Education Management

Name of employee (alphabetical, by first name)	Post name and level	Education qualifications	Professional experience and career results before joining the Ministry	Career path in the Ministry
Simone Naidoo	Education Office Manager:	B.Ed.	Math and science remedial lessons for students who struggled (worked from home while raising children)	**1992 — 2000:** Teacher for math and science at 3 secondary schools **2000 — 2004:** Head teacher of Gillford Primary school **2000 — current:** Education Office Manager

Annex A: World Bank Organogram Showing Position of Independent Evaluation Group (October 2008)

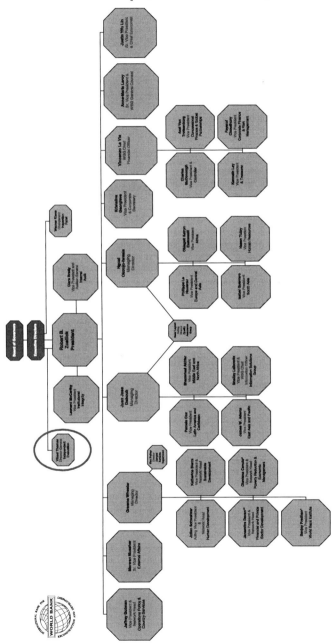

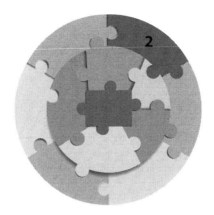

Chapter 2
Human Capacity for M&E Systems

Chapter Aim

The aim of this chapter is to enable you to build the skills that people need to fulfill their M&E responsibilities (develop human capacity) so that the M&E system works well.

Chapter Knowledge and Skills

By the end of this Chapter, you should be able to:

a) Explain the most important human capacity development terminology and definitions.

b) Identify the key implementation issues concerning human capacity development.

c) Manage and undertake a Human Capacity Assessment for the M&E system.

d) Manage the development of a Human Capacity Development Strategy and Plan.

Before You Begin...

Take a few minutes to read through the questions below. You may find it helpful to write down your answers. As you work through the chapter, compare your answers to the views of the authors.

- Are your organization's mission and goals written down?

- Does everyone in the organization understand how their job contributes to the organization's goals (alignment)?

- Are there incentives for successfully achieving the goals of the organization?

- Does your organization have the mandate and authority to carry out monitoring and evaluation tasks?

- Is everybody clear on their monitoring and evaluation responsibilities?

- Do the parts of the organization involved in M&E have relevant job descriptions that include adequately defined M&E functions and are these posts filled?

- Do the organization and its staff feel responsible for monitoring and evaluation functions just as they do for other aspects of the work?

- Are staff supported by their managers in carrying out their M&E tasks?

- How is technical support for M&E managed in your organization?

These questions remind us that, without people, an organization's M&E system cannot work. People need to be motivated to complete their M&E tasks. They must be clear on what their tasks are and be rewarded if they complete their tasks well. This chapter will teach you how to design organizational structures with M&E functions embedded in them and how to design the job descriptions for staff with M&E functions.

Component 2: Human Capacity for M&E Systems

1. Introduction

> *"The primary stakeholders are policymakers like us because*
> *without information, things are done arbitrarily and one becomes*
> *unsure of whether a policy or programme will fail or succeed. If we*
> *allow our policies to be guided by empirical facts and data, there*
> *will be a noticeable change in the impact of what we do."*

Director of Policy, National Action Committee on AIDS (Nigeria), 2003

Human capacity is part of the *"people, partnerships and planning"* ring of the 12 Components of an M&E system (see introductory chapter for more information). Just as it is essential that M&E responsibilities of an organization and its staff are clearly defined and authorized (Component 1), so it is essential for staff to have the necessary skills to execute their tasks well.

How this chapter is organized: This chapter begins with selected background information and definitions related to human capacity concepts, development and assessments (Section 2), followed by suggested results for this component of the M&E system (Section 3). The benefits of strong human capacity are presented in Section 4. Implementation issues related to human capacity development are presented in Section 5. Specific steps involved in undertaking and managing a Human Capacity Assessment for the M&E system follow in Section 6, and steps involved in developing a Human Capacity Development Strategy are provided in Section 7. The Chapter closes with a summary of lessons learned (Section 8) and a practical exercise in Section 9 to cement what you have learned in the chapter.

2. Background Information and Definitions

Capacity: The ability to perform appropriate tasks effectively, efficiently, and sustainably. Capacity focuses on three levels, as illustrated in Figure C2-1:

- *System capacity (Level 1):* The ability of a system to deliver the goal and objectives of a process and thereby contribute toward fulfilling the organization's objectives. In a systems context, capacity is defined as a set of entities that operate to achieve a common purpose and according to certain rules and processes (Hopkins, 1994). This definition implies that capacity is a continuing process, that human resources are central to capacity development, and that the overall context within which organizations undertake their functions are key considerations in strategies for capacity development.

- *Organizational capacity (Level 2):* The capacity of the organization and its processes to deliver the organization's goals and development objectives. (This component does not focus on organizational capacity).

- *Individual (human) capacity (Level 3):* The ability of individuals to perform functions effectively, efficiently and sustainably.

Figure C2–1: The Three Levels of Capacity and Capacity Development

Level 1 is the broader response environment within which the M&E system needs to be implemented. This level is often referred to as the "situation," the "market," the "action environment" or simply the "environment."

Level 2 consists of the organization(s), both formal and informal, and the internal sub-organizational units responsible for functions associated with the M&E system.

Level 3 consists of the individual(s) functioning within the various organizations. A major dimension of capacity is at the individual level — people. This covers individuals within organizations involved in executing M&E functions, and those who are beneficiaries or are otherwise impacted by the M&E system or the things it measures.

Source: Adapted by authors from UNDP, 1997

Capacity development: Improvement of human resources and operational capabilities of systems, institutions/organizations and individuals so they can perform better (Lamptey et al., 2001). Capacity development focuses on three levels (see Figure C2-1):

- **Systems capacity development (Level 1):** Improvements in the ability of systems (single systems or groups of systems) to effectively perform the tasks for which they have been designed (for example, developing tertiary education institutions' ability to deliver training).

- **Organizational capacity development (Level 2):** Improvements in the ability of institutions and organizations (public, private and NGOs) to singly, or in cooperation with other organizations, perform appropriate tasks (UNDP, 1997), for example, by providing computers in all offices.

- **Human capacity development of individual/s (Level 3):** The development of skills and the effective use of managerial, professional and technical staff and volunteers (for example, through training). This involves identifying the appropriate people to be trained, providing an effective learning environment for training and education, in-service and field supervision for continued skills transfer, and long-term mentoring (Lamptey et al., 2001).

Capacity assessments: A structured and analytical process whereby the various dimensions of capacity are measured and evaluated within the broader environmental or systems context, as well as specific entities and individuals within the system. Special emphasis must be given to looking at existing capacities (BPPS/MDGD and FMP International, 1997).

As can be seen, all three concepts (capacity, capacity development and capacity assessments) can focus on three levels: the systems level, organizational level, and individual level. This focuses on the individual level with building the M&E skills of people involved in the M&E system (executing M&E functions, or managing employees with M&E functions), at the national, sub-national, or service delivery level.

The other two levels are also important. M&E systems need to be developed holistically: the overall system needs to be assessed and strengthened through better and more effective coordination and documentation (Level 1 in Figure C2-1); and organizational systems, processes, and resources need to be strengthened to enable organizations to effectively fulfill their M&E mandate (Level 2 in Figure C2-1).

3. Results to Be Achieved When Implementing This Component

Long-term result: Ensure M&E human resources are adequately skilled and able to effectively and efficiently complete all activities defined in the M&E work plan.

Short- and medium-term results:

- Defined skill set for people responsible for HIV M&E functions
- Human capacity assessment, including career paths for M&E
- Human capacity development plan
- Standard curricula for M&E capacity building
- Local and/or regional training institutions that offer good quality M&E training courses
- Supervision, in-service training, and mentoring as mechanisms for continuous capacity building

---

For reflection 1:

Reflect on the human capacity within your organization.

How many of the short- and medium-term results listed here are visible in your organization? Does your organization have adequate, skilled human resources for your M&E system? Who is responsible for defining and ensuring adequate M&E human capacity within your organization? Is this task formally assigned to one or more posts or units in the organization? Is your organization achieving the long-term result defined above?

---

4. Benefits of Human Capacity as Part of an M&E System

"No skilled people, no M&E system."
(Workshop participant)

The M&E system cannot function without skilled people who effectively execute the M&E tasks for which they are responsible. Therefore, understanding the skills needed and the capacity of people involved in the M&E system (undertaking human capacity assessments) and addressing capacity gaps (through structured capacity development programs) is at the heart of the M&E system, as illustrated in Figure C2-2.

Figure C2–2: Human Capacity Assessments and Human Capacity Development Are at the Heart of M&E System Implementation

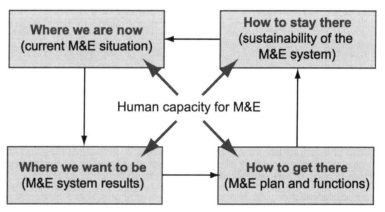

Source: Adapted by authors from UNDP, 1997

Focusing on human capacity for M&E will improve the quality of the M&E system. In an ideal scenario, the M&E system would be designed in advance, skill requirements for it established, and human capacity development (HCD) planned and undertaken before the M&E system was implemented. In *real life*, we know that it does not always happen in this way; M&E skills are often developed while the M&E system is being implemented.

The increased interest of development partners in M&E has made more funding available for M&E capacity development.

"Recognizing that capacity building is central to achieving economic growth, reducing poverty and equalizing opportunity, foundations and bilateral and multilateral funding agencies have taken a new-found interest in this fundamental area. The timing seems right. Not only is the information revolution upon us, trends towards democratization, government decentralization and economic liberalization have profoundly reshaped how universities, NGOs and other public-interest organizations do their work, thus, presenting them with new challenges and opportunities. National governments, for example, play a much smaller role in developing policy and delivering services than they once did. With less public funding, public-interest organizations must have a strong concept of a relevant knowledge-based economy, and they must have a greater market orientation — not necessarily as commercial entities per se, but rather as organizations attuned to issues once considered the purview of business: management, finance, innovation, customer service, marketing, and the capacity to help clientele themselves acquire and communicate knowledge" (Moock, undated).

5. Implementation Issues Related to Human Capacity Development for M&E Systems

5.1. At what levels should capacity be assessed?

Since capacity gaps exist at the system, organizational and individual levels, capacity also needs to be assessed at these levels. The GAMET HIV M&E Electronic Resource Library (ERL) contains guidelines for and examples of M&E capacity assessments that have been done at all three levels. You can access the library by going to http://gametlibrary.worldbank.org and clicking on Component 2.

5.2. Whose M&E capacity should be developed for the M&E system to be fully functional?

All stakeholders involved in the M&E system need to have certain competencies in order to effectively execute their part in the operation of the M&E system. Annex A of this chapter includes a list of skills that an M&E specialist may need, a list of individuals whose capacities may need to be developed, as well as more specific typical skill sets needed by people doing various M&E tasks at national and decentralized levels.

5.3. What human capacities are typically needed for the M&E system?

Experience has shown the need for holistic M&E capacity development programs that focus on the technical (i.e., technical skills to make the 12 Components functional) and managerial aspects of M&E systems (i.e., managing the M&E system and managing the staff involved in it). More detail is found in Annex A.

5.4. In what ways should human capacity be developed?

Developing capacity entails more than education and training (Hopkins, 1994) and should not take place only in a workshop format for the following reasons: (i) workshops take people away from their places of work and, thus, from doing the things for which they are responsible; and (ii) knowledge retention in workshop-only capacity development programs is not very high (IEG, 2007). Therefore, additional capacity development strategies need to be included in a Human Capacity Development Strategy and Plan. Examples of such additional strategies are provided below (Errkola, 2007; FHI, 2002; Nzima, 2007).

Examples of Capacity Development Strategies for Those Involved in M&E

i.   **Provide M&E technical assistance as an opportunity for on-the-job (in-service) training**. Technical assistance for in-country, full-time staff can be provided in different ways: local M&E consultants, international M&E consultants, or international M&E staff of development partners. This technical assistance can be used, if managed well, as a form of HCD by:

   • Establishing twinning arrangements

   • Developing specific capacity transfer objectives and targets for the M&E technical support person to achieve

   • Developing a scope of work for the M&E technical support person, so that the person does not become another member of staff (This is a risk for long-term, residential, technical support providers.)

   • Periodically evaluating the performance of the M&E technical support persons

   • Targeting technical assistance so that it focuses on specific areas of need

   • Building in specific mentorship visits and processes as part of technical support — where the country, not the consultant, is responsible for producing the technical support output (The chapter for Component 1 contains more information about different modalities of M&E technical support and how to manage it.)

ii. **Conduct professional meetings and regional conferences to share experiences and develop capacity**.

iii. **Establish and maintain regional knowledge networks** where people can share experiences.

iv. **Develop distance-learning and modular training courses as continuing education options**. Existing distance learning courses provide ready-made delivery mechanisms for capacity development in M&E and are greatly under-utilized. Capitalizing on this delivery system involves understanding the networks, media and learning methods of existing programs and then adding M&E to them. These courses should be academically accredited so that classes can take place at universities in the evenings and over weekends.

v. **Include M&E content in all pre-service courses at the tertiary level (M&E is a cross-cutting issue)**, thereby reducing the amount of in-service training in M&E that needs to be done.

vi. **Arrange targeted exchange visit and study tours**. Such tours should be very specific in their focus and should visit venues where best practice is in evidence.

Examples of Strategies to Develop the Capacity of Individuals and Institutions Responsible for M&E Capacity Development

i. **Support and provide in-service training for in-country training institutions to provide M&E courses**. Potential training institutions need to be identified and their instructors' capacity developed to run M&E training courses.

ii. **Implement a professional development program for local M&E consultants**. Such a program would reduce reliance on international (external, fly-in/fly-out) M&E expertize.

iii. **Develop and implement "twinning" programs for capacity development**. A new, emerging training institution interested in M&E may, for example, want to *twin* its efforts with an institution that has years of experience in M&E.

iv. **Create standardized curricula**. This is another strategy that can be used to make it easier to train service providers to deliver training. Currently, there are no global standards or accredited M&E training materials; a given country's National Qualifications and Accreditation Authority (if one exists) usually accredits these materials. Accreditation takes time. If accreditation of materials is not possible, then M&E curricula should at least be standardized so that different training service providers use the same curricula when conducting training. Many countries have elected to start by developing three M&E curricula:

- M&E concepts and an introduction to the national M&E system
- Reporting routine data in the national routine reporting system
- Managing data received from the national routine reporting system

Standard M&E curricula should be accompanied by teaching aids (facilitator guides, presentation slides, answers to group work exercises, etc.), learning aids (participant summary handouts, group work exercises, etc.), and evaluation tools such as pre-training assessments.

5.5. Who should provide human capacity development?

Depending on the capacity development strategy, either individuals (such as freelance consultants) or organizations (training institutions, universities or others) can be responsible for capacity development. The most important factor to consider is the training relevance (does the curriculum match the capacity needs?) and quality (do people have the identified skills after the training?). Wherever possible, training should be provided by local, in-country institutions, as this helps to assure the sustainability of capacity development efforts. If there is no local capacity for training, the capacity of training service providers can be built through:

- Building capacity of in-country institutions to provide M&E training. This will reduce travel costs, and increase the supply of M&E professionals in a country.

- Creating a local cadre of skilled M&E trainers. Standard curricula and teaching and learning aids are of no use if there is no one to deliver the training. M&E trainers could be sourced from outside the country but it is much better in the long run for the training to be provided by local trainers. If a country does not have an adequate supply of local M&E trainers, a group should be identified and trained to form a new cadre of accredited M&E trainers. Ideally, they should include trainers who have skills in adult learning, as the addition of technical M&E skills is less challenging than the acquisition of adult learning skills.

5.6. How can human capacity development strategies be adapted to deal with the high demand for skilled M&E staff?

The scarcity of M&E skills has been exacerbated by high turnover of M&E staff. Experience has shown that, as soon as a person has been trained in M&E, these highly marketable skills lead to other job opportunities. It is, therefore, necessary to develop strategies to ensure that skilled staff responsible for M&E remain in key positions. Such strategies may include:

- Introducing mass training programs to alter the supply-demand balance (If there were a greater supply of persons skilled in M&E, their skills would not be in such great demand, and they might remain in the same positions for longer.)

- Contracting trained staff to the organization for a given period and requiring them to repay the cost of training if they break their contract

- Building institutional memory within the organization by ensuring that every person who receives training is responsible for training at least one other person in the organization and developing a structured handover process as part of this training

- Ensuring management and organizational commitment in identifying the right people to attend training, that is, the people who will actually use the skills to perform their jobs better.

5.7. How can a database be used to track HCD efforts?

Though not essential, it is possible to use a database to track individual HCD efforts over time and prevent duplication, as part of a national database (see Component 10). For such a system to work effectively, each person must be uniquely *identifiable*. Such a system should not only track details of the trainees but also details of available training courses in M&E in the country and sub-region, as well as the cadre of local trainers who have been accredited by the relevant authority to provide M&E training. A training management information system could, for example, include the following information (Source: Adapted from: http://www.jhpiego.org/about/what/tims.htm):

Courses

- How many courses (by training center, district, or province) have been held?
- Which courses have been held on a specific topic in a given time frame, who sponsored them, and how many people attended each course?

Participants

- How many course participants received training through each funding agency or award?
- In what types of organizations do the people who were trained work?
- What levels of training skill competency have participants attained?
- Are people attending complementary or duplicate courses?

Trainers

- How many trainers of each rank or type has a program trained?
- Which trainers have been conducting courses and how many people have they trained?
- When were trainers' skills last assessed and are they currently active as trainers?

Assessments

- Which course participants have received a follow-up assessment of their skills?
- What are the results of training follow-up visits to a specific course participant?

It should be noted that databases are not essential for capacity development efforts.

It is possible to do capacity building without a database. However, irrespective of whether a database is used, capacity development efforts should be recorded and tracked to avoid duplication.

5.8. How can human capacity development efforts be evaluated?

Evaluating the effects of capacity development is not straightforward and the short- and longer-term perspectives need to be considered. In the short term, increases in knowledge and skills can be measured and, in the longer term, one can measure whether people are doing things differently as a result of the capacity building, that is, whether they have applied the skills they learned. (You can go to http://gametlibrary.worldbank.org to download a manual about how to evaluate capacity development. Search for the manual under "Evaluating Capacity Development".)

One way to evaluate the longer-term results of capacity development is to ask participants to prepare *Portfolios of Work* showing what they have done differently as a result of attending the training and to present them at a follow-up workshop. There could also be a non-financial incentive/reward scheme where, for example, the best portfolios are showcased in an annual publication.

6. HowTo Guide 2-1: Undertaking a Human Capacity Development Assessment for the M&E System

Different approaches to undertaking an HCD assessment

In addressing human capacity gaps in the implementation of M&E functions, there are two approaches: bottom-up and top-down. In the bottom-up approach, stakeholders involved in the M&E system are asked which areas of their capacity need to be developed in order for them to fulfill their M&E functions. The HCD plan is then developed based on these responses. This approach views stakeholders as *experts* who are able to gauge their own level of knowledge and capacity development needs.

In the top-down approach, capacity gaps and development needs are determined by comparing the capacity required by the system with the capacity that exists in those participating in the system. A *top-down* approach does not mean that capacity building needs are imposed in any way but rather that the starting point is what the system requires and not what stakeholders believe they need. The *top-down* approach can be summarized by the following mathematical equation:

	Full range of human capacity required	(collective skills set)
LESS (-)	Existing human capacity	(collectively)
EQUALS (=)	**Human capacity gaps**	**(collectively)**

Perhaps because M&E is a new area, the *bottom-up* method has not worked well for assessing human capacity needs for M&E systems. Where this approach has been used, participants were usually only able to state that they needed M&E training, but were not able to pinpoint exact areas of need. For these reasons, this HowTo Guide describes the process steps for doing a *top-down* HCD assessment.

Whether to carry out new HCD assessments

HCD assessments should be undertaken periodically as the M&E system is being implemented. Integrating HCD assessments in the design process will help ensure an appropriate HCD strategy. Doing an HCD assessment as the system is being implemented will also ensure that HCD objectives are being met. Doing an HCD assessment as the M&E system is being evaluated will help ensure the long-term availability of skilled human capital and long-term investment in human capital.

It should be noted that it is not always necessary to undertake a new HCD assessment. Often, other assessments have been done that can provide general information about capacity gaps. Experienced officials may already know what the capacity gaps are based on their practical work experience. Since capacity gaps will take time to resolve, it makes sense to draw first on previous HCD assessments (even if done a few years ago) before undertaking a new one.

Step 1:   Plan the HCD Assessment

Planning a Human Capacity Assessment will help ensure that its objectives, purpose and outputs are clear. The following questions should be asked in planning such an assessment (FHI, 2002):

- Does the country have a comprehensive plan for assessing human capacity issues related to the program served by the M&E system?
- Does the country have a database of available human capacity and areas of technical competence?
- Is any key sector developing human resource policies? Have staff job descriptions changed?
- Do program managers have suggestions about how best to link with domestic and regional networks to support implementation of the M&E system?
- What is the status of distance-learning programs (if any) in the country and are they reaching district implementers or community-based implementers?

- Is radio used to offer distance education to any group within the program (not necessarily M&E of the program)?

- Are there group-learning opportunities such as regional workshops or skills-exchange visits on M&E?

- What strategies (if any) are used at the moment to address the short- and long-term skills development of implementers and service providers in the program and people responsible for monitoring and evaluating the program?

- What strategies (if any) are used to develop systems for improving performance and ensuring quality?

- What strategies (if any) are used to ensure the basic infrastructure exists to allow individuals to meet/communicate for capacity development?

- What strategies (if any) are used to develop resource pools of local trainers/facilitators?

- Have the resources for M&E from domestic, regional and international networks been researched and fully utilized?

Based on the answers to these questions, a **Concept Note and Project Plan** for the Human Capacity Assessment can be developed. This document will define the following aspects:

a)   Objectives of HCD assessment which may include:

- Summarizing the human capacity required to implement the M&E system

- Determining the current capacity for M&E among those involved in implementing the M&E system

- Identifying the gaps in M&E human capacity (differences between capacity required and current capacity)

- Identifying the challenges to HCD and suggesting methods by which HCD M&E gaps can be overcome

b)   The benefits and use of the HCD assessment results for the organization and the positive impact of using them to help achieve the organization's goals and objectives

c)   Who will manage, implement, govern, review, and approve the HCD assessment

d)   Which stakeholders will be targeted by the HCD assessment and what will be required of them

e)   The methodology and sampling frame (if applicable) that will be used for the HCD assessment

f)   The time frame and cost of the HCD assessment and how resources will be mobilized for it

g) How the quality of the HCD assessment will be assured (peer review mechanism and other quality control processes)

h) How communications will be managed in conducting the HCD assessment in different sectors

Deliverables: Concept Note and Project Plan. These need to be discussed and approved (from a technical proficiency point of view) by the M&E Technical Working Group (see Component 3).

Step 2: Obtain political and senior management buy-in and approval

Once the Concept Note and Project Plan have been approved by the M&E TWG, these documents can be submitted to the organization's management for consideration, approval and funding allocation. It would be helpful for management to be aware of the assessment planning before the Concept Note and Project Plan is presented to them.

If the HCD assessment is approved and resources mobilized, the next step is to assemble the HCD team and the other governance structures (e.g., peer review team), as defined in the Concept Note.

Deliverables: Approved HCD assessment Concept Note and Project Plan, secured funding, and constituted committees/groups to oversee the process.

Step 3: Determine the M&E competencies required

The competencies required for implementing the M&E system are embedded in the job descriptions of M&E staff. If an organization has already included M&E functions and posts in its organizational structure, there already should be job descriptions for M&E staff. Even if job descriptions have not been developed, the skills required for the M&E system can still be defined by:

a) Looking at the performance objectives (results/goals) of the organization for its M&E system

b) Using expert input of persons who have experience in developing M&E systems

c) Using similar human capacity assessments from other countries (M&E skill requirements are fairly uniform across countries.)

d) Reading the M&E system documentation to see if any human capacity requirements are stated or implied in the documentation

Having a defined skills set (i.e., knowing who needs to be able to do what) is the starting point in developing human capacity for the M&E system. Each M&E system's skills set may look different. Experience suggests that there are generally two types of skills needed for M&E systems: (a) general management and coordination skills, and (b) technical skills related to the 12 Components of an M&E system.

Deliverables: Clear, documented description of the required skills set for the M&E system.

Step 4: Design the HCD assessment data collection instruments and train team members

The information found in Step 3 should assist in the design of appropriate data collection instruments based on the approved Concept Note and Project Plan. The Electronic Resource Library contains an example of an assessment tool.

Once the data collection instrument has been designed, it needs to be piloted (rapidly field-tested with a few respondents) and then submitted for approval to the peer review group (if one has been established).

Deliverables: Set of data collection instruments and training of all team members in their use.

Step 5: Collect data for the HCD assessment

Use the data collection instruments and methodology described in the Concept Note and Project Plan to collect relevant data. Keep data confidential and capture it using the method defined in the Concept Note. If only a few qualitative questionnaires or records of focus group discussions are envisaged, no electronic data capture is needed. However, if large quantities of quantitative data are to be collected, then some data capture (using statistical software) may be required to make data analysis easier.

Deliverables: Data collected on existing capacities (and captured, if needed).

Step 6: Analyze data and prepare an HCD Assessment Report

Analyze the data that has been compiled, keeping in mind that:

a) The purpose of the HCD assessment is to understand general capacity gaps so that a few standardized curricula for M&E can be developed. Grouping similar capacity needs will help to identify which M&E curricula would be most useful. This is also known as a thematic analysis.

b) The purpose is not to develop an individual learning or professional development plan for each person interviewed.

c) The main focus should be on comparing the required skills to the actual existing capacities in order to understand capacity gaps.

Once data have been analyzed, the results and recommendations for action need to written up in a human capacity assessment report.

Deliverables: Draft HCD assessment report ready for approval by the relevant governance structures and peer review processes defined in the Concept Note and Project Plan.

Step 7: Present HCD assessment results

Once the peer review group has approved the human capacity gap report, it can be presented to management for input and feedback. One of the main points to be made during a presentation of these results is that the report is only one step in a process of human capacity development and that the next step entails detailed planning to address the identified gaps.

Deliverables: Approved HCD assessment report.

7. HowTo Guide 2-2: Developing a Human Capacity Development Strategy and Plan

Step 1. Seek political and senior management buy-in

Usually, a Human Capacity Development Strategy is a national (or at least regional or sectoral) strategy. Therefore, the relevant governance structures [(e.g., M&E TWG (see Chapter 3) or others] should not only know about the plans to develop the strategy but should also be involved in its development. This will help ensure that the HCD strategy and plan links to other development efforts and that funding is available for its implementation. HCD efforts in the public sector should also carry the approval of the agency responsible for managing all public sector employees (i.e., the Public Service Commission or its equivalent).

Deliverables: Written approval to proceed with a strategy development (e.g., minutes of TWG meetings).

Step 2: Put a team together to develop the strategy

Seek team members who:

- Represent various sectors and institutions involved in M&E
- Have high-level authority and have demonstrated leadership in HCD and/or M&E
- Have a history of successful collaboration in issues to do with M&E or HCD
- Are knowledgeable about human resource policy and issues
- Understand the staffing requirements for M&E
- Can think creatively and comprehensively

Deliverable: A team for the task, with clearly defined roles for each team member.

Step 3: Carefully review the HCD Assessment (or conduct one if not yet done)

Carefully review the findings and recommendations of an existing HCD assessment if one has been done recently or, if not, do one (see Section 6 for more information on how to do an HCD assessment).

Deliverable: HCD assessment findings reviewed carefully.

Step 4: Prioritize the HCD issues that need to be addressed

The HCD assessment will reveal areas of human capacity to be developed. The team should work together to identify the most critical skills required and prioritize attention to address them. Principles of prioritization of human capacity may include prioritizing:

- Capacity needs of full-time people responsible for implementing and managing the M&E system. Without their leadership in the M&E system, it will not be fully operational.
- Capacity needs of people responsible for collecting, capturing, and reporting routine data, the rationale being that routine data systems are the backbone and often most neglected part of M&E systems
- Capacity needs of people responsible for interpreting and using the data because data use is the raison d'être of M&E systems (Without data use, all other M&E processes are of little value.)

Deliverable: A list of HCD priorities.

Step 5: Identify constraints to addressing the human capacity gaps

A review of possible constraints and their causes will help facilitate a partnership approach to identifying and implementing solutions. Human capacity development constraints may include:

- Lack of willingness by senior management to invest in the M&E system by investing in human resource capacity development
- Lack of local training institutions or trainers to provide M&E capacity building
- Lack of funds for M&E capacity building
- Lack of standardized and approved curricula, leading to inconsistent quality of training
- Lack of coordinated training efforts, leading to repetition and sub-optimal use of the limited funds for capacity building
- One-dimensional capacity building strategies such as relying only on workshops
- *Workshop culture* where workshops are associated with additional per diems and a day *away from the office*, instead of an opportunity to build skills
- Lack of demand for data and M&E, leading to low levels of attendance at M&E training courses

Deliverable: A set of constraints on M&E-related HCD and ways to address them.

Step 6: Identify the most suitable HCD strategies/approaches

A range of HCD strategies should be followed to ensure good knowledge retention and application by those whose capacity is to be developed. (See Section 5 (d) for a range of possible HCD strategies.)

Deliverable: A set of HCD strategies/approaches for inclusion in the HCD strategy

Step 7: Develop a draft HCD Strategy and Plan, and ways to advocate for it

Develop a draft HCD strategy and action plan with timelines and recommendations that deal with the most pressing issues first but do not neglect entrenched HCD problems. Also consider how the strategy will be implemented: some advocacy for the new strategy may be needed (e.g., a launch, meetings with key persons, having a senior champion and so forth). (See Chapter 6 for more details about advocacy strategies.) Include such advocacy activities for the new HCD strategy in the action plan.

Submit the draft strategy and plan to the M&E TWG, Public Service Commission, or other concerned agency for approval.

Deliverable: An approved HCD strategy and costed action plan for its implementation

Step 8: Implement, monitor and report on capacity-strengthening activities and progress

Monitoring and evaluating capacity development is important and should be planned for. Monitoring human capacity development involves counting the number of training sessions and the number of people trained. A training database could be used but is not essential. Evaluating human capacity development involves assessing the medium- to long-term results of capacity development efforts (i.e., are people whose capacity has been built doing their jobs better and have they internalized the capacity development effort through changing their behavior, attitudes or practices?). The ERL contains more information on evaluating capacity development.

Seek leadership (i.e., a multi-sectored team of decision-makers) to help implement the action plan and monitor its results.

Deliverables: Capacity development progress reports; improved human capacity for M&E system.

For reflection 2:

Reflect on the human capacity processes within your organization. Will these steps for HCD assessment and/or strategy development work? What are some of the pitfalls in following these steps? Will these steps address all the concerns that you may have? What are some of the challenges for HCD within your organization? Why have previous HCD strategies failed?

8. Summary of Chapter 2 Knowledge and Skills

In this chapter, you learned about human capacity development for the M&E system, focusing specifically on the individual level, that is, people at the national, sub-national and service delivery levels who execute M&E functions or manage those responsible for M&E. You learned about theory and technical process steps for conducting an M&E Human Capacity Assessment as well as an M&E Human Capacity Development Strategy and Plan. You learned about the benefits of human capacity development for M&E systems as well as challenges you might face as you try to customize and incorporate the steps for HCD in your own organization. You learned about the importance of political and senior management buy-in at the start of the process, the need to identify/prioritize capacity needs and strategies, and the importance of monitoring and reporting on capacity in order to strengthen the process for the future.

9. Learning Activity

a) Review Section 6 (undertaking an HCD assessment).

b) Read Section 7 carefully (developing a HCD strategy and plan).

c) Now, imagine that an HCD assessment has been conducted in a Ministry of Agriculture. This assessment showed that the following groups of people lacked M&E skills.

> **GROUPS THAT REQUIRE CAPACITY BUILDING IN M&E:**
> - Directors of the Ministry of Agriculture
> - Finance staff of the Ministry of Agriculture
> - Extension officers working in district council offices
> - Members of the parliamentary committee on agriculture

d) Discuss, in your groups (or reflect on your own), the kind of knowledge and M&E skills each of these groups needs, and the best ways in which their capacity could be built. **'Knowledge'** is what the person should KNOW or KNOW ABOUT and **'skills'** refers to what the person should be able to DO. If a person has both the knowledge and skills not only to do something but to teach it to others, the person is said to be fully competent in that area. You can refer to Annex B for a sample list of the kinds of skills that evaluators should have (please remember this is about skills in monitoring and evaluation, not just evaluation; the competencies for evaluators are provided as an example for you to consider in completing the exercise).

Please note that the knowledge and skills referred to in this exercise are **knowledge about and skills relating to monitoring, evaluation, and M&E systems,** and **not** the knowledge and skills that these persons need to do their broader jobs.

Document your answer in a table that looks like this:

Group that requires M&E capacity building	Types of knowledge and skills ABOUT M&E they need to have	How can their capacity be built?
Directors of the Ministry of Agriculture	The person needs to know about (KNOWLEDGE): • The information that the M&E system will generate • The financial resources that the M&E system will need • The information products (reports) that the M&E system will generate The person needs to be able to (SKILLS): • Interpret the data from the different surveys received • Be a champion for M&E and encourage other directors in the department to set up M&E systems	Technical workshop in survey design and data interpretation Study tours with other ministries that have successfully implemented M&E systems

Source: Authors

Annex A: Information to Use When Assessing M&E Capacities

A: Skill profile for an M&E Specialist

The skill profile for an M&E Specialist includes four critical domains: Institutional Analysis, System Design and Applications, Methodological Tools, and Information/Knowledge Utilization (Source: Kusek and Rist, 2004). Briefly consider each:

Institutional Analysis:

- Ability to assess the relevant political situation as to the demand for/ interest in building an M&E system

- Ability to understand the role of M&E in the larger context in a country (e.g., public sector reform, donor relations)

- Ability to conduct needs assessments of an organization's requirements for an M&E system

- Ability to conduct institutional capacity assessments within targeted institutions, on their strengths relevant to building an M&E system

- Ability to identify individual *champions* in organizations, and successfully work with them to build understanding of, and support for, an M&E initiative

System Design and Applications:

- Ability to conceptualize and contribute to the design of an M&E system for a public sector organization/ministry/bureau

- Ability to see applications of an M&E system for various levels and components of government

- Ability to see applications of an M&E system for various public sector activities (projects, programs and policies)

- Ability to see the linkage of an M&E system to other core functions such as budget, accountability and oversight

- Ability to design at least a minimal statistical collection strategy on relevant M&E variables/indicators

Methodological Tools:

- Ability to understand the logic and applications of data collected through an M&E system

- Ability to assess the quality of data and statistical information collected in an M&E system, i.e., have some understanding of reliability and validity

- Ability to specify the appropriate data collection tools for various variables/indicators used in the M&E system

- Ability to conduct appropriate analysis from relevant data

Information/Knowledge Utilization:

- Ability to understand the applications of M&E data to organizational information needs
- Ability to target appropriate information to appropriate officials
- Ability to understand how to accumulate, over time, longitudinal or trend information on policy areas of concern

B: Typical M&E posts at all levels and in all sectors

This table (see next page) summarizes the typical M&E posts, both full-time and part-time, that countries may consider as they build their network of organizations with M&E functions.

		National level	Sub-national level	Service delivery level
Government	**Public Sector**	**NCA** **M&E Unit with 4 full-time persons** • National manager • Database manager • Officer responsible for routine data • Research officer	**Decentralized coordinating committee** Linked to Local Government Authority structures • Person at Local Government Authority responsible for M&E	Not applicable
		Ministry of Local Government **Program Focal point,** and/or **M&E officer**	**Local Government Authorities** • Program M&E officer, OR • M&E officer for LGA, OR • Program Focal point with M&E responsibilities (i.e. part-time M&E)	Not applicable
		Key Ministry Implementing the Program **M&E unit with 3 full-time persons** • Epidemiologist/Analyst • Statistician • Persons responsible for routine data collection	**Local Key Implementing Ministry Management Team** • Person responsible for Management Information System (MIS) • Person/s responsible for data capture and quality control	**Ministry Service-Providing Units** (e.g. health facilities) • Person/s responsible for data recording, collation, reporting and quality control

	National level	Sub-national level	Service delivery level
Government / **Public Sector**	**NCA** **M&E Unit with at least 4 full-time persons** • National Manager • Database Manager • Officer responsible for routine data • Research officer	**Decentralized coordinating committees** Linked to Local Government Authority structures • No M&E person as part of committee: M&E provided by person at Local Government Authority responsible for M&E	Not applicable
	Ministry of Local Government Program Focal point, and/or M&E officer	**Local Government Authorities** • Program M&E officer, OR • M&E officer for LGA (not only), OR • Program Focal point with M&E responsibilities (i.e. part-time M&E)	Not applicable
	Key Ministry Implementing the Program **M&E unit with at least 3 full-time persons** • Epidemiologist/Analyst • Statistician • Persons responsible for routine data collection	**Local Key Implementing Ministry Management Team** • Person responsible for Management Information System (MIS) • Person/s responsible for data capture and quality control	**Ministry Service-Providing Units** (e.g. health facilities) • Person/s responsible for data recording, collation, reporting and quality control

	National level	Sub-national level	Service delivery level
Government	Other Government Ministries (programs whose implementation involves several ministries) • **Program Focal point with M&E responsibilities**	Local coordinating teams/officers, e.g., district education office • Person responsible for collating, reporting and verifying M&E data, as part of or parallel to the education management information system (EMIS) • Person/s responsible for electronic data capture and quality control	Other facilities that provide government services, e.g., schools • Part-time Focal Person (most likely not full-time) tasked with recording, summarizing, reporting, analyzing and verifying the quality of data relevant to the program
National Partners — Civil Society Sector	Umbrella organization/s for civil society organizations **Program Focal point with M&E responsibilities** Umbrella organization/s for associations of program beneficiaries **Focal point with M&E responsibilities**	Regional offices of civil society organizations coordinating activities • Person responsible for collating, reporting and verifying M&E data, as part of the organization's monitoring system Umbrella organizations in countries with vast geographic areas, may also have sub-national coordinating offices • Person responsible for collating, reporting and verifying M&E data, as part of the umbrella organization's monitoring system • Person/s responsible for electronic data capture and quality control	Civil society organizations implementing services • Part-time Focal Person (most likely not full-time) tasked with recording, summarizing, reporting, analyzing and verifying the quality of data Associations of beneficiaries (membership organizations) • Part-time Focal Person (most likely not full-time) tasked with recording, summarizing, reporting, analyzing and verifying the quality of data

	National level	Sub-national level	Service delivery level
National Partners — Private Sector	**Umbrella organization for the business sector** • Focal point with M&E responsibilities **Head offices of companies** • Focal point with M&E responsibilities	**Regional offices of businesses coordinating activities** Person responsible for collating, reporting and verifying M&E data, as part of the organization's monitoring system	**Businesses that have mainstreamed program into their operations** • Part-time Focal Person (most likely not full-time) tasked with recording, summarizing, reporting, analyzing and verifying the quality of data received
National Partners — National research sector	National Research Council, University Research Institutes, Ethical Review Boards, etc.	Not applicable	Not applicable

		National level	Sub-national level	Service delivery level
International Partners	**Funds and foundations**	National office of the organization	Not applicable	Not applicable
	Research institutes	National office of the organization Focal Point with M&E responsibilities	Not applicable	Not applicable
	Bilateral agencies	National office of the organization M&E officer	Not applicable	Not applicable
	Multilateral agencies	National office of the organization Technical support adviser, e.g., UNAIDS M&E advisor, UNICEF M&E officer	Not applicable	Not applicable
	International NGOs	National office of the organization	Not applicable	Not applicable

C: Key functions of full-time M&E posts

(Adapted from the World Bank's write-up on the 11 Components of functional M&E systems.)

The full-time officers within the network of organizations responsible for M&E have different roles and responsibilities. Suggested roles and responsibilities have been summarized here.

At the National Level

1. National M&E Manager

- Coordinate the creation and review of M&E system documentation.
- Manage and supervise the M&E unit staff.
- Manage the M&E system (i.e., provide technical oversight).
- Coordinate M&E plan costing and annual review.
- Chair the M&E Technical Working Group (TWG) and coordinate its work.
- Play a key role in coordinating the planning, implementation and dissemination of findings of all surveys and surveillance (in collaboration with the focal institution on this aspect).
- Advocate for and communicate about M&E in all sectors at the decision-making level to build strong M&E partnerships.
- Develop and oversee M&E capacity building strategy, accompanying activities, and play a key role in mobilizing resources for this.
- Coordinate and act on supervision and data auditing report results.
- Create information products (annual report, etc.).
- Oversee all data dissemination and feedback processes.
- Represent the organization/ministry at M&E forums in the country.
- Act as a Liaison with poverty monitoring and other relevant groups.

2. Data Officer

- Create and manage a national database in line with national M&E needs
- Import data from government ministries/organizations and decentralized coordinating units and conduct analysis as required by the M&E Unit
- Install database at decentralized levels and oversee its operation
- Train decentralized structures on database use
- Trouble-shoot database problems with decentralized structures
- Provide data for all organization/ministry information products

3: Research Officer

- Coordinate the development of a research and learning strategy and agenda.
- Coordinate implementation of the strategy.
- Act as a Liaison with the Research Council regarding ethical approvals for all research.
- Ensure that research and learning agenda is managed and implemented.
- Represent organization/ministry at all sub-national research forums.
- Lead research funded by the organization/ministry.
- Disseminate research results in academic journals, research conferences, special university lectures, political/decision-making forums, etc.

4: Routine Monitoring System Officer(s)

- Implement scheduled and/or agreed activities in the annual M&E work plan (road map).
- With support of the leadership of the organization/ministry, agree on data reporting commitments (including timelines) with data providers.
- Coordinate supervision and auditing of program monitoring data.
- Coordinate with the Data Officer about electronic capture of data into the national database.
- Act as a Liaison with the health (or other relevant) ministry regarding health sector data collection.
- Coordinate dissemination of output level data.
- Advocate for the use of output monitoring data.

At Regional/District (Local) Government Authority

This section is relevant where activities are coordinated at decentralized government structures, e.g., district councils, municipalities. The following M&E resources should exist at the decentralized levels (linked to and part of the local government offices):

1. District/Regional M&E Officers

- Undertake M&E advocacy at the decentralized and implementation levels.
- Coordinate M&E capacity building (e.g., training and mentorship of partners).
- Coordinate implementation of program monitoring system at the decentralized level.

- Liaise with stakeholders concerning implementation of program monitoring system.
- Manage program monitoring system data submission, capture and export to main M&E system.
- Manage program monitoring data dissemination.
- In collaboration with the Research Officer, support coordination of surveys at the decentralized level.
- Advise on M&E issues at decentralized level.
- Manage M&E capacity building at the decentralized level.
- Analyze and present M&E data as requested at decentralized levels.
- Disseminate information products.
- Promote data use during decision making and planning of interventions and use data for decision making.
- Manage the program implementers' registration system at the decentralized level.
- Act as a Liaison with the national organization that manages the M&E system on all M&E issues at the decentralized level.

At the Service Delivery Level

Some organizations have full-time staff members and others do not. Irrespective of whether there is a full-time staff member responsible for M&E, each organization implementing activities should nominate a person to amend daily record keeping tools to ensure compliance with the national program monitoring system (or create these if they were not in existence). This will involve:

- Keeping daily records of the implementation of activities
- Compiling program monitoring system forms and submitting completed data forms
- Attending decentralized program monitoring system feedback meetings
- Promoting the use of program monitoring system data when planning interventions

Annex B: Evaluation Competencies

1. Evaluation knowledge competencies

   1.1. Appreciates the social and political role played by evaluation

   1.1.1. Shows awareness of evaluation history and knowledge.

   1.1.2. Appreciates the linkages and differences between evaluation and social research.

   1.1.3. Understands program theory and its implications.

   1.1.4. Can relate evaluation to policy environments.

   1.1.5. Demonstrates familiarity with theories of causality and attribution.

   1.1.6. Shows awareness of different modes of generalization.

   1.2. Understands evaluation methods and approaches

   1.2.1. Uses appropriate evaluation concepts and terms.

   1.2.2. Knows how to design and structure an evaluation.

   1.2.3. Comprehends the value of diverse evaluation approaches.

   1.2.4. Demonstrates appropriate use of these in specific contexts.

   1.2.5. Shows familiarity with quantitative and qualitative methodologies, and their underlying philosophical assumptions.

   1.2.6. Grasps the potential and limits of quantitative methods (including randomized experiments, cost benefit analysis, survey) and qualitative methods (including case study, interview and observation).

   1.3. Shows ability to use evaluation tools of data collection and analysis to:

   1.3.1. Design case studies, surveys, interviews, observations.

   1.3.2. Set up and use evaluation monitoring systems.

   1.3.3. Determine appropriate indicators and questions for evaluation task.

   1.3.4. Analyze and interpret data with variety of strategies.

   1.3.5. Establish criteria for validity and for "valuing" the evaluation.

   1.3.6. Report fairly and objectively to agreed audiences in the public interest.

2. Professional practice competencies

   2.1. Demonstrates capacity to deliver evaluations

      2.1.1. Ascertains the evaluative context.

      2.1.2. Appraises policy logic and program theory.

      2.1.3. Selects appropriate approaches, methods and tools.

      2.1.4. Chooses judicious and relevant evaluation criteria.

      2.1.5. Knows when to involve evaluators with different skills.

      2.1.6. Demonstrates effective management of the evaluation.

      2.1.7. Makes sensitive ethical decisions in practice.

      2.1.8. Interprets evaluation results in context.

   2.2 Demonstrates interpersonal skills

      2.2.1. Writes fluently and communicates clearly.

      2.2.2. Is able to work independently and in a team.

      2.2.3. Uses sound and sensitive negotiating skills.

      2.2.4. Demonstrates cultural/gender sensitivity.

      2.2.5. Nurtures professional relationships.

3. Qualities and disposition competencies

   3.1 Upholds ethical and democratic values

   3.2 Respects clients, stakeholders, and participants

   3.3 Is responsive and flexible in changing context

   3.4 Exercises sound, rigorous and fair judgment

   3.5 Is able to handle conflict and remain impartial

   3.6 Displays self-knowledge and pursues professional development

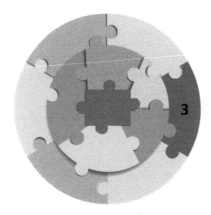

Chapter 3
Monitoring and Evaluation Partnerships

Chapter Aim

The aim of this chapter is to enable you to understand the importance of establishing and maintaining strong M&E partnerships as a way of bringing diverse people from different organizations together, to work around similar objectives and goals. M&E partnerships are especially important, given that many of the people involved do not necessarily work in the same institutions.

Chapter Knowledge and Skills

By the end of this chapter, you should be able to:

a) Explain to others the different types of partnerships, the benefits of partnerships and different partnership mechanisms.

b) Recognize the implementation issues establishing and maintaining partnerships.

c) Establish and maintain a national M&E TWG as an M&E partnership mechanism.

d) Organize a joint mission/trip with other development partners.

Before You Begin...

Take a few minutes to read through the questions below. You may find it helpful to write down your answers. As you work through the chapter, compare your answers to the views of the authors.

- Why are partnerships important in M&E?
- When is a partnership successful?
- Why do partnerships fail?
- What makes a partnership strong?
- How do I build partnerships with M&E persons?
- Who should I build partnerships with?
- Why should I participate in a monitoring and evaluation technical working group?
- How can I coordinate efforts with partners working in the field of M&E?

M&E is a cross-cutting issue and many people are involved in it over time. These questions remind us that not only does the M&E system need skilled people, they need to plan and work together to ensure the success of the M&E system. These partnerships for M&E are important even if you are a small organization implementing a program.

This chapter will teach you more about building and keeping strong partnerships for the M&E system.

Component 3: M&E Partnerships

1. Introduction

> *"The grip of AIDS will only be broken by effective*
> *programmes at country level. The difficulty is that agencies and funders...*
> *operate quasi-independently of one another.*
> *What never happens is an event or process to develop integrated*
> *country strategies that focus only on the country – not on the*
> *interests of the agency, funder, or constituency..."*

Richard Horton, *The Lancet,* Vol. 368, August 26, 2006: pp. 716-718

M&E partnerships are part of the *people, partnerships and planning* ring of the 12 Components of a functional M&E system. Establishing and maintaining strong partnerships is a way in which a group of diverse people from different organizations can work together around the same set of objectives. This is especially important for an M&E system, given that many of the people involved do not work in the same institutions or come from the same sector.

Component 3 outline: This component begins with background and definitions relating to M&E partnerships, the types of partnerships that exist, and mechanisms to assist in establishing and maintaining them (Section 2). Sections 3 and 4 describe the desired results for this chapter (in developing and maintaining M&E partnerships) and their benefits. Implementation issues related to M&E partnerships are presented in Section 5. These include understanding the principles of partnership development, characteristics of successful partnerships, and mechanisms for developing and maintaining an M&E Technical Working Group (TWG). Section 6 is directed to people responsible for M&E system partnerships and focuses on how to establish and maintain a national M&E TWG. Section 7 discusses how development partner representatives, who are planning technical support in a country, can undertake joint trips or missions with other development partners. The chapter closes with a summary of lessons learned (Section 8), and a practical exercise to cement what you should have learned in the chapter (Section 9).

2. Background Information & Definitions

a) **Partnerships for M&E:** A partnership is an agreement between two or more parties to work together to achieve common aims. Partners (individuals and institutions) share resources, ideas and experience, to support and enrich each other's capacity and better achieve common goals.

Partnerships can also be seen as two or more groups working collaboratively towards meeting common goals while, at the same time, meeting their own individual goals. An M&E partnership is a special type of partnership. It refers to a cooperative relationship between people or groups who agree to share responsibility for implementing the M&E system. Such partnerships are characterized by a commitment to cooperation, shared responsibility, and the achievement of a common goal.

b) **Types of M&E Partnerships:** The types of M&E partnerships will depend greatly on the organization's M&E system. A small organization will, for example, have less elaborate partnerships than a national Ministry of Education trying to operationalize a uniform M&E system for the entire education sector. National M&E systems involve the most complex partnerships and will be internal (e.g., between units within an agency) and external (e.g., between an agency and its partners). The external partners may be in different sectors (multi-sectored), LGAs and communities (multi-level). These two types of partnerships for a national M&E system are illustrated in Figure C3-1.

Figure C3–1:   Types of M&E Partnerships in the M&E System

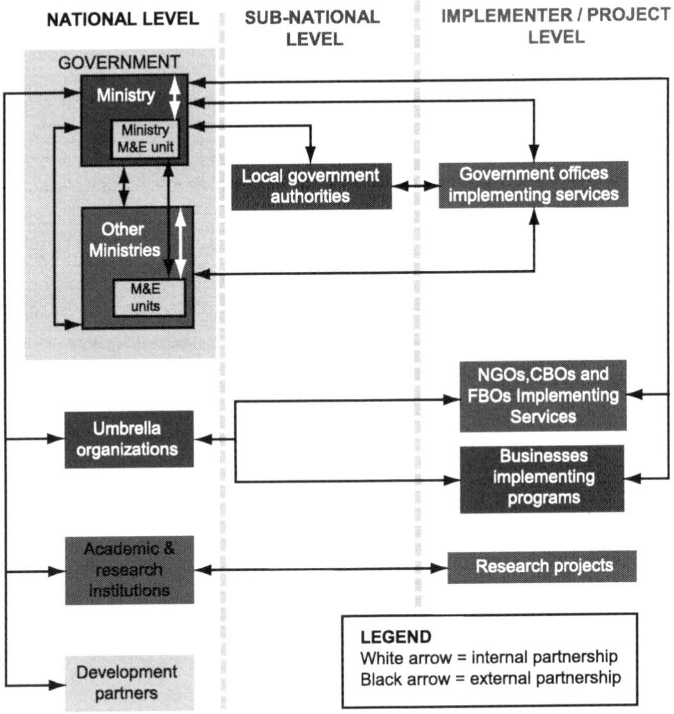

Source: Authors

Making Monitoring and Evaluation Systems Work

c)   There are different partnership mechanisms through which M&E partnerships can be established and maintained:

- **Task force:** A temporary grouping of persons mandated by a permanent structure to fulfill a specific, often short-term, objective.

- **M&E technical working group:** This involves a group of experts who meet on a regular basis to discuss technical M&E developments and approve key M&E documentation. Such groups have fixed invitation-only membership and usually consist of stakeholders from all sectors.

- **Joint study tour:** This is an opportunity for groups of nominated persons from one country to visit similar groups in other countries that have similar interests, to learn more about how they operate their programs.

- **Joint evaluation:** This involves more than one partner undertaking an evaluation of a program together. Guidelines on conducting joint evaluations have recently been prepared by OECD/DAC. The benefits are: shared capacity development, harmonization and reduced transaction cost, participation and alignment, objectivity and legitimacy, and broader scope. Challenges include the complexity of evaluating a multi-agency or multi-sector program, as well as the cost and complexity of coordinating joint work (OECD DAC, 2006).

- **Joint M&E missions/trips:** This involves more than one development partner's representatives (all of whom support the country in one or more aspects of its M&E system) agreeing and planning a joint trip to the country concerned. Good experiences relating to joint M&E missions/trips have recently been documented. (Search the ERL for "Getting Results–M&E Partnerships".)

3. Results to Be Achieved When Implementing This Component

Long-term result:

- Establish and maintain internal and external partnerships to strengthen the M&E system

Short- and medium-term results:

- Inventory of all M&E stakeholders
- Mechanism to coordinate and communicate with all M&E stakeholders
- Participation in a National M&E Technical Working Group
- Local leadership and capacity for stakeholder coordination

4. Benefits of M&E Partnerships for an M&E System

1. **M&E partnerships increase and improve communication**, participation and shared accountability among stakeholders involved in M&E. Improved communication facilitates a coordinated approach to managing the M&E system and helps to create a joint vision for it.

2. **M&E partnerships enable the lead agency to coordinate** the M&E efforts of development partners, government agencies, civil society, and the private sector. In a 2003 OECD/DAC assessment, governments reported that uncoordinated efforts by development partners impose the third highest burden on development support (OECD, 2003:13). Improved coordination reduces confusion and duplication, facilitates shared learning and, therefore, lowers the costs associated with M&E systems.

3. **M&E partnerships help to simplify, harmonize and align** the M&E and reporting procedures of government, civil society, the private sector and development partners. A strong partnership could enable organizations to prepare one standard report for all partners rather than expending unnecessary time and money preparing multiple reports. This approach helps build a common platform for sharing information, plans, results, tools and strategies.

4. **M&E partnerships help to mobilize required technical and financial support for implementing the M&E system**. When stakeholders involved in the M&E system communicate regularly and effectively, everyone concerned understands the human, financial and technical support required for M&E work. M&E functions can be divided rationally among stakeholders, who are then better able to share their technical skills efficiently and effectively. Such partnerships also help to link M&E processes to the budgets of stakeholders and support the clear division of labor.

5. **M&E partnerships help to achieve the goal of** *one harmonized M&E system:* Harmonized M&E systems (as in the *Three Ones* principles designed

to make AIDS support more effective and efficient[1]) were designed to guard against the proliferation of strategies, committees and monitoring systems, which add confusion, duplicate effort and increase transaction costs for countries. Strong M&E partnerships are key to achieving this goal.

6. **Undertaking joint missions/trips has specific additional benefits** for development partners working in a country. Partnerships through joint missions enable consolidated feedback to be shared over a shorter period of time, assist country-level M&E technical advisers to develop new strategies or find new solutions, introduce new country-level staff and explore possible solutions to country level challenges, raise the credibility of development partners, and provide the agency being supported with an opportunity to advocate for rationalized support.

5. Implementation Issues Related to Establishing and Maintaining M&E Partnerships

5.1. Principles for effectively managing and sustaining M&E partnerships

- There should be mutual trust between partners. This can be built through open dialogue and exchanges of views in a respectful setting that accommodates different views. Such actions will make partners feel valued and help to keep them involved.

- Partners should be accountable to each other so that they honor their rights and responsibilities as M&E stakeholders.

- Partnerships are dynamic. Changes are bound to occur as individuals representing institutions change, and as institutional priorities change. Maintaining partnerships is an ongoing effort. Partnerships need to be flexible and adaptable to change.

- Partnerships should be purposeful. Partnerships should have predefined objectives and intended results so that everyone concerned can see the value of the partnership. The results may, for example, include the production of four information products every year.

- Internal partnerships (between the M&E unit and the rest of the agency) and partnerships with M&E units of ministries involved in the program being monitored, are very important and should be developed.

- Harmonization to improve aid effectiveness and *managing for results* are both global priorities for development partners and corporate priorities for most development agencies. The momentum created by the international harmonization and "managing for results" agenda can be used to encourage partners within the country to become involved in the M&E system.

- In successful partnerships, the complementary skills and contributions of all partners are recognized. An agreed-upon division of partner responsibilities can streamline contributions and prevent gaps. A budgeted M&E work plan (see Component 5) that captures the responsibilities of all partners should help with assigning specific roles to specific partners.

5.2. Characteristics of successful M&E partnerships

Partnerships are successful when:

- There is a shared vision of what may be achieved with clear and shared mandates or agendas.
- Partners are legitimate constituency groups that are interested in M&E and agree that a partnership is necessary.
- There is respect and trust between different interest groups, commitment of key interest groups developed through a clear and open process, and a critical mass of balanced representation and influence at all levels and in all relevant bodies and processes.
- Time is taken to build the partnership and to develop compatible and flexible ways of working together (including sensitivity to the specific needs and challenges of all partners).
- There is timely and effective communication and collaborative decision making, with a commitment to achieving consensus.
- There is effective organizational management and coordination within sectors and effective leadership.
- Partners have access to adequate, appropriate and timely information.
- Training and technical support is provided to partners in order to foster professionalism and a culture of equity and transparency.
- There is evidence of non-discriminatory involvement of all partners, shared ownership, responsibility and commitment.
- The partnership is underpinned by efficient administrative support, such as adequate advance notice of meetings and processes.

5.3. Using an M&E Technical Working Group as a partnership mechanism

The M&E TWG is a multi-sectored partnership normally representing all M&E stakeholders in a given country and is usually established for national-level M&E systems. M&E TWGs fulfill a variety of functions in different countries. They may include coordinating M&E activities, advice on technical M&E issues, and providing a partnership or consultation forum. Here are some tips to keep an M&E TWG active and functioning:

Formation, Mandate, and Functions of M&E TWG:

i. Include the formation of an M&E TWG in the National Strategic Plan to give the M&E TWG legitimacy and authority to make decisions or provide advice.

ii. TWG members should receive the same allowances as other similar standing committees, e.g., Partnership Forum or Board of Commissioners.

iii. The government should chair M&E TWG so that it is seen to be a legitimate government-run mechanism of coordination.

iv. Develop a Terms of Reference for the M&E TWG. The GAMET HIV M&E resource library includes guidelines for M&E TWG Terms of Reference and example TORs from different countries. (It is accessible at http://gametlibrary.worldbank.org: Click on the M&E partnerships puzzle piece or M&E partnerships on the left hand side of the screen, once you are in the library.)

v. Ensure that the M&E TWG oversees the implementation of the M&E work plan (see Component 5). This implies that individual TWG members would, for example, report back on the previous quarter's M&E activities assigned to their organizations in the national M&E work plan. In this way, the meeting is not dominated by the coordinating agency and other participants are not passive in the meeting but have an equal role and contribution.

vi. The TWG may need to form sub-committees from time to time, with short-term objectives and a defined life span to deal with specific issues (e.g., a specific survey). Such committees should be chaired by government representatives and should report back to the main M&E TWG on progress.

Membership of M&E TWG and attendance at meetings:

All organizations that have been assigned M&E functions in the national M&E work plan should be represented in the M&E TWG (including government departments concerned with M&E, decentralized structures, civil society organizations).

i. Development partners are more likely to attend regularly if they have a specific role to play, see the benefits to their organizations, perceive that the meetings are productive, and that progress is being made.

ii. The involvement and interest of key partners can be improved by giving them a prominent role in the TWG (e.g., chairperson or deputy chairperson).

iii. Civil society umbrella organizations that are members of M&E TWGs should provide feedback on M&E activities to their members.

iv. At the inception of the M&E system, the M&E TWG needs to meet more regularly than may be necessary once the system has matured. TWG members must be made aware that they need to meet once a month for the first 18 months of system implementation and on a quarterly basis thereafter, to ensure participation and a sense of progress.

5.4. Specific activities to strengthen the M&E partnership with civil society

Table C3–1: Specific Activities to Strengthen Civil Society's role in M&E Partnerships

Support community sector representatives by:	Community sector representatives can support partnership by:
• Being non-discriminatory and welcoming the involvement of all members of the community sector	• Understanding the many pressures and responsibilities faced by the secretariat
• Giving adequate advance notice of meetings and processes	• Providing appropriate and timely information (e.g., about the process for selecting the community sector's representatives)
• Providing administrative support (e.g., taking and distributing minutes of meetings)	
• Making general information about the coordination body or process freely and easily accessible	• Providing community resource people (e.g., experts to participate in working groups)
• Providing information about opportunities for the community sector to give input	• Communicating information to the broader community sector via focal points, such as networks
• Providing a contact point for the community sector (e.g., partnership officer)	

Adapted from: ICASO, AfriCASO, the Alliance, 2007

5.5. Specific activities for development partners to strengthen the partnership with government

Development partners can contribute to building partnerships around the M&E system by supporting the institutions (financially and technically) that lead the M&E TWGs and link their own planning and budgeting processes with those of government. Development partners should be aware of the latest information about partnership developments, and communicate in a coordinated and coherent way with government to ensure they are familiar with the latest government policies.

6. HowTo Guide C3-1: Establishing and Managing an M&E TWG

As mentioned in 5.3, M&E TWGs are one mechanism for creating an M&E partnership in the country. These steps describe how to set up an M&E TWG. NOTE: Many of the steps below could also be used, with some adaptation, to strengthen an existing M&E TWG.

Step 1: Collect necessary information about M&E and other partnerships, and determine strengths and weaknesses

When planning to establish M&E partnerships, find out:

- What is the government's strategy for M&E partnership? (To avoid compromising or accidentally circumventing this strategy)
- Are there any existing plans for partnerships?
- What is the government's intention in coordinating technical support in the country?
- Is there a national M&E work plan for the country and how is it used?
- Is there an M&E technical working group in the country and, if functional, how does it operate?
- Has a recent M&E system assessment been carried out? If so, what does it say about the nature and strength of partnerships?
- Who are the key M&E partners in the country?

Once you have found out all this information, obtain a list of partners and introduce yourself to other partners in the field. Ask these partners what their partnership needs are and ensure a clear understanding of their perceived and stated partnership needs. Establish what M&E activities these partners are involved in. Aim to understand, through these initial introductions, in-country sensitivities and formal and informal relationship protocols.

Conduct an informal SWOT analysis of M&E partnerships: Determine through initial interviews and discussions with partners (Step 1) the internal strengths and weaknesses (i.e., within the coordinating agency's control) and the external threats and opportunities (i.e., outside its control) in forming a national M&E partnership. The ERL contains information about how to do a SWOT analysis and a SWOT analysis template.

Deliverable: SWOT analysis of M&E partnership strengths and weaknesses.

Step 2:   Plan the M&E TWG

Brainstorm ideas with colleagues: When thinking of establishing a partnership, ask some preliminary and exploratory questions of a few trusted colleagues, perhaps, in a brainstorming setting:

- What are the government's aims and objectives in forming an M&E partnership?
- Will the partnership be composed of individuals, organizations or both?
- How will this new national M&E partnership link with existing partnership groups/forums?
- Is there a core group with the capacity to network during the planning phase?
- Who else needs to participate in the partnership within the next 1-3 years?
- Who may be connected in the future?
- What can each potential member contribute (e.g., staff time, money, work space, data, media relations, credibility and skills)?
- Do the individuals provide a representative range of different constituency groups or cultural perspectives? Are any groups or perspectives missing?
- Will certain organizations or individuals need incentives to join? What will they gain by joining the effort (e.g., increased skills, networking, and access to policy-makers)?
- What constitutes membership within the community partnership? Are there different levels of membership or membership dues?
- Is there an enabling environment for inter-agency partnership?
- What mechanisms exist to promote M&E partnerships?
- How have M&E partnerships improved and/or deteriorated over the past two to five years? What lessons can be learned from these experiences?
- What strategies could be recommended to optimize support for the M&E system?
- Who will benefit and who may oppose the M&E partnership? For what reasons? How can those who will oppose the partnership be convinced that the partnership is a good idea?

Plan the M&E TWG: When planning for the M&E TWG, ensure that it is grounded on solid partnership principles (see Step 4 below) and that one partner does not dominate. Plan the partnership by inviting initial partners to a meeting to:

- Reach consensus on roles and responsibilities (including leadership of the partnership).
- Agree on a common platform to share information.
- Develop a framework within which the partnership will work.
- Agree how partners will work together so as to maximize participation.

- Define how any differences or conflicts will be addressed.
- Assess available financial, human and technological capacity to support the partnership.
- Outline how valued resources will be shared.
- Define how the partnership will fit in with the government plans.
- Agree on the name for the M&E partnership (the name most often used is M&E TWG).

Develop Terms of Reference for the M&E TWG. Annex A contains guidelines for what to include in the Terms of Reference of an M&E TWG.

Deliverable: Draft M&E TWG TOR.

Step 3: Set up the M&E TWG

Launch the M&E TWG: Invite organizations that agreed to be members of the national M&E partnership to select representatives and have an initial launch meeting of the M&E TWG. Their TOR should be finalized during the launch meeting. In addition to the regular members, invite senior representatives of all partner organizations to co-chair the meeting, as this will increase the perceived importance of the TWG (and motivate individuals to attend).

Provide an induction for members: Not all persons who are representatives of the M&E TWG would necessarily know about the M&E system in the country. An induction course may be necessary to provide them with the requisite information and skills.

Raise awareness of the work of the technical working group by

Why do partnerships fail?

- A history of conflict among key interest groups
- Unequal balance of power and control among the partners, with a few partners manipulating and dominating processes
- Lack of clear purpose in all that the partnership does
- Partners setting unrealistic goals that are never achieved
- Tension caused by philosophical and methodological differences among the partners
- Lack of communication among the partners
- Weak participation or interest in partnership activities by certain members
- Lack of honesty and openness or hidden agendas among partners
- Differences in values and ideologies
- Personality conflicts
- Unclear and misunderstood communication and attempts by certain partners to control power, decisions, and resources

planning a specific communication and advocacy campaign (see Component 6) as one of the first tasks of the new or reconstituted M&E TWG.

Deliverables: Approved M&E TWG TOR; constituted TWG.

Step 4:   Maintain the M&E TWG

Different options for maintaining partnerships include:

a)   Having partnership meetings as scheduled and prepare and circulate minutes of the meeting soon after it has taken place

b)   Recognizing and publish the achievements of the partnership and communicate these to senior members of stakeholder organizations

c)   Building information-sharing platforms at the regional and national level, e.g., regional M&E partners' forum and national technical working groups

d)   Supporting decisions and actions taken by the members of the partnership

e)   Providing ongoing training and technical support for members of the par, astnership the need arises (e.g., if a new type of evaluation methodology for M&E is to be used in the country)

f)   Supporting the coordinating agency to nurture the following values for the M&E TWG:

- Openness, generosity, flexibility, shared vision and transparency

- Trust, shared values and team spirit

- Link the partnership to ongoing processes within the national program.

- Ensure sustainability through the partners contributing their own resources.

- Ensure a sense of ownership is nurtured among the partners.

- Recognize the power of all partners.

- Reflect a positive spirit of collaboration.

- Ability to negotiate and compromise where conflicts arise.

- Democracy and power sharing among partners

Also, one needs to monitor and evaluate the strength the M&E partnership established through the M&E TWG. **Monitoring** options include keeping records of the percentage of members who attend, the follow-through on decisions made, and the number of relevant national policy events in which the TWG is asked to be represented. Also, **evaluate** the effectiveness, success or failure of the partnership to understand its strengths and weaknesses and address areas of failure. Assessments could be carried out as part of a wider partnership assessment (e.g., using the UNAIDS Country Harmonization and Alignment Tool — "CHAT"), or as a more focused assessment. Make the necessary changes subsequent to the partnership evaluation.

Deliverable: TWG in which members attend and actively participate in meetings

For reflection 2:

Reflect on the M&E partnerships within your organization. Is your organization part of a national M&E TWG? Do you know if it is functioning, if there is one? What would be worthwhile for you from such a national M&E partnership? What are some of the pitfalls in following the steps listed in this chapter for developing and maintaining partnerships? Will these steps address all the concerns that you might have? What are some of the challenges for M&E partnerships within which your organization participates?

7. HowTo Guide C3-2: Planning and Undertaking a Joint M&E Mission/Trip

NOTE: Specific guidance has been developed on roles and responsibilities in undertaking joint missions to assess M&E systems. The steps listed here are general steps for a joint mission, irrespective of its purpose. If the purpose of the joint mission is to do a joint assessment of the status of the M&E system, then consult the relevant multi-partner operational guidance on conducting M&E assessments and choosing M&E assessment tools.

Step 1: Gather information before the mission

Contact the government to *bring it into the loop* of discussions about a joint mission. This step should start by contacting the government organization that requested the support to be provided through the planned M&E mission. The government contact person should be told of plans to contact other agencies, as well as the purpose of these contacts (to establish partnership opportunities). Efforts should be made to confirm the following with the government contact person:

- The government's strategy for the M&E partnership so that this is not accidentally circumvented

- Whether there are already plans for a joint mission

- What the government's intention is for coordinating technical support in the country

- Whether there is a work plan for M&E in the country. (If one exists, request a copy. The ideal would be a national multi-partner, multi-year work plan with information on M&E functions and who executes them.)

- Whether there is an M&E technical working group in the country
- Whether an M&E system assessment has recently been carried out. (If so, ask for a copy.)

If there is no national budgeted M&E work plan in the country, find out who the in-country and *remote* partners are (i.e., those who fly in, fly out) through other means, e.g., contact regional development partner offices, ask the government contact person, etc.

Deliverable: Statement of Mission Objectives and deliverables prepared.

Step 2: Create and explore opportunities for joint missions with partners

Single organization activities are easier and require less coordination, but the potential benefits for clients are reduced. When trying to organize a joint mission, try to fit in with government plans where possible and remember that one partner does not always have to dominate.

Going to the country on the same dates as partner organizations is a good start, even if the mission objectives of the various partners are different. It also helps the country to focus its efforts on the mission and not get distracted by repetitive missions, all of which take up the time and effort of country representatives.

- **Introduce yourself to other partners in the country.** Understand the nature of their M&E activities, schedule of visits, and any other relevant information. Remember to contact the in-country representatives of international partners (and then also the relevant regional/HQ representatives).

- **Initiate discussions about joint missions.** Discussions to determine the viability of a joint M&E country mission can be initiated through the coordinating agency or with one or more development partners based in the country. The decision to proceed with a joint mission should at all times be with the agreement and guidance of the host country.

- **Have preliminary meetings via telephone, videoconference, or in person.** Preliminary meetings provide a forum for various partners to compare their strategic objectives for M&E technical support to the country and to harmonize them. The meetings also offer an opportunity to discuss the perceived and stated needs of the host country for technical assistance. Joint missions are most productive if the relationships initiated during preliminary meetings are nurtured and developed, and are responsive to the changing needs of the host country.

- **Finalize joint mission objectives.** The joint mission objectives will form the basis of further planning. They may also identify gaps in the technical assistance implementation plan and provide the opportunity to engage other partners. Usually, the initiating partner produces the first draft of the mission objectives with other mission participants adding to the draft. The objectives will determine the work plan and schedule and should be developed with the country/client and shared with all relevant stakeholders once developed.

- **Develop a joint mission schedule.** The initiating partner may take the lead in formalizing other partners' participation, to consolidate scheduling, logistics, and facilitation of meetings with host country agencies and other mission partners. Prior to the joint mission, a thorough review of relevant information pertaining to the host country's M&E agenda is of paramount importance. The information should normally be provided several weeks before the visit to ensure that all participating partners have ample time to read and digest materials.

Deliverables: Partners for joint mission identified; Joint mission program developed.

Step 3: Undertake the joint mission

- **Keep in contact with each other during the mission. Share findings, develop joint strategies, and link with** local M&E partners, to ensure a seamless interface between the development partners. Help in-country M&E partners see these links, even if the terminology or jargon is different.

- **Promote principles of sharing** in thought, word, and action, while still fulfilling the organization's mandate and the mission's terms of reference.

- **Have a joint debrief** at the end of the joint mission with the coordinating agency management and the M&E TWG.

Deliverable: Joint mission debrief prepared.

Step 4: Write and disseminate a joint mission report

- Develop a joint mission report that describes the activities completed by the mission and the short-term activities following the mission. Writing the joint mission report should follow the same process as the drafting of the joint mission objectives. The initiating partner produces the first draft of the report, with other mission participants adding to it. In addition to being an information product, the joint mission report may also be viewed as a management tool, which guides follow-on activities after the mission.

- Post relevant information about the joint mission on any websites that may become available or relevant for future use.

- Share the joint mission report with each agency manager and the Regional M&E Partner's Forum (if one exists) to ensure they are informed of the latest developments and status in the region.

Deliverable: Joint Mission Report.

8. Summary of Chapter 3 Knowledge and Skills

In this chapter, you learned about M&E partnerships and their benefits/importance. You learned about theory and technical process steps to establish and maintain both internal and external partnerships, and about the characteristics of successful partnerships. You learned about the formation, mandate and functions of an M&E Technical Working Group.

You will have gained skills in how to set up an M&E technical working group, and how to strengthen activities for partnerships between the M&E coordinating agency, other government entities, and civil society. Lastly, you learned what steps are necessary to plan and undertake a joint M&E mission/trip in order to conduct assessments of the M&E system.

9. Learning Activity

Assume that there is currently no M&E Technical Working Group in your country. Your group's task is to develop a Terms of Reference for a national M&E Technical Working Group for a new national government-wide M&E system. Follow the instructions in this chapter on how to develop a TOR as a basis for your work group. Refer to Annex A for assistance and guidance on what to include in the TOR.

Learning Activity Output: Terms of Reference for the M&E TWG.

Annex A: What to Include in Terms of Reference for a National M&E TWG

- Background to the TWG
- Main purpose of the TWG
- TWG mandate (explains on whose authority/request the TWG is set up) and the time frame for which the TWG was set up
- Members of the TWG and process for selecting new members
- TWG chairperson and procedure for selecting a new chairperson
- Secretariat services for the TWG
- Specific roles and responsibilities of the TWG need to be clearly stated (the main part of the TOR), including the TWG's ability to review and approve materials or advise on content (i.e., the limits of the decisions that TWG members might take)
- Who the TWG has to report to, in which format, and at what frequency
- Whether products approved by the TWG will carry agency logos on them
- How and when the TWG membership will be reviewed

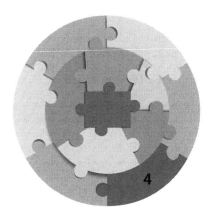

Chapter 4
M&E Plans

Chapter Aim

The aim of this chapter is to enable you to develop or review your organization's M&E plan. This plan, together with a costed M&E work plan, is at the heart of an M&E system. It describes the purpose of the system, the data the system will collect and how the system will operate.

Chapter Knowledge and Skills

By the end of this chapter, you should be able to:

a) Know what an M&E plan and a national M&E plan are, and how they differ from M&E frameworks and M&E work plans.

b) Understand the linkage between a national M&E plan and the M&E plans of individual organizations.

c) Explain to others what to include in an M&E plan.

d) Develop or review an M&E plan, at the national level or at the organizational level.

e) Develop a sub-national or sector M&E plan linked to a national M&E plan.

143

Before You Begin...

Take a few minutes to read through the questions below. You may find it helpful to write down your answers. As you then work through the chapter, compare your answers to the views of the authors.

How do I know when an M&E plan is good and how do I know if it contains all the necessary sections?

- What is the difference between an M&E plan and an M&E work plan?
- How is an M&E plan different to an M&E framework?
- What is the difference between an M&E plan and an M&E system?
- Which indicators should be in the M&E plan?
- What is the optimal number of indicators?
- What is an optimal timeframe for an M&E plan?

These questions remind us that not only do we need to have people (Component 1), who are skilled (Component 2) and prepared to work together (Component 3), we also need to have a structured and planned way of making the M&E system operational. For this, we need an M&E plan. This chapter will teach you all about what should be in an M&E plan, and how to develop one.

Component 4: M&E Plans

1. Introduction

> *"Organizing is what you do before you do something,*
> *so that when you do it, it's not all mixed up."*

Winnie the Pooh

M&E plans are part of the *people, partnerships, and planning* ring of the 12 Components of a functional M&E system. An M&E plan, together with a costed M&E work plan (see Component 5), is at the heart of an M&E system. It describes the purpose of the system, the data the system will collect, and how the system will operate. The M&E plan includes the list of indicators to be measured but is much more than this. The M&E plan is a comprehensive *recipe book* for setting up the entire M&E system and keeping it functioning.

How this chapter is organized: This chapter begins with background information, definitions and distinctions between an M&E plan, M&E system and M&E work plan (Section 2). The desired result of this chapter and the benefits of a national M&E plan follow in Sections 3 and 4. In order to reach and implement the desired results (developing and maintaining a functional M&E system), one needs to have a clear understanding of what an M&E plan and M&E system are, of the relationship of the M&E plan to the strategic plan of the program to be monitored, and of the program itself. Section 5 describes these links and other implementation issues. Section 6 provides steps and guidance on how to develop (or update) a national M&E plan. The next section (7) describes the steps for how to link a sub-national or sector-specific M&E plan with a national M&E plan. The chapter closes with a summary of lessons learned (Section 8), and a practical exercise to cement what you should have learned (Section 9).

2. Background Information and Definitions

M&E plan: An M&E plan is a comprehensive narrative document on all M&E activities. It describes the key M&E questions to be addressed; what indicators are to be measured; how, how often, from where — and the indicator data that will be collected; includes baselines, targets, and assumptions; how the data will be analyzed or interpreted; how or how often reports on the indicators will be developed and distributed; and how the 12 Components of the M&E system will function (Rugg, Peersman and Carael, 2004).

National M&E plan: A national M&E plan is a special type of M&E plan that focuses on how a national M&E system (for example, for HIV, the education sector, health sector, non-governmental sector, or others) would work. Typically, a national M&E system (and, therefore, a national M&E plan) requires the M&E systems (and, therefore, the M&E plans) of different institutions to be linked and aligned with each other. A national M&E plan, therefore, defines the key M&E questions to be addressed at national level (i.e., how to measure achievement of a national set of objectives such as those in the country's National Development Plan, National Poverty Reduction Plan, or National HIV/AIDS Strategy.

Difference between an M&E plan and M&E system: The *M&E plan* documents all aspects of the *M&E system*. The M&E system consists of people and processes that work together in an enabling environment to achieve the 12 performance goals of an M&E system.

Difference between the M&E plan and M&E work plan: The M&E plan is a narrative document that describes, in detail, how the M&E system will operate (see M&E plan definition above). An M&E work plan is an activity-based budget showing M&E tasks, responsibilities, time frames, and costs. Put another way, the M&E work plan (see Component 5) is a costed list of activities for implementing an M&E plan to make all 12 Components of the M&E system function. An M&E work plan can be (and often is) an annex to an M&E plan. Figure C4-1 illustrates, visually and from a content point of view, the difference between these two types of documents:

Figure C4-1: Difference between an M&E Plan and an M&E Work Plan
A: M&E Plan

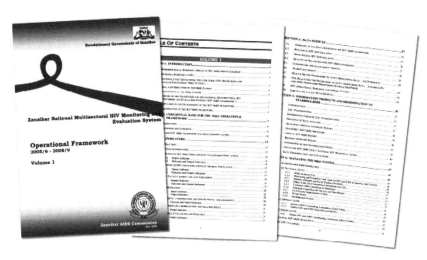

Source: Zanzibar National AIDS Commission, 2005

Making Monitoring and Evaluation Systems Work

B: M&E Work Plan

No.	Activities	Lead Agency	Supporting Partner Agencies	2008 Jan - Mar	Apr - Jun	Jul - Sept	Oct - Dec	2009 Jan - Mar	Apr - Jun	Jul - Sept	Oct - Dec	2008 costs Cost	Funding Source	2009 costs Cost	Funding Source
M&E Work plan															
Component 1: Organizational Structures for M&E Systems															
Performance Objective: Establish and maintain an effective network of organizations responsible for HIV M&E at national, sub-national and service delivery level															
1.10	Revise job descriptions	CNLS	CDLS									2,000	UNAIDS		
1.20	Conduct routine monitoring	All organizations	not needed									9,400	Each organization	10,000.00	Each organization

Difference between an M&E plan and an M&E framework: One of the most frequently asked questions concerning an M&E plan is 'What is the difference between an M&E plan and an M&E framework?' They generally refer to the same thing. Terminology and definitions often vary. Even in the example in Figure C4-1, the M&E plan is called an *Operational Framework*. In this course, we use the term M&E plan to refer to a document that describes, in a narrative format, the indicators of the M&E system (linked to goals and objectives), the way the M&E system will function, and other features of the M&E system. This is quite often called an *M&E framework*. It should be noted, however, that in other writing and training on M&E, the term *M&E framework* is sometimes used to refer to what we call a *Results Framework or Logical Framework* (See Annex A for more details.)

3. Results to Be Achieved When Implementing This Component

Long-term result: Develop and update periodically an M&E plan for your organization that addresses these aspects: identified data needs, national standardized indicators; data collection tools and procedures, and roles and responsibilities in order to implement a functional M&E system.

Short- and medium-term results:

* Participation of all relevant stakeholders in developing the M&E plan

* The M&E plan meets these requirements: (a) indicators are derived from, and linked to, the strategic/program objectives that these indicators are intended to measure; (b) describes the implementation of all 12 Components of an M&E system; and (c) adheres to international and national technical standards for M&E.

- The M&E plan and its revisions are based on the findings of periodic M&E system assessments.

- Sector-specific, sub-national and organizational M&E plans are linked to the national M&E plan.

For reflection 1:

Reflect on your organization's M&E plan for a moment. If possible, get a copy of this plan for you to think about and consider before answering the questions here.

Does your organization have an M&E system, M&E plan and/or an M&E work plan in place? If so, how is the M&E plan connected or related to the M&E system as a whole? When is the last time your organization's M&E plan was updated? What is in the M&E plan for your organization? Are you aware of a national M&E plan? Is your organization's M&E plan linked to the national M&E plan? How many of the short- and medium-term results listed above are visible in your organization's M&E plan?

4. Benefits of an M&E Plan as a Component of an M&E System

1. **An M&E plan provides a common vision of what a successful M&E system will look like.** The M&E plan defines all aspects of what the M&E system will measure and how the M&E system will operate. Therefore, the M&E plan can be used by different professionals at different times to develop a common vision of what the M&E system will look like, when fully operational.

2. **An M&E plan is used as a benchmark against which to measure progress in implementing the M&E system.** Because an M&E plan describes what the M&E system should look like when fully functional, it can be used as a benchmark against which to measure performance of the system implementation.

3. **An M&E plan standardizes and validates the mandates, authorities, and responsibilities of M&E stakeholders.** Without defined mandates and authority to carry out M&E functions, organizations responsible for this work are much less likely to carry out their M&E responsibilities. An M&E plan provides a way for all stakeholder M&E system mandates, authority, and responsibilities to be clearly defined, approved, and validated by government, civil society, and the private sector.

4. **An M&E plan assigns specific responsibilities to specific organizations.** Given that the M&E plan defines stakeholder mandates and authorities for the M&E system, it also assigns clear responsibility for specific M&E functions to specific organizations (or even posts within the organization). This is incredibly helpful when preparing an M&E work plan and when reporting back on progress in implementing the M&E system.

5. **An M&E plan can be the basis for deciding which M&E activities to implement.** The information in an M&E plan on who is responsible for which aspect of the M&E system can be used to prioritize M&E activities and to decide who should implement each of the activities in the M&E work plan.

6. **A national M&E plan provides a common *recipe for implementation*.** In addition to the benefits of an M&E plan already mentioned, a national M&E plan has the added benefit in that it is a common *recipe book* for individual implementers to follow. It helps them comply with national reporting requirements and it also helps them know what types of data they can expect from the national M&E system.

5. Implementation Issues Related to M&E Plans

5.1. Link between a strategic/program plan and M&E plan

The purpose of an M&E system is to measure the achievement of the objectives of a program, be it a country's educational goals, national HIV response, or the program of a specific organization.

Because an M&E plan describes an M&E system and a strategic/program plan describes the strategies and programs to address the problem/s, the first link between an M&E plan and strategic/program plan is that the indicators in the M&E plan are directly derived from (and respond to) the objectives of the strategic/program plan (see Figure C4-2). If the objectives in a program or strategic plan change, the indicators in the M&E plan also need to change.

For the M&E system to work well and have a solid mandate, the objectives and strategies to make the M&E system functional should be included in the strategic/program plan providing the second link. The third and final link is slightly broader. It is that the information from the M&E system is used to inform decisions about the future of the program response.

Figure C4-2:   Link between Program Plan/Strategy and M&E Plan

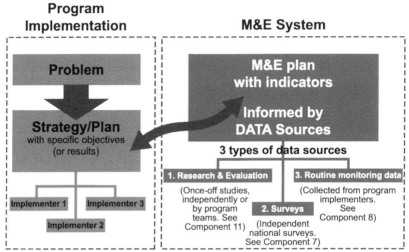

NOTE: Indicaters determine what is measured to know we have been successful
with achieving objectives (or results)

Source: Authors

The three links between the program plan and M&E plan suggest a five-fold
focus on M&E during the review or development of a program plan/strategy as
illustrated in Figure C4-3 and described below:

AREA A.   **Data from the M&E system will help identify gaps**
in program service delivery, data and research, etc.
Understanding the gaps and the reasons for them will help to
develop evidence-based strategies in the new program plan/
strategy (Step 1 of Figure C4-3).

AREA B.   **The functioning of the M&E system itself should be
assessed** so that appropriate M&E strategies to address M&E
system weaknesses can be included in the program plan/
strategy. There are standard M&E assessment tools that can be
used (Step 1 of Figure C4-3).

AREA C.   **The program plan/strategy should have an M&E section**
that defines specific M&E strategies to address weaknesses in
the M&E system (Steps 3 and 4 of
Figure C4-3).

AREA D.   **The M&E plan should be developed/reviewed in tandem
with the program plan/strategy** (Step 5 of Figure C4-3).

This will enable you to:

- (Re-)align the indicators in the M&E plan with the new or revised objectives of the program plan/strategy.

- (Re-)align the data sources and information products to the indicators.

- Address weaknesses pointed out in the M&E system assessment (see Area B).

- Include the M&E strategies of the program plan/strategy in the M&E plan and related documents.

AREA E.   **The M&E work plan may need to be reviewed** (Step 6 of Figure C4-3). After the M&E plan has been reviewed, the national, sectored and sub-national M&E work plans may need to be developed or reviewed (see Component 5). Section 6 in Component 5 contains step-by-step instructions on how to develop or review national, sector, or sub-national M&E work plans.

Figure C4-3:   Five-fold Focus on M&E during a Strategic/program Planning Cycle

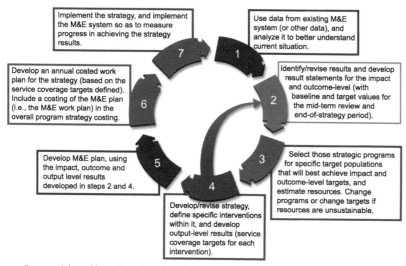

Source: Adapted by authors from Rodriguez-Garcia and Kusek, 2007

5.2. Link between the national M&E plans of different sectors

Managing for results is a growing global priority. As a result, different sectors (of government, in civil society, and in the private sector) have been developing monitoring and evaluation systems and, therefore, (should) have M&E plans. A national M&E system in one sector may need to draw data from the M&E systems of other sectors and may need to provide data to M&E systems in other sectors to avoid duplication, overlap and overburdening the implementers of programs. Figure C4-4 shows the potential links between the M&E systems of different

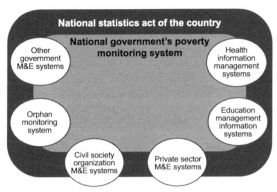

Source: Authors

Figure C4-4:   Linkages between the National M&E Systems of Different Sectors

sectors, from the perspective of a cross-cutting M&E system (for example, for HIV or poverty programs).

5.3. Link between a national M&E plan and M&E plans of individual organizations

Another type of linkage that needs to be understood is between a national M&E plan and an M&E plan of an individual organization. In the education sector, for example, the Ministry of Education may have developed a national education monitoring and evaluation plan. The question is, "How does the M&E plan of a training college or of a school, or an NGO that trains teachers, link to this national education M&E plan?"

A national M&E plan provides a common *recipe book* of what should be reported to the national ministry and what will be reported by the national ministry. Each individual organization should include in its indicator set all national-level indicators on which it needs to report (to the Ministry of Education, per the example in the previous paragraph) and should use relevant data generated by the national ministry (summary data) for its own planning purposes. Figure C4-5 illustrates the relationship between national-level indicators and objectives, and program-level indicators and objectives (and, therefore, between national M&E plans and the M&E plans of individual organizations).

In this example (Figure C4-5), the national strategic plan contains 2 types of objectives, OVC and PMTCT objectives (relating to programs for Orphans and Vulnerable Children, and to prevent mother-to-child HIV transmission). These objectives are measured in the national M&E system by including one indicator in the M&E plan linked to every national strategic plan objective. At the program implementation level, the program implementation guidelines include

Figure C4-5:   Linkages between the National M&E System and M&E Systems of Individual Organizations

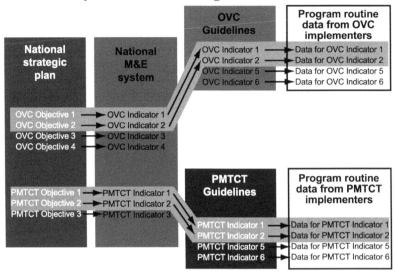

Source: The World Bank GAMET Team, 2008

the national level indicators but also specify indicators that implementers need to collect. The implementers collect all the data specified in the program guidelines and send only what is necessary to the national office to measure the national-level indicators.

5.4. Contents of an M&E plan

An M&E plan should provide background information, define what the M&E system will measure (indicators linked to the objectives of the strategic/program plan being monitored and evaluated), and how the M&E system will operate to enable these measurements to take place. These requirements for the contents of an M&E plan broadly translate into three sections:

Section 1 of the M&E plan:	General background information
Section 2 of the M&E plan:	Results Framework or Logical Framework with program objectives and indicators (see Annex A for an example of a Results Framework or Logical Framework)
Section 3 of the M&E plan:	How will the M&E system be managed?

In Annex B, a detailed description of the typical contents of each of these three sections of an M&E plan is provided. This annex can also be used as a checklist to review the contents of existing M&E plans when deciding how to update an M&E plan.

Some frequently asked questions about the contents of an M&E plan are answered here:

i.   **What types of indicators should my M&E plan have?** Indicators are usually defined within what is known as a *results chain* that documents the sequence of results (and, therefore, the sequence of indicators) that need to have been achieved in order for an intervention or a strategy to be successful. An example of a results chain is illustrated in Figure C4-6.

Figure C4-6:   The Results Chain for the Agriculture Sector in Goldstar State, with Accompanying Results Framework

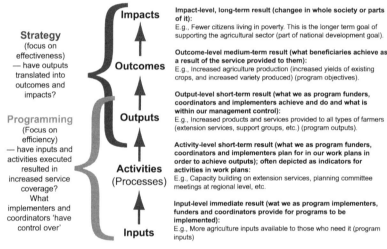

Source: Adapted by authors from Rodriguez-Garcia and Zall Kusek, 2007

ii. **How many indicators should my M&E plan have?** Indicators are linked to objectives and, therefore, the first factor that determines the number of indicators is the number of objectives in the strategic/program plan. However, not all objectives need indicators as it may be possible to measure more than one objective with the same indicator. Also, every indicator does not necessarily need a separate data source. In fact, it is better to focus on the number of data sources needed to produce indicator values than on the actual number of indicators. An M&E plan with 20 indicators from 20 routine data sources is much more difficult and time-consuming to implement than one with 60 indicators where all the indicator data come from only two surveys. As a general guideline, we recommend designing an M&E system that does not depend on more than 6 to 8 data sources (both routine data sources (see Chapter 7) and episodic data sources (see Chapter 8).

Results	Indicators	Baseline		Target	
Impact-level, long-term result: Fewer citizens living in poverty. This is the longer-term goal of supporting the agriculture sector (part of national development goal).	**Impact-level indicator:** Percent of Goldstar citizens living under $2 dollar per day	34% in 2004		25% in 2009	
Outcome-level, medium-term result: Increased agriculture production (increased yields of existing crops, and increased variety produced) (program objectives)	**Outcome-level indicator:** Yield in agriculture production, by type of produce	Coffee	300 tons in 2003	Coffee	500 tons by 2009
		Tea	20 tons in 2003	Tea	60 tons by 2009
		Cassava	5 tons in 2003	Cassava	15 tons by 2009
				Vanilla	3 tons by 2009
				Fruit	10 tons by 2009
Output-level, short-term result: Increased products and services provided to all types of farmers (extension services, support groups, etc.) (program outputs)	**Output-level indicators:** Percentage of districts with demonstration plots for new crops	4% of districts in 2004		50% of districts by 2007 65% of districts by 2009	
	Percentage of districts with local markets that operate at least once a week	6% of districts in 2003		50% of districts by 2009	
	Average number of hours of extension support by agriculture extension workers per registered farmer per year	3 hours per year in 2004		12 hours per year by 2007 24 hours per year by 2009	
Input-level immediate result: More agriculture inputs available to those who need them (program inputs)	**Input level indicators:** Percentage of subsistence farmers provided with agriculture inputs	21% of subsistence farmers in 2002		30% of subsistence farmers by 2007 60% of subsistence farmers by 2009	
	Percentage of agriculture sector funding expenditure for providing agriculture inputs (seeds, etc.)	8% of expenditure in 2003/2004 financial year		10% of expenditure by the 2006/2007 financial year 15% of expenditure by 2009/2010 financial year	
	Average number of farmers per agriculture extension workers	350 farmers per extension worker in 2001		300 farmers per extension worker by 2007 200 farmers per extension worker by 2009	

It is, however, important to note that the *levels* in a results chain are relative and depend on the point of view of who develops them. By way of illustration, training materials are usually seen as inputs, but for a training organization, the training materials may be the outputs or even outcomes of all their efforts. This concept of *point of view* is illustrated in Figure C4-7.

Figure C4-7: **Linkages between the National M&E System and M&E Systems of Individual Organizations**

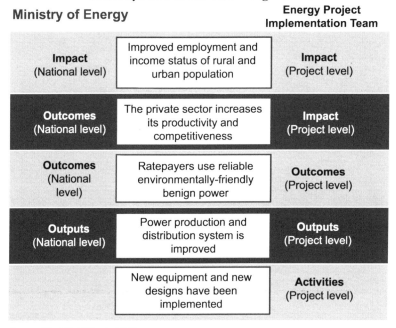

Source: The World Bank, 2005

iii. **What is a good quality indicator?** Over time, different criteria have been used to determine the quality of an indicator. The same criteria may not apply in all settings. Annex C contains a summary of criteria for good indicators, as well as a suggested indicator selection process. There is also another guideline that you can follow to help you select and grade indicators that have been developed. It is a more formal process whereby an indicator is assigned a rating across five rating criteria and is a thorough and comprehensive process for selecting indicators. Although this guideline has been developed for an HIV context, the rating criteria equally apply to this context (UNAIDS and MERG, 2009):

1. The indicator is needed and useful.

2. The indicator has technical merit.

3. The indicator is fully defined.

Chapter 4

4. It is feasible to measure the indicator.

5. The indicator has been field-tested or used operationally.

6. In addition, where indicators are presented as part of a set, this should be coherent and balanced.

Each of these six indicator criteria then has a set of specific questions, with suggested rating scales associated with each question. This allows one to test each indicator and to assign a score to each indicator, making the selection and improvement of the way in which indicators are defined, much easier.

iv. **How should indicators be defined?** Each indicator needs an indicator protocol, which fully defines the indicator. (UNAIDS and MERG, 2009):

- The indicator has a clearly stated title and definition.
- The indicator has a clearly stated purpose and rationale.
- The method of measurement for the indicator is clearly defined, including the description of the numerator, denominator, and calculation, where applicable (4 points).
- The collection method for the indicator data is clearly stated.
- The measurement frequency for the indicator is clearly defined.
- Any relevant data disaggregation is clearly defined.
- There are clear guidelines to interpret and use data from this indicator.
- Strengths, weaknesses and challenges in using the indicator are clearly stated.
- Relevant sources of additional information on the indicator are cited.

The UNAIDS and MERG Guidelines on Indicator Standards (accessible at www.worldbank.org/aids > tools and guidelines) also contain more details about indicator definitions, and is a recommended resource.

v. **What should be the time frame of the M&E plan?** M&E plans are not developed in a vacuum or as stand-alone documents. The M&E plan should cover the same time period as the strategic/program plan (e.g., a national HIV response strategy for 2004–2008 would have a national HIV M&E plan for 2004–2008). The reason the M&E plan coincides with the time frame of the strategic plan is to ensure that there are strategies for monitoring and evaluating the strategic plan throughout its lifespan.

vi. **Is it a framework or plan?** Some countries have an M&E plan, some have an M&E framework, while others have both, or even an M&E operational framework. The name and number of documents do not really matter; it is the content of the M&E plan that is important. Throughout this 12 Component Skills Building Course, the term "M&E plan" is used to refer to narrative documents that describe and define how the M&E system operates (recipe book for the M&E system) and what the M&E system measures (i.e., the results framework that indicators measure results in the organization/government's strategy).

A final word of advice about M&E plans. Keep the language plain and clear. M&E plans need to be detailed enough to contain all relevant technical information while still being clear and easily understandable. GAMET's electronic M&E resource library (accessible at http://gametlibrary.worldbank.org; click on the red puzzle piece in the middle called "Data Dissemination and Use") contains resources on professional writing styles, and how to construct easy-to-read sentences and paragraphs.

6. HowTo Guide C4-1: Developing or Reviewing a National M&E Plan

This section guides you in developing a national M&E plan but the steps could easily be adapted for developing an M&E plan for an organization.

Step 1: Collect information and assess the scope of the M&E work to be done

This step should take place 6 to 8 months before the implementation of the program being monitored.

Assess whether the following exist, collect and read the relevant documents:

- Comprehensive, up-to-date information about the most important factors affecting program targets
- An existing M&E TWG
- An existing M&E plan
- An existing M&E work plan
- An assessment of the national M&E system
- Any other assessments that contain M&E information
- Relevant information produced by the M&E team
- Any relevant research on the effectiveness of program interventions

Deliverable: Collection of all existing documents relevant to the M&E system.

Step 2: Undertake situation analysis to determine key challenges in the program area

This step is dependent on whether data already exist and, if undertaken, should begin at least 6 months prior to the strategic plan and M&E system review process.

This step involves understanding the nature of the problems and the response to date, using current M&E system information (Step 1 of Figure C4-3).

A situation analysis needs to be undertaken in order to understand the following key questions:

a) What are the trends, magnitude, and causal factors relating to the problems being experienced?

b) Are policies and strategies in line with the latest evidence on intervention effectiveness?

c) Which programs are implemented for which target populations and to which coverage levels?

d) Are programs being implemented in the most efficient ways?

e) Is money spent on the most effective programs?

f) Is the program managed in the most effective ways?

Deliverable: Report with an understanding of the program challenges.

Step 3: Obtain M&E system assessment results

Getting M&E system assessment results is a necessary step when reviewing a strategic plan and should be undertaken at least 4 months prior to the strategic plan review and M&E system review process. M&E system assessment results can be obtained from either an existing M&E system assessment or from conducting a new M&E system assessment. Deciding how to obtain M&E system assessment results is a logical process as detailed in the following steps:

a) **Determine whether a new M&E system assessment is needed** as part of the strategic plan review process. Annex D contains a helpful decision tree for this (Step 1 of Figure C4-3).

If an M&E system assessment is needed...

b) **Plan the M&E system review process** by writing a Terms of Reference for the M&E assessment process. In the M&E Assessment Terms of Reference, detail:

- Which M&E assessment tool will be used (see box to the right)

- How the M&E system assessment process will be carried out

- Budget required for the M&E system assessment

- How the M&E system assessment process will link with the strategic/program plan review or development process

c) **Determine technical resources required for the M&E system assessment.** Determine whether there is sufficient technical expertise and time available in the M&E unit to execute steps 4 to 10 of this guide, keeping in mind that such a review will take at least 30 to 50 days of work.

d) **Present the M&E Assessment Terms of Reference with budget to the M&E TWG**, if in existence (see Component 3), for technical inputs and resource mobilization. Include the M&E system assessment

Range of M&E System Assessment Tools

There are many options to conducting M&E system assessments. Guidance varies in terms of:

a) The level of guidance provided on to how to undertake the assessment. Guidance ranges from a one page summary as suggested by Mackay (2007) or by UNAIDS on HIV M&E system assessments as part of their 'Three Ones' assessment process (see Annex I), to detailed guidance and spreadsheet tools that provides M&E system ratings as per the 12 Components. The most detailed tool that the authors know of, is the Comprehensive 12 Component M&E System Assessment Tool, which is available at www.worldbank.org/aids > tools and guidelines or at www.unaids.org (search for the tool name).

b) The number of components focused on, and the depth with which each component is assessed. M&E assessment tools that focus only on one or some of the components include the routine Data Quality Assurance tool that focuses specifically on the component and not on all.

c) How the assessment is undertaken. Some guidance suggests an outsider-view, with the assessment undertaken by individuals outside the M&E system, other tools recommend self assessment.

You have to choose the most appropriate tool available for the purpose of the assessment: be it to understand the overall status of the M&E system in order to develop M&E system strengthening programs or to do a detailed audit of one of the components, in order to improve, for example, routine monitoring or improve all surveys in the country.

Alternatively, you do not need to use an existing M&E assessment tool to assess the status of your M&E system. You could simply look at (a) the long-term results that you have defined for each of the components of your M&E system and (b) the work plan for your M&E system. By assessing progress towards achieving the long-term result of each component and progress with activities in the M&E work plan, you should have a good idea of the status of your M&E system.

concept note in the strategic/program plan review process, so it is clear to everyone concerned that the reviews are linked and that the results will influence each other. Consult with the M&E TWG (if in existence) to determine whether an external consultant is needed to undertake the assignment.

e)   If an external consultant is needed, **develop a Terms of Reference** for the consultant, have it approved, and obtain funding for the review.

f)   **Undertake the M&E system assessment** and present the findings for validation to the M&E TWG.

If an M&E system assessment is NOT needed...

Obtain the latest M&E system assessment report and study it in detail to ensure that you understand all the M&E system assessment challenges.

Deliverable: Understanding of the strengths and weaknesses of the M&E system.

Step 4:   Review the strategic plan objectives once developed

This is an essential step and the start of the strategic plan review itself.

This step is a quality control step for the strategic plan itself. As the strategic plan objectives are developed, specific data will be referred to. The purpose of this review is to ensure that those responsible for the strategic plan review have consulted all relevant data in their decision-making process. M&E TWG members may undertake this review as part of strategic plan working groups (Step 2 of Figure C4-3).

Deliverable: New strategic plan has SMART objectives or results (objectives that are Specific, Measureable, Achievable, Realistic, and Time-bound).

Step 5:   Develop M&E objectives to include in the strategic plan

This is also an essential step for every strategic plan. The M&E system assessment will point to strengths and weaknesses of the M&E system and enable you to identify the M&E objectives that, if met, would address the weaknesses in the M&E system and to develop, together with the M&E TWG, the most appropriate M&E strategies to achieve the objectives (Step 2 of Figure C4-3).

Deliverable: M&E objectives or results for inclusion in strategic plan.

Step 6: Develop strategic plan indicators

Once the objectives for the strategic plan have been agreed upon, appropriate indicators can be developed (Step 2 of Figure C4-3). Developing indicators is a systematic process that involves a number of tasks and criteria. It should be done collaboratively with all development partners involved in the program (preferably through the M&E TWG) so that the indicators are unanimously endorsed.

Developing indicators requires the following tasks to be implemented:

Task 1.   Clarify the objectives or results and identify what needs to be measured. This is what *success* would look like for the organization of the program that is being measured. The goals are not directly measured but must be translated into indicators that **are** measured to determine if the program is on track to meet its goals or objectives and being implemented as planned (Kusek and Rist, 2004).

Task 2.   Brainstorm a list of possible indicators for your goals, objectives, or results.

Task 3.   Assess each potential indicator from a technical perspective. Indicator selection criteria can be found in Annex C.

Task 4.   Select the most relevant indicators based on the assessment (Task 3).

Task 5.   Determine whether baseline values for the indicators exist. Baseline values should exist (relying on routine monitoring data) for all output indicators in the results framework. If baseline values for outcome indicators do not exist, include funding to collect the data needed in the national M&E work plan (see Component 5).

Task 6.   Record the baseline values for indicators (even if baseline values for all indicators do not exist), and circulate these widely.

Task 7.   Compile protocols for the project indicators. An indicator protocol is a detailed definition of the indicator [see section 5.4 (iv) for a detailed description of what is included in an indicator protocol].

Task 8.   Refine indicators and protocols and finalize the indicator selection.

Deliverable: List of indicators (with protocols) to monitor progress toward the objectives of the strategic plan.

Step 7: Review the M&E plan (or develop one if it does not exist)

When the strategic plan (including indicators) is completed and endorsed, the M&E plan can be developed and reviewed (Step 5 of Figure C4-3). To do this:

a)   Ensure that the operational requirements of all strategic plan M&E strategies have been defined in the M&E plan.

b)   Ensure that relevant information on laws, policies, and strategies related to M&E has been included.

c)   Ensure that all indicators and data sources are aligned to the goals, objectives or results of the program strategic plan.

d)   Address the weaknesses of the 12 Components of an M&E system at national, sub-national and sector-specific levels.

Annex B can be used as a checklist for what to include in a national M&E plan. Subsequent to reviewing the national M&E plan, you may want to review the sub-national and sector-specific M&E work plans. Guidance on how to align a sector or sub-national M&E plan to a national M&E plan can be found in the HowTo Guide in the Section 7 of this chapter.

Deliverable: New/revised national M&E plan.

Step 8.   Develop or review national M&E work plans

The final technical step is to review the developed M&E work plans (see Chapter 5) to implement the M&E plan so that national strategic plan costing can be included (Step 6 of Figure C4-3). The How To Guide in Section 6 of Chapter 5 provides detailed instructions on how to develop or review a national, sub-national, and sector M&E work plan.

When developing the national M&E plan and work plan, ensure that the time frame specified is the same as that of the program plan so that M&E strategies exist to measure program implementation throughout its lifespan.

Deliverable: New/revised national M&E work plan.

Step 9.   Advocate for, communicate about, and build capacity for the new M&E system

After the technical work has been done, it is essential to disseminate the M&E plan and related work plans to all relevant senior-level stakeholders, including the organization coordinating the program to be monitored. Ensure, through this mechanism, that M&E priorities for the years are known; that resource mobilization (government and other sources) has been addressed; and that the progress of the M&E system has been reported. Ensure that the M&E plan and work plan is at the core of the coordination work done by the M&E TWG (see Component 3).

Deliverable: All stakeholders aware of, understand, and supportive of the new M&E plan.

For reflection 2:

Reflect on the process for developing your country's national M&E plan for a moment. Were you involved in the process, or do you know about it? How was it done? Was it linked to the development or review of the national program plan? Will the steps listed here work for your country or your sector? Why or why not? How can the steps be adapted to suit your country's situation?

---

7. HowTo Guide C4-2: Developing Your Organization's M&E Plan Linked to the National M&E Plan

Step 1: Obtain senior-level buy-in

Senior level buy-in and advocacy should be ensured so that the plan will be understood, accepted, and supported by senior management in the organization. This will also help ensure that there is senior-level support for the M&E system and that funding is available.

Deliverable: Funding for and commitment to the M&E planning process from senior management.

Step 2: Determine your organization's objectives in the program area

Obtain and read the country's national program plan or national development plan. Also, read any sector strategies relating to your sector and at your level, including any decentralization policies. Based on these strategies, identify your organization's role in achieving the objectives of the national plan. These roles may include coordination, planning, management, and/or implementation and, of course, monitoring and evaluation.

Now, develop objectives for your organization that are linked, or contribute to the national program objectives.

Deliverable: Objectives/results for your organization's contribution to the national or other higher-level program.

Step 3:   Assess the status of your organization's M&E system

Do an assessment to understand the status of the 12 Components of a functional M&E system, including strengths and weaknesses. Follow the same steps as outlined in HowTo Guide C4-1 Step 3. If an assessment has been done, you do not need to do a new assessment.

Deliverable: M&E system assessment report.

Step 4:   Design indicators for your organization's objectives

Once the objectives and strategies for your sector, sub-national organization or project have been developed, appropriate indicators can be defined. Developing indicators is a systematic process that involves a number of tasks and selection criteria. This should be done collaboratively with all development partners involved in the program (preferably through an M&E working group) so that the indicators are unanimously endorsed. Follow the same steps as suggested in HowTo Guide C4-1, and remember that criteria of good indicators are found in Annex C.

Deliverable: Indicators for the objectives/results of your organization's program.

Step 5:   Design the components of the M&E system

Based on the M&E system assessment, design all 12 Components of the M&E system. Keep in mind that not all 12 Components may be applicable to your organization. A starting point is to discuss, component by component:

*   What would work in your organization in terms of this component?
*   How could it link with or draw data from existing sources of data?
*   How could it be linked to the national level?
*   How could it build on what is already in place for M&E in your sector?

Deliverable: Clear and common understanding of how your organization's M&E system will work.

Step 6:   Design the routine monitoring procedures

Routine monitoring includes both program monitoring and financial monitoring. It requires good data management procedures to ensure good quality data are captured and reported. The HowTo Guide in Section 6 of Chapter 8 provides more information about how to design a program monitoring system with guidelines, data flow, and data collection tools to collect all the routine data needed to measure the indicators that have been selected. Where possible, use existing data collection tools and improve on them.

Deliverable: Data collection tools and data flow charts for all routine monitoring data for your organization.

Step 7:   Write the M&E plan

Once the program monitoring procedures have been designed, the next step is to write the M&E plan. An M&E plan usually contains the following information:

- The organization's objectives and need for an M&E system
- The data (management information and indicators) that will be collected by the organization (Annex A is an example of a Results Framework or Logical Framework that contains all the relevant information.)
- The source, method, frequency and schedule of data collection [(summarized in a data source matrix (see Annex E)] which includes the team or individuals responsible for data collection
- How data will be analyzed, compared, reviewed, and presented and how associated tools will be utilized can be summarized in an information product matrix (see Annex F)
- Plans, schedules, and tools for communicating information can be summarized in a dissemination matrix (see Annex G)
- Partnerships and collaborations for success
- Plans, schedules, and tools for evaluating information
- Management of the M&E system, specifying roles, work plans, supervision, data auditing, software, and review of the plan

Annex B can be used as a checklist of what to include in your project's M&E plan.

Deliverable: M&E plan for your organization.

Step 8.   Develop an M&E work plan

Once the M&E plan (narrative) has been developed, the next step is to develop the work plan. The HowTo Guide in Section 6 of Chapter 5 provides detailed instructions on how to develop or review an M&E work plan.

Deliverable: Costed M&E work plan for your organization.

Step 9. Initiate advocacy, communications, orientation, and capacity building

After this technical work has been done, it is essential to disseminate the M&E plan and related work plans to everyone in your organization. Ensure, through this mechanism, that M&E priorities for the coming years are known, that resource mobilization (of government and other sources) has been addressed, and that the progress of the M&E system has been reported. Ensure that the M&E plan and work plan guides the M&E work done by your organization and how your organization reports on the activities that you have implemented.

Deliverable: Relevant stakeholders aware of, understand, and supportive of the new M&E plan.

8. Summary of Chapter 4 Knowledge and Skills

In this chapter, you learned about M&E plans and their benefits/importance in developing an M&E system. You learned about the links between a national M&E plan, national strategic plan for the program to be monitored, and M&E work plan. You also learned about the linkages between a national M&E plan and an organization's M&E plan. Then, you learned about theory and technical process steps required to develop or review a national M&E plan including identifying data needs, national standardized indicators, data collection tools and procedures, and roles and responsibilities in order to implement a functional national M&E system. Lastly, you learned about how to develop an M&E plan for your organization that is linked to the national M&E plan.

9. Learning Activities

LEARNING ACTIVITY 1: CRITIQUE EXISTING M&E PLANS

Chapter 4 is all about the M&E plan for the organization. Therefore, in this activity, we will look at the M&E plans of a number of organizations, and ask you to identify the strengths and weaknesses of each. Please read Sections 5, 6 and 7 carefully. Be sure that you have also spent some time on the reflections, as this will assist you in your tasks below.

Read through the three example M&E plans (Tables of Contents) provided in Annex H of this chapter. Review these three plans in terms of their comprehensiveness (see the criteria in Annex B).

M&E plan criteria	Does M&E plan 1 fulfill this criterion?	Does M&E plan 2 fulfill this criterion?	Does M&E plan 3 fulfill this criterion?

LEARNING ACTIVITY 2: THINK ABOUT HOW TO IMPROVE THE M&E PLANS

2.1 What have you learned through doing M&E plans and the use of the 12 Components?

2.2 Suggest improvements to the three M&E plans.

Annex A: Example of a Logical Framework and Results Framework

EXAMPLE 1: Logical Framework for economic development project

Sector-related goal	Sector indicators	Sector/country reports	(from goal to bank mission)
Strengthen public policy and implementation capacity	% of population in transitioning towns whose incomes increases	National Survey	
Project development objective	**Outcome indicators**	**Project reports**	**(from objective to goal)**
Resource poor towns effectively: undertake economic development in a self-reliant manner	1. x% of participating towns rate their ability to better plan and implement investment programs (control systems, planning, supervision) as satisfactory or better, attributing this to project by xx,xx,xx	1. Survey of towns	Towns currently unable to obtain support, are able to get the needed support from other donors
	2. % of participating towns increase their own revenue share of all current municipal revenues by at least x% by xx,xx,xx	2. National Monitoring System	
	3. % of participating town sub-projects achieve their economic development outcome and maintain the impact by xx,xx,xx	3. National Monitoring System	

Source: The World Bank, 2005. Logical Framework Handbook

Chapter 4

EXAMPLE 2:   Logical Framework for rural development project

Country assistance strategy goals	Indicator	Data sources	Country assistance strategy goal to bank mission
Improved health status of rural population	1. Reduced incidence of endemic diseases by 5% annually for '93 to '99	1.1.1. World Health Organization Reports	1) Improved health increases workers' productivity
	2. Mortality rate reduced to 120/1000 by 2000	1.2.1. World Health Organization Reports	2) Other social infrastructure projects achieve their World Bank Country Assistance Strategy Goals
	3. Morbidity rate reduced to 100/1000 by 2000	1.3.1. World Health Organization Reports	

Project development objective	Indicator	Data sources	Development objective to country assistance strategy goal
The rural population uses improved secondary health care	1.1 Number of patients served by local hospitals increased by 20%	1.1.1 Independent National Study: Ministry of Health	1) No major outbreaks of diseases
	1.2 65% of the children in service areas are inoculated	1.2.1 Independent National Study: Ministry of Health	2) Current level of food security is maintained
	1.3 70% of population in need of services use these services	1.3.1 Independent National Study: Ministry of Health	

Source: The World Bank, 2005. Logical Framework Handbook

EXAMPLE 3:   Results Framework for National HIV Response

IMPACT of all the efforts [Long-term result (accomplishment in 5 years)]

QUESTION TO ASK: What do we want to see? *The ideal future*

Results to be achieved	Indicator to measure whether result has been achieved
Continue to reverse the spread of HIV and AIDS by 2013.	Modeled HIV incidence rate
	% of infants, born to HIV-infected mothers, who are infected
HIV-positive persons live longer by 2013.	% of adults and children with HIV still alive and known to be on treatment 12 months after initiation of antiretroviral therapy
	% of women and men aged 15-49 expressing accepting attitudes toward people living with HIV
	% of persons in need of impact mitigation services who express satisfaction with the services that they receive
	Ratio of orphans and non-orphans aged 10-14 who attend school
HIV response is managed effectively by 2013.	National Composite Policy Index assessment score

OUTCOMES of all the services [Intermediate result (accomplishment in 2 to 3 years)]

QUESTION TO ASK: What prevents this future from happening? Therefore, which changes need to take place for the ideal future to become a reality?

Results to be achieved	Indicator to measure whether result has been achieved
Reduced exposure to HIV	% of never-married young women and men aged 15-24 who have never had sex
	% of women and men aged 15-49 who have had sexual intercourse with more than one partner in the last 12 months
	% of young women aged 15-24 who have had sexual intercourse before the age of 15
	% of persons who have had sex in return for gifts or favors in the last 12 months
	% of women aged 15-24 who have a sexual partner 10 years or more older than them
	% of persons who have long-term concurrent sexual partners

Results to be achieved	Indicator to measure whether result has been achieved
Reduced transmissibility	% of HIV-infected pregnant women who received antiretrovirals to reduce the risk of mother-to-child transmission
	% of persons who require pre-exposure prophylaxis (medicine to avoid HIV transmission) as per national guidelines that receive them
	% of HIV-negative men who have been circumcised
	% of men and women with advanced HIV infection receiving highly active antiretroviral therapy
Better access to HIV-related services	% of estimated HIV-positive incident TB cases that received treatment for TB and HIV
Social norms have changed to encourage positive HIV-related behaviors and attitudes.	% of community leaders who have spoken about concurrent sexual partners at a public meeting at least twice in the past 12 months
	% of women and men aged 15-49 who have had more than one sexual partner in the last 12 months reporting the use of a condom during their last sexual intercourse
Social norms have changed to encourage positive HIV-related behaviors and attitudes.	% of men and women who feel that it is justified for a women to refuse sex or insist on condom use if her partner has an STI
	% of persons who find it acceptable that condoms are given to 12–14 year olds
Communities support HIV positive persons and their families in the ways that they need support.	% of orphaned and vulnerable children aged 0-17 whose households received free basic external support in caring for the child
	% of vulnerable homesteads that report they receive all the services that they need

Provide SERVICES (OUTPUTS) [Immediate results (Accomplishment immediately after work plan activities have been implemented)]

QUESTION TO ASK: Do we need to help these changes become a reality?

Results to be achieved	Indicator to measure whether result has been achieved
HIV PREVENTION PROGRAM	**HIV PREVENTION PROGRAM INDICATORS**
Prevention of mother-to-child transmission: All pregnant women and their partners know their HIV status, and receive prevention counseling, support and treatment, as appropriate.	% of pregnant women and their partners who were tested for HIV and who know their results
Family planning and HIV prevention for HIV-positive persons: HIV-positive women do not have unplanned children.	% of HIV-positive women who have accessed family planning services
Blood safety: All blood and blood products are free of HIV.	% of donated blood units screened for HIV in a quality-assured manner

Results to be achieved	Indicator to measure whether result has been achieved
HIV PREVENTION PROGRAM	**HIV PREVENTION PROGRAM INDICATORS**
Social change communication for youth (15–24) and adults (25 and older): All persons–young and old–receive appropriate messages and acquire competencies to help them make decisions that would protect them against HIV transmission.	% of population who have participated in at least 2 HIV prevention services
	% of schools that provided life skills-based HIV education in the last academic year
	% of peer education programs that provide specific messaging around MCP-related social norms
Condom distribution: Sufficient condoms are available to all persons who need them.	Total number of male and female condoms available for distribution nationwide during the last 12 months per person aged 15–49, and per person aged 15–19
Male Circumcision: All uncircumcised men have been circumcised.	% of primary health care clinics that offer male circumcision services
HIV TREATMENT AND CARE PROGRAM	**HIV TREATMENT AND CARE PROGRAM INDICATORS**
HIV testing and counseling: Men, women, and couples of all ages know their HIV status and are referred to appropriate support services.	% of women and men aged 15-49 who received an HIV test in the last 12 months and who know their results (by location where service is provided)
Antiretroviral therapy: All men and women who need HIV treatment, during any stage of their illness, receive it	% of adults and children with advanced HIV infection receiving antiretroviral therapy
	% of tuberculosis patients who had an HIV test result recorded in the tuberculosis register
	% of estimated HIV-positive incident tuberculosis cases that received treatment for tuberculosis and HIV
	% of ART facilities that provide nutrition support
Community and home-based care: Vulnerable individuals, families, the homesteads and communities they live in, are supported and cared for through home-based care, rehabilitation, and other services.	% of vulnerable households that received home-based care support at least once every week for the past 6 months
	% of child-headed households that received home-based care at least once every week for the past 6 months
Traditional health therapies and alternative health therapies: Traditional health therapists and alternative health therapists operate according to an agreed service provision framework that is complementary to services provided at health facilities.	% of registered practitioners who have been trained in providing HIV-related services

Results to be achieved	Indicator to measure whether result has been achieved
HIV IMPACT MITIGATION PROGRAM	**HIV IMPACT MITIGATION PROGRAM INDICATORS**
Community system for coordinating impact mitigation services: Communities are able to identify those who need HIV impact mitigation services, make decisions about who should receive what kind of HIV impact mitigation services at which point in time, and then plan for, coordinate and implement HIV impact mitigation services. Service providers partner with community structures in the coordination and implementation of HIV impact mitigation services.	% of care centers that have a register, that has been updated at least once in the past 3 months, of vulnerable homesteads and the impact mitigation services provided to them
	% of service providers who report to and meet in person with the care centers about the HIV impact mitigation services they have provided
Demand-driven and integrated impact mitigation service provision: Vulnerable individuals and households are able to access the services that they need and improve their livelihood.	% of vulnerable homesteads in need of impact mitigation services, reached by such services
	% of vulnerable persons in need of IMS, reached by impact mitigation services (disaggregated by type of service and sex)
Strengthening of social capital: Communities are able to identify and take collective responsibility to care for vulnerable homesteads, adults, and children.	% of vulnerable homesteads that feel they can turn to family, friends, or neighbors in time of need
MANAGING THE HIV RESPONSE	**MANAGING THE HIV RESPONSE INDICATORS**
Coordination and partnerships: Stakeholders know their role in the HIV response, and work together in implementing their roles.	% of development partner work plans that reflect the National HIV Strategic Plan results and HIV interventions that they intend to support
	% of stakeholders that express satisfaction that NAC, the sectors, sub-sectors, and regions have implemented their coordination roles as defined in the National HIV Strategic Plan
Human resource development: Adequate and competent human resources are available every year in all sectors to implement all aspects of the HIV response.	% of posts, needed for an effective HIV response, which are vacant
	% of staff in posts who can competently perform all the HIV-related tasks in their job descriptions
Joint annual planning: Stakeholders that work in the same sector jointly plan their HIV response interventions every year, keeping in mind the principles of results-based management, gender, and human rights.	% of stakeholders (regions, sectors, sub-sectors, National AIDS Commission, and implementers) that have submitted annual HIV plans using the national HIV planning template

Results to be achieved	Indicator to measure whether result has been achieved
MANAGING THE HIV RESPONSE	**MANAGING THE HIV RESPONSE INDICATORS**
HIV M&E and research: Accurate and comprehensive information about the HIV epidemic and response available when needed to improve decisions about the HIV response	% of HIV research from the national HIV research agenda that have been conducted and research results disseminated
	% of planned information products (quarterly and annual HIV response report) disseminated on time in the last 12 months
	% of regions, sectors, and sub-sectors that have adapted HIV strategies and their annual HIV work plans based on new HIV-related information from joint reviews, research, and other sources
Resource management: Sufficient and appropriate human, technical and financial resources are available on time to implement and manage the HIV response.	Domestic and international AIDS spending by categories and financing sources
	% of required funding for the National AIDS Action Plan that is available on time
	% of implementers, National AIDS Commission, regions, sectors, and sub-sectors who have experienced delays with receiving funding for their HIV work plans
Legal, ethical, and social rights provision and protection: Laws and acts support persons living with HIV and persons affected by HIV	National Composite Policy Index score

Annex B: Checklist of What Should be Included in an Organization's M&E Plan

Broadly, an M&E plan consists of 3 sections. Section 1 provides background information about the plan: its mandate, how it was developed, and the overall objectives of the M&E system. Section 2 answers the question, "What will we measure?" by stating the objectives (from the program plan) being measured, together with indicators for these objectives. Section 3 helps to define "how will we measure the objectives?" by defining the M&E system's 12 Components [every M&E system, irrespective of the level where the M&E system operates, should have all (or most) of the 12 Components]. Proposed content for these 3 sections is provided in this example (as a general guideline, but it needs to be adapted to the country context).

Section 1 contents: BACKGROUND, IMPORTANCE, AND RELEVANCE OF M&E PLAN; and AUTHORITY OF THE M&E SYSTEM

Content to be in M&E plan	(Check if included)
Objectives of M&E plan	
Structure of the M&E plan	
Reference to relevant laws, policies and strategies that contains M&E mandates and authority of governments and other organizations, e.g., the National Statistical Act may specify that the National Bureau of Statistics is responsible for all data collection in the country, other national/ organization policy, poverty reduction strategy, etc.	
Acknowledge the existence of, and describe the linkages to other M&E systems	
Vision and long-term results of M&E system	

Section 2 contents: WHAT WILL BE MEASURED WITH THE M&E SYSTEM?

Content to be in M&E plan	(Check if included)
Results Framework or Logical Framework (see Annex A), linked to the specific objectives or results of the strategic plan/program, or organization strategy	
Detailed indicator definitions & protocols (or at least reference to where these can be found)	
Data source matrix (see Annex E)	

Section 3 contents: HOW WILL THE M&E SYSTEM FUNCTION?

	Content to be in M&E plan	(Check if included)
1. Organizational structures for M&E systems	The overall organizational structure for the organization showing where M&E fits in	
	The detailed organizational structure of the M&E unit (if a separate unit is to be created)	
	Job descriptions, M&E career paths, and performance measurements of M&E posts	
2. Human capacity for M&E systems	Target audiences for M&E capacity building	
	Knowledge, skills, and competencies for persons in M&E posts or the process through which they will be developed	
	Typical capacity building mechanisms	
	Process through which (and interval) for assessing human capacity development needs in M&E	
3. M&E partnerships	Process of developing and updating an inventory of all M&E stakeholders	
	Mandate and purpose of M&E TWG	
	Process and criteria for selection of M&E TWG members	
	Other partnership mechanisms and routine communication channels	
4. M&E plans	How the M&E plan will be reviewed	
5. Costed M&E work plans	Description of the annual process for developing/reviewing the costed M&E work plan	
	How the M&E work plan will link with the government's budgeting cycle	
	Definition of available resources, and potential resource gaps	
	Costed, multi-sectoral, multi-year, and multi-level M&E work plan	
6. M&E advocacy, communications, & culture	Key target audiences with whom to communicate	
	Key messages to be conveyed to these target audiences	
	Typical communications and advocacy strategies	

	Content to be in M&E plan	(Check if included)
7. Routine monitoring	Standard data collection tools	
	Description of six routine monitoring data management processes	
	Description of the linkage between planning and routine program monitoring	
8. Surveys and surveillance	Types of surveys to be done to address indicator requirements, including protocols to be used (inventory of surveys)	
	Who will manage each survey	
	How data will flow between the various actors–can use a flow chart to explain	
9. Databases useful for M&E systems	Statement of M&E system information needs	
	Inventory of and linkages with existing data systems	
	Database development and maintenance requirements	
10. Supervision and data auditing	M&E supportive supervision and data auditing processes (use same data flow diagram as for routine data)	
	Requirement to develop guidelines for M&E supervision and data auditing	
11. Evaluation and research	Inventory of completed and ongoing country-specific evaluation and research studies, or process for developing it	
	Process for developing a research strategy	
	Process for developing an annual research agenda	
	Linkages to existing research institutions	
	Procedures for ethical review, and reference to guidelines on evaluation and research standards	
	Research dissemination strategies	
12. Using information to improve results	Information product matrix (see Annex F)	
	Information product templates with data tabulation plans	
	Dissemination matrix (see Annex G)	

Annex C: Selecting Good Quality Indicators

Indicator Selection Process

Adapted from: McCoy, KL., Ngari, PN., and Krumpe, EE. 2005. *Building monitoring, evaluation and reporting systems* For HIV/AIDS *programs*. PACT: Washington DC, pp. 41 and 42.

Step 1:   Clarify the results statements; identify what needs to be measured

Step 2:   Develop a list of possible indicators for your results through brainstorming and research

Step 3:   Assess each possible indicator

Step 4:   Select the best indicators

Step 5:   Draft indicator protocols

Step 6:   Collect baseline data

Step 7:   Refine indicators and protocols and finalize your selection

Ten Criteria for Assessing Indicators

Adapted from: McCoy, KL., Ngari, PN., and Krumpe, EE. 2005. *Building monitoring, evaluation and reporting systems for HIV/AIDS programs*. PACT: Washington DC, pp. 41 and 42.

Indicator selection criteria	Examples – good and bad
1. **Measurable:** It can be quantified and measured using some scale. Quantitative indicators are numerical. Qualitative indicators are descriptive observations. While quantitative indicators are not necessarily more objective, their numerical precision is conducive to agreement on interpretation of results data, making them usually preferable. However, even when effective quantitative indicators are used, qualitative indicators can supplement them to provide rich information that brings the program results to life.	NO! People's feelings about the elections YES! Percentage of the population who voted
2. **Practical:** Data can be collected on a timely basis and at reasonable cost. Managers require data that can be collected frequently enough to inform them of progress and influence decisions. Organizations should expect to incur reasonable but not exorbitant costs for obtaining useful information. A general rule is to plan on allocating 3 to 10 percent of total program resources for monitoring and evaluation.	NO! Number of targeted population who understand their voting rights (census) YES! % of targeted population who understand their voting rights (representative sample, through a poll)

Indicator selection criteria	Examples – good and bad
3. **Reliable:** Data can be measured repeatedly, with precision by different people. While the data that a program manager needs in order to make reasonably confident decisions about a program do not have to be held to the same rigorous standards research scientists use, all indicators should be able to be measured repeatedly with relative precision by different people.	NO! Number of people receiving quality care and support services through workplace programs YES! Number of people who were tested for HIV at work in the last 12 months
4. **Relevant:** Attributable at least in part to the program being monitored. A result is caused to some extent by program activities. Attribution exists when the links between the program outputs and the results being measured are clear and significant.	NO! Agriculture production yield in the country YES! Agriculture production yield in the district where the project is being implemented
5. **Useful to management:** Information provided by the measure is critical to decision making. Avoid collecting and reporting information that is not used to support program management decisions.	EXAMPLE INDICATOR: LEVEL OF INSTITUTIONAL CAPACITY NO! Number of computers; number of staff meetings YES! Amount by type of resources mobilized YES! Number by type of critical organizational systems fully operational
6. **Direct:** The indicator closely tracks the result it is intended to measure. An indicator should measure as closely as possible the result it is intended to measure; e.g., condom use is a direct measure of the result of efforts to increase use of condoms. But number of service providers trained would not be a direct measure of improved service delivery. Just because people are trained does not necessarily mean they deliver better services. If using a direct measure is not possible, proxy indicators might be appropriate; e.g., sometimes, reliable data on direct measures are not available at a frequency that is useful. Proxy measures are indirect measures linked to the result by one or more assumptions; e.g., in rural areas, it is often difficult to measure income levels directly. Measures such as percentage of village households with roofs (or radios or bicycles) may be a useful, if somewhat rough proxy. The assumption is that, when villagers have higher income, they tend to purchase certain goods. Select proxy indicators for which convincing evidence exists of the link to the result (e.g., research data).	RESULT: INCREASED VARIETY IN AGRICULTURE PRODUCTION NO! Number of types of agriculture seeds distributed YES! Volume of production by type of agriculture produced

Indicator selection criteria	Examples – good and bad
7. **Sensitive:** The indicator serves as an early warning of changing conditions. A sensitive indicator will change proportionately and in the same direction as changes in the condition or item being measured, thus sensitive proxy indicators can be used as an indication (or warning) of results to come.	NO! Gross Domestic Product YES! Amount of rice consumed per household per year
8. **Responsive:** What the indicator measures can be changed by program actions. Indicators should reflect change as a result of program activities and thus indicators reflect results that are responsive to program action.	NO! % of population unemployed YES! % of secondary school students who graduate with a passing grade of 60% or higher
9. **Objective:** The measure is operationally precise and one-dimensional. An objective indicator has no ambiguity about what is being measured. That is, there is general agreement on the interpretation of the results. To be one-dimensional means that it measures only one phenomenon at a time. Avoid trying to combine too much in one indicator.	NO! Number of expanding and successful parent/teacher associations YES! Number of parent/teacher associations experiencing an annual increase in membership of at least 5%
10. **Capable of being disaggregated:** Data can be broken down by gender, age, location, or other category where appropriate. Disaggregating data by gender, age, location, or some other category is often important from a program or reporting point of view. Experience shows that development activities often require different approaches for different groups and affect those groups in different ways. Disaggregated data help track whether or not specific groups participate in and benefit from activities intended to include them.	YES! Gender, age, location, ethnic group

Chapter 4

Annex D: Decision Tree to Help Decide If an M&E Assessment Is Necessary

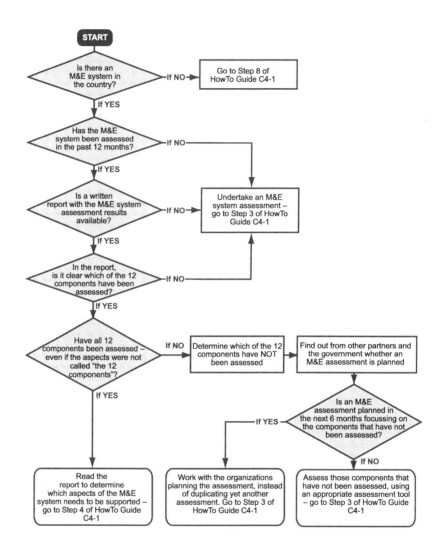

START

Is there an M&E system in the country? — If NO → Go to Step 8 of HowTo Guide C4-1

If YES ↓

Has the M&E system been assessed in the past 12 months? — If NO →

If YES ↓

Is a written report with the M&E system assessment results available? — If NO → Undertake an M&E system assessment – go to Step 3 of HowTo Guide C4-1

If YES ↓

In the report, is it clear which of the 12 components have been assessed? — If NO →

If YES ↓

Have all 12 components been assessed – even if the aspects were not called "the 12 components"? — If NO → Determine which of the 12 components have NOT been assessed → Find out from other partners and the government whether an M&E assessment is planned

If YES ↓

Is an M&E assessment planned in the next 6 months focussing on the components that have not been assessed? — If YES →

If NO ↓

Read the report to determine which aspects of the M&E system needs to be supported – go to Step 4 of HowTo Guide C4-1

Work with the organizations planning the assessment, instead of duplicating yet another assessment. Go to Step 3 of HowTo Guide C4-1

Assess those components that have not been assessed, using an appropriate assessment tool – go to Step 3 of HowTo Guide C4-1

Annex E: Example of a Data Source Matrix

Example from a National HIV Monitoring and Evaluation Plan

Data source	Time period covered in data source	Publication date	Frequency of data collection	Institutional responsibility	Level of readiness	
ROUTINE DATA SOURCES						
1. **Financial Management System Report**	January – December	January (1st one by Jan 2004)	Collected continuously, reported monthly	Financial Management Agency	Data specifications	Defined in contract
					Methodology	Agreed in contract
					Budget	Prepared — in Financial Management Agency contract
2. **Quarterly Service Coverage Report** (XE "Core Data Sources: Quarterly Service Coverage Report")	3 calendar months (preceding quarter)	4 weeks after end of the quarter (1st one by Dec 03)	Collected continuously, reported quarterly	Providers of HIV-related services	Data specifications	Defined in this plan
					Methodology	Agreed in contract with each implementer
					Budget	Should be part of each implementer's budget
3. **National HIV/AIDS research database**	Cumulative data submitted to database	Not relevant – available online	Periodic updates as and when information is submitted	National AIDS Commission	Data specifications	Partly defined in this plan
					Methodology	To be agreed
					Budget	Development budget in this plan
EPISODIC DATA SOURCES (SURVEYS)						
4. **Workplace survey**	Survey data collection period	January (1st one by Jan 2005)	Biennial	Ministry of Labor and Vocational Training	Data specifications	Defined in global guidelines
					Methodology	To be agreed with Ministry of Labor and Vocational Training
					Budget	To be prepared

Data source	Time period covered in data source	Publication date	Frequency of data collection	Institutional responsibility	Level of readiness	
5. Health facility survey	Combined with health facility supervision (July)	November (1st one by Nov 2003)	Annual	Ministry of Health & Population – Planning Unit	Data specifications	Defined in this plan
					Methodology	To be agreed with Ministry of Health and Population
					Budget	To be prepared
6. Behavioral Surveillance Survey	Survey data collection period	January (1st one in 2004)	Biennial	Ministry of Health & Population – Epidemiology Unit	Data specifications	Defined in this plan
					Methodology	Agreed: international practice
					Budget	To be prepared
ONCE-OFF DATA SOURCES (RESEARCH AND EVALUATION)						
7. Clinic research (basic science research) to determine most effective treatments	Period of study	May 2009	Once-off	Ministry of Health & Population – Research Unit	Data specifications	Study protocol to define
					Methodology	Study protocol to define
					Budget	Study protocol to define
8. Operations research to identify problems with delivery of HIV prevention programs	Past 2 years	June 2010	Once-off	Ministry of Health & Population – Research Unit	Data specifications	Study protocol to define
					Methodology	Study protocol to define
					Budget	Study protocol to define
9. Evaluation of acceptance among patients of the new testing guidelines	Since the use of the new guidelines	June 2009	Once-off	Ministry of Health & Population – Research Unit	Data specifications	Evaluation protocol to define
					Methodology	Exit interviews
					Budget	Evaluation protocol to define

Annex F: Example of an Information Product Matrix

Information Product Matrix for an M&E System of the National Ministry of Tourism

Name of information product	Frequency	Contents	Distributed to	Publication date
Quarterly Tourism Statistical Bulletin	Every 3 months	Statistics on tourism volumes and number of role players in the sector	All registered tourism establishments All regional tourism offices	15th of the month following the end of the quarter
Annual Tourism Bulletin	Once a Year	Contribution of tourism to Gross Domestic Product Most popular tourism sites Results of tourism satisfaction survey	All registered tourism establishments All regional tourism offices All other government departments All local councils All private sector providers of tourism	3 months after the start of the governmental financial year
Biennial Tourism Situation Analysis	Every Two Years	Progress of the tourism sector in achieving the country's national tourism goals Results of global branding survey which shows how the country is perceived globally Contribution of tourism sector to country's economy in the last two years Plans for the future	All registered tourism establishments All regional tourism offices All other government departments All local councils All private sector providers of tourism	2 months before the end of the governmental financial year

Annex G: Example of a Dissemination Matrix

Example from an Education Sector M&E Plan

Information products and data sources that need to be disseminated

To whom information needs to be disseminated

Stakeholders	Monthly school attendance summary	Research on teacher morale	Annual education report
Minister	Executive summary by e-mail	Paper copy, presented in person	Paper copy, presented in person
Regional government officials	Full report by e-mail	Paper copy, post	Paper copy, post
Community-based Organizations	Full report by e-mail	Presentation at workshop	Summary in vernacular
Ministries	Full report by e-mail	Paper copies	Full report file sent by email
Private sector education stakeholders	Full report posted on website, e-mail link	Annual research conference	Full report posted on website, e-mail link

How information will be disseminated
(dissemination channels)

Annex H: Examples of M&E Plans (Tables of Contents)

TABLE OF CONTENTS 1

TABLE OF CONTENTS 2

Chapter 4

SECTION 2:   WHAT THE M&E SYSTEM WILL MEASURE

4.   National results framework

    4.1   National indicators

    4.2   Relationship between the National and Program-Level M&E systems

SECTION 3:   HOW THE NATIONAL M&E SYSTEM WILL OPERATE
                   TO ENABLE IT TO MEASURE THE NATIONAL
                   TRANSPORT SECTOR STRATEGIC PLAN

5.   Introduction to the 12 Components of a functional M&E System

6.   Description of Routine Data Sources for Indicators

7.   Description of Surveys and Surveillance as Periodic Data Source for Indicators

8.   Management of Transport Sector M&E System Data

    8.1   Database system

    8.2   Electronic Repository for M & E related data and information

9.   Dissemination and Use Transport Sector M&E System Data

    9.1   Data Dissemination Strategies

    9.2   Production of Information Products

        9.2.1   Quarterly District-level Transport Volume Report

        9.2.2   Annual Transport Sector Progress Report

        9.2.3   Regular Information Updates

        9.2.4   Ad Hoc information needs

10.   Human Capacity Building in Monitoring and Evaluation Relating to the Transport Sector

11.   Data Audits and Supportive Supervision

12.   Evaluation & Research

13.   Coordination and Roles of Stakeholders in the Transport Sector M&E System

14.   Advocacy and communication for the National Transport Sector M&E System

15.   Review of national Transport Sector M&E plan

TABLE OF CONTENTS 3

1.   Introduction to the M&E system

    • Why an M&E system?

    • What the M&E system will try to achieve

Making Monitoring and Evaluation Systems Work

- How other M&E systems will work with this one
- How will the M&E system help to achieve the role of the education sector?

2. Indicators
    - Which indicators will be used to measure the education sector goals and objectives?

3. Data Sources in the M&E system
    - Routine data — how routine data will be managed, how data quality will be assured
    - Surveys to be undertaken
    - Other evaluation and research to be done

4. Information products
    - What information products the M&E system will produce
    - How it will be organized
    - Who will approve the information products, and how analysis will be done

5. Dissemination to stakeholders
    - What are stakeholders' information needs?
    - How will information be disseminated to these stakeholders?

6. Management of the M&E system
    - Capacity building in the M&E system
    - Ideal culture for M&E to which the organization will strive
    - How organizations will work together in M&E
    - How information will be captured electronically
    - How M&E planning will be done as part of the government's annual budget process
    - When the M&E system and the M&E plan will be reviewed and which assessment tools will be used

Annex I: M&E System Assessment Tools

1.   M&E System Diagnostic Tool by Mackay (2007)

Aspect of the government M&E system to be diagnosed [from Mackay (2007) p 69, Box 12.1]
1.   **Genesis of the existing M&E system**—Role of M&E advocates or champions; key events that created the priority for M&E information (for example, election of reform-oriented government, fiscal crisis)
2.   **The ministry or agency responsible for managing the M&E system and planning evaluations**—Roles and responsibilities of the main parties to the M&E system, for example, finance ministry, planning ministry, president's office, sector ministries, the Parliament or Congress; possible existence of several, uncoordinated M&E systems at the national and sector levels; importance of federal/state/local issues to the M&E system
3.   **The public sector environment and whether it makes it easy or difficult for managers to perform to high standards, and to be held accountable for their performance**—Incentives for the stakeholders to take M&E seriously, strength of demand for M&E information. Are public sector reforms under way that might benefit from a stronger emphasis on the measurement of government performance, such as a poverty-reduction strategy, performance budgeting, strengthening of policy analysis skills, creation of a performance culture in the civil service, improvements in service delivery such as customer service standards, government decentralization, greater participation by civil society, or an anti-corruption strategy?
4.   **The main aspects of public sector management that the M&E system supports strongly**—(i) Budget decision making, (ii) national or sector planning, (iii) program management, and (iv) accountability relationships (to the finance ministry, to the president's office, to parliament, to sector ministries, to civil society): •   Actual role of M&E information at the various stages of the budget process: such as policy advising and planning, budget decision making, performance review and reporting; possible disconnect between the M&E work of sector ministries and the use of such information in the budget process; existence of any disconnect between the budget process and national planning; opportunities to strengthen the role of M&E in the budget •   Extent to which the M&E information commissioned by key stakeholders (for example, the finance ministry) is used by others, such as sector ministries; if not used, barriers to utilization; any solid evidence concerning the extent of utilization by different stakeholders (for example, a diagnostic review or a survey); examples of major evaluations that have been highly influential with the government

Aspect of the government M&E system to be diagnosed [from Mackay (2007) p 69, Box 12.1]
5. **Types of M&E tools emphasized in the M&E system:** regular performance indicators, rapid reviews or evaluations, performance audits, rigorous, in-depth impact evaluations; scale and cost of each of these types of M&E; manner in which evaluation priorities are set—focused on problem programs, pilot programs, high expenditure or high visibility programs, or on a systematic research agenda to answer questions about program effectiveness
6. **Who is responsible for collecting performance information and conducting evaluations** (for example, ministries themselves or academia or consulting firms); any problems with data quality or reliability or with the quality of evaluations conducted; strengths and weaknesses of local supply of M&E; key capacity constraints and the government's capacity-building priorities
7. **Extent of donor support for M&E in recent years; donor projects that support M&E at whole-of-government, sector, or agency levels**—Provision of technical assistance, other capacity building and funding for the conduct of major evaluations, such as rigorous impact evaluations
8. **Conclusions:** Overall strengths and weaknesses of the M&E system; its sustainability, in terms of vulnerability to a change in government, for example, how dependent it is on donor funding or other support; current plans for future strengthening of the M&E system

Source: Mackay, 2007

2. M&E System assessment tool, as part of the *Three Ones* assessment, by UNAIDS

a) A recognized authority for coordinating and operationalizing national M&E

Does it exist?

If yes,

- Where is that authority located (e.g., Ministry of Health)?
- What authority does this body have and where does it come from? (By law, other legislation, technical specialties?)
- Is there a budget allocation?
- How many staff does it have?
- Does a systems map exist of who is conducting M&E activities?
- Is there a strategy for sharing information and what role does the coordinating authority play?

If no,

- Is there any plan for the establishment of a coordinating authority?
- Which organizations conduct M&E now?
- Is information shared among different stakeholders?

b) **One national M&E Working Group for coordination**

Does it exist?

If yes,

- Is there a defined Terms of Reference?
- Is there a budget allocation?
- How many staff does it have?
- Who are the participants (e.g., ministries, donor agencies, UN system organizations, academic institutions, civil society)? Obtain the list of participating agencies.
- How often do they meet?
- What are major products from this forum?

If no,

- Is there a plan to establish a coordination working group with representation from all major stakeholders?

c) **A common national level data management system that includes relevant information and databases**

- Where does this system reside?
- Who enters data into the system?
- How many different databases comprise the system?
- Has CRIS (Country Response Information System) been installed and does it play a role in this plan?
- Is there a CRIS implementation plan?
- Is there way to synchronize CRIS with other national databases?

d) **Reporting and use of data**

- Are there routine reports available for decisions makers?
- Is there routine reporting to high-level policy-makers (e.g., Parliament)?
- Obtain copies of recent reports containing M&E data

e) **One national multi-sectoral M&E action plan endorsed by major stakeholders?**

Does it exist?

If yes,

- When was the plan endorsed?
- What time period does it cover?
- Is there a set of standardized indicators endorsed by all major stakeholders? (Which stakeholders have endorsed this plan?)
- Is there a sub-set of indicators from the global guidelines on indicators?
- Is there a strategy for data collection?
- Is there a budget for management and implementation?
- Is there a data dissemination and use strategy?
- Is there a strategy for assessing quality and accuracy of data?
- Is there an M&E capacity building plan?

    If yes to an M&E capacity building plan,

    - When was it approved and by whom?
    - Does it define the number of people to be trained?
    - Does it identify the technical and management areas to be strengthened?
    - Is there a database/list of people who have been trained in the past?
    - Is there a strategy for building M&E capacity at the sub-national level?

    If no to an M&E capacity building plan,

    - Is there any proposal to produce such a plan or draft for it?

If no,

- Is there a proposal to produce a national action plan?
- Is there any draft plan that is currently being used?

f) **Data management system**

Does the data management system contain the following data?

- Serological and behavioral surveillance
- Coverage of essential services
- Assessment of quality of services
- Financial tracking
- Impact of the epidemic including vital registration statistics

- Assessment of the policy environment for implementing HIV/AID programs
- An inventory of current and proposed evaluation research activities that are taking place in the country

g) Evaluation

- Has a joint assessment taken place that includes national, donor, UN, and civil society representation?
- How many individual donor evaluations were conducted last year?
- Among them, how many missions were joint missions?
- Were these mission reports shared with the national AIDS authority?

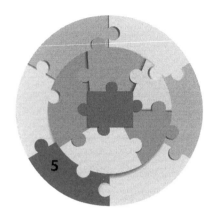

Chapter 5
Costed Monitoring and
Evaluation Work Plans

Chapter Aim

The aim of this chapter is to enable you to develop, cost, and prioritize an M&E work plan and mobilize resources for it. The M&E work plan is an action plan that includes activities, responsibilities, time frames, and costs to make each of the 12 Components of an M&E system work.

Chapter Knowledge and Skills

By the end of this chapter, you should be able to:

By the end of this chapter, you should be able to:

a)   Know the different costing methods

b)   Develop an M&E work plan

c)   Cost an M&E work plan (using the ABC costing method)

d)   Use the M&E work plan for management purposes

Before You Begin...

Take a few minutes to read through the questions below. You may find it helpful to write down your answers. As you work through the chapter, compare your answers to the views of the authors.

- What is the difference between the M&E plan and the M&E work plan?

- What should be in my M&E work plan?

- To what level of detail should one plan? Should all the individual tasks of staff members in the unit be included in the work plan or only those activities for which the unit is responsible?

- What time period should the M&E work plan cover?

- How should activities be worded, and from whose perspective, personal or institutional?

- When revising the work plan, should completed activities be deleted?

- Who should be indicated in the responsibility column, all agencies or only the lead agency?

- Can software be used for this planning process and which is the best to use?

These questions should indicate to you the difference between the holistic, overall focus of the M&E plan and the specific and detailed focus of the M&E work plan. This chapter will teach you how to develop a multi-year, multi-sectoral, and multi-level M&E work plan; how to cost the work plan; and how to use that plan in managing the M&E system.

Component 5: Costed M&E Work Plans

1. Introduction

> *"Planning without action is futile, action without planning is fatal."*
>
> Anonymous

For a national M&E system at the country level to become and remain operational, it is essential to coordinate the efforts of all stakeholders involved in the M&E system. Such coordination is easier, especially when there are **many stakeholders** involved, if one inclusive set of M&E activities is developed. Such activities should include all components of the system and should assign individual organizations to take the lead on specific activities. A costed, multi-year, multi-sectoral, and multi-level M&E work plan is a very useful tool for prioritizing, planning, and coordinating activities relating to the M&E system.

How this chapter is organized: Chapter 5 begins with background information and definitions relating to costed, multi-year, multi-sectoral, and multi-level M&E work plans (Section 2). The desired result for this chapter and the benefits of costed M&E work plans[1] follow in Sections 3 and 4. The next three sections provide steps and guidance related to M&E work plans. Section 5 presents steps for developing/updating an M&E work plan by developing a joint set of prioritized activities linked to the 12 Components of a functional M&E system. Section 6 provides specific steps on costing and mobilizing resources for an M&E work plan, determining the human and financial costs of each activity in the work plan, and the required annual cash flow. Section 7 explains how to use the M&E work plan to manage the M&E system. This means using this multi-year, multi-sectoral and multi-level M&E work plan to manage the work of an M&E unit. The Chapter closes with a summary of lessons learned and a practical exercise to cement what you have learned.

2. Background Information and Definitions

What is a costed M&E work plan?

A costed, multi-year, multi-sectoral and multi-level M&E work plan describes and budgets for all M&E activities that are necessary to implement an M&E system over a defined time period (1-2 years, usually). A work plan can be

---

[1] Throughout Chapter 5, reference is made to the "M&E work plan." This could refer to the national M&E work plan, a sector-specific M&E work plan or the M&E work plans of individual organizations. The steps in Sections 5-7 would apply in all cases, with suitable adaptations.

developed for an individual organization or for an entire national M&E system. A common work plan, if thoroughly developed, will provide one common vision for all stakeholders and a single operational framework within which individual organizations can develop their approach.

A work plan needs to be **costed** in order to accurately determine funding requirements, mobilize resources, and assign appropriate levels of funding.

A **national M&E work plan** is usually **multi-year, multi-sectoral,** and **multi-level**.

1. **Multi-year** because:

    *   The M&E plan is itself a multi-year plan corresponding to the time frame of the program being monitored;
    *   Government budgeting has become a multi-year process; and
    *   A multi-year budget enables a country to develop cash-flow estimates and include M&E funding requirements in resource mobilization proposals to government and development partners.

2. **Multi-sectoral** because there are many stakeholders involved in the M&E system. Each of the stakeholders needs resources to implement the M&E activities for which they are responsible. By including in the work plan the activities for which each M&E stakeholder is responsible and the costs that they would incur, it becomes clear what resources need to be mobilized and assigned to meet these requirements.

3. **Multi-level** because it is not only ministries at the national (head office) level that are involved in M&E activities but also (most likely) umbrella organizations or local government authorities at the sub-national levels.

A national M&E work plan, however, is **not** only the M&E work plan for government ministries but is a joint work plan for all stakeholders involved in M&E activities in the country. It allows M&E stakeholders to plan and work together in a complementary and harmonized way toward one common vision for the M&E of the national program.

Types of activities in the costed M&E work plan

Activities in a costed M&E work plan must include both the one-off or periodic activities required when establishing an M&E system (such as developing training materials) and the recurring activities that must be implemented regularly, at defined intervals, to ensure the continued operation of this system (e.g., processing routine monitoring data).

Difference between M&E work plan and M&E plan

The M&E plan (see Component 4) is a narrative document that describes, in detail, how the M&E system will operate. The M&E work plan, on the other hand, is an

Making Monitoring and Evaluation Systems Work

action plan (with activities, responsibilities, time frames, and costs for each of the 12 Components). An M&E work plan is usually an annex to an M&E plan.

3. Results to Be Achieved When Implementing This Component

Long-term result: A multi-partner and multi-year M&E work plan is used as the basis for planning, prioritizing, costing, mobilizing resources, and funding of all M&E activities.

Short- and medium-term results

- The M&E work plan contains activities, responsible implementers, time frames, activity costs calculated using a unit cost table, and identified funding.

- The M&E work plan links to the program work plans and to the government's medium-term expenditure framework and annual budgets.

- Resources (human, physical, and financial) are committed to implement the M&E work plan.

- All relevant stakeholders are committed to implementing and contributing to the national M&E work plan.

- The M&E work plan is developed/ updated annually, based on performance monitoring.

> **For reflection 1:**
>
> Reflect on your organization's M&E plan for a moment. Does your organization have an M&E system, M&E plan and/or an M&E work plan in place? If so, is it really used? How is it used? For day-to-day management and priority setting? Or mainly for budgeting? Is your M&E work plan included in your organization's broader budgets and work plans? How many of the short- and medium-term results do you see in your organization's existing M&E work plan?

4. Benefits of Costed M&E Work Plans as Part of an M&E System

Organizations that have implemented their M&E systems based on an M&E work plan have found that the joint development and budgeting for all M&E activities has the following benefits:

1. **It helps to clarify and facilitate execution of M&E system mandates.**
    Having mandated roles and specific responsibilities assigned in the M&E system
    is a good start. Having a work plan that defines what activity main M&E
    stakeholders will do and what this will cost provides a more powerful tool to
    ensure that M&E system mandates are executed. For national M&E work plans,
    the work plan is strengthened by including it in government budgets.

2. **It provides a useful management tool for coordinating the M&E
    system.** The organization responsible for overseeing the M&E system can
    refer to the M&E work plan to know what each stakeholder's responsibilities
    and duties are within the M&E system. Staff can follow up with
    stakeholders about specific activities, track progress, and proactively manage
    any potential delays and bottlenecks.

3. **It enables real partnerships to be formed.** The agreement and commitment
    to develop an M&E work plan enables M&E stakeholders in different sectors
    and at all levels in a country to plan thoroughly and therefore work together in
    building one M&E system.

4. **It enables the assessment of the types of M&E support required.** M&E
    technical working groups should assess objectively whether or not the country
    requires specific M&E technical support or resources that may be offered
    from time to time, to support the agreed-upon work plan. With a clear and
    detailed plan in place, decision makers may be able to decide which external
    support is needed and which is not, and to avoid *supply-driven* technical and tied
    financial support that are not consistent with the work plan.

5. **It forms a basis for determining membership of the M&E Technical
    Working Group.** Representatives of all the organizations listed in the
    "responsibility column" of the M&E work plan should be involved and
    included as members of the M&E TWG.

6. **It helps mobilize and rationalize resources for the M&E system.**
    A costed work plan will enable the country to determine the level of
    financial and human resources needed. A clearly costed work plan enables
    development partners effectively to tailor their M&E support to the
    prioritized M&E needs of the country and commit to supporting specific
    aspects of the M&E system. The costed work plan has many uses:

    -   It justifies the actual amount of domestic and international resources
        required (instead of relying on the general recommendation to dedicate
        "7% to 10% of the program budget to M&E";

    -   It can be used when proposals to development partners are written to
        describe resource shortages;

    -   It can be used to motivate reallocation and prioritization of available
        resources; and

    -   It enables government ministries, agencies, and LGA to include M&E

costs in their budgets and the finance ministry to include these costs in the medium-term expenditure framework of the country.

7. **It helps to track progress in implementing the M&E system.** In addition to being a planning tool that defines tasks and responsibility, the M&E TWG can use the national M&E work plan to follow up and assess M&E system implementation and progress. If all M&E work plan activities have been implemented on time to the required standard, the M&E TWG should be able to report that M&E system implementation in the country is on track.

5. Implementation Issues Related to This Component

5.1. Ensure leadership support at all levels and government ministries

Senior management should be aware of, buy into, and drive the process of creating, maintaining and updating the national M&E work plan. The M&E TWG should lead the development, costing and updating of the national M&E work plan. Finance directors of organizations with M&E responsibilities should also be involved in costing and understanding how the plan, once budgeted, will impact on and link with the broader budgets of their organizations.

5.2. Involve all stakeholders meaningfully in all facets of the process

Development partners need to be committed to the development of a national M&E work plan. This can be facilitated by involving program coordinators and implementers, decentralized structures involved in coordinating the national program being monitored; national ministries, research and academic institutions, the team responsible for reviewing the national program strategy and work plan, and beneficiary representatives when developing the work plan.

5.3. Link the M&E work plan to the main organization's (e.g., government) budgeting mechanism and cycle

The M&E work plan needs to be developed in time for government's annual budgeting cycle and needs to be used as a basis for the main stakeholders' M&E units to develop their Medium-Term Expenditure Framework (MTEF) estimates and annual work plans. Also ensure that the M&E work plan budget is included as the M&E component of the overall budget for the program being monitored.

5.4. Include all types of activities

Include activities for all M&E strategies in the national program and include all types of M&E activities (both one-off and recurrent).

5.5. Synchronize time periods

Develop a multi-year M&E work plan that covers at least the same time period as the national program plan and the M&E plan.

5.6. Budget for development partners' technical assistance contributions

Assign a standard unit cost to the professional time and support provided by development partners, even though this is not funded from country-level resources.

5.7. Extract individual M&E activities which each stakeholder is responsible for from the multi-year, multi-sectoral and multi-level plan

Use the multi-year work plan for annual planning and setting milestones, even for the weekly management of M&E units. Link the work plan to daily activities and weekly management as a live management tool.

5.8. Use project planning methodologies, strategies and software

Developing, costing and using an M&E work plan is an integral part of project management. Use project management principles and available project management and planning software.

6. HowTo Guide C5-1: Developing/Updating a National M&E Work Plan

Please note that, although this HowTo Guide has been developed for designing a national M&E work plan, the same steps can be used to develop an M&E work plan for your organization.

Step 1: Advocate for the development and use of a national M&E work plan

Early political buy-in will ensure that the M&E work plan is implemented. Use the successes or failures of the previous work planning cycle to adjust your current planning process for the new M&E work plan. Find a champion to motivate and mobilize resources for the M&E work plan implementation and seek development partners to use the work plan as a basis for their own planning. Present the planning process to relevant stakeholders early to ensure inclusivity and shared ownership.

Deliverable: Champion for national M&E work plan.

Step 2: Carry out a national M&E systems assessment, if needed

A system assessment helps stakeholders to *focus on, prioritize, and phase-in the activities in the M&E work plan.* This will ensure that attempting to implement all 12 Components of the M&E system simultaneously does not overwhelm the designated team. In line with agreements with development partners, an M&E system assessment should not be done if one has been done in the past 12 months.

Deliverable: National M&E system assessment or capacity assessment for your organization.

Step 3: Obtain copies of work plans and budgets from all relevant stakeholders

The work plans of other units within your organization or other ministries (e.g., Ministry of Health, or Education, or National Bureau of Statistics) are important in confirming what M&E activities are already planned and what they perceive the funding priorities to be.

It should be emphasized that the national M&E work plan is not intended to be a conglomeration of existing M&E work plans. The national M&E work plan should be a mutually agreed-upon list of prioritized activities designed to implement the 12 Components of a national M&E system, irrespective of whether the government or its development partners have planned to implement these prioritized activities or not.

Deliverable: Copies of M&E work plans and budgets from all relevant stakeholders.

Step 4: Ensure that the M&E TWG has wide representation from all stakeholders

All stakeholders that are expected to fulfill M&E functions and those currently funding or interested in funding M&E activities should be represented at the planning and costing workshop.

Deliverable: Representation of stakeholders/funders with M&E functions in the group developing the M&E work plan activities list.

Step 5: Brainstorm a wish-list of activities for the M&E work plan

First, agree on the time frame of the work plan. It should coincide with the time frame of the national M&E plan and, in turn, coincide with the time frame of the national program strategy.

- Experience suggests that approaching this component-by-component is most effective. For example, consider Component 1 (M&E organizational alignment and structures). Briefly discuss the current status (with reference to the latest M&E systems assessment), refer to the performance objective (the component's *ideal state*), and only then develop a list of activities, both one-off and recurrent, to ensure the component's functionality. Once complete, move on to the next component.

- Not all activities for each component need to (or can) be implemented in a single year. It is important in prioritizing and phasing activities to recognize that these might have short-, medium-, and long-term objectives and implications that require careful phasing.

- The work plan should not only contain activities needed to strengthen the M&E system but also activities that may already be working well and need to be maintained for the system to remain functional (e.g., routine surveillance). This work plan and costing, therefore, covers the total M&E system implementation and not only M&E system strengthening activities. In this way, the government remains in control of M&E system implementation and coordination, as agreed upon by its international development partners.

Deliverable: Agreed-upon time frame and draft list of activities for the M&E work plan.

Step 6: Build consensus around the activities to be included

- After a zero draft list of activities has been developed (Step 5), some iterations and discussions are likely to be necessary. The discussions should focus on which M&E system activities to prioritize, such as activities that will yield *quick wins*, as well as activities that are most important for building the national system.

- One agency should be assigned responsibility for executing each activity. Some countries divide the responsibility column into two: a lead agency and agencies to support this lead agency.

- Customize an M&E work plan template for the country's use. Do this by adding a sufficient number of years in the time frame columns of the M&E. The time frame of the M&E work plan should ideally correspond with the time frame in the plan of the program being monitored and the national M&E plan.

- Complete the M&E work plan template (see Annex A).

- After agreeing on each activity, specify when the activities will take place and illustrate this on the work plan template bearing in mind the short-, medium-, and long-term time frames of other activities and links between activities. Finally, the work plan needs to be costed (refer to the next section).

Deliverable: Completed and customized M&E work plan template that specifies agreed upon activities, time frames, estimated costs, and responsible agency.

Step 7: Submit the M&E work plan for approval to the M&E TWG

A formal M&E TWG meeting with a quorum present and sufficient time to complete the task should be convened. The decisions taken will affect all development partners' allocations for M&E so it is important that they are present at this meeting.

Given the possible implications of the work plan, it is strongly recommended that the Director of finance and administration of the lead M&E agency also attends this meeting (or a follow-up meeting where a draft costing is presented), so that she or he is aware of the work plan activities, the estimated costs, and the importance of including these activities in the government's annual and medium-term budgeting process. Directors of finance or administration from key government ministries should also attend, particularly those from the key stakeholder ministries.

Deliverable: Formal approval by M&E TWG of M&E work plan.

Step 8: Update and finalize the membership of the M&E TWG

After the work plan is finalized and the *responsibility* column is reviewed, there may be organizations with M&E functions that have inadvertently been excluded from the M&E TWG. Although this should be rectified if practically possible, care should be taken that the M&E TWG does not become too large. Experience suggests that the group should have no more than 15 to 20 members.

- Regularly update the membership (and, therefore, the TOR) of the M&E TWG to ensure that all relevant organizations are represented at the M&E TWG.
- The work plan can be used as a basis for updating the M&E TWG on progress made in implementing the M&E system. Flowing from this, every partner can then report back to its own constituency on the progress made with the activities for which it is responsible.

Deliverable: Updated membership in the M&E TWG.

Step 9. Use the M&E work plan during M&E TWG meetings to assess the status of each activity

This will ensure that the work plan is a *live* management tool and that the TWG remains focused on its responsibilities and activities. It is also a good idea to develop quarterly milestones from this work plan. In this way, the TWG can focus every quarter on the milestones planned for that particular quarter (and the milestones rolled over from the previous quarter, if any).

Deliverables: Assessment of the status of activities in the M&E work plan as well as a review of quarterly milestones developed from the M&E work plan.

Step 10. Review and update the M&E work plan annually

The timing of the M&E work plan update should coincide with the governmental financial year and budgeting time frames so that the results of the national M&E work plan's costing can be included in government budgets. Make sure that the M&E unit of the agency coordinating the M&E work knows the budgeting cycles and time frames of all development partners, so that they can submit requests for M&E funding on time, too.

Deliverable: Reviewed and updated M&E work plan prior to development partners' budget deadlines.

Practical tips for National M&E Work Plan Development

a) **Align years in the work plan with government financial years:** If the government's financial year runs from April to March, then use this as the calendar period within the work plan (i.e., Year 1 is from April 2008 to March 2009, Year 2 is from April 2009 to March 2010, etc.).

b) **Describe activities with a focus on the person/organization responsible for action:** This multi-partner work plan includes the activities of many partners. Therefore, there are different ways in which the activities could be worded, depending on organizational perspective. It is better to describe an activity from the perspective of the organization performing the action. For example, consider the alternative perspectives in this example from a draft work plan:

Activity	Responsibility	Comments
Receive comments from M&E TWG members.	Head of M&E Unit	✖ The M&E Unit is not the lead agency responsible for actually completing the activity; there is a danger that, if the activity is described this way, when the TWG looks down the "Responsibility" column, it might overlook the fact that it needs to develop the comments.
Comment on draft document and submit it to the lead M&E agency or ministry.	M&E TWG	✓ The M&E TWG must perform the activity, so it is best to describe it from its perspective.

c) **How to decide on the level of planning detail:** When developing a work plan, it is important to plan an appropriate level of detail. GAMET's experience suggests that the best option is to plan in terms of activities, where an activity is defined (for this purpose) as a group of actions or tasks that can be realistically led by an individual in an organization, over a reasonable period of time, and for which specific costs can be assigned. A useful distinction is to think of activities as *whole activities*. Thus, the work plan should include descriptions of the highest level of activity that can be done by any individual organizational unit.

Consider the following examples:

Too aggregated	Reason
Implement a survey.	A survey consists of many steps involving many stakeholders, e.g., government needs to appoint the contractor; one agency or ministry manages the work; and the M&E TWG provides technical input and approval. Make sure that each activity can be effectively led by one stakeholder.
Too much detail (Tasks)	**Reason**
Phone Ministries to obtain names of field workers.	This is only one task within the *whole* activity of conducting a survey.

Appropriate level of detail (Activities)	Reason
Plan for program survey (specific ministry). Approve program survey TOR (M&E TWG). Procure services of contractor (govt. procurement dept). Conduct the survey (survey team). Analyze data and write report (survey team). Approve program survey report (M&E TWG).	Each task is a *whole task* for which one organization is responsible (see illustrative names in brackets, against every task).

d) **Use of software for planning:** The work planning itself can be done manually or using available spreadsheet or project management software. The advantage of using software is that it is easier to make changes (provided that the software is used appropriately). The disadvantage is that people need to know how to use, maintain and make changes to the software. Be careful before allowing a consultant to develop work plans using non-standard software that may be difficult to use or maintain after the consultant leaves. Project management software may be a better option than spreadsheet software, as it enables the user to determine the critical path, analyze activities, and present them in different ways.

e) When developing a new work plan (or updating the most recent one), **do not delete the completed activities of the previous year.** Only start a new work plan when the M&E plan's time period has expired.

f) **Divide the *responsibility* column of the work plan into two sections**, one for the lead agency and one for support agencies, with the lead agency usually being a government entity, given that government usually plays the coordinating/leading role).

g) **It is possible to use the activity-based costing (ABC) method** (see below) even if it has not previously been used. When using the ABC method, it is important to group the activity costs by type (e.g., salary costs, procurement costs, or consultancy costs), so that you can provide those cost categories (and actual costs per category) to the team developing your government's annual or multi-year budget (government budgets are not usually prepared on an activity basis but by type of activity.)

7. HowTo Guide C5-2: Costing a Multi-Year, Multi-Sectoral, and Multi-Level M&E Work Plan

Step 1: Select a costing methodology

Carefully consider which planning and costing methodology to use before embarking on this process. There are four possible methods for estimating the costs associated with implementing the M&E system:

1. **Conventional Cost Accounting (CCA):** This method focuses primarily on determining financial costs based on categories of direct and indirect costs associated with a particular product, service, or process (e.g., salary costs, procurement costs, or consultancy costs) as illustrated in the example below. CCA works well in organizations with regulated or standard business processes, such as government offices.

Salary costs of all teachers	$10,000
Maintenance costs of school buildings	$4,000
Textbooks	$8,000
Operational costs	$8,000
TOTAL	**$ 30,000**

2. **Mathematical modeling:** In mathematical modeling, formulas are used (derived from specific numerical inputs into a model) to calculate the anticipated costs of a program.

3. **Unit cost method:** In this method, the unit costs of specific functions or processes are determined and then multiplied by the number of people intended to receive the particular service. The unit cost method works well for repetitive processes where the unit costs are known. The GOALS model by the Futures Group is an example of a unit cost method. In the GOALS model, the estimated coverage of services is determined, the unit cost of providing the services is determined, and the two numbers are then multiplied by each other, as illustrated in the following example:

Service coverage.................................1000 children need to be in primary school

Unit cost of providing services...........$60.00 per year to provide primary education to a child

Calculation to determine total cost:
1000 children x $ 60.00/child = **$ 60,000** to provide primary education to 1000 children

4. **Activity-based costing (ABC):** Assigns costs to all the resources needed to carry out a particular business activity. It also accounts for indirect *soft* operating costs as illustrated in the example below. The result is a fuller financial picture than is usually produced with other accounting methods (e.g., standard costing), and provides a useful distinction between activities that add value and those that do not. ABC can be used to help pinpoint and control costs and increase the efficiency and effectiveness of organizations.

Activity	Duration	Cost
Train teachers.	3 weeks	50 teachers x 15 days x $15/day/person = **$11,250**
Purchase textbooks.	2 weeks	3 subjects x 1000 books/subject x $3/book = **$ 9,000**
Deliver textbooks.	1 week	1 truck x 550 kilometers (the truck has to drive to all the schools) x $1 per km = **$550**
Paint buildings.	4 weeks	20 schools x $400/school = **$8,000**
Pay for monthly office telephone costs.	Monthly	$100/month x 12 months = **$1,200**
		TOTAL COST = $30,000

A hybrid of ABC and unit costing works best for costing a multi-sectoral, multi-level and multi-year M&E work plan for the following reasons:

a) ABC has proved to work best where people's time is the main resource required for implementing activities.

b) Implementing an M&E system is not a constant, repetitive series of processes. There are significant annual variations depending on the priorities of the M&E system. The costs of implementing a national M&E system may vary significantly from year to year. For example, a large population-based survey might cost about as much as all other combined M&E activities in the budget that year.

c) The costs in the first two years of implementing an M&E work plan can be two or three times the annual cost of maintaining a functional M&E system. This may distort a mathematical or unit cost model.

d) CCA would not work in an environment where a significant part of the costs are for sub-contractors. CCA also does not allow the contribution made by development partners who provide direct M&E technical support to be costed.

e) There are significant differences in the types of costs associated with each of the 12 Components. Some components require funding in some but not in all years (e.g., surveys or research), while other components (e.g., M&E partnerships) require a constant, steady flow of funds.

Other costing methodologies may be selected for various reasons. These may include the need to simply determine a global M&E system estimate, in which case a detailed work plan is not needed and the GOALS model may be more applicable. Alternatively, if the M&E system has reached a level of maturity where there are only recurrent activities occurring for which unit costs can be accurately determined, the unit cost model might work better.

Deliverable: Selected costing methodology based on needs and context.

Step 2: Brainstorm a list of types of costs likely to be incurred in executing work plan activities

When brainstorming this list, do not repeat a series of activities in the work plan. Instead, try to list, from the work plan, all the different types of costs. When identifying the types of costs, write down the *unit* that needs to be costed (e.g., kilometer, daily rate per person, etc.). These units will then be costed and multiplied by the *number of units* to determine the total cost of an activity. Examples of cost types are:

- Annual salary costs of the M&E unit staff, per type of post (junior, middle and senior management)
- Road travel (per km)
- Air travel (per local/international flight)
- Local/international consultant rate — junior/senior (per person per day)
- Workshop attendance cost for non-residential workshop (per person per day)
- Workshop attendance cost for residential workshop (per person per night away from home)

In the example below, there are different *units of costing* for residential and non-residential workshops: for non-residential workshops, it is per person, per day; for residential workshops it is per person, per night away from home. The reason for this differential is the need to be able to count the number of nights for which per diem has to be paid in a residential workshop.

Deliverable: Brainstormed list of categories or types of costs for activities in the M&E work plan.

Step 3: Develop a unit cost table

Access existing unit cost tables. Find out from the government and from other development partners if they already have developed unit cost tables for some of the types of costs that have been brainstormed. For example, governments often have fixed rates for road travel, per diems, travel costs, maximum consulting rates to contractors, etc. There are also other unit costs that may be used. For example, some technical support agencies publish the typical costs of conducting, for example, sentinel surveillance, a DHS, etc. Also refer to previous unit cost tables (e.g., development partner unit cost tables). If the country has prepared a Global Fund proposal, it would have had to prepare a similar unit cost table that should be available. (Global Fund proposal costing uses ABC.)

Match the types of costs (as listed in Step 2) to the unit cost tables (collected from various sources of unit cost tables, such as the government, development partners, or your organization's financial department) and identify any units for which costs are not available. Start to compile the unit cost table, as follows:

Unit of costing	Unit cost	Source of unit cost
Annual salary costs of NCA M&E unit staff — junior, middle and senior management (per type of post)	500,000	Government records
Road travel (per km)	5.00	Government rate
Air travel (per local flight)	2,000	Global Fund rates
Air travel (per international flight)	8,000	Global Fund rates
Local consultant rate — junior (per person per day)	300	Estimates
Local consultant rate — senior (per person per day)	400	Estimates
International consultant rate (per person per day)	500	Government regulations
Workshop attendance fee for non-residential workshop (per person per day)	100	Calculation
Workshop attendance fee for residential workshop (per person per night away from home)	300	Calculation

NOTE: No currency is specified in the above table and the amounts are provided for illustrative purposes.

Deliverable: Unit cost table for the M&E work plan.

Step 4: Determine the number of units required of each activity

Now estimate the number of units required for each activity and write these down in the M&E work plan template, in the column headed *cost description* (see Annex A, M&E work plan). Do this for every year that the activity will take place, as a work plan is required that indicates costs on an annual basis. Perform the calculations and capture the cost totals for each activity in each year that the activity will take place. If the work plan runs over more than one year, have different costing columns for the different years.

When determining the number of units required and assigning costs to the activities, keep in mind that not all activities need to generate additional costs. Some activities could be combined or implemented simultaneously with other activities.

Deliverable: M&E work plan template containing estimated number of units required for each activity and cost totals for each activity per year.

Step 5: Determine total resources to be mobilized

Resource mobilization involves first understanding what resources are required. The amount and type of resources required for M&E are calculated as follows:

	Amount & type of resources needed (from Step 4)
LESS	Amount & type of resources already available and planned for (see below)
EQUAL	**Amount of resources to be mobilized** (from different sources)

To determine the resources available and those anticipated (i.e., those planned for or committed but not yet released), discussions with the heads of finance of the organizations or ministries involved may be necessary, as well as bilateral discussions with development partners to see where resources are available and which work plan activities each partner can support. Once this step is completed, the estimated total amount of funding required to be mobilized from domestic and international resources should be known.

Deliverable: Estimated amount of additional funding required from domestic and international resources.

Step 6: Assign available resources to specific activities and determine resource gaps, by activity

After completing a costed list of activities (Step 4), it is possible to assign available/planned-for resources (see Step 5) to individual activities. Note that available resources for an activity may differ from year to year. If the work plan time frame is longer than one year, ensure that there are additional columns for each year in the costing section of the work plan.

When assigning resources, make sure that these comply with development partner conditions (e.g., some types of development partner funding can only be used for certain activities). Government resources should be assigned to where they are most needed and to activities identified as priorities. Work plan activities should be prioritized to ensure that the most important and urgent activities are funded first from the resources already in hand.

Once available resources have been assigned, there may be resource gaps. Study these resource gaps to see if they can be grouped together logically (i.e., a group of activities relating to the conducting of a survey) and note these groups of activities.

Deliverable: Identified resource gaps for specific activities or groups of activities

Step 7: Mobilize and secure domestic and international resources

Identify domestic resources and potential international resources. It is essential to secure resource commitments in writing. The ERL contains information about how to write proposals and about resource mobilization.

Deliverable: Secured and written commitments from domestic and international resources.

Practical tips when costing

a) **Use of software for costing:** Costing can be done most effectively using spreadsheet software or project management software.

b) **Include the costing of national M&E work plans in the costing of national action plans:** This will help ensure that M&E is mainstreamed within the organization's planning and costing processes.

c) **Avoid getting too caught up in the process:** ABC is a tool to make costing easier but using it can become *all-consuming*.

d) **Do not underestimate the task:** Setting up and maintaining ABC can be daunting. Organizations may need to prepare a preliminary cost estimate to keep the exercise within realistic bounds. Nevertheless, a certain level of detail is essential. For example, time studies can be done to estimate the time taken for a new task or you can simply ask someone who has already done similar work to estimate how long it should take to complete an activity. Other methods may need less input but could be so subjective that the whole exercise is compromised. Moreover, they may not identify precisely where staffing is being used inefficiently (or vice-versa), or miss significant trends.

e) **Be careful of using the wrong tools:** If an organization tries to embark on ABC without the help of appropriate computer software, it may become a time-consuming waste of money and effort. ABC is a complex process and needs to be automated as much as possible and in the most appropriate ways.

f) **Maintain the system:** Like any other accounting method, ABC is an ongoing activity that needs constant updating as circumstances develop and change.

g) **Be prepared for and anticipate the implications:** ABC has the potential to turn the spotlight on any area of an organization and to expose its deficiencies, as well as to identify what works well. If an organization decides to adopt ABC, it needs to be ready to grasp the nettle and act on its findings in order to really reap the benefits.

8. HowTo Guide C5-3: Using the M&E Work Plan to Manage the M&E System

A multi-year, multi-sectoral and multi-level M&E work plan is usually bulky. To have value, it needs to be used, especially for the day-to-day management of the M&E system. Four main uses of the M&E work plan are described here but note that there may be others.

1. **Any organization with M&E responsibilities** can use the M&E work plan to develop a budget and work plan for its own M&E activities, as part of the organization's wider budgeting process, as follows:

    Step 1:   Extract the activities, time frames and costs for which the organization is responsible from the multi-year, multi-sectoral and multi-level work plan.

    Step 2:   Study these activities and break them down into a further level of detail (tasks).

    Step 3:   Cost these tasks in the same way that the M&E work plan was costed.

    Step 4:   Assign individuals in the organization (posts in the organogram) to complete specific tasks in the work plan.

    Step 5:   Determine available resources, consider zero-budget and concurrent activities where possible, as well as resource gaps.

    Step 6:   Mobilize additional resources for these tasks.

2. **The M&E unit can use the M&E work plan to manage the activities of their own unit** and staff on a daily, weekly, monthly or quarterly basis, as follows:

    Step 1:   Extract the activities, time frames, and costs for which the organization is responsible from the multi-year, multi-sectoral and multi-level work plan for a one-year period.

Step 2: Study these activities and break them down into a further level of detail (tasks).

Step 3: Cost these tasks in the same way that the M&E work plan was costed.

Step 4: Assign individuals in the organization (posts in the organogram) to complete specific tasks in the work plan.

Step 5: Expand the time frames in the work plan to create weekly time frames.

Step 6: Use the work plan every week to review activities done in the previous week and activities planned for the following week.

Step 7: Summarize the activities to be implemented every quarter and do quarterly reviews of these milestones.

3. **Any organization with M&E responsibilities can use the M&E work plan to update (if the plan is already in existence) or develop (if not yet in existence) the job descriptions of their staff with M&E responsibilities, as follows:**

Step 1: Extract the activities, time frames, and costs for which the organization is responsible from the multi-year, multi-sectoral and multi-level work plan for a one-year period.

Step 2: Study these activities and break them down into a further level of detail (tasks).

Step 3: Assign individuals in the organization (posts in the organogram) to complete specific tasks in the work plan.

Step 4: Update the job descriptions of the individual posts with the responsibilities assigned to them as per the work plan.

4. **The M&E TWG can use the M&E work plan to track the progress of developing/building the M&E system, as follows:**

Step 1: Extract the activities, time frames, and costs for the current financial year from the multi-year, multi-sectoral and multi-level work plan.

Step 2: Summarize activities to be implemented every quarter as quarterly milestones.

Step 3: At every quarterly M&E TWG meeting, review the milestones of the previous quarter, receive progress reports, and plan milestones for the next quarter.

9. Summary of Chapter 5 Knowledge and Skills

In this chapter, you learned how a costed, multi-sectoral and multi-leveled M&E work plan can be a useful tool for prioritizing, planning and coordinating activities related to the M&E system. You learned how the M&E work plan provides one common vision for all the stakeholders concerned so that each knows which approach and activities they will undertake within a single operational framework. You learned about theory and technical process steps that are required to develop and update a multi-year, multi-sectoral and multi-level M&E work plan and how to cost out that plan using the ABC costing method. Lastly, you learned four main uses of the M&E work plan for day-to-day management.

10. Learning Activities

LEARNING ACTIVITY 1: CRITIQUE AN EXISTING M&E WORK PLAN

Annex B contains the main findings of an M&E system assessment for the Ministry of Education in Goldstar State, the unit cost table, and a costed M&E work plan. Critique this work plan by looking at the following aspects:

- Do the activities in the work plan respond to the main M&E system challenges that came out of the M&E system assessment?
- Do the budget priorities reflect the main M&E system challenges?
- Are the budgeted amounts appropriate for the priorities for the M&E system?
- Is the work plan in a format that can also be used for management purposes (see Annex A for a template)?
- Are the activities worded correctly and pitched "at the right level" (see HowTo Guides for more details)?

Once you have critiqued the work plan, suggest ways in which the work plan could be improved (by adding or removing activities, changing columns, adding columns, and changing funding priorities).

LEARNING ACTIVITY 2: PRIORITIZATION OF ACTIVITIES IN THE M&E WORK PLAN

Assume that you have only been given G4,100,000 (G = Goldens, the Goldstar State currency) to implement the work plan that can be found in Annex B, in the next financial year (2010). Detailed budget forecasts for 2011 to 2013 are not yet available but it is unlikely to exceed G4,000,000 per year (in today's value).

- Improve the work plan by implementing the suggestions that you gave in Learning Activity 1. This means that you have to develop a NEW WORK

PLAN using the template in Annex A.

- When developing the new work plan, remember the budget limitation that you have been given for the financial year 2010, and for the following financial years. You will have to **prioritize** the most urgent and important activities, or find less costly ways of implementing the same set of activities, or scale down activities.

LEARNING ACTIVITY 3:   USE OF THE M&E WORK PLAN

How would you recommend to the Ministry of Education they use the work plan provided in Annex B (once improved) to manage their M&E system on a weekly basis?

LEARNING ACTIVITY 4:   M&E OF THE M&E SYSTEM

Given the M&E system challenges, what would be the one indicator that you would use to track the progress with the education M&E system over the next four years?

Annex A: M&E Work Plan Format

Activity Number and Description	Current Implementation Status	Time Frame for Implementation Q = Quarter				Documents required for activity to be completed	Responsible organization (1 lead organization, with supporting organizations)	Cost description	Cost calculation	Cost (for each year of implementation)	Funding Source
		Q1	Q2	Q3	Etc.						

Chapter 5

Annex B: M&E Work Plan Example for Learning Activity

Goldstar State Ministry of Education M&E System Assessment Results

Component of M&E System	Status of this Component of the M&E System at the national and district levels	Status of this Component of civil society M&E systems that provide data
1. **Organizational structures for M&E systems**	At the national level, the MOE has an M&E unit that is currently understaffed due to 2 resignations. Each of the 10 districts in Goldstar State has a MOE Data officer	A civil society capacity assessment showed significant shortages in M&E staff at civil society level.
2. **Human capacity for M&E systems**	MOE has undertaken some capacity building of CSOs in M&E, but not to a sufficient level or sufficient numbers.	A civil society capacity assessment showed significant shortages in M&E skills of civil society organizations that implement education programs.
3. **M&E partnerships**	A national M&E technical working group has been established. Both membership and meeting frequency have not been as initially planned and need improvement.	Some civil society organizations participate in national-level forums, and inter-civil society discussions take place through the national civil society forums, but partnerships around M&E between specific civil society organizations (CSOs) at the district and implementer level are not in place.
4. **M&E plans**	A national M&E plan is in place, and was reviewed in Oct 2008 subsequent to an M&E systems assessment that was undertaken.	A civil society capacity assessment has revealed that not all CSOs have M&E plans in place. Where plans are in place, the focus is on program monitoring data collection and reporting, and less on evaluation or the use of information to improve programming or planning.
5. **Costed M&E work plans**	A national M&E work plan has been developed but not yet validated and not yet costed.	A civil society capacity assessment showed that M&E is mostly not included in COS budgets. Where funds have been assigned, it has mostly been for program monitoring and supervision.
6. **Communications, and culture**	Communication and advocacy efforts have been limited and not coordinated, leading to a lack of clarity about the purpose and value of M&E within the education sector.	No specific focus from CSOs.
7. **Surveys**	National behavioral surveillance need more frequent measures and behavioral surveillance to be undertaken.	Not applicable — CSOs can access national surveys and surveillance, although there are challenges in data interpretation.

Component of M&E System	Status of this Component of the M&E System at the national and district levels	Status of this Component of civil society M&E systems that provide data
8. Routine monitoring	GOMSES (Goldstar State Output Monitoring System for Education Sector) has been developed as a system to collect all routine data about education services in the country. For data about education services delivered in community venues, forms have been designed for CSOs and government ministries to use. No financial monitoring data are collected.	Some CSOs have program monitoring systems in place, some do not, and some do not collect any data.
9. Databases	A national database exists, but it is different from the system used at the district level; data are also not captured in it.	Only large, urban-based, CSOs have information systems in place.
10. Supervision and data auditing	National guidelines have recently been developed but not yet implemented. No supervision data auditing is taking place.	Not in place — CSOs do not do supervision.
11. Evaluation and research	Education sector research is not yet coordinated in an efficient manner; data have not been disseminated appropriately about education sector research.	Extent of program evaluations by CSOs not known and not well communicated — but the sense is that these are limited in scope and frequency.
12. Data analysis, information dissemination and use	At the national level, the MOE produces an annual education sector progress report in which it reports all the latest indicator data available in the country, as well as other information relating to the status of the national education system. Two such reports have been prepared to date but the data in the reports have not been verified and the reports have only contained data from education censuses and surveys, not any other routine data from schools or district education offices. In the first report, MOE was able to report on 7 out of 21 indicators, and the next year, it was able to report on 14 out of 21 indicators.	Civil society organizations use data, to a limited extent. When data are used, it is primarily their own data and not in triangulation or working in partnership with other CSOs.

Goldstar State Ministry of Education Unit Cost Table for M&E Work Plan

Type of Cost	Unit Cost
Local consultant	G1,000 /day
Regional consultant	G2,000 / day
Printing costs	G150/average manual
Local flight	G4,000/flight
Regional flight	G10,000/flight
Workshop cost (non-residential)	G250 per person per day (all inclusive cost, including transport, venue costs, and the costs of printing materials)
Workshop cost (residential)	G650 per person per day (all inclusive cost, including transport, venue costs, accommodation and per diem costs, and the costs of printing materials)

Goldstar State Ministry of Education M&E Work Plan

	Activity	2010	2011	2012	2013	Total
1	Coordination & Roles of Stakeholders in the M&E system					
	Printing and dissemination of M&E plan	G20,000	G20,000	G20,000		G60,000
	Technical working group meetings and retreats	G35,000	G35,000	G35,000	G35,000	G140,000
	Joint Annual Review	G200,000	G200,000	G200,000	G200,000	G800,000
2	Routine Data Sources					
	Monthly collection of data at the district level	G250,000	G250,000	G250,000	G250,000	G1,000,000
3	Surveys & Surveillance as Periodic Data Sources					
	Modeling of exam outcomes	G30,000	G30,000	G30,000	G30,000	G120,000
	Vocational skills survey	G200,000		G200,000		G400,000
	Learning quality assessment	G100,000	G150,000	G150,000	G150,000	G550,000
4	Management of M&E System Data					
	Electronic Repository for M&E-related data and information both at national & district levels	G100,000		G100,000		G200,000
	GIS establishment	G50,000		G50,000		G100,000
	Establish linkages between relevant database	G20,000	G20,000	G20,000	G20,000	G80,000

	Activity	2010	2011	2012	2013	Total
5	**Dissemination and Use of Education Sector M&E System Data**					
	Disseminate annual education sector report	G100,000	G120,000	G120,000	G120,000	**G460,000**
	Country profile update on website	G100,000	G120,000	G120,000		**G340,000**
	Ad hoc information needs	G50,000		G50,000		**G100,000**
6	**Human Capacity Building**					
	Training of district data officers	G60,000	G60,000	G60,000	G60,000	**G240,000**
	Training of implementers	G300,000	G300,000	G300,000	G300,000	**G1,200,000**
	Post-graduate certificate/diploma	G7,000,000	G7,000,000	G7,000,000	G7,000,000	**G28,000,000**
	Training of Trainers	G500,000		G500,000		**G1,000,000**
	Mentorship and Coaching	G250,000	G250,000	G250,000	G250,000	**G1,000,000**
	Customize the existing M&E curriculum	G50,000		G50,000		**G100,000**
7	**Evaluation & Research**					
	Mobilize Research Fund	G300,000	G300,000	G300,000	G300,000	**G1,200,000**
	Maintain & update the research agenda	G250,000		G250,000		**G500,000**
	Update research database					
	Facilitate Revision of research ethnic guidelines	G50,000		G50,000		**G100,000**
	Training of researchers on HIV & AIDS techniques	G150,000	G150,000	G150,000	G150,000	**G600,000**
	Research ethnic working committee meetings	G20,000	G20,000	G20,000	G20,000	**G80,000**
8	**Data Audits & Supportive Supervision**					
	Development of data audit & verification guidelines & tools			G300,000		**G300,000**
	Development data verification plan			G20,000	G25,000	**G45,000**
	Conduct data audit and verification visits & spot-checks	G130,000	G130,000	G130,000	G130,000	**G520,000**
9	**NAC Monitoring and Evaluation Human Resources**					
	M&E Unit salaries	G2,600,000	G2,900,000	G3,200,000	3,500,000	**G12,200,000**

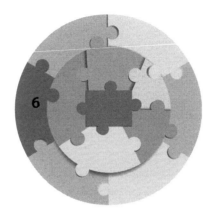

Chapter 6
Advocacy, Communication, and Culture for Monitoring and Evaluation

Chapter Aim

The aim of this chapter is to enable you to plan, develop and manage an advocacy and communication strategy for your organization or country's M&E system. The purpose of an advocacy and communication strategy is to help ensure knowledge of and commitment to M&E and the M&E system among policy-makers, program managers, program staff and other stakeholders.

Chapter Knowledge and Skills

a) Explain to someone else the difference between advocacy and communication

b) Know why advocacy and communications for M&E are important

c) Know how advocacy and communications can contribute substantially to creating a positive culture for M&E in your organization

d) Plan and manage the advocacy and communication plan for your country's M&E system

e) Be familiar with different communication strategies and channels

Before You Begin…

Take a few minutes to read through the questions below. You may find it helpful to write down your answers. As you work through the chapter, compare your answers to the views of the authors.

- What is the difference between advocacy and communications?
- Why should we undertake advocacy for M&E work?
- Why is it so important to try and see things from the point of view of the person/people to whom your advocacy is directed?
- Who are the M&E champions in your organization?
- What should be in an M&E advocacy and communications strategy?
- How do you develop an M&E advocacy and communications plan for your organization?
- What are the *carrots and sticks* for M&E to become functional in an organization?

These questions remind us that, although organizations may have advocacy and communication strategies for various programs, many do not have advocacy and communication strategies for monitoring and evaluation. This chapter will teach you how to develop and implement an M&E advocacy and communications plan for your organization.

Component 6: Advocacy, Communication, and Culture for M&E Systems

1. Introduction

> *"If you think you're too small to have an impact,*
> *try going to sleep with a mosquito."*

Anita Roddick

Many organizations have developed advocacy and communications strategies to define how they plan to communicate messages about their programs to the general public and to other, more specific target audiences. However, not many of these strategies refer to the need to communicate about, and advocate for, monitoring and evaluation. Advocacy, communication and culture for M&E systems comprise the last component of the *Planning, Partnerships and People* ring of the 12 Components of a functional M&E system. It was included in this ring because a positive culture for M&E is an essential and important part of having an enabling environment for your organization's M&E system in place.

How this Chapter is organized: The chapter on Component 6 begins with background and definitions relating to the concepts of advocacy, communication and culture (Section 2). The desired result for this chapter is in Section 3. Why are advocacy and communication important for M&E? The benefits of advocacy and communication are listed as well as important questions and issues to ponder when implementing processes for advocacy and communication (Sections 4 and 5). Section 6 offers some ideas for making the organization's culture more positive for M&E. Section 7 outlines steps for developing and implementing a national advocacy and communication plan for M&E. The chapter ends with a summary of lessons learned (Section 8), and a practical exercise to cement what you should have learned in the chapter (Section 9).

2. Background Information & Definitions

1. **Advocacy:** The act of arguing on behalf of something, such as a cause, idea, or policy. Advocacy is intended to educate, sensitize, influence and change opinion. Advocacy can motivate action, for example, by creating and implementing a favorable policy. Advocacy requires passion and commitment to advance the cause or interest of another. It motivates the advocate to take the lead and do more than what is required routinely. The advocate should have a sense of urgency and challenge the status quo.

2. **Communication:** A process of exchanging information using various means or media. Good communication is characterized by a clear purpose; content; reliable source; appealing form; effective transmission channel; defined or targeted receivers; and is effectively delivered to the intended recipient.

3. **M&E culture:** Shared set of values, conventions, or social practices about M&E. A positive M&E culture is where M&E is accepted, welcomed, encouraged and valued by all members of the team as an essential part of achieving implementation success.

4. **Advocacy and communications to create a positive M&E culture:** The exchange of information about M&E to change attitudes, actions, perceptions and behavior relating to M&E. By influencing people, organizations, systems and structures at different levels, M&E advocacy and communication efforts create a shared set of positive values about the importance and value of M&E.

3. Results to Be Achieved When Implementing This Component

Long-term result: Knowledge of, and commitment to, M&E and the M&E system among policy-makers, program managers, program staff, and other stakeholders.

Short- and medium-term results:

- M&E communication and advocacy plan, as part of the national communication strategy (if it exists). The plan should identify the objectives of the advocacy and communications efforts, the target audiences, key messages to be communicated, and the communication and advocacy channels.

- M&E reflected in the planning and policies of the national program being monitored.

- M&E champions among high-level officials for endorsement of M&E actions. *An M&E champion* is usually a senior decision-maker or person of influence who is positive about, and fully values and understands the benefits of using information for decision making. An M&E champion would speak, act and write on behalf of those responsible for managing the program's M&E to promote, protect and defend the creation of a functional M&E system.

- Targeted, structured and planned M&E advocacy activities.

- M&E materials for different audiences to communicate key M&E messages (as defined in the M&E advocacy and communications plan) (see Annex A for examples of M&E advocacy and communications materials).

4. Benefits of Advocacy and Communication for an M&E System

Effective advocacy and communication for M&E are critically important for the following reasons:

1. **Help to overcome misconceptions and knowledge gaps:** Advocacy and communications are effective tools to overcome any misconceptions or lack of information about M&E among senior program managers and decision and policy-makers who often have very little understanding of the subject.

2. **Help to mainstream monitoring and evaluation as one of the organization's main functions:** This helps to establish a positive culture of M&E within the organization. M&E is a crosscutting issue and requires a standard question to be asked whenever any aspect of the program is discussed: "How does this link with, or affect our M&E system or, can our M&E system contribute to it?"

3. **Help to influence policies and strategies so that they include adequate provision for M&E:** On a political level, advocacy can be used to incorporate requirements for monitoring and evaluation into national laws, policies and strategies. Examples include: the Statistics Act; the NGO Registration Act; the Education Act; the National HIV Policy and Strategy; or the National Poverty Reduction Strategy. Obtaining political support to promote transparency and accountability around any given program will help support and make it more effective.

4. **Help to convince and encourage organizations and individuals to carry out their M&E functions.** On an organizational and personal level, strategic communication can play a large role in making individuals more positive about M&E, as well as their participation in M&E systems.

5. **Help to create demand for data.** If policy and decision-makers demand data (a demand to which advocacy and communication efforts contribute), the development and sustainability of an M&E system is more likely to be a priority, and to be allocated sufficient resources.

6. **Help to reduce double-reporting systems.** If all stakeholders are clear about the purpose, focus and outputs of the M&E system, everyone would want to contribute to the system and reporting requirements that may inadvertently lead to double reporting, could be reduced.

5. Implementation Issues Related to Advocacy, Communication, and Culture

5.1. Why is it so important to think about the point of view, needs, and interests of the person/people to whom your advocacy is directed?

To motivate someone to be positive about M&E and support the M&E system, they need to see M&E as relevant and valuable to them, their jobs or team. If you can see M&E from their perspective, and explain how M&E could help them do their job better, or achieve their goals, you are much more likely to convince them of its value. M&E has a clear purpose to help a program or organization be more successful, or to identify and resolve problems. So, for example, by explaining to someone how M&E could help to address a challenge they are facing, it becomes relevant and more compelling. Effective advocacy for M&E makes M&E *real* and relevant to the target audience. It explains M&E from that person's perspective rather than expecting people to be convinced by an M&E expert's passion or technical information.

5.2. Who should lead advocacy and communications efforts?

For government M&E systems, the M&E units of national ministries or agencies and M&E TWG members should all communicate about the M&E system. Advocacy efforts to influence and motivate senior decision-makers about the M&E system should be coordinated by the organization with primary responsibility for the M&E system, and advocacy efforts directed at leaders at the sub-national level should be coordinated by the LGAs. Specific ministries should be responsible for all communication and advocacy efforts that relate to

M&E for the sector relevant to each ministry. For M&E systems of individual organizations, advocacy and communications about M&E can be led by any person in the organization who is positive and knowledgeable about M&E.

5.3. Typical M&E issues for communication and advocacy

M&E issues to be communicated about depend on the challenges facing the M&E system. Some examples of key messages could be:

- Monitoring and evaluation is not a policing function. It is useful and indeed essential for each stakeholder involved in the program (use specific examples that are relevant to your audience to reinforce this message).

- Because M&E can help the program to improve and achieve its results, staff and funding should be dedicated to it. The recommended level is 7–10% of program funding.

- M&E systems create data and information that make it possible to recognize and correct problems, and encourage and reward success.

- The information that an M&E system provides enables sound decisions to be made.

- The agency/ministry/organization responsible for coordinating a program is also responsible for monitoring and evaluating it.

- Especially when there are many implementers of a program, they need to report data regularly to enable the coordinating agency to fulfill its role.

- With an M&E system in place, stakeholders should expect and demand progress reports.

- Capacity needs to be built for a monitoring and evaluation system to be successful.

- Funders (national and international) want to know what results are being achieved.

5.4. To whom should communications and advocacy efforts be directed?

The target audiences depend on the messages to be conveyed and who is opposed to M&E in the organization and beyond. The target audiences are likely to include both internal staff (i.e., from your organization) and other persons external to the organization:

- Internal target audiences for M&E advocacy and communications
  - Your organization's managers
  - Your colleagues
- External target audiences for M&E advocacy and communications
  - Senior management in national ministries

- Ministry program staff
- Cabinet ministers, principal secretaries and other heads of government departments
- Local assembly chief executives
- Heads of civil society organizations and heads of private sector organizations
- Academic and research institutions
- Technical and program staff of organizations that implement program services
- Funders of programs
- Beneficiaries of program services (i.e., target groups who receive services)
- The media

5.5. What types of communication channels work best?

There is no single communication channel that works best for advocacy and communications efforts. Creating a positive culture for M&E will take time, diplomacy, effort, and a well-tuned understanding of why certain people behave the way that they do or hold certain opinions when it comes to M&E. M&E advocacy and communications are definitely not *one size fits all*. To give you an idea of your range of options, the main types of communication channels are listed as follows:

- **Personal channels:** Identify, equip and support an *M&E champion* (e.g., a high-level official who can promote M&E among his or her peers); conduct strategic meetings with different stakeholders (e.g., heads of all umbrella organizations); arrange business breakfasts with key stakeholders and the media to help the media become M&E *literate*. For example, training the media in M&E would help ensure that they are able to interpret and report on M&E results.

- **Printed materials:** Information packs about the M&E system; brochures on the program monitoring system; and key aspect reminders on summary postcards.

- **Standard PowerPoint presentations:** These should summarize the M&E system and provide key speaker notes, so that persons involved in M&E can confidently speak and explain the program's M&E system to others.

- **Radio messages:** Radio messages could remind program implementers to submit their program monitoring forms, affirm the importance of doing this and also remind the beneficiaries of services to request information about the program from their LGAs.

5.6. What advocacy techniques work best?

Advocacy techniques vary from low to high pressure approaches. Advocacy messages should be organized and presented in a succinct and clear manner, and communicated through different channels, ranging from print and electronic to verbal *folk media*. Printed messages may use media like newspapers, books, magazines, brochures, posters, fliers, banners, printed caps or tee-shirts. Electronic messages may be channeled through email, internet, radio, television, video, and cell phones. *Folk media* can communicate verbally through meetings, drama, songs, dances and other social events. There is no simple rule for what will work best; it depends on the message and the audience.

5.7. Implementing M&E advocacy and communications plans

Assign the responsibility of implementing the advocacy and communications plan to someone (or a small team) who understands the M&E system and its value and who can communicate clearly. Advocacy activities need to be reflected in costed annual implementation work plans and M&E work plans.

To influence an organization other than your own, it is often a good idea to use trusted colleagues in that organization to do the advocacy on your behalf.

5.8. Monitoring, evaluating and reporting on advocacy and communication for M&E

Advocacy work is normally monitored and reported on within the framework and requirements of the M&E system. Where an M&E system does not exist, then a simplified plan to monitor, evaluate and report on the advocacy work is developed and implemented.

6. HowTo Guide C6-1: Creating a Supportive Organizational Culture and M&E Leadership

An organization's culture can embrace *managing for results*, or can be ambivalent, or even actively resist such efforts. The result may be that employees of the organization support, passively resist or openly undermine the M&E system set up to measure results that the organization does (or does not) achieve.

Who creates an organization's culture? How, and by whom, can the organizational culture be changed? This *HowTo Guide* provides suggestions on how to influence the organizational culture to be positive towards *managing for results*. Within such an organizational culture, employees would support, strengthen and keep the M&E system functional and they would value data from the organization's M&E system because it would help them plan more accurately, better manage, and improve their organization's performance.

Step 1: Assess the organization's readiness to manage for results and the organization's overall culture

Before implementing efforts to address potential weaknesses in the organization's culture, the organization's readiness to *manage for results* needs to be assessed. This assessment determines the organization's political willingness to monitor and evaluate its goals and develop a performance-based framework. It will also help to distill the underlying nuances and complexities of the environment in which the M&E system should function, as it is often this environment that makes M&E systems succeed or fail (Kusek and Rist, 2005).

A readiness assessment does not necessarily entail a formal or even public assessment report but rather a team that asks and finds answers to the following key questions (Kusek and Rist, 2005):

- What potential pressures are encouraging the need for the M&E system within the organization and why?
- Who is the advocate for an M&E system?
- What is motivating the champion to support the M&E effort?
- Who will own the system?
- Who will benefit from the system?
- How much information is really required?
- How will the system directly support better resource allocation and the achievement of program goals?
- How will the organization, the champions, and the staff react to negative information generated by the M&E system?
- Where does capacity exist to support a results-based M&E system?
- How will the M&E system link project, program, sector and national goals? This last question is only applicable if the focus is on a national M&E system.

The answers to these questions will help guide the process of changing the organizational culture to support and actively work towards making and keeping the M&E system functional. You can read more about doing readiness assessments in Chapter 1 of Kusek and Rist's book, *"Ten Steps to a Results-Based Monitoring and Evaluation System."* (Also available online in Spanish, French and Vietnamese.)

Deliverables: Readiness assessment completed, organization's culture understood.

Step 2: Identify potential M&E resistors in the organization

A readiness assessment helps identify potential champions of the M&E system. One should also identify those who may passively resist or be opposed to the M&E system. How are these champions and resistors relevant to an organization's culture with regard to managing for results? They are not necessarily the leaders/managers in an organization, but are often vocally opposed or supportive of monitoring and evaluation efforts. Vocal or outspoken people can have a great influence over the perceptions and attitudes of other employees about the organization. Employee attitudes drive their behavior related to M&E processes.

If a leader or manager of an organization champions M&E, it will be reflected in the organization's planning and management systems and processes. If the manager is negative about M&E or does not clearly understand its benefits in enabling him/her to manage the organization better, it will be reflected in funding levels for M&E; whether there are dedicated M&E posts in the organizational structure; and in the level of attention that M&E receives in the day-to-day running of the organization.

Champions and resistors are not only found at the managerial level. Other employees could also fall into one of these categories and influence the attitudes of those around them with regard to monitoring and evaluating the goals of the organization (positive, negative, or ambivalent).

If possible, it is important to try to identify why the resistors feel the way that they do about M&E. A relaxed conversation, perhaps over a cup of coffee outside of the regular office space, could encourage a resistor to open up and talk freely about his/her concerns without being defensive or attacking.

Deliverable: Resistors (counter-reformers) identified as well as what drives them.

Step 3: Develop and implement strategies to influence the organizational culture

To influence the organizational culture, one needs to influence the champions and resistors to help change the perceptions and attitudes of employees around them. Changes in organizational culture take time to implement. It is a process that is implemented over time and cannot be fixed in a one-off workshop.

Table C6-1 suggests some practical strategies that leaders and subordinates can implement to create a supportive culture for M&E.

Chapter 6

Table C6-1: Suggested Actions by Subordinates and Leaders to Create a Supportive M&E Culture in an Organization

Suggested actions by subordinates
• Organize study tours for your organization leaders to experience the positive benefits of the M&E system themselves
• Arrange opportunities for leaders to interact with leaders of other organizations that have already incorporated M&E
• Find an M&E champion at senior level
• Deliver M&E products when planned so that senior management can rely on them
• Actively search for advocacy opportunities
• Remove *M&E jargon* from M&E documents circulated to senior management
• Be proactive by finding and actively pursuing opportunities to mainstream M&E into the organization's operations and help other units see the benefits (not burdens) of the M&E system for them
• Fulfill all M&E functions so that senior management can use the M&E unit as an example to other employees

Suggested actions by leaders
• Create a reliable, robust and attractive vision for the future of the M&E system that people will respect and believe in
• Communicate your M&E vision
• Learn about M&E and the M&E system so that you feel confident to advocate for the system, and so that the employees respect your views and statements on M&E
• Motivate your M&E staff to work hard and reward their performance
• Become a data user yourself by asking for and demanding information products (reports, data) when decisions are made about future plans (in a firm but fair way)
• Be an example by making decisions based on data even if they are difficult decisions
• Help M&E staff build trusting relationships with colleagues to mainstream M&E into all the functions of the organization
• Understand and use group dynamics to ensure that people who do not comply with M&E system requirements are the exception and not the rule

Deliverable: Strategies for changes in organizational culture implemented.

7. HowTo Guide C6-2: Developing and Implementing an M&E Advocacy and Communication Plan

These steps follow a results-based approach to M&E-related advocacy and communications. They start with understanding the advocacy and communications challenges, and defining communications objectives before deciding on the target audiences you need to communicate with and what to say to them about M&E.

It is important to remember that advocacy and communication is an incremental process that often takes a long time (years) to accomplish and succeed fully. These efforts take place in a dynamic and ever changing environment and external factors can affect whether or not you are able to achieve your advocacy and communications objectives (Constella Futures, not dated).

Step 1: Understand the results that you want to achieve with your M&E advocacy and communications efforts

List all the challenges that have a negative effect on your organization's M&E system. You may use the results of a recent M&E systems assessment, if they are available, or other relevant assessments. (If there is no recent assessment, there is no need to do a full assessment.)

From this list of M&E challenges, identify all those that can be addressed, even in part, through M&E advocacy and communications. For each of these challenges, write down the negative impacts that not addressing the challenge has on the M&E system and on the program being monitored and evaluated. Then arrange the list of challenges in order, from the greatest to the smallest negative impact.

It is important to understand the policy context in which you are working that could impact on the M&E system: e.g., Is the director about to be replaced, is an election on its way that may bring in a new Minister of Health?

Think what the situation will look like when the challenge has been addressed (e.g., "managers are positive about M&E and ask for M&E reports"). Develop M&E advocacy and communication objective(s). Remember that objectives for M&E-related advocacy and communications are not objectives to do with data use and dissemination of information but rather with a positive M&E culture in the organization.

Once objectives have been defined, the next step is how to realize the outcomes (intermediate outcomes). What activities can you implement to achieve these intermediate outcomes? (outputs). Table C6-2 shows an example of this kind of logical approach for an M&E advocacy effort.

Table C6-2:   Example of Results Logic/Chain for Your M&E Advocacy and Communications Efforts

Long-term outcome	Intermediate outcomes	Outputs
M&E culture in organization is supportive of M&E efforts	M&E positions in the organization are included in the organogram of the organization	• 5 meetings about benefits of M&E held • Report on organizational structure design with M&E shared with HR manager
	M&E is a standard item on the agenda of monthly meetings	• Office manager briefed on M&E system • Office manager aware of the benefits of M&E for the organization

Deliverables: List of main challenges affecting the country's M&E system that can be addressed, even in part, through advocacy and communications efforts, in order from greatest to smallest negative impact, results logic for your M&E advocacy and communications efforts.

Step 2:   Identify the target audiences

Based on the advocacy and communication objective(s) defined in Step 1, identify the individuals and groups that need to be influenced in order to achieve the advocacy and communications objectives. The target audiences may include individuals (e.g., Prime Minister); organizations (e.g., civil society organizations or LGAs); or sub-populations (e.g., M&E officers of all organizations).

Deliverable: List of individuals and organizations to be targeted with advocacy and communications efforts.

Step 3:   Identify your allies and form a team of advocates with specific roles and responsibilities

List the anticipated benefits of fully realizing the advocacy and communication objectives. List organizations, groups or individuals who would directly benefit or be positive if the advocacy and communication objectives were realized. This group would constitute key allies and communicators. Invite these allies to form a team of advocates and ask each ally to list the strengths and benefits they bring to the advocacy work. List all the key roles and responsibilities that must be allocated. Assist each of these allies to identify their strategic niche and commit to their role and responsibilities.

Making Monitoring and Evaluation Systems Work

Deliverable: Team of identified advocates with specific roles and responsibilities.

Step 4:   Lead advocates in agreeing on the key advocacy and communication messages

Review and discuss the M&E-related communications and advocacy objectives (see Step 2). With your team of advocates, brainstorm what you want to communicate to targeted decision-makers. Agree on the key messages which you need to communicate to each of the target audiences. The messages that will get most attention are those most relevant to the audience that address their needs, problems, challenges and goals. What is likely to be most important to each audience? How could M&E help them? What specific benefits could the M&E system deliver for that audience?

Table C6-3 provides examples of advocacy and communications messages for different target audiences. As you can see from the example, a table that links each target audience to specific messages is very useful for developing a strategic and focused approach to M&E-related advocacy and communications.

Table C6-3:   Example of Target Audiences and Communications Messages (follows-on from the example in Table C6-2)

Target audiences	Key message
CEO	M&E can help the organization perform better
Implementers	M&E provides data on results and achievements that helps justify continued funding

Deliverable: Agreement on key messages to be communicated to different target audiences.

Step 5:   Guide advocates in selecting the advocacy approaches and communication channels

Use different resources to draft a list of possible advocacy and communications techniques and channels to be used. Supplement this list through a brainstorming session in which you creatively explore options for advocacy and communications. This is an ideal opportunity to consider zero budget options. For example, consider where M&E advocacy and communications activities and messages could be added to existing communications, training, information sharing or capacity building opportunities without costing more money. Also, remember that individual one-on-one meetings are important and need not be expensive.

Given that M&E is a cross-cutting issue and tool, there are often many ways in which M&E could be *mainstreamed* into the organization's operations. If, for example, another unit is conducting a workshop, the M&E team could be given a few minutes at the start of the workshop to communicate important M&E information to the participants. Table C6-4 provides examples of communications channels to reach different target audiences.

Table C6-4: **Example of Communications Channels for Different Target Audiences (follow-on from example provided in Table C6-2)**

Target audiences	Key messages	Advocacy approaches / Communications channels
CEO	M&E can help the organization perform better	Breakfast with CEO of a company that already has full-time M&E staff
Implementers	M&E provides data on results and achievements that helps justify continued funding	Work-planning meetings, technical workshops, memo on new source of funding

Deliverable: List of possible advocacy approaches and communication channels.

Step 6: Design communications materials

Identify people who are good at developing advocacy and communication messages. Facilitate their working with the advocates to analyze the advocacy messages and brainstorm ideas for communication materials. Schedule sufficient time for the experts to develop the communication materials. Pre-test the communication materials on a selected and suitable audience. Finalize the communication materials. See Annex A for sample advocacy and communications materials.

Deliverable: A plan to facilitate and support identified advocates in analyzing advocacy messages, designing materials, pre-testing the materials on the target audience and finalizing them.

Step 7: Design a plan to monitor and evaluate advocacy and communications efforts

It is important to think about evaluating advocacy and communications efforts. To evaluate, you need to determine how you will evaluate the advocacy and communications objective/outcome that you have set and how you will monitor the implementation of your efforts.

However, it is important to remember that because changes as a result of advocacy and communications can take a long time to achieve, "it is as important to be able to measure progress towards the desired goal, the incremental successes of your efforts over time, as it is to assess whether you actually achieve the goal" (Constella Future, not dated). In addition, advocacy efforts, objectives and the environment in which these efforts take place frequently changes (Weiss, 2007).

"There are many ways to evaluate the effectiveness of an advocacy effort, from simple tracking systems to rigorous research conducted by outside professionals. The type of evaluation should be chosen by the goals and objectives and by the resources available" (Shannon, 1998). Coffman further suggests that evaluating advocacy efforts requires that one understand and implement the following principles (Coffman, 2007):

a) **Provide real-time information to the advocacy team:** Because of the changing environment, it is essential to get M&E information about advocacy efforts collected, analyzed and communicated quickly. This may imply more frequent reporting and reviews than for other projects.

b) **Give interim results the respect they deserve:** It is important to assess progress with advocacy efforts by looking at short-term outputs and outcomes, as well as long-term impacts.

c) **Choose simple evaluations and be creative:** Choose simple ways to evaluate that do not complicate advocacy efforts and find creative, innovative ways to evaluate advocacy efforts.

Deliverable: A jointly designed plan to monitor and evaluate the advocacy and communications strategies and their implementation within the framework of the M&E system.

Step 8: Support advocates in developing an advocacy work plan and budget

Provide support for advocates who produce a specific work plan that shows what, how, and when identified activities will be carried out. Guide them in developing a budget for implementing the work plan and divide and agree roles and responsibilities within the work plan to be implemented by the advocates.

Deliverable: Advocacy work plan and budget as part of the M&E work plan and budget. (See Component 5 for more information about an M&E work plan and budget for the organization's M&E system.).

Step 9: Work with advocates to mobilize resources and implement the advocacy work plan

Assign responsibilities for mobilizing resources to finance work plan activities, among the advocates. For those activities that are not financed, list possible sources to address the funding gaps. Approach these possible funding sources and appeal to them to support the activity.

Deliverable: Mobilization of resources to enable implementation of the advocacy work plan.

Step 10: Organize the advocates to monitor, evaluate and report on the advocacy work

Often remind advocates of their responsibilities to monitor and evaluate their advocacy work and to report on their efforts. Ensure, as far as possible, that their M&E reports are used to influence and change policies accordingly.

Deliverable: Plan to organize advocates for monitoring, evaluating and reporting their work and M&E findings.

For reflection 2:

Reflect on the advocacy and communication efforts for M&E that exists within your organization for a moment. Why is it important to undertake advocacy for M&E work? What are some M&E challenges within your organization and how may advocacy and communication strategies address these challenges? How do you envision an effective advocacy and communications strategy? How would you implement the above steps in your organization?

---

8. Summary of Chapter 6 Knowledge and Skills

In this chapter, you learned about the importance of advocacy and communication in creating a positive M&E culture as well as how an advocacy and communication strategy can help to ensure that all stakeholders (national and local policy-makers, program managers, program staff and others) have knowledge of and commitment to M&E and the M&E system. You learned about the benefits of advocacy and communication; specifically how they help to overcome miscommunication, assist in influencing program policies and strategies as well as assist organizations to carry out their M&E functions. Last but not least, you learned about theory and technical process steps that are required to develop and implement an M&E advocacy and communication plan. You also learned that advocacy efforts need to be evaluated and that M&E advocacy and communications efforts are approached differently than for other types of programs.

9. Learning Activities

Chapter 6 is all about communications and advocacy for the M&E system, so that managers and senior decision makers can get excited about, supportive of, and use data when making their decisions.

LEARNING ACTIVITY 1:   PREPARE ADVOCACY AND COMMUNICATIONS MATERIALS

a)   Write a speech of 10 minutes for your organization's Executive Chairperson to motivate for a 200% increase in M&E funding, and mechanisms through which these resources can be secured. When you develop this speech, keep in mind the importance of the message you are trying to convey and how best this message can be expressed so that the chairperson will clearly understand what is needed (read more about this in Annex B).

b)   Develop a brochure about the national M&E system, specifically for the civil society organizations that will attend a national civil society conference.

LEARNING ACTIVITY 2: INCENTIVES FOR M&E SYSTEMS

Write down all the *carrot* incentives (attractive, pleasant incentives) and *stick* incentives (not-so-pleasant, more punitive type incentives) that you could develop for the M&E system in your organization.

Annex A: Examples of Advocacy and Communications Materials for M&E Systems

Example from Swaziland: Posters to Summarize the Routine HIV Data Flow Process (SHAPMoS = Swaziland's HIV and AIDS Program Monitoring System) and who is involved in it

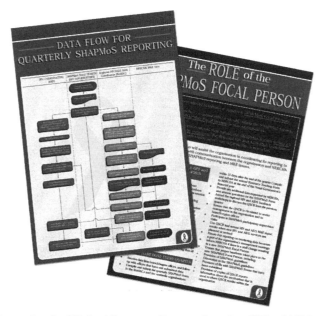

Source: Swaziland National Emergency Response Council on HIV and AIDS

Example from Swaziland: brochure to explain the routine HIV data collection system

Source: Swaziland National Emergency Response Council on HIV and AIDS

Example from Zanzibar: M&E brochure in the vernacular (kiSwahili) to increase levels of understanding

FRONT OF BROCHURE

8 Vipi taasisi yako itafaidika kutokana na Mfumo wa Ufuatiliaji na tathmini"?

Zipo faida nyingi itakazopata taasisi yako ikishiriki kutekeleza Mfumo huu:

- Itaweza kupanga mipango madhubuti ya baadae na kupanga vizuri rasilimali za taasisi.
- Itatambulika na kuingizwa katika mipango ya kuzijengea uwezo taasisi zinazopambana na UKIMWI
- Utaisaidia kutumia vyema takwimu zilizopo kuibua mapungufu na kuimarisha huduma.
- Itasaidiwa kuimarisha au kuweka "utaratibu wa ndani wa taasisi wa ufuatiliaji na tathmini"
- Itapata ushaumu juu ya masuala ya ufuatiliaji na tathmini na hivyo kuinua uwezo wa taasisi husika
- Itaimarisha mawasiliano baina ya Tume ya UKIMWI na wadau wengine na kujenga mahusiano yatakayosaidia kuinua viwango vya utekelezaji.

9 Hitimisho

Ili Mfumo wa Ufuatiliaji na Tathmini uweze kufanyakazi unategemea sana mashirikiano ya wetekelezaji wote wa shughuli za UKIMWI nchini. Kila mmoja wetu akumbuke kutimiza wajibu wake. Mfumo huu ni kwa manufaa yako na taifa lako. Piga vita UKIMWI kwa kutoa taarifa za taasisi yako kila baada ya miezi mitatu (robo mwaka).

Kwa taarifa zaidi wasiliana na:-

Mkurugenzi Mtendaji
Tume ya UKIMWI Zanzibar
P O. Box 2820
ZANZIBAR, Tanzania
Tel: (+255) (0)24-223 1152
Fax: (+256) (0)24-223 1152
Email: zac@zanlink.com
Website: www.zacaids.com

4

Mfumo Wa Taifa Wa Ufuatiliaji Na Tathmini Kwa Shughuli Za UKIMWI Zanzibar

1 Utangulizi

Katika kupambana na UKIMWI Zanzibar, jitihada imefanyika ili kuzishirikisha taasisi zote katika jamii kuelekeza nguvu zao katika mapambano katika ngazi zote. Hivi sasa kuna taasisi nyingi zinazopambana na UKIMWI nchini. Tume ya UKIMWI Zanzibar imepewa jukumu la kuratibu, kufuatilia na kutathmini harakati zote za kitaifa za kupambana na UKIMWI. Hivyo, Tume ya UKIMWI Zanzibar kwa kushirikiana na wadau wote imelayarisha Mfumo wa Taifa we Ufuatiliaji na Tathmini kwa shughuli za UKIMWI Zanzibar.

2 Nini Mfumo wa Taifa wa Ufuatiliaji na Tathmini kwa shughuli za UKIMWI Zanzibar?

Mfumo wa Taifa wa Ufuatiliaji na Tathmini kwa shughuli za UKIMWI Zanzibar ni utaratibumaalum ulioandaliwa na unaoruhusa mtirinko mzuri wa taarifa kutoka kwa wadau wote walioko ngazi ya chini (jamii) hadi ya taifa. Taarifa hizo zitakusanywa, zitachambuliwa, zitahifadhiwa nakusambazwe kwa ajili ya kutathmini muelekeo na utekelezaji (maendeleo) ya harakati za taifa za kupambana na UKIMWI zenye kulenga maeneo yafuatayo: Kukinga masambukizo ya virusi vya UKIMWI na UKIMWI, kukabiliana na athari zinazotokana na UKIMWI, utafutaji rasilimali, ufuatiliaji na tathmini. Mfumo huu umeelezwa kwa ufasaha katika kitabu maalum kinachoitwa" Zanzibar National Multi sectoral HIV Monitoring and Evaluation System: Operational Framework, 2005/06 - 2008/09.

BACK OF BROCHURE

3 Kwa nini tunahitaji mfumo wa ufuatiliaji?

- Ili Tume ya UKIMWI Zanzibar iweze kutekeleza vyema majukumu yake, inahitaji muongozo unaofahamika ambao unaelezea jinsi ya kukusanya taarifa za UKIMWI kutoka kwa wadau wote wanaohusika na kazi za kupambana na UKIMWI hapa Zanzibar.
- Ni muhimu kufahamu na kutathmini mafaniko yanayopatikana na matatizo yanayojitokeza katika kupambana na UKIMWI katika taifa.
- Itapelekea kupatikana kwa taarifa zilizosahihi zitakazochambuliwa na kutoa picha inayoonesha klasi cha utekelezaji wa mpango wa taifa wa kupambana na UKIMWI.
- Utaratibu maalum wa ufuatilaji utakaofuatwa na wadau wote katika ngazi mbali mbali utawezesha kugundua namna ya kuelekeza mbinu za mapambano kwa uhakika zaidi.

4 Shabaha ya Mfumo wa Ufuatiliaji

Mfumo huu unalenga katika kuweka utaratibu utakaoiwezesha Tume ya UKIMWI Zanzibar pamoja na wadau wake wote kufuatilia uenejai na athari zinazotokana na UKIMWI, kufuatilia ubora na kutaithmini ufanisi wa harakati za kupambana naUKIMWI nchini kwa kutumia taarifa zilizo sahihi zitakazotolewa na wadau.

5 Mfumo huu umejengwa vipi?

Mfumo huu umejengeka katika mambo yafuatayo:
- Viashiria vitakavyotumika kupima utekelezaji wa shughuli za UKIMWI
- Vyanzo vitakavyohusika kutoa taarifa zinazohitajika
- Njia zitakazotumika kutoa ripoti zinazotokana na uchambuzi wa taarifa zilizokusanywa
- Namna Tume ya UKIMWI na wadau watakavyouendesha mfumo mzima ili uwe. Endelevu

6 ZHAPMoS ni nini?

Ni utaratibu au mfumo uliowekwa kufanya ufuatiliaji wa shughuli za kila siku za programu zinazotekelezwa na taasisi zote (taasisi za Serikali, taasisi za Serikali, sekta binafsi, asasi za kijamii, Kamati za UKIMWI wilaya na shehia). Kutakuwa na fomu maal um za ZHAPMoS ambazo wadau wote isipokuwa sekta ya afya wanalazimika kuzijaza katika kipindi cha robo mwaka na kuziwasilisha watakakoelekezwa.

Mchoro 1: Muundo wa utekelezaji wa Mfumo wa Taifa we Ufuatiliaji na Tathmini wa Shughuli za Ukimwi Zanzibar

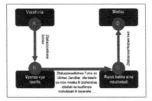

7 Vipi taasisi yako itasaidia kutekeleza mfumo huu?

Kama wewe ni mdau utasaidia kutekeleza mfumo huu kwa:

Kujaza fomu za ZHAPMoS pamoja na kutoa taarifa / ripoti ya shughuli unazotekeleza kwa kuziwasilisha katika ngazi husika na kwa wakati uliowekwa.

Kutumia ripoti zitakazotolewa zinazotokana na taarifa za ufuatiliaji na tathmini ili kuboresha upangaji na utekelezaji wa shughuli zako.

Kuwashawishi wenzako nao washiriki katika kuutekeleza mfumo huu na kubadilishana uzoefu unaopatikana.

Source: Zanzibar AIDS Commission

Annex B: Communication Channels

Communication mainly serves one or a combination of three purposes, to inform, instruct, and influence. There is a difference between the message that is intended to be communicated, the message that actually gets communicated, the message that is heard by the recipient, and the message that the recipient remembers and uses to take action (Vercic, undated). When developing communication messages, it is important to keep the intended message (what the person wants to communicate) as close as possible to the perceived (and internalized message). The figure below summarizes specific actions that one can take to increase the likelihood of the intended and internalized message being as close to each other as possible.

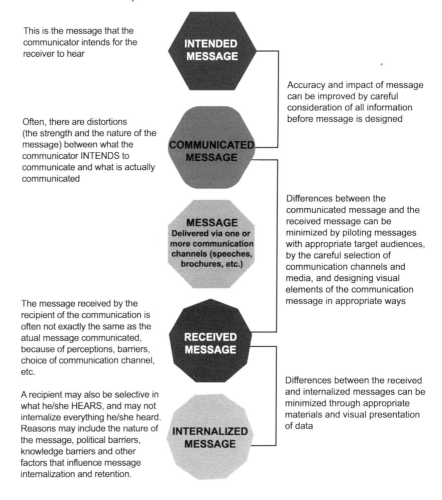

This is the message that the communicator intends for the receiver to hear

INTENDED MESSAGE

Accuracy and impact of message can be improved by careful consideration of all information before message is designed

Often, there are distortions (the strength and the nature of the message) between what the communicator INTENDS to communicate and what is actually communicated

COMMUNICATED MESSAGE

MESSAGE
Delivered via one or more communication channels (speeches, brochures, etc.)

Differences between the communicated message and the received message can be minimized by piloting messages with appropriate target audiences, by the careful selection of communication channels and media, and designing visual elements of the communication message in appropriate ways

The message received by the recipient of the communication is often not exactly the same as the atual message communicated, because of perceptions, barriers, choice of communication channel, etc.

RECEIVED MESSAGE

A recipient may also be selective in what he/she HEARS, and may not internalize everything he/she heard. Reasons may include the nature of the message, political barriers, knowledge barriers and other factors that influence message internalization and retention.

INTERNALIZED MESSAGE

Differences between the received and internalized messages can be minimized through appropriate materials and visual presentation of data

Making Monitoring and Evaluation Systems Work

Chapter 7
Routine Monitoring

Chapter Aim

The aim of this chapter is to enable you to manage the different types of routine monitoring data that your organization needs to collect, report on, and use to its best advantage.

Chapter Knowledge and Skills

a) Understand the benefits of routine monitoring for interpreting program outcomes and impacts

b) Explain to others and implement the six routine data management processes

c) Include attention to data quality in every data management step

d) Know how to link your organization's routine data management efforts to that of the national government ministry or other main system of your organization and how to build national reporting requirements into your organization's routine monitoring system

e) Know how to link program monitoring data to financial data in your organization

f) Design and develop a new routine monitoring system for your organization

g) Write routine monitoring guidelines for your organization

Before You Begin...

Take a few minutes to read through the questions below. You may find it helpful to write down your answers. As you work through the chapter, compare your answers to views of the authors.

- What are the types of routine monitoring data?
- What are the main challenges for routine monitoring data?
- How does routine data flow in your organization?
- Are there delays in reporting routine data?
- Are all routine data in your organization of good quality?

There are many types of data that can inform organizations about the effectiveness and operations of their programs. If we properly manage our routine monitoring data, we can take what may seem an overwhelming amount of information and systematically work with it to make it really useful for our organizations. This chapter explains the benefits of routine monitoring within an organization, the six standard data management processes for routine data, and how to design and develop a routine monitoring system.

Component 7: Routine Monitoring

1. Introduction

> *"Not everything that can be counted counts and not*
> *everything that counts can be counted."*
>
> Albert Einstein (1879-1955)

The *fuel* of an M&E system is its data. The data that the M&E system requires
to *run* are determined by the indicators and the research questions in the M&E
plan (see Chapter 4: M&E plans). The different indicators (input indicators,
output indicators, outcome indicators and impact indicators) in the M&E system
require three types of data sources: routine, periodic, and one-off, as Table C7-1
illustrates.

Table C7-1:   Types of Data Sources for Different Types of Indicators

Indicator type	Data collection time frame	Types of data sources
Input/Process	Continuously	Routine data sources such as statistics about education or other government services
		Routine data sources such as routine monitoring data about training materials developed for schools
Output	Quarterly, semi-annually, or annually	Routine data sources such as statistics about education or other government services
		Routine data sources such as routine monitoring data about teacher absenteeism or the number of visits by agriculture extension officers
		Periodic data sources such as exit interview surveys
Outcome	1 to 3 years	Periodic data sources such as population-based surveys
		One-off data sources such as special studies (research or evaluation)
Impact	2 to 5 years	Periodic data sources such as surveillance
		Periodic data sources such as population-based surveys
		One-off data sources such as special studies (research or evaluation)

Source: Authors adapted from the Global Fund and WHO M&E toolkit, 2006

Each of these three types of data sources are components of the middle ring (data
collection, capture and verification) of the 12 Components of a functional M&E
system and are covered in this training course in the following chapters:

*   Routine data sources (Chapter 7: Routine Monitoring – **this chapter**)
*   Periodic data sources (Chapter 8: Periodic Surveys)

- One-off data sources (Chapter 11: Evaluation and Research)

How this chapter is organized: Chapter 7 begins with background information and definitions relating to routine monitoring systems (Section 2). The desired results for this chapter follow in Section 3. The benefits of routine monitoring as part of a national M&E system are presented in Section 4, which explains that routine monitoring data provide information on program impact and size, and on input/output issues such as funding sources and program implementation protocols. Implementation issues are presented in Section 5. There is one HowTo Guide for this Component: how to design a new program monitoring system (Section 6). The Chapter closes with a summary of lessons learned (Section 7), and a practical exercise to cement what you have learned in the Chapter (Section 8).

2. Background Information and Definitions

a) **Routine monitoring data:** Routine monitoring data are data generated as part of the implementation of a program, activity or service e.g., attendance registers completed at schools every day. Routine monitoring data can be distinguished by the nature of the data (census data about the demand for services, routine program monitoring data about the supply of services, and routine financial monitoring data), or by the location where the data are generated (e.g., at health facilities or in the community), or by the types of organizations that generate the data (public sector, private sector and civil society).

1. **Types of routine data based on the nature of the data**

    When categorizing routine data by type, you would usually ask, "What are the data?" Three general types of routine data can be distinguished:

    - **Census-type data about the need for (or demand for) services.** These are data about the persons or groups who are in need of services, such as orphans and vulnerable children, poor households that are not coping with the economic downturn, or something similar. These data can also, for example, be about local government offices that need support, or community groups that need to be supported. These data are typically collected through either registers (e.g., a register of orphans in the district council offices) or through a census that determines who is in need. The fact that a person/group/organization is on a register or a list of *who needs the service*, does not mean that services will necessarily be provided. But it is useful to use such a list as a starting point for deciding which services need to be delivered in which areas and to which groups. If such data are regularly maintained, they could be used to determine service coverage (see Section 3 for more details).

- **Routine program monitoring data (or data about the *supply* of services)** are data about processes and outputs achieved as the immediate consequences of implementing an activity by service providers. Colloquially, it is sometimes referred to as *bean counting* (number of persons at a workshop, number of new text books distributed, etc.) and is used primarily to **monitor** progress in implementing programs. Program monitoring data usually count outputs. Put in a different way, these are "data used to track activities and services through a monitoring system that ensures that all partners submit regular, structured program reports that are externally verified" (Wilson, 2004:103).

- **Routine financial monitoring data** are data about the inputs used to implement activities, that is the funding for programs. They monitor financial expenditures through either a manual or computerized financial management system for the organization.

2. **Types of routine data based on the location where the data are generated**

   It may be important for a routine monitoring system to distinguish data flows and data management processes based on the location where the data are generated. To make such a distinction, ask "Where is the first place the data are recorded?" It may be, for example, important to distinguish between data about HIV services implemented at health facilities and data about HIV services generated in other work places or at community venues.

3. **Types of routine data based on the type of organization generating the data**

   It may be important for the sake of understanding the data flow to separate data by the type of organization generating the data. Three main types of organizations can be distinguished: private sector organizations (businesses); public sector (government departments, ministries and agencies); and civil society.

   Combining the types of routine data

   It is possible to combine the types of routine data to better understand how the different types of routine data relate to each other. Table C7-2 illustrates these relationships using an example from the education sector.

For the ministry of education to have comprehensive data, it needs to collect the same data from government schools and community schools, operated by both the ministry of education and non-governmental organizations.

b) **Routine data management processes:** When managing any type of routine data, every organization should aim to implement six routine data management processes (Kemerer (ed.) et al., 2007):

- **Data sourcing:** The first data management process entails writing down or typing data onto standard forms designed for the purpose. The forms may be paper forms, registers, or electronic forms on a computer (e.g., workshop attendance registers). Without this step being implemented, there will be no data to manage.

- **Data collection:** Data need to be collected regularly and collated from the various data source locations. For example, facilitators may be asked to send all workshop attendance registers to one person in the organization.

- **Data collation:** Once the routine data have been collected, the next step is to collate them. This means to add up or tally the individual data into summary data. For example by entering data into a monthly workshop report form that summarizes workshop data from many sources.

Table C7-2: **Combining Types of Routine Data**

		Location where data are generated (the same as the location where the service is provided)	
		Government schools (schools built by the government)	**Community schools** (local schools built by the community)
Type of organization generating the data	**Schools operated by ministry of education**	• Registers with the number of pupils enrolled in each class • Program monitoring data about teacher and pupil attendance • Financial monitoring data about the school's expenditure	• Registers with the number of pupils enrolled in each class • Program monitoring data about teacher and pupil attendance • Financial monitoring data about the school's expenditure
	Schools operated by non-governmental organizations	• Registers with the number of pupils enrolled in each class • Program monitoring data about teacher and pupil attendance • Financial monitoring data about the school's expenditure	• Registers with the number of pupils enrolled in each class • Program monitoring data about teacher and pupil attendance • Financial monitoring data about the school's expenditure

Nature of the data: The table contains "census data" about the number of children enrolled in school, program monitoring data about their attendance, and routine financial data about the school's finances.

- **Data analysis:** Once tallied (collated), the data can be analyzed. You may want to analyze data by seeing how the summary data (e.g. number of persons who have attended workshops) change over time, or by comparing the number of persons who attended training with the number that you planned would attend. You may also want to perform basic descriptive statistical calculations (such as calculating the mean, mode, and median).

- **Data reporting:** In addition to analyzing data, it is almost always necessary to report data to another location such as an organization's head office, or ministry headquarters. However, reporting the data to another organization is **not** the main purpose for collecting the data. First and foremost, your organization should be collecting the routine data that it needs to monitor the implementation of its program in order to answer the question, "Are we implementing what we said we would in our annual plan?"

- **Data use:** Finally, and most importantly, you should use the data to help you make decisions. Finding out, for example, that fewer people were trained than planned enables you take remedial action by speaking to the staff concerned and then addressing the reason/s for the shortfall. Routine data can also only be used to maximum effect if, during planning, you set targets for your program for the year. This concept is explained below in more detail in Section 5(e) of this manual.

c) **Data quality:** Data quality refers to the extent to which data adheres to the six dimensions of quality; accuracy, reliability, completeness, precision, timeliness and integrity (Table C7-3 provides detailed definitions of each of these dimensions) (USAID, 2007). "For good quality data to be produced by, and flow through a data-management system, key functional components need to be in place at all levels of the system" (The Global Fund et al., 2008). Therefore, data quality is an integral part of routine data management. When managing routine data, it is essential to consider issues of data quality throughout these six data management processes. Data quality is, therefore, not an additional data management process as one needs to consider how these six dimensions of data quality can be assured during each of the data management processes and be implemented accordingly.

Table C7-3: Operational Definitions about Data Quality

Dimension of data quality	Operational definition
Accuracy	Also known as validity. Accurate data are considered correct: the data measure what they are intended to measure. Accurate data minimize error (e.g., recording or interviewer bias, transcription error, sampling error) to a point of being negligible.

Dimension of data quality	Operational definition
Reliability	The data generated by a program's information system are based on protocols and procedures that do not change according to who is using them and when or how often they are used. The data are reliable because they are measured and collected consistently.
Completeness	Completeness means that an information system from which the results are derived is appropriately inclusive: it represents the complete list of eligible persons or units and not a fraction of the list.
Precision	Precision means that the data have sufficient detail. For example, an indicator requires the number of individuals who received HIV counseling & testing and received their test results, differentiated by the sex of the individual. An information system lacks precision if it is not designed to record the sex of the individual who received counseling & testing.
Timeliness	Data are timely when they are up-to-date (current), and when the information is available on time. Timeliness is affected by: (1) the rate at which the program's information system is updated; (2) the rate of change of actual program activities; and (3) when the information is actually used or required.
Integrity	Integrity is when data generated by a program's information system are protected from deliberate bias or manipulation for political or personal reasons.

Source: USAID, 2007

d) **Relationship between data quality and routine data management processes:** One of the most frequently asked questions is why data quality control/assurance/ management is not one of the six data management processes. The answer is that data quality should be an integral part of every routine data management step: sourcing, collecting, collating, analyzing, reporting and using data.

3. Results to Be Achieved When Implementing This Component

Long-term result:

- Timely and high quality routine data are used for routinely assessing program implementation and for taking decisions to improve programs.

Short- and medium-term results:

- Routine monitoring forms, data flow, and manual
- Defined data management processes for routine data (sourcing, collection, collation, analysis, reporting, and use)
- Routine procedures for data transfer from sub-national to national levels

---

For reflection 1:

What types of data are routinely gathered and monitored by your organization? Are data sent to your organization from other organizations? Is there a coordinated effort to align systems for monitoring these data? How do the six routine data management processes function in your organization? Can you list them? How many short- and medium-term results listed here are visible in your organization?

---

4. Benefits of Routine Monitoring as Part of an M&E System

When implementing M&E systems, you might wonder, "Is it really necessary to collect routine data?" The answer is YES for the following reasons:

a) **Routine monitoring provides data to explain changes at the outcome and impact levels.** Interventions are needed to bring about higher-order changes in behavior and in society. The implementation of such programs and the inputs supplied to deliver them need to be monitored; the data help to interpret positive or negative changes (or the lack thereof) at the higher-order level.

b) **Routine monitoring provides real-time data that can be used for day-to-day monitoring, coordination, and program planning.** Routine monitoring data track changes over time, unlike surveys and surveillance data (see Chapter 8) that provide a single *snapshot* in time. Routine monitoring data can be used to validate program service-coverage data generated through surveys and surveillance. Both routine monitoring data and survey data can be used to estimate program coverage but there are some differences (see Table C7-4). Routine monitoring data show program service delivery by geographic.area and can be disaggregated by sub-national level, which is not always possible with survey data.

Table C7-4: Differences between Using Routine Monitoring Data and Sample Surveys for Determining Service Coverage

Routine monitoring system	Sample survey for program coverage
Collects census type data about all who need services (individuals, groups, or organizations that will be targeted with services)	Selects a representative sample of beneficiaries
Collects routine monitoring data about implemented programs, from organizations that implement programs	Collects data from beneficiaries of programs (i.e., individuals, groups, or organizations that receive programs services/benefits)
Collects data from all organizations that implement programs	Selects respondents on a sample basis
Depends on implementers of programs to report data	Actively collects data from respondents
Provides feedback to implementers of programs	Provides no feedback to individual survey respondents
Covers all geographic areas where programs are implemented	Only covers areas selected in the sample. (If the sample is not representative of the country, then the survey results are equally unrepresentative.)
Organizations collect data daily and summarize quarterly for report back (i.e., routinely)	Survey respondents are selected only when a survey is being undertaken and surveys are only undertaken periodically, typically every two years
Not expensive to implement	Expensive to implement
Targets the implementers of programs and makes them responsible for data collection	Does not directly target the implementers of programs or involve them in data collection

Source: Authors

Section 5.7 explains how to calculate service coverage data from either routine monitoring data or sample surveys.

5. Implementation Issues in Routine Monitoring of Programs

5.1. Collect only the data you need

One of the main downfalls of routine monitoring is often the sheer volume of data that are sourced and need to be collected, collated, analyzed, reported and used.

When designing program-monitoring forms, the main principle to keep in mind is whether or not you will use the data. You should not collect data *just in case*. It is most likely not necessary, for example, to collect data about school pupils' grandparents.

> If I'd known they wanted me to use all this data, I would never have asked for it!

5.2. Reporting rates with new monitoring systems usually start out low but actions can be taken to improve the reporting rate

One of the major challenges that organizations face with program monitoring systems is how to improve the reporting rate. In some cases, the coordinating agency may ask organizations it does not fund to report. Actions that have proven successful in improving the reporting rate include the following:

- Ensuring that the LGAs responsible for coordination of programs understand that managing the program monitoring system is part of their responsibility to ensure good governance (good governance involves three linked aspects: flow of information; transparency; and accountability). For this reason, a program monitoring system is more than simply a tool for collecting data. Properly implemented and functional, it can serve as a coordination mechanism to ensure data flow at sub-national levels and assist the LGA to improve governance of the program.

- If reporting is required, reporting program-monitoring data to a national entity such as a national ministry of health or education, should be made compulsory. If the requirement to report program monitoring data are included in relevant country program policies and strategic plans, it will help mainstream M&E and ensure compliance with reporting.

- If it is a national routine monitoring system, consider developing an advocacy and communications plan (that includes mass media communication materials) for the program monitoring system. This should include strategies to encourage funders that provide funds directly to implementing organizations to include the requirement to report data to various channels in contracts or agreements with implementers.

- Publishing a regular (quarterly or biannual) program report that shows the extent of program coverage in the country. This gives stakeholders a *data dividend* in the form of a tangible report presenting data that all stakeholders have submitted (as part of the quarterly program report).

- Publishing a list of organizations that have submitted program data.
- Publishing a separate program monitoring report for each sub-national unit (e.g., district, region, or other administrative unit).
- Holding dissemination and planning workshops every quarter at the sub-national level at which the program data are discussed with all stakeholders. To ensure that these workshops take place, it is necessary to include them in the work plans of the sub-national units and to provide funding.
- Registration of civil society organizations. Some countries have opted to register organizations which provide programs and to apply the laws of the country which state that only registered organizations may provide particular services and to insist that only registered organizations may be funded. Such measures enable the country to better control the quality of services and to better target all organizations that need to submit program-monitoring data.

5.3. Capacity building in monitoring systems is essential

When designing capacity building for routine monitoring systems, remember that:

- Many program implementers have not collected monitoring data before. It is necessary, therefore, for capacity building to focus on basic M&E skills in addition to training on how to use the program monitoring forms.
- Staff reporting on and using program-monitoring data also need an introduction to a spreadsheet program to facilitate rapid analysis of the data and generation of information products.
- A one-off workshop or training course usually is not sufficient; and long-term, on-going support should be provided. Mentorship or supportive supervision visits should be considered to help each trainee internalize their understanding of the routine monitoring system. Technical support should also be provided in designing or customizing program data collection tools.
- Capacity building with added mentorship visits or supportive supervision visits immediately after training may add to the cost of implementing the system but is a good investment in human resources.
- Use dummy data sets during training so that participants build practical skills in tallying data from daily registers onto a quarterly form.
- Use the opportunity of training in the routine monitoring system to create a cadre of local trainers who are certified to conduct training in the routine monitoring system and M&E, in general.

5.4. Developing a system to collect standardized routine monitoring data at the national level

If a country wishes to create a national routine monitoring system, standardizing and regulating data collection will minimize the amount of data that cannot be analyzed or aggregated due to inconsistent data collection or operational definitions (see Figure C7-1).

5.5. Program supply and demand need to be monitored

Routine program monitoring data are needed about the provision of programs (i.e., which program implementer is delivering which service to which target group), collected from the implementers of programs (i.e., the service providers). In addition, census-type data about the demand for programs (how many persons/groups or organizations in each area need support) are also needed to determine the coverage of, or gaps in, program provision. For example, if organizations that support vulnerable children do not know which households have vulnerable children (i.e., where demand for services is located), they cannot accurately target their support or cover the *target area* (i.e., supply of services). Measuring the demand for programs may require community registers of households or other data collection tools that are periodically updated as the situation changes.

Figure C7-1: Why Receiving and Reporting Standardized Data are Important

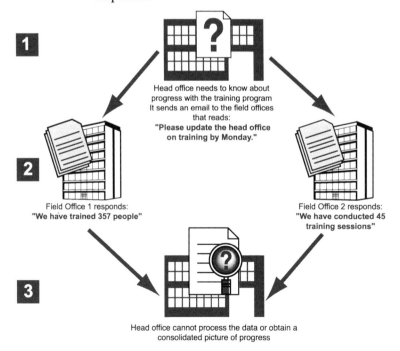

Source: Authors

Routine Monitoring

5.6. Linking monitoring systems to planning processes

Routine monitoring systems should be linked to planning processes and time frames to ensure that monitoring data can be used to help implementers track whether they have implemented what they planned. The example below explains how this would work.

Example using Routine Data to Plan and Monitor Progress

1. A register of orphans is kept at each district council office and updated.

2. All district councils report the number of orphans in their district to the Ministry of Social Welfare at national level on a given date.

3. The Ministry of Social Welfare determines that there are 200 orphans in total and that, as a target, the 40% orphans most in need must be reached (80 orphans). This is the national target

	Number of orphans on register as of 1 January 2009
District 1	60
District 2	40
District 3	80
District 4	20
TOTAL	**200**

4. Now organizations start planning how many orphans they will reach in which district:

	District 1	District 2	District 3	District 4	TOTAL
NATIONAL TARGET	24	16	32	8	80
Organization 1 target	6	10	24	0	40
Organization 2 target	2	6	8	24	40

5. Each organization develops a work plan and a budget to show how they will reach the targeted number of orphans (see next page).

ORGANIZATION 1

Activity	Q1 Target	Q1 Budget	Q2 Target	Q2 Budget	Q3 Target	Q3 Budget	Q4 Target	Q4 Budget	
Train orphan caregivers	5	$10,000	3	$8,000	0	$0	0	$0	
Procure materials for support	40 uniforms 40 books	$5,000	weekly food parcels for 20 households	20,000	weekly food parcels for 30 households	$35,000	weekly food parcels for 40 households	$50,000	
Support orphans	0	0	20	$15,000	30	$18,500	40	$40,700	cumulative target
TOTAL		$15,000		$43,000		$53,500		$90,700	$202,200

ORGANIZATION 2

Activity	Q1 Target	Q1 Budget	Q2 Target	Q2 Budget	Q3 Target	Q3 Budget	Q4 Target	Q4 Budget	
Procure materials for support	4 weekly food parcels for 20 households	$50,000	weekly food parcels for 20 households	$50,000	weekly food parcels for 30 households	$50,000	weekly food parcels for 40 households	$50,000	
TOTAL		$132,300		$132,300		$132,300		$132,300	$529,200

6. Every quarter, organizations report on how many orphans they have actually reached

ORGANIZATION 1

Activity	Q1 Reached	Q1 Spent	Q2 Reached	Q2 Spent	Q3 Reached	Q3 Spent	Q4 Reached	Q4 Spent	
Train orphan caregivers	2	$12,400	4	$4,000	2	$3,000	0	$0	
Procure materials for support	20 uniforms 40 books	$2,400	weekly food parcels for 25 households	$17,000	weekly food parcels for 30 households	$32,000	weekly food parcels for 44 households	$53,100	
Support orphans	0	0	25	$24,000	30	$19,600	37	$37,800	cumulative target $37,800
TOTAL		$14,800		$45,000		$54,600		$90,900	$205,300

ORGANIZATION 2

Activity	Q1 Reached	Q1 Spent	Q2 Reached	Q2 Spent	Q3 Reached	Q3 Spent	Q4 Reached	Q4 Spent	
Procure materials for support	weekly food parcels for 20 households	$25,000	weekly food parcels for 35 households	$24,100	weekly food parcels for 40 households	$56,000	weekly food parcels for 32 households	$42,050	
Support orphans	35	$45,980	35	$34,000	40	$82,300	32	$37,800	cumulative target $37,800
TOTAL		$70,980		$58,100		$138,300		$109,050	$376,430

7. National coverage (percent of targeted number) is determined every quarter, and implementation progress is known

	Orphans reached		Funding	
	Planned	**Actual**	**Budgeted**	**Spent**
Quarter 1	40	35	147,300	85,780
Quarter 2	60	60	175,300	103,100
Quarter 3	70	70	185,800	192,900
Quarter 4	80	69	223,000	199,950
TOTAL	**80**	**69**	**731,400**	**581,730**

Coverage	86% of target reached
Expenditure	80% of funding spent

5.7. At the national level, the routine monitoring systems of different agencies often need to be linked

Exchanging data and creating harmonized/joint reports at the national level means that routine data from different sources often need to be combined and linked. This process of linking may be challenging for the following reasons:

•   Different organizations and institutions are involved

•   Relationships between some of the institutions may not be strong or may even be competitive

•   Some ministries or organizations may already have existing information systems to which the new system has to be linked

•   The M&E systems of different institutions may not be at similar levels of maturity

•   Reporting mechanisms between institutions and organizations may not be clearly defined or mandated

Different solutions have been offered to address this challenge, including:

•   Joint development of a government ministry M&E framework and a national M&E framework

•   Harmonizing indicators so that the various actors can report on the single set of target indicators in the national M&E plan

•   Greater involvement of coordinating agency M&E staff in the databases of ministries or other organizations from which data need to be collected so that data extraction for reporting can be automated

•   Involvement of senior-level officials (e.g., Permanent Secretary or Minister) to agree on reporting requirements

- Joint planning and execution of feedback workshops
- Joint writing of reports on program service coverage

5.8. The difference between using routine data and using sample surveys to determine service coverage

The illustration below demonstrates the difference.

PRINCIPLE

$$\text{SERVICE COVERAGE} = \frac{\text{Supply of services}}{\text{Demand for services}}$$

USING SAMPLE SURVEY	USING ROUTINE DATA
$\text{SERVICE COVERAGE} = \dfrac{\text{Number in survey who received}}{\text{Number in survey interviewed}}$	$\text{SERVICE COVERAGE} = \dfrac{\text{Number given services by service providers}}{\text{Number who need services, according to census data}}$
Example	**Example**
Coverage of persons reached with anti-smoking messages	Coverage of persons reached with anti-smoking messages
$\text{SERVICE COVERAGE} = \dfrac{\text{Number in survey who received}}{\text{Number in survey interviewed}}$	$\text{SERVICE COVERAGE} = \dfrac{\text{Number of persons reached with message}}{\text{Number of persons needing to receive the message}}$
$\text{SERVICE COVERAGE} = \dfrac{\text{Number of respondents reached}}{\text{Number of respondents asked}}$	$\text{SERVICE COVERAGE} = \dfrac{\text{Number of persons reached by service providers}}{\text{Population age 10 and older (as per census)}}$
$\text{SERVICE COVERAGE} = \dfrac{345 \quad \text{said YES in survey}}{800 \quad \text{were asked}}$	$\text{SERVICE COVERAGE} = \dfrac{456\,782 \quad \text{were reached}}{956\,045 \quad \text{in the population 10 or older}}$
$\text{SERVICE COVERAGE} = 43\%$	$\text{SERVICE COVERAGE} = 48\%$
NOTES Sample survey value is valid for the entire population provided that the sample of respondents are selected randomly, that the sample is large enough, and that the sample's characteristics are the same as the characteristics of the general population aged 10 and older.	NOTES This method works well, provided that the denominator is known. Often the denominator is either not known or is a crude estimate. In this event, a survey may be needed.

Chapter 7

5.9. Qualitative monitoring data to complement quantitative monitoring data

Although monitoring data are important, other data should also be collected to provide insight into the quality and effectiveness of programs. Qualitative data may be collected periodically and integrated with quantitative data. Some examples of innovative qualitative data collection techniques include a methodology called Most Significant Changes (MSC), sometimes known as *monitoring-without-indicators*. MSC has already been used in some programs. You can go to: www.mande.co.uk/docs/MSCGuide.pdf to download MSC guidelines and learn more about this method.

6. HowTo Guide C7-1: Designing a New Routine Monitoring System

This guide deals with the design of a new routine monitoring system at the national level (e.g., the national education management information system or HIV routine data management system). Following similar steps can also improve existing routine monitoring systems or develop an organization's own routine monitoring system.

Step 1: Obtain senior management buy-in for the creation of a new data collection system

Obtain senior management buy-in for developing the system to ensure its sustainability and maintenance over time. Management buy-in and financial support will be needed for the long-term existence of the system. When advocating the concept of the system to senior management, it would be beneficial to:

a) Use examples/case studies from other countries to show how the systems have worked and the results they have generated;

b) Show what data the system will collect;

c) Show the long-term cost-efficiency of the system by comparing the costs of regular surveys;

d) Prepare management for the relatively high system initiation costs due to the extensive capacity building that needs to be done but note the value of this investment in human resources.

Deliverable: Agreement (preferably in writing) by senior management of the organization.

Step 2: Discuss creating the new system with development partners, national staff, and the M&E TWG

Development partners have agreed to use country-level M&E systems. This implies that once a national routine monitoring system is functional, they should draw their data from it instead of instituting parallel monitoring systems. These partners need to be aware of the purpose of developing one harmonized system and need to be informed of the development timetable so that they can participate in discussions and agreements about how to collect the necessary data.

Discussing the creation of the new system with development partners at this early stage will also help prevent a scenario in which they do not buy into the new system or keep their own systems once the new system is operational.

Deliverable: Agreement (preferable in writing) by development partners and the M&E TWG to use data from one system, rather than using parallel monitoring systems.

Step 3: Develop an inventory of routine monitoring systems in the country

The purpose of developing an inventory is to determine which systems already exist for collecting routine monitoring data; the level of functionality of each system; how the data flow works within each system; and the data being recorded through each system. This will enable interested parties to draw data from existing sources and avoid duplication. Developing the inventory involves:

a) Making a list of all program data that are required for the indicators in the M&E plan;

b) Asking stakeholders (i.e., Ministry of Health; Ministry of Education; Ministry of (Child) Welfare or Social Development; Ministry of Local Government; Ministry of Finance; National Coordinating Authorities; Bureau of Statistics; development partners; and national private sector and civil society umbrella organizations) about the existence of routine program monitoring and financial monitoring systems (whether functional or not).

c) Collecting and sorting the data collection tools (instruments) and guidelines from each of these monitoring systems. The tools can be organized into two types: those for daily data capture and those to report aggregate data that have been summarized (by grouping and adding up the daily values). Ensure that both sets of tools are accessed and obtained.

d) Sketching the data flow processes for each monitoring system.

e) Documenting the information products that the systems generate.

f)   Documenting the databases and/or other electronic means (e.g., spreadsheets) in which existing data sets relating to the program targets are being captured and stored.

g)   Determining how data are verified and the data quality and supervision process associated with each type of monitoring data.

h)   Determining what percentage of organizations that are required to report, have done so in the past 12 months (this is a measure of the level of functionality of the data).

i)   Recording the name of the agency responsible for managing the data monitoring system in each case.

j)   Capturing the answers in a structured format (see Annex A for an example).

Deliverable: Inventory of existing routine monitoring systems in the country.

Step 4:   Develop a list of data that are not yet collected through any existing system

a)   Extract from the national M&E plan a list of required routine monitoring data by carefully interrogating the denominator and numerator of each input and output level indicator.

b)   Obtain from development partners any additional routine monitoring data needs they might have.

c)   Use the results of the monitoring system inventory in the following way: Take the data collection forms of all systems where more than 60% of contributing organizations reported data in the last 12 months and record a list of program monitoring data already captured on these forms.

Compare the routine monitoring data required and the list of additional data needs to the routine monitoring data already captured. This will help identify data gaps and, therefore, what data needs to be included in the new system.

Deliverable: List of data that are not collected via existing monitoring systems.

Step 5:   Design and agree on how the data will flow

If it is a government system being designed, it is vitally important that the data flow be linked with the existing, regularized flow of government data (e.g., annual planning and budgeting data). If data were to flow separate to that of government, it could create bottlenecks, conflicts, and reduce the prospects for sustainability. After agreeing on how the data will flow, it is advisable to illustrate the data flow in a schematic of some kind. Annex B discusses the schematic options available to you and also provides examples of data flow schematics.

Deliverable: Cross-functional flow chart that shows the data flow in the routine monitoring system.

Step 6: Design the data collection tools and pilot them in the field

Completion of Step 4 will have confirmed what data gaps exist and guide development of appropriate data collection tools. When designing them, remember to design both the daily registers and the summary report forms. Examples of forms are available in Annex C.

Deliverables: Data collection tools and report on the piloting of the tools.

Step 7: Design and agree how the six standard data management processes will be handled at each level

At each of the *nodes* where data will be aggregated and through which the data flow will pass (e.g., service delivery level, sub-national or LGA level, umbrella organization level, and national level), the six data management processes need to be considered. Several key questions arise in this regard, as follows:

• Do they have the mandate and authority to manage data?

• Do they have the skills to manage data?

• How can they be supported in their work?

• How will data quality be handled at this level?

Deliverable: Six data management processes defined for each location in the data flow (see example in Annex D).

Step 8: Write guidelines for the routine monitoring system and then pilot and approve them

Because a system for collecting routine data requires uniformity, guidelines are essential. Different types of guidelines may be necessary depending on the complexity of the system and depending on the types of routine data (census-type data, program monitoring data, and financial monitoring data) that needs to be collected (see Table C7-5).

Table C7-5: Types of Guidelines for Routine Monitoring Systems (example of education sector)

	Data about education programs in the community	Data about programs at education facilities
Guidelines for IMPLEMENTERS (at the service delivery or implementer level)	Guidelines for civil society and the private sector entities that implement education programs at venues in the community (Guidelines A)	Guidelines for education sector staff at schools about how to manage data (Guidelines C)
Guidelines for MANAGERS OF ROUTINE MONITORING DATA (at sub-national, sectoral, and national levels)	Guidelines for LGAs, umbrella organizations and M&E units to explain their role in managing the routine monitoring data (Guidelines B)	Guidelines for district education offices and national education offices about how to manage data (Guidelines D)

Source: Authors

The guidelines should be simple, concise, and easy to understand. They should include the following information:

	Proposed Content of Guidelines
Guidelines for IMPLEMENTERS (at the service delivery or implementer level)	• Benefits of reporting • Types of data to be sourced: census-type (demand) data; program monitoring data; and financial monitoring data • The forms to be used for census-type (demand) data; program monitoring data; and financial monitoring data • Data element definitions for each data element on each form • Description of six data management processes for each type of data • Description of data quality assurance mechanisms • Use of the data • Frequently asked questions

	Proposed Content of Guidelines
Guidelines for MANAGERS OF ROUTINE MONITORING DATA (at sub national, sectoral and national levels)	Everything that is in the Implementer's Guidelines, PLUS: • Reporting formats for organizations to report on programs implemented themselves and on how they have managed the data that they have received • Data quality procedures, including supportive supervision and data auditing (see Chapter 10) • Job aids to support them in their tasks (a job aid is a standard template that will help to manage the data such as a template of a register to record all incoming forms)

Source: Authors

In most cases, the routine monitoring guidelines and data collection tools should be piloted by the groups concerned, after which they should be approved by the M&E TWG and the senior management of the organization. Once the routine monitoring guidelines have been approved, they may need to be translated into local languages, depending on country context and protocols, to ensure that they can be understood easily.

Deliverables: Approved routine monitoring guidelines.

Step 9: Prepare for implementation of the routine monitoring system

After the routine monitoring guidelines are approved, one prepares for full-scale implementation by:

a) Developing specifications for the database(s) that will be used to capture the routine monitoring data. Ensuring that Terms of Reference and funding are available for designing and customizing the database(s).

b) Signing agreements with organizations that will supply other routine monitoring data to supplement the data collected in the routine monitoring system, so that all these systems can be linked and harmonized.

c) Developing training materials and initiating capacity building for the routine monitoring system. This training should be for technical personnel involved in the system and should also include decision-makers, such as mayors, district executive directors, and other LGA staff who should be aware of the system.

d) Implementing an extensive communication and advocacy program, in conjunction with the national advocacy and communications office (or the public relations officer), that is integrated with other activities of the organization (see Chapter 6).

Deliverables: Database specifications and development/customization procedures, training materials, communications and advocacy materials and mechanisms.

Step 10. Launch the routine monitoring system

The final step is to launch the routine monitoring system. This is an important starting point for implementation. If the routine monitoring system is to be managed at sub-national levels, sub-national launches should also be considered.

Deliverables: Coordinated launch of routine monitoring system (at national and sub-national levels).

For reflection 2:

Reflect on the different types of routine data gathered and monitored by your organization. Now that you have learned the steps involved in preparing, developing, and then finally launching a routine monitoring system, what challenges do you anticipate in your context when designing a routine monitoring system? Can you think of ways to support this process? Has your organization followed the steps above?

---

7. Summary of Chapter 7 Knowledge and Skills

In this chapter, you learned about the entire gamut of input, output, outcome, and impact data needed to inform organizations about how well programs are meeting communities' needs. You learned that routine monitoring provides data to explain changes at the outcome and impact levels, which can be used for day-to-day monitoring, coordination, planning, and improvement of programs, as well as validating service-coverage data generated through surveys or surveillance. You learned about implementation issues such as the necessity of a systematic way to capture and use routine data, how to improve reporting rates, and the importance of capacity building. You learned about the technical process steps required to design and develop a routine monitoring system for routine monitoring data. And lastly, you learned how to prepare for its launch nationally and/or sub-nationally.

8. Learning Activities

LEARNING ACTIVITY 1:   DEFINING DATA MANAGEMENT PROCESSES
IN YOUR ORGANIZATION

Make a list of all the different routine monitoring data (census-type data, program monitoring data, and financial monitoring data) that your organization manages or in which it participates. Draw a data flow schematic for one of these types of routine data. To give you some ideas and help you understand the options available in terms of data flow schematics, read Annex B. It summarizes the three data flow schematic options available and provides examples.

LEARNING ACTIVITY 2:   DEFINING DATA MANAGEMENT PROCESSES
IN YOUR ORGANIZATION

Define the data management processes in your organization, using the same data flow schematic that you developed in Learning Activity 1. Capture these data management processes as follows:

		Locations where the data will be managed (e.g., from individual organizations (Place 1), to district council offices (Place 2), to the national ministry of education (Place 3)		
		Place 1	**Place 2**	**Place 3**
Data management process	Data Sourcing			
	Data Collection			
	Data Collation			
	Data Analysis			
	Data Reporting			
	Data Use			

LEARNING ACTIVITY 3:   DATA QUALITY EMBEDDED IN DATA
MANAGEMENT PROCESSES

Read through the six dimensions of data quality described in Section 2 of this chapter. Describe how you would manage data quality during implementation of the data management processes you defined in Learning Activity 2.

Making Monitoring and Evaluation Systems Work

Capture your answer in table format, following the example in the table template below.

		Locations in the data flow diagram where data are managed		
		Place 1	Place 2	Place 3
Data management process	Data Sourcing	Periodically and randomly observe the data sourcing at different locations to ensure that all source data are correctly and comprehensively completed		
	Data Collection			
	Data Collation			
	Data Analysis			
	Data Reporting			
	Data Use			

Annex A: Example of an Inventory of Different Types of Routine Monitoring Data Managed by an Organization

Type of routine HIV data	Data collection system	Focus	Agency responsible for managing it
Routine data about medical HIV services provided at health facilities and at stand-alone sites	Through HMIS or separate vertical systems for collecting HIV data	All routine data in the health sector	MOH
Routine data about HIV services provided in the community	New system to be created only for this type of data	HIV services delivered in the community (not at health facilities)	NACA and LGAs (Since no other institution is involved in collecting HIV data about community-based interventions in a uniform manner, this will be the major focus of NACA M&E units and LGAs.)
Routine data about support to vulnerable children	Orphan and Vulnerable Child register	All data about OVC	Ministry of Child Welfare / Social Services
Routine data about education services, including HIV life skills education	Education Management Information System	All routine data from schools in the country, including data about supervision visits, numbers of vulnerable children in schools, etc.	MOE
Financial data about grants that NACA awards	NACA grants management system	All financial data about HIV grants that the NACA awards	NACA
Financial data about HIV services being funded and delivered	Financial systems of development partners Financial systems of organizations that implement HIV services	Financial figures relating to HIV services being delivered	Various development partners and implementers of HIV services
Routine data from umbrella organizations	Database of members	Data about NGOs and CBOs in the country	NGO networks Networks of persons living with HIV

Type of routine HIV data	Data collection system	Focus	Agency responsible for managing it
Routine data from implementers of HIV services to their funders	Detailed information, line-by-line, about the types of HIV services that implementers of HIV services have provided	Detailed data about the implementation of individual HIV activities in implementer workplans	Funders of HIV services Implementers of HIV services
Routine data about all services provided at the LGA	Local Government Monitoring System	Detailed data, from all sectors (water, education, health, etc.) of the services provided at the LGA level	Each LGA

Source: Authors

Chapter 7

Annex B: Data Flow Schematics

A: Data flow schematic options available

Data need to be sourced, collected, collated, analyzed, reported, and used. Reporting the data usually involves data *flowing* from one location to another, as the data are reported. Such data *flow* could be paper-based, where data are captured on paper forms and then sent via fax, post, or hand delivered. Alternatively, data could be captured electronically into a computer database using an application software, and then emailed, sent via a network connection, or using a cell phone, to a central location. Completing a paper form on a computer and emailing it is only superficially an electronic form of data flow if the information is captured in a word processing program. In order to be analyzed, the data must be in a database that facilitates various kinds of analyses.

The principle of data flow is that it flows from one location to another, at specific points in time. Usually, data flows between different organizations (or different branches/offices of the same organization) that are based in different geographic locations.

This data flow between entities over a period of time can be described narratively (in words) or through a schematic (illustration) of some kind. It is usually helpful to describe the data flow in both words and illustrations, as some people internalize words better, while others find it easier to interpret an illustration.

This Annex summarizes three options available to illustrate the flow of routine data: data flow schematics; flow charts (regular and cross-functional flow charts); and data management charts.

Using data flow schematics to illustrate the data flow

The first option is to draw a data flow schematic (which is a special form of a business process diagram), as illustrated in the 2 examples in this annex. In this schematic, rectangular blocks represent organizations (or branches of organizations, or groups of similar organizations). These rectangular blocks are arranged to represent the different levels of authority in the government system (see Example 1 that shows the levels from village, wards, districts, regions and national). *Blocks* (organizations) are drawn as they appear at each level.

The distinguishing feature of a routine data flow schematic is that the arrows indicate the flow of data from one organization to the other. It may be a bi-directional arrow, in which the dual directional flow suggests that data (feedback) is given back to those who reported the data.

Also note that, in Example 2, the actual forms organizations have to use to report are also included in the illustration.

Making Monitoring and Evaluation Systems Work

The **advantages** of a data flow schematic are that it is simple and relatively easy to draw and that most people intuitively understand them. It is also an effective workshop and facilitation tool to conceptually illustrate how the data will flow. These schematics can also be used to illustrate how feedback will be provided, how funding will flow, and how supervision will be done (usually supervision is done in *reverse* to how data flows. If districts report to regions and regions report to national, then usually national supervises the regions who, in turn, supervise the districts) (See Chapter 9 for more information about supportive M&E supervision and data auditing.).

The **disadvantages** are that these schematics do not contain sufficient amounts of detail about the processes entailed in the data management process or about the data management processes. For this reason, one might want to consider a more detailed schematic such as a flow chart (discussed in Section B of this Annex) or a data management chart (discussed in Section C of this Annex).

Example 1: Data flow schematic of routine data flow in the Ministry of Education

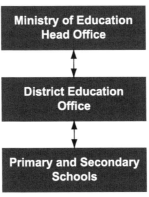

Example 2: Data flow schematic (of the same routine monitoring system illustrated in example 1 but with added detail)

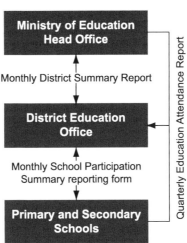

Source: Authors

B: USING FLOW CHARTS TO ILLUSTRATE THE DATA FLOW

A flow chart is a schematic that shows a series of process steps and their dependencies (what activities/process steps need to be done, in what order, and what will impact on whether the activity can/should be implemented). Example 3 shows the process for hiring a new person in an organization. In a flow chart, standard meanings have been assigned to specific shapes, as indicated below.

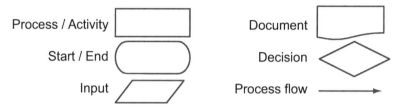

The difference in schematic notation between a data flow schematic and a flow chart is important to note: whereas a block in the data flow schematic represents an institution, the block (rectangle) in a flow chart represents a process step (in other words, an action).

A cross-functional flow chart (also called a deployment flowchart) is a special kind of flowchart that has all the features of a regular flow chart, with one exception. It **also** shows the names of the persons/groups responsible for each process step. Such a flow chart is, therefore, a how-to guide for *who needs to do what* (Smartdraw, 2009).

The **advantages** of a cross functional flow chart are that it provides more detail than a data flow schematic. At the same time, it is also more time consuming to develop and not everyone is familiar or comfortable with the logic of a flow chart. It is, however, great to show *who does what, when* at a glance.

The **disadvantages** are its level of detail and that many users are not familiar with reading them. Such flow charts need to be developed incrementally; first at the higher level and then more detailed flow charts over time.

C: DATA MANAGEMENT CHART

A data management chart looks like a cross-functional flowchart as it has boxes, columns, and column headings. The main difference is that in a data management chart, the row headings are the different data management processes (data sourcing, data collection, data collation, data analysis, data reporting, and data use), whereas the column headings are the organizations (Kemerer (ed) et al., 2007). Example 5 illustrates how the cross functional flow chart shown in Example 4 would look if it was drawn as a data management chart.

The **advantages** of data management charts are the level of detail that they contain, and the logical way in which the responsibilities of all stakeholders in terms of the six data management processes are described.

The **disadvantages** of data management charts are that the level of detail that they contain may be daunting for some stakeholders, especially policy makers or decision makers who only want a quick overview, without all the details.

Example 3: Regular flow chart (of the same routine monitoring system illustrated in example 1)

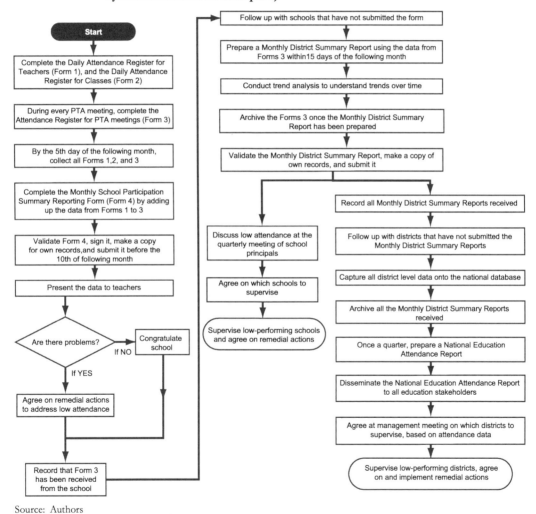

Source: Authors

Example 4: Cross-functional flow chart (of the same routine monitoring system illustrated in example 1)

Primary and Secondary Schools	Education District Offices	Ministry of Education Head Office

Start

On a daily basis, complete the Daily Attendance Register for Teachers (Form 1), and the Daily Attendance Register for Classes (Form 2)(see Annex C for template)

During every PTA meeting, complete the Attendance Register for PTA meetings (Form 3)(see Annex C for template)

By the 5th day of the following month, collect all Forms 1, 2, and 3

Complete the Monthly School Participation Summary Reporting Form (Form 4) by adding up the data from Forms 1 to 3

Validate Form 4, sign it, make a copy for own records, and submit it before the 10th of following month

Present the data to teachers

Are there any problems? → If NO → Congratulate school

If YES

Agree on remedial actions to address low attendance

Education District Offices column:

Record that the form has been received

Follow up with schools that have not submitted the form

Prepare a Monthly District Summary Report using the data from Forms 3 within 15 days of the following month

Conduct trend analysis to understand trends over time

Archive the Forms 3 once the Monthly District Summary Report has been prepared

Validate the Monthly District Summary Report, make a copy of own records, and submit it

Discuss low attendance at the quarterly meeting of school principals

Agree on which schools to supervise

Supervise low-performing schools and agree on remedial actions

Ministry of Education Head Office column:

Record all Monthly District Summary Reports received

Follow up with districts that have not submitted the Monthly District Summary Reports

Capture all district level data onto the national database

Archive all the Monthly District Summary Reports received

Once a quarter, prepare a National Education Attendance Report

Disseminate the National Education Attendance Report to all education stakeholders

Agree at management meeting on which districts to supervise, based on attendance data

Supervise low-performing districts, agree on and implement remedial actions

Source: Authors

Example 5: Data management chart (of the same routine monitoring system illustrated in example 1)

	Primary and Secondary Schools	Education District Offices	Ministry of Education Head Office
1. Data sourcing	• Complete, daily, the Daily Attendance Sheet for Teachers (Form 1 in Annex C) • Complete, daily, the Daily Attendance Sheet for Classes (Form 2 in Annex C) • Complete, at every PTA meeting, the Attendance Sheet for PTA Meetings	• Record that the Forms 3 that have been received into the Monthly School Summary Reporting Form register	• Record all Monthly District Summary Reports received
2. Data collection	• By the 5th day of the following month, collect all Forms 1, 2, and 3	• Follow up with schools that have not submitted the form	• Follow up with districts that have not submitted the Monthly District Summary Reports
3. Data collation	• Complete the Monthly School Summary Reporting Form (Form 4 in Annex C) every month • Archive the Forms 1 and 2 once the Monthly School Summary Reporting Form has been prepared	• Prepare a Monthly District Summary Report using the data from Forms 3 within 15 days of the following month • Archive the Forms 3 once the Monthly District Summary Report has been prepared	• Capture all district level data onto the national database • Archive all the Monthly District Summary Reports received
4. Data analysis	• Validate Form 4, sign it, and make a copy for own records. • Perform trend analysis to understand trends over time at the school, and look for patterns amongst teachers and students with higher absenteeism	• Validate the Monthly District Summary Report, and make a copy of own records • Perform trend analysis to understand trends over time	• Once a quarter, prepare a National Education Attendance Report by month end following the reported quarter • Perform trend analysis to understand trends over time
5. Data reporting	• Submit the Monthly School Summary Reporting Form to the District Education Office before the 10th of the month following the reported month	• Submit the Monthly District Summary Report to the National Education Head Office before the 20th of the month following the reported month	• Disseminate the National Education Attendance Report to all education stakeholders
6. Data use	• Use the data to decide which schools to supervise • Supervise the schools, agree on remedial actions to improve weaknesses (See Module 10 for more details about Supportive Supervision and Data Auditing) • Follow up to ensure that remedial actions have been implemented	• Discuss low attendance at the quarterly meeting of school principals • Agree on which schools to supervise • Supervise low-performing schools and agree on remedial actions	• Agree at management meeting on which districts to supervise, based on attendance data • Supervise low-performing districts, agree on and implement remedial actions

Chapter 7

Annex C: Examples of Routine Monitoring Forms

Example 1: Example of a Daily Register

DAILY ATTENDANCE REGISTER FOR TEACHERS (FORM 1)

School Name:..

Register Sequence Number:...

School District: ....

Date	Teacher Name	In attendance?	If absent...			
			Was school notified of absence by 10 am?	Reason for absence?	Name of replacement teacher	Sick leave check

DAILY ATTENDANCE REGISTER FOR CLASSES (FORM 2)

School Name:..Date: ....

School District: ....

Grade:.................Class Number...............Homeroom Teacher:.............................

Number	Student Last Name	Student First name	Tick the appropriate blocks		
			At school today?	On time?	Homework book signed?

Example 2: Example of a Routine Workshop Attendance Register

ATTENDANCE REGISTER FOR PARENT TEACHER ASSOCIATION MEETINGS (FORM 3)

School Name:..Meeting Date:..................

School District:...
....Meeting Number:.............

Meeting Venue:...

Parent Attendance						
Name	Surname	Physical Address	Names of children in school	Grades of children in school	Email address	Wish to receive school updates via cell phone messaging?

Teacher Attendance						
Name	Surname	Teaching grades	Teaching subjects	Email address	Extra curricular activities	Number of meetings attended this year

Chapter 7

Example 3: Example of a Month Summary Form That Draws from the Register and the Workshop Attendance Register

MONTHLY SCHOOL PARTICIPATION SUMMARY REPORTING FORM (FORM 4)

School Name: ....

Month and Year of Reporting: ....

School District: ....

Teacher Attendance	
Percentage of school days in the month with no teachers absent	
Percentage of teachers with more than 3 days absent in the school month	
Student Attendance	
Percentage of students not absent in the past school month	
Percentage of students absent for 1 or 2 days in the past school month	
Percentage of students absent for more than 2 days without reason in the past school month	
Parent Attendance of PTA Meeting	
Percentage of school teachers in attendance	
Percentage of school's students with at least one parent in attendance	

General comments: ....
....
....
....

Report validated:

Signed: ....

Name: ....

Designation: ....

School Stamp

When completed and validated, submit to District Education Manager, by the 10th of the following month

FOR DISTRICT OFFICE USE	
Received by and Date Received	
Verified by and Date:	
Captured by and Date:	
Filed by and date:	

Annex D: Example of Data Management Processes Description

	Locations in the Data Flow Schematic		
	All schools (including community schools)	**Ministry of Education district office**	**Ministry of Education head office**
Data Sourcing	Attendance registers of students Attendance registers of teachers Exam results records of students	Record attendance of its own staff	Record attendance of its own staff
Data Collection	Collect attendance registers every day from teachers Collect exam results from teachers within 10 days of exam end	Collect school attendance record summaries from schools Collect median and average exam records from schools	Collect summary of attendance records from districts
Data Collation	Tally all attendance registers onto a school attendance record summary Tally exam results for the school onto exam result summary sheet	Collate all school attendance summaries to determine average attendance per school Collate its own attendance registers	Collate attendance register data to determine annual average
Data Analysis	Analyze attendance trends Determine median and average scores per subject	Analyze attendance trends in schools and in own office Determine median and average scores per subject	Analyze attendance trends Determine median and average scores per subject per district
Data Reporting	Report exam results to district education office Report school attendance record summary to district education office	Report exam results to national office Report school attendance summary sheets to national office Report its own staff attendance records to national office	Compile a national school performance and school attendance report

Data Management Process (row label, left side)

Locations in the Data Flow Schematic		
All schools (including community schools)	**Ministry of Education district office**	**Ministry of Education head office**

| | Data Use | Use data to motivate teachers to perform better

Use data to identify students who problems with attendance | Use data to identify well-performing schools

Use data to identify staff with high absenteeism

Use data to identify schools with poor attendance records | Use data to identify well-performing district management teams

Use data to identify well-performing schools |

Data Management Process

Source: Authors

Making Monitoring and Evaluation Systems Work

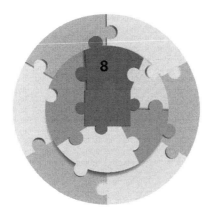

Chapter 8
Periodic Surveys

Chapter Aim

The aim of this chapter is to enable you to decide whether you require a survey to collect the data you need and, if a survey is necessary, to design and implement a good quality survey.

Chapter Knowledge and Skills

By the end of this Chapter, you should be able to:

a) Decide whether or not a survey is useful for the type of data you need to collect.

b) Know the steps involved in planning, designing and implementing a survey.

c) Design each step of the survey.

d) Implement a survey with as little bias as possible.

e) Know the process steps involved in calculating a sample size.

Before You Begin…

Take a few minutes to read through the questions below. You may find it helpful to write down your answers. As you work through the chapter, compare your answers to views of the authors.

- Have you ever used a survey?
- Can you use survey results to measure the outcomes of your program?
- Why is it necessary to have both surveys and routine monitoring data?
- When is it better to use a survey and when is it better to use routine monitoring data for the indicator values in your M&E system?
- How do you design a survey?
- What can you do to ensure that your survey results can be generalized?
- What are the pitfalls to avoid when conducting surveys?
- How do you best calculate a sample size?
- How do you know if your survey results can be generalized for the whole population?

This chapter explains how to decide whether or not to do a survey and how to undertake one. It takes you through all the steps involved in doing a survey, shows you all the important decisions you need to make along the way, and offers tips that will help you implement a better survey.

Component 8: Periodic Surveys

1. Introduction

> *"Everyone takes surveys. Whoever makes a statement about human behavior has engaged in a survey of some sort."*[1]
>
> Andrew Greeley, 2008

The *fuel* of an M&E system is its data. The data that the M&E system requires to *run* are determined by the indicators and the research questions in the M&E plan (see Chapter 4: M&E plans). The different indicators (input indicators, output indicators, outcome indicators and impact indicators) in the M&E system require three types of data sources: routine, periodic, and one-off, as Table C8-1 illustrates.

Table C8-1: **Types of Data Sources for Different Types of Indicators**

Indicator type	Data collection time frame	Types of data sources
Input/ Process	Continuously	Routine data sources such as statistics about education or other government services
		Routine data sources such as routine monitoring data about training materials developed for schools
Output	Quarterly, semi-annually, or annually	Routine data sources such as statistics about education or other government services
		Routine data sources such as routine monitoring data about teacher absenteeism or the number of visits by agriculture extension officers
		Periodic data sources such as exit interview surveys
Outcome	1 to 3 years	Periodic data sources such as population-based surveys
		One-off data sources such as special studies (research or evaluation)
Impact	2 to 5 years	Periodic data sources such as surveillance
		Periodic data sources such as population-based surveys
		One-off data sources such as special studies (research or evaluation)

Source: Adapted from the Global Fund and WHO M&E toolkit, 2006

---

[1] Extracted from BrainyQuote.com on 5 October 2008 at http://www.brainyquote.com/quotes/quotes/a/andrewgree180244.html

Chapter 8

Each of these three types of data sources are components of the middle ring (data collection, capture, and verification) of the 12 Components of a functional M&E system and are covered in this training course in the following chapters:

- Routine data sources (Chapter 7: Routine Data)
- Periodic data sources (Chapter 8: Periodic Surveys – **this chapter**)
- One-off data sources (Chapter 11: Evaluation and Research)

How this chapter is organized: The chapter begins with background information and definitions relating to selected types of surveys and surveillance (Section 2). The desired result for this chapter is presented in Section 3. Section 4 describes the benefits of surveys and surveillance: how each helps to form the bedrock of an M&E system; and how each provides data that inform stakeholders of program impact and outcome. Implementation issues are briefly presented (Section 5) to provide context for the HowTo Guide on how to undertake a survey for this component. Steps are provided in detail in Section 6. The chapter closes with a summary of lessons learned (Section 7) and a practical exercise to cement what you have learned (Section 8).

2. Background Information and Definitions

Types of Data Sources: Within an M&E system, three types of data sources can generally be distinguished: one-off data sources, periodic data sources and routine data sources.

- **One-off data sources:** Data sources are one-off when data are collected: (1) once only to answer a specific research or evaluation question; and (2) there is no expectation that similar data collection, using similar data collection instruments, will be done again. Most **evaluations and** research are one-off data sources (see Chapter 11 of this Training Course).

- **Periodic data sources:** Data sources are periodic when data are collected: (1) independently of interventions; (2) at significant intervals in time; (3) using the same data collection tool (often a quantitative questionnaire) so that data can be compared over time. An example of a periodic data source is a **survey** (discussed in this chapter). Survey data are not collected only in areas where interventions have been implemented (satisfying condition 1); are collected only every year (or less often) when the survey is undertaken (satisfying condition 2); use the same questionnaire, protocol and data analysis techniques every time the survey is conducted (satisfying condition 3).

- Surveys could collect data from an entire population (census) or from a sample population (sample survey). In sample surveys, if the demographic characteristics (e.g., age and sex) of the sample are the same as the characteristics of the entire population and the survey results satisfy certain statistical tests, the answers provided by the sample are said to be representative of the answers that the entire population would provide (i.e., the survey results from the sample are *generalizable* to the population at large).

- For surveys to be *independent of interventions* implies that the sample population is selected to be representative of the entire population, rather than from only the areas where the intervention has been implemented. A survey done only in intervention areas would lead to results that are not representative of the whole population, i.e., biased results (see definition of "bias" later in this section).

- **Routine data sources:** Data sources are routine when data are collected on an ongoing basis as activities are implemented. Examples of routine data sources are attendance registers or registers of peer education sessions. Attendance registers are *routine* because new data are added on an ongoing basis, for example, every time that a meeting is held, an attendance register is filled out. Routine data cannot be collected on a sample basis because for routine data to be meaningful, standardized data are required from all places where the activity is implemented, usually using standard data collection tools.

Example

To explain the contrast, consider a non-governmental organization (NGO) that keeps records of all its drama shows that promote HIV prevention. Every time a drama is conducted, a form is filled out. This is an example of ongoing data collection and the completed forms are a routine data source. In contrast, once a year the NGO may undertake a survey to find out what people who attend the drama shows think of the show. This survey is an example of a periodic data source.

- **Survey:** A method of collecting information from respondents — who can be either a sample of the population or selected, targeted, organizations (or facilities). This may involve gathering information either at a point in time (cross-sectional survey) or tracking a group of people over a period of time (longitudinal survey or panel data). Information generated through surveys can include factual information; levels of knowledge; attitudes; personality types; beliefs and preferences. For many national-level surveys, standard protocols have been developed to ensure that the survey gets conducted in the same way every time it is done. This enables trend analysis over time and comparisons.

Surveillance: Surveillance includes biological and behavioral surveillance. Biological surveillance involves collecting specific biological data through repeated cross-sectional surveys in a representative population. Behavioral surveillance refers to repeat cross-sectional surveys of behavior in a representative population (UNAIDS and WHO, 2000). Surveillance is often used to collect information about the prevalence of a specific disease amongst populations being surveyed, either populations that are more or less representative of the general population or specific populations at high risk for the disease.

Bias: A bias is a "feature of the study which makes a particular result more likely — like a football pitch which slopes from one end to the other" (Leung, 2001a), also known as non-sampling errors. Non-sampling errors can be generated by various problems in executing the survey: such as incorrect sampling, non-interviews, too few respondents, lack of understanding or knowledge by respondents, desire by participants to conceal the truth, loaded questions, processing errors, or interviewer errors. Different types of biases exist (Macdonald, 2001):

- **Information bias** occurs when systematic differences are introduced in measuring the response. Two examples are recall bias and observer bias.

   i.   **Recall bias** is when a difference occurs because one/some groups of respondents are more likely to remember an event than another group. This is typical in a case control study when the cases are more likely than the controls to remember an adverse event.

   ii. **Observer bias** can result from differences between observers (inter-observer) or with the same observer (intra-observer). To eliminate this, it is important that all observers use a standardized method of measuring or collecting data. If you are the only observer, you will still need to have a standard and systematic method for measuring or collecting your data to make sure that your results are not affected by your mood.

- **Non-response bias** arises when those who respond to a questionnaire (responders) differ in some relevant way from those who don't (non-responders). Most researchers try to reduce this as much as possible by trying to (a) maximize the response rate by sending out reminders, having incentives for responding etc., or (b) by identifying the relevant characteristics of the non-responders (age, sex, education, etc.) so they can see whether they are any different from the responders. They can then make adjustments in their analysis for the non-responders.

- **Selection bias** results when the sample group you have chosen is not representative of the population for which you want to generalize your results. Random sampling can stop this from happening in your survey.

- **Sampling** is the process of selecting respondents for the survey. Sampling can be done in different ways. Respondents can be selected purposively, randomly, or respondents can nominate each other to participate in the survey (respondent-driven sampling). Sampling involves deciding on the sampling unit (e.g., persons, households, or health facilities), determining the sampling frame (the population from where the sample will be selected), determining the overall sample size and the sample size of the strata. If the sample is stratified, then the sample size is proportional to strata size, equal

Making Monitoring and Evaluation Systems Work

sample sizes should be drawn from all strata and the required sample size is bigger the more strata vary from each other.

Respondent: The person who answers questions during an interview.

Sampling unit: The unit that is selected during the process of sampling. If you select teachers in the education system from a list of teachers, the sampling unit is a teacher.

Basic sampling unit: the sampling unit at the last stage of sampling. In a multi-cluster survey, if you first select villages, then select households within the village, the basic sampling unit is the household.

Sampling universe: The entire group of sampling units (commonly households or persons) who are eligible to be included in the survey sample.

Sampling frame: A list of all members of the population being studied, so that each has an equal chance of being included in the sample (Scheuren, 2004). It is, therefore, a list of all the sampling units from which you will choose your sample (UNHCR, The World Bank and GLIA, 2008). A sampling frame can be a list of individual names, or a list of households, or a list of facilities, or a list of schools. Whatever the sampling unit chosen, the sampling frame should provide a list of the sample *population* (persons, buildings, geographic areas, etc.). The sampling frame and sampling universe should be the same, as closely as is possible.

Sample size is the number of units that will be selected from the sample frame, to produce statistically reliable results. It needs to be statistically calculated as there is no fixed or ideal sample size.

Sampling methodology is the method you apply to select respondents for the survey sample. Different sampling methods exist but random sampling methods are generally preferred to ensure that the survey is generalizable. "Virtually all surveys taken seriously by social scientists and policy-makers use some form of random sampling" (Scheuren, 2004: 18). Annex A contains an overview of the classes of sampling methods.

3. Results to Be Achieved When Implementing This Component

Long-term result:
Surveys that: answer relevant objectives, are unbiased and accurate, generalizable, ethical and economical are undertaken or existing survey results are used, as required by the program's data needs.

Short- and medium-term results:

- Inventory of relevant surveys already conducted.

- Specified schedule for future surveys (to be conducted by the organization or from where the organization should draw its own data).

- Protocols for all surveys based on international or national standards (if in existence).

For reflection 1:

What types of data collection are the preferred methods in your organization? Has your organization conducted surveys or surveillance of any type? If so, how were the surveys designed and by whom? Did the surveys serve all stakeholders' needs? How was the sampling done in the surveys that you know of? Did the surveys have a sampling frame and a sampling strategy? How many short- and medium-term results listed here are visible in your organization?

---

4. Benefits of Periodic Surveys as Part of an M&E System

a) **Generate objective impact-level and outcome-level data:** Surveys and surveillance data are essential for an M&E system because they help generate certain impact and outcome-level data. These survey data avoid bias by collecting data in intervention and other areas and usually provide an objective, independent view on the impacts and outcomes and may be more credible than data collected by a project itself.

b) **Surveys can provide generalizable data:** Surveys collect data that can be generalized to the entire population from which the sample was selected, provided that survey results pass certain statistical tests of significance and validity. This implies that every program or organization does not necessarily need to do its own survey as they can all use the results of a representative survey.

c) **A survey costs less than a census.** Because a survey can generate generalizable data, it is possible to get views, opinions, and other information about an entire population without having to survey the entire population and this greatly reduces costs.

d) **Surveys enable trend analysis over time:** Provided that the survey protocol is set up appropriately and the survey is conducted in the same way (same method), and collects the same kind of data (same questionnaire), trend analysis over time is possible.

5. Implementation Issues Related to Periodic Surveys

5.1. Deciding whether or not to undertake a survey

A decision about whether or not a survey should be undertaken depends on the type of indicator for which data are needed and the indicator measurement unit (*number of* or *percentage of*).

* If the indicator starts with ***Number of***, then a sample survey ***cannot*** be used because surveys can only collect percentage data (e.g. the percentage of all respondents who said YES).

* If the indicator starts with ***Percentage of***, then either a survey OR routine data can be used to calculate the indicator value. The decision tree in Figure C8-1, and the information provided in Table C8-1 can help you decide whether a survey or routine data are needed.

In Figure C8-1, it is important to understand how to interpret the two different types of indicator values that will be generated through the two different data

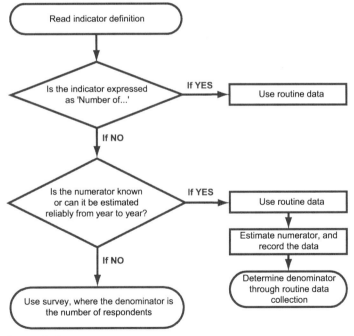

Source: Authors

Figure C8-1: **Decision Tree to Help Decide Whether an Indicator That Starts with "Percentage of" Should Be Collected through Routine Data or Surveys**

sources. If routine data are used for the denominator and estimates are used for the numerator, the indicator value is representative of the general population as long as the denominator data (routine data) were collected from all possible sites and locations. Low reporting rates (used for denominator) or estimations (used for the numerator) will skew the indicator value. If a survey is used as a data source, the survey design needs to enable generalizable data (i.e., a probability sampling method) so that the percentage generated from the survey is a percentage that is valid for the entire population from which the sample was drawn.

Also refer to Section 5.8 of Chapter 7 that provides a detailed example of how one could use either routine data or survey data.

5.2. Governance and execution of national surveys

National surveys should be led by the most suitable agency. This may be the Ministry of Labor (for workplace surveys) or Ministry of Health (for all biological and health facility surveys). Behavioral surveys are coordinated by the National Statistical Office in some countries and in others by the Ministry of Health. The National Statistical Office should be involved in, and approve, all surveys that are done in a country so it is good practice to include this agency in the peer review group for the survey.

Survey design should be scientifically sound, use experts, and involve the M&E team so that survey data are collected, analyzed, and presented in such a way that indicator values can be extracted easily from the survey report.

5.3. Ethical processes to follow during survey execution

In implementing surveys, there are some basic ethical protocols and principles to consider so that respondents are treated fairly and their responses remain confidential (FHI, 2001). Respondents should have:

- The choice to participate or not to participate in the research (the ability to opt-out entirely from the survey);
- An understanding of why the research is being carried out, the possible positive outcomes associated with the research, and the possible negative outcomes associated with the research;
- A clear understanding of the possibility that there will be no individual impact of the research;
- The knowledge that they are free to withdraw from the survey at any point during the survey;
- The knowledge that they are free to refuse to answer any questions they do not want to answer;
- The reassurance that their answers are strictly confidential, will be

aggregated with no name identifiers, and will not be attributed to any particular individual.

Each survey needs a **statement to inform and request consent** from potential respondents that is tailored to the particular issues being investigated and the populations being interviewed. In cases where interviews are being conducted with children, for example, permission needs to be secured from a responsible adult. In the case of household-based surveys, parental/caregiver permission is required to interview non-adults (the consent age varies but often is set at eighteen). In the case of institutional interviews, for example in schools, generally it is acceptable to secure the approval of school authorities, although the situation varies from country to country and depends on survey content.

How does one guarantee the **confidentiality** of respondents? Feber et al (1980:7) have a few practical suggestions:

- Use only code numbers to refer to a respondent on a questionnaire and keep the code separate from the data
- Refuse to give names and addresses of survey respondents to anybody outside the survey organization
- Destroy questionnaires and identifying information about respondents after entering and checking the data
- Omit names and addresses of survey respondents from computer analysis
- Present statistical tabulations by broad enough categories so that individual respondents cannot be identified

5.4. How much does a survey cost?

Experience has shown that the typical kinds of costs included in a survey budget are as follows (Schreunen, 2004; UNHCR, The World Bank and GLIA, 2008):

- Staff time for planning the survey, doing the sample selection, designing the questionnaire, and general survey oversight
- Labor and material costs for pre-testing the questionnaire and field procedures (more than one iteration of pre-testing may be needed)
- Costs for field staff (enumerators) and supervisors during data collection and data cleaning
- Enumerator field and travel costs for collecting data
- Labor costs for data entry and data checking
- Labor costs for quality control and spot checking
- Labor costs for data tabulation and data analysis
- Labor costs for report preparation and finalization
- Report printing and dissemination costs

- Renting space (training, data entry, other needs)
- Printing and photocopying
- Office supplies such as pens, notepads, Post-It® notes, colored tags (handy for marking questionnaires), easel paper, folders, staplers, paperclips
- Communication including SIM cards for mobile phones, radios, e-mail, local and international calls
- Computer rental
- Software
- Car rental for data collection and for travel between survey sites
- Car maintenance
- Fuel costs
- Accommodation, when necessary
- Participant incentives, if appropriate
- Supplies for field staff such as folders to carry questionnaires and other documents, umbrellas to keep off rain/sun, rain boots and raincoats, strong shoes if long distances have to be covered
- Name tags to identify survey members and their affiliation to local leaders and participants
- Meals during training and other activities
- Certificates

A general principle to remember is that surveys involving a large number of interviews tend to be cheaper on a per-interview basis than surveys with fewer interviews. This is particularly so when the sample size is less than 1000. The reason is that the same *tooling up* costs (all the survey preparatory activities) are involved for a survey of any size. Consequently, the greater the number of interviews the lower the preparatory costs per interview. (Schreuner, 2004).

5.5. Types of questions in survey questionnaires

Questionnaires have two main types of questions: (i) open-ended questions (non-structured) and (ii) closed (fixed or structured) questions (Fehrer, 1980; Kenneth Lafferty Hess, 2008). Examples are provided in Table C8-2.

Table C8-2:   Examples of Open-Ended and Closed Questions

Open-ended question	Closed question (choice of categories)
How did you experience the training course?	How did you experience the training course? (choose one answer) 1. Relevant for my needs 2. Too difficult to understand 3. Just what I needed
Closed question (rating or Likert scale)	**Closed question (differential scales)**
(When you want to quantify opinions. Avoid a 5-point Likert scale (people tend to choose the middle option more often), and include an option for non-response. Please describe your feelings at the end of the training course: 1. Unsatisfied 2. Somewhat satisfied 3. Satisfied 4. Very satisfied	How do you rate the training? Extremely dull = 1: Extremely good = 10 1 2 3 4 5 6 7 8 9 10
Closed question (ranking)	**Closed question (checklists)**
(sometimes you want the respondent to compare items) Rank all of the training courses you have attended in the last 12 months from most to least relevant to your training needs: Data analysis Team building Creative drawing	Circle all the sessions in the training course that you found useful: Session 1: Data use Session 2: Managing for results Session 3: Supervision Session 4: Data quality assurance

Partially-closed question

How do you intend to use the training course materials (please select all that apply)?

• To train others

• To improve my own knowledge

• To show other people at work

• Other

Source: Author examples, with categories drawn from Leung (2001b) and Kenneth Lafferty Hass (2008)

Each type of question has advantages (Leung, 2001b) — see Table C8-3:

Table C8-3: Advantages of Open-Ended and Closed Questions

Open-ended question advantages	Closed question advantages
Allows exploration of the range of possible themes	Easy and quick to fill in
Can be used even if a comprehensive range of alternative choices cannot be compiled	Minimize discrimination against less literate or less articulate people
Data can be qualitatively coded and frequency of themes displayed in a histogram	Easy to code, record, and analyze results
	Easy to report results

Source: Leung, 2001b:144

Open-ended questions will yield qualitative data for which qualitative data analysis techniques are needed whereas closed questions will yield quantitative data to which quantitative data analysis techniques (descriptive and inferential statistics) can be applied.

The wording of questions can determine whether or not a person answers the question. You need to be clear, unambiguous, and make sure that all respondents will understand your question in the same way. Here are some principles to remember (Leung, 2001b).

- Use short and simple sentences
- Ask for only one piece of information at a time
- Avoid negatives, if possible
- Ask precise questions
- Ensure that those you ask have the necessary knowledge
- Ask for the exact level of detail required
- Minimize bias by avoiding leading questions
- Phrase questions about sensitive issues carefully

In addition to deciding how best to ask each question (what type of question and the precise wording), questionnaire design also involves deciding how to sequence and group the questions. Questions are often organized from easier to more difficult or from general to particular, factual to abstract, and closed questions before open questions (Leung, 2001b). This is so that respondents can relax and feel comfortable with the survey process before difficult, sensitive, or particular questions are asked.

Making Monitoring and Evaluation Systems Work

5.6 General pitfalls to avoid when designing and conducting surveys

Schreuner (2004:26) said that, "If anything can go wrong (in a survey), it will… if you did not check on it, it did (go wrong)". Table C8-4 summarizes general lessons learned about planning and implementing surveys. Possible solutions and remedies to these challenges are provided in the last column of the table. Remember that the quality of a survey is not determined by the number of problems but by whether problems that occurred were properly documented and handled in a professional and appropriate way.

Table C8-4: Pitfalls and Sources of Biases when Conducting a Survey, and How to Handle Them

Survey Step (See HowTo Guide C8-1)	Possible pitfalls and biases	Possible precautions/ remedies
Survey preparation	Question not understood as intended	Make the purpose of the survey explicit from the start
	Time period for survey not sufficient	Develop a detailed action plan with time line and responsibilities upfront
Sampling	Relevant people not studied	Clearly define the study population
	Lack of baseline denominator information	Consider various sources of baseline denominator information
	Sample not representative of population studied	Use appropriate probability sampling method
	Convenience sampling chosen	Use appropriate probability sampling method
	Sample size insufficient to answer the intended question	Calculate sample size, using statistical means, before carrying out the survey
Questionnaire design	Essential information not collected	Consider carefully what data are required
	Long questionnaires or interviews (from collecting unnecessary information) cause a low response rate	
	Leading question influences the answers provided	Rephrase the question after testing it on a small number of persons
	Not pre-testing the questionnaire	Pre-test all questionnaires: the only way to find out *if everything works*
Collect the data	Invalid measurement of information	Use validated measurement tools to carry out pilot studies
		Pre-test all questionnaires

Chapter 8

Survey Step (See HowTo Guide C8-1)	Possible pitfalls and biases	Possible precautions/remedies
Collect the data	Sloppy field work and inadequate controls	Check and supervise every facet of the survey. Supervisor re-do some surveys to see if similar results are achieved.
	Not sufficiently following up on non respondents (low response rate makes survey results questionable)	Ensure proper procedures that are all carried out
	Inability by respondents to recall information that is difficult to recall	Encourage participants to use records to help them remember OR shorten the required recall period
	Biases: Non-consent and non-response bias, Social undesirability bias, or Observer bias	Approach and explain survey carefully and politely Train enumerators well
Record and analyze the data	Inaccurate recording of results	Use optical scanning, computer assisted questionnaires, validate data as they are being captured
	Wrong analysis	Use statistical packages
	Sampling errors not known	If a probability sample was used, calculate the sampling error in the report
	Imprecise findings	Increase the sample size or choose a stratified sample
	Incomplete survey coverage	Work out the percentage not covered and adjust the findings by this weighting

Sources: Authors compiled it from Leung, 2001; Schreunen, 2004; NERCHA, 2009; UNHCR, The World Bank and GLIA, 2008

6. HowTo Guide C8-1: Undertake a Periodic Survey

Various manuals and handbooks have been written on how to plan and undertake a survey. This section provides a summary of the different sources summarizing the action steps required. At the end of the HowTo Guide, links to a website are included for you to learn more about planning and undertaking surveys.

Step 1: Survey preparations

During survey preparation, one needs to collect information including previous surveys, census data, maps, population and household lists, local interventions. A vital step is to determine clearly the objectives of the survey and core indicators. Generally, a survey has one of two classes of objectives (Leung, 2001a):

- **In a descriptive survey, the purpose may be to learn the frequency of occurrence of particular characteristics.** An example would be the proportion and characteristics of students who read a specific magazine or practice certain behaviors or the proportion and characteristics of people who use a particular product. Such purposes can be achieved by collecting information from a sample of students at one point in time (cross sectional survey). If the cross-sectional survey is repeated periodically, information about the time trends can be gathered, for example, whether the magazine is becoming more popular, or the behaviors less or more common.

- **In an analytic survey, the purpose may be to learn something about the causes of certain characteristics.** An example would be how students' learning styles at the start of a course affect their final results. A cohort (longitudinal) study following a group of first-year students until they graduate is more likely to yield the required information as this allows initial learning styles to be accurately assessed without being influenced by prior knowledge of their course results.

With the objectives and data requirements clear, the next tasks are to define the survey population and geographic area, and determine sampling methodology and sample sizes (see HowTo Guide C8-2). At the same time, it is important to build partnerships with community leaders, UN and government agencies, NGOs and local authorities, and generate consensus on survey objectives. Ask the appropriate people to help communicate with populations to be surveyed about the purpose of the survey in order to help ensure a high participation rate.

In addition, resolve timing, access, participation, and security issues, and obtain ethical clearance. It is also necessary to define survey team composition and roles, the preliminary survey time frame and preliminary budget (see Section 5.4 for a list of sample survey costs).

Deliverables: Clear and explicit purpose of survey, survey plans and time frames, ethical clearance, community support, and a draft survey budget.

Step 2:   Decide on all aspects related to sampling

Leung (2001a) points out that sampling design involves defining exactly who should be studied and that it is crucial to ensure that this definition corresponds to the purposes of the survey. This usually includes specific personal, time and place criteria. For example, in an investigation of the reasons for the non-attendance by women for cervical cancer screening, those who are not eligible for such screening must be excluded from the study population. For example, women above or below the recommended screening age or those who have had a total hysterectomy would not be included. If they were included,. the results would not provide a valid answer to the original question.

Therefore, one needs to calculate the sample sizes (see HowTo Guide C8-2), validate the accuracy of population data, and fill any information gaps (UNHCR, The World Bank and GLIA, 2008). A final decision is needed on the sampling methodology. The sample chosen must be representative of the sampling frame. To ensure that the sample is representative, each sampling unit in the sampling frame must have an equal chance of being sampled (Leung, 2001b).

After the sample size and sample methodology have been finalized, the number of field staff and days needed to achieve the desired sample size can be calculated and the budget and time frame finalized (UNHCR, The World Bank and GLIA, 2008).

Deliverables: Defined sample frame, sample size, and sample methodology that correspond to the purpose of the survey; an almost-final survey budget; field staff numbers and final budget agreed upon.

Step 3:   Develop the questionnaire and determine procedures for obtaining informed consent

First, develop the core or expanded questionnaire and carefully determine and make any necessary adaptations to the questionnaire and consent form. Then, translate into all locally relevant languages and field test the documents. Revise the questionnaire and consent form based on field test results, back-translate all documents, and finalize and print the questionnaire (UNHCR, The World Bank and GLIA, 2008).

Section 5.5 (above) provides more details about questionnaire design. When designing the questionnaire, always start with the data collection goals of the survey and remember to collect data for **dependent variables** (e.g., performance in the assessments of various components of the course) and **independent variables** that may explain changes in the dependent variables (e.g., the number of hours a week the student works). In this example, however, it may not be part-time work which directly affects course results but that students from poor families may be more likely to take on part-time work as well as more likely to do worse in assessments. In this case, coming from a poor family is a **confounding variable**. Data should also be collected for possible confounders (Leung, 2001b).

Deliverable: Final survey questionnaire.

Step 4:   Prepare survey documentation

This step entails developing or adapting the survey protocol for local field conditions, and developing additional fieldwork forms (such as household information sheets). It also entails determining the step-by-step process of data collection, including roles and responsibilities of the team. It is important to document each step in the process of data collection, management, and analysis in an operational manual. Based on all this information, the time frame and budget can be finalized (UNHCR, The World Bank and GLIA, 2008).

Deliverables: Survey protocol (see Annex) and final survey budget.

Step 5:   Put the team together and train the team members

For this step, one would first determine the field team composition and qualifications, and then recruit field staff and supervisors. When training all field staff and supervisors, include mock data collection activities. In many surveys, more people than needed are trained and, then, after reviewing the abilities of each member of the team, final members are selected (UNHCR, The World Bank and GLIA, 2008). This also safeguards against some people not completing the training. One of the main purposes of the training is to ensure that all enumerators follow the same interview protocol. All interviewers should adopt the same approach in explaining the survey, phrasing particular questions, and recording the responses. This will minimize observer bias.

Deliverable: Trained survey team members.

Step 6:   Collect the data

First, you need to finalize a detailed schedule for data collection and then recruit respondents. Once respondents have been identified, you can set up sites and conduct interviews (UNHCR, The World Bank and GLIA, 2008). There are several possible methods of collecting data (e.g., postal questionnaires to individuals or via organizations; computer assisted questionnaires; email questionnaires; online questionnaires; face-to-face interviews; telephone interviews) (Leung, 2001a). At each stage of the data collection process thorough quality control is necessary. Security measures are important such as collecting fieldwork forms each day and storing them in a locked place. Also, remember to debrief with your team every day so that you can discuss problems and find solutions together (e.g., non-response – see section 5.6). Bear in mind that everything done or not done in a survey could affect the validity of the results (Schreuner, 2004; UNHCR, The World Bank and GLIA, 2008).

One of the most important aspects during the data collection phase is to minimize non-response which is an important source of bias. Those who respond to the survey are likely to differ from those who do not. Hence, it is very important to maximize the response rate. Carefully explaining the purpose of the survey and how the results will be used helps, so does approaching people politely and courteously, and sending reminders to non-responders (or calling back, or re-visiting) (Leung, 2001a).

Deliverables: Completed questionnaires and all field supervision forms.

Step 7:   Manage the data

Although for small scale surveys it is easy to record results by hand and carry and analyses using calculators, larger surveys are more efficiently conducted using technology such as optical scanners and statistical packages for analysis of more complex data (Leung, 2001a).

Should you use software for data entry, you first need to develop a data entry program with quality control checks and then train all data entry clerks on the questionnaire and data entry procedures. A data entry schedule should be developed and questionnaires and other field work information entered into the data set according to the schedule. Once entered, you need to clean all data sets rigorously prior to beginning analysis, combine and/or rename data sets if needed, and collect and store questionnaires and fieldwork forms in a central, secured location upon completion (UNHCR, The World Bank and GLIA, 2008).

Deliverable: Cleaned data set.

Step 8:   Develop a report and disseminate it

After updating the coding and analysis guide, you need to first conduct an analysis of proportions and means. Next analyze core indicators. Review the analysis for accuracy and document all results in results templates (standard data tabulation formats/templates). If needed, conduct additional analysis of important findings and document results.

Once all analyses have been done, you need to share the findings with key collaborators and population members to develop conclusions and recommendations. With them, determine best methods for disseminating findings to important audiences and other ways of using the data. Document the entire survey process and the results in technical reports and other mediums. Once these documents have been approved, disseminate findings widely to local and international partners, population members, and decision-makers.

Deliverable: Report finalized and disseminated and findings used.

For reflection 2:

Reflect on the different types of data collection strategies used in your organization. Is there a defined protocol for the surveys you undertook? If so, what is the protocol and how does it compare to the steps outlined in this chapter's HowTo guide? Will your organization need to implement surveys or can it draw data from existing surveys? What pitfalls do you anticipate for your organization when implementing surveys? What remedies would be appropriate in your context?

7. HowTo Guide C8-2: Calculate a Sample Size

How many people need to be surveyed? Clearly, a larger sample size would yield more precise results. On the other hand, resources are always limited and constrain size. The sample size required for a survey will depend on the reliability needed which, in turn, depends on how results will be used (Fehrer, 1980).

The sample size needed depends on several factors: the purpose of the survey (e.g., descriptive or analytic); how common the main dependent variables are among the sample population; the amount of variation of the factor of concern; and how precise the results need to be (Schreuner, 2004). You cannot decide sample size based on other surveys or the size of your budget. The sample size will affect the precision with which you are measuring the key indicators in the survey and your ability to measure trends in behavior over time, so it must be tailored to your individual survey and specific context (UNHCR, GLIA and The World Bank, 2008). In order to determine your sample size, you must go through each of the following steps.

Step 1: Define your sampling universe

What populations are you including in the survey? Do you want to be able to analyze each of the populations separately and compare them, or are you going to group them together during the analysis? What geographic areas are you including in the survey? Do you want to be able to analyze each of the geographic areas separately or are you going to group them together during the analysis? If you are surveying refugees in several camps that are close to each other, do you want to look at behavioral risk factors separately for each of the camps or are you going to combine the camps in your analysis? If you have two areas of the country with large numbers of displaced people, do you want to analyze their results separately or will you aggregate the data as a single population group?

The definition of your sampling universe will depend on the objectives of your survey. If a key objective of your survey is to describe HIV risk behaviors in different refugee populations residing in three areas of the country, then you will have three separate sampling universes for the refugees. If another objective of your survey is to compare the behavioral risks and access to interventions among the three refugee populations and their surrounding communities, the host populations will comprise three additional sampling universes. In total you would have six separate samples in your survey, meaning the sample size will be applied to each of these populations separately. You cannot calculate a sample size and spread it across all of the populations in your sample or you will lose the power to analyze the different refugee and host population groups separately, and compare the results.

Example from Uganda

In Uganda, there were two areas of the country where HIV programs were being designed for populations in refugee settlements and their surrounding communities. The survey objective was to measure differences in behaviors and access to interventions between the two different refugee areas, and also to measure differences between the refugee populations and the surrounding communities. In one survey area, there were two refugee settlements abutting each other. The two settlements were similar in composition and relevant characteristics and were to receive the same HIV interventions. These settlements were combined as a single survey population with the understanding that the results from the two settlements would not be analyzed separately. In total, four distinct populations, or sampling universes were included in the survey.

Step 2: Determine the key indicators that you want to measure

Determine the key indicators you want to measure, the precision with which you want to measure them, and whether you will be evaluating changes over multiple survey rounds (i.e., trends).

While budgets should not be the determining factor in calculating the sample size of your survey, restrictive budgets are a reality. For this reason, understand which indicators your sample size will allow you to measure with high precision and where you will have to sacrifice tight confidence intervals for a wider and less precise estimate of an indicator.

Measurements of behaviors at a single point in time require a smaller sample size than measuring changes in behaviors between multiple survey rounds. If one objective of your survey is to measure behavioral trends over time, then your sample size will be somewhat larger than if the survey is intended to be a one-off description of a population.

When measuring behavioral trends, determine the baseline estimated prevalence of the behavior being measured at the time of the survey and what magnitude of behavioral change you wish to be able to measure. Previous research in the region among similar populations may provide reasonable estimates of the baseline behavioral prevalence. The minimum percentage increase (or decrease) in a behavior that you need to measure should be decided on the basis of previous research and program targets. When this information is unavailable, it is common to use a 10% or 15% change between survey rounds for behavioral indicators but this can vary depending on the indicators of interest, the amount of time between surveys, and the intensity of interventions in the area aiming to bring about the change. This means that your sample size will be sufficiently large to measure, for instance, a 10% or larger change in the behavior from baseline prevalence but it will not be able to measure significant statistical differences between survey rounds that are smaller than 10%. The smaller the percentage of change that you wish to be able to measure between survey rounds, the larger your sample size will need to be (see the table below for illustrative sample sizes).

Example from Uganda

A behavioral survey in Uganda was designed to measure several key indictors but it was not feasible to use all the indicators in calculating the sample size. For instance, transactional and casual sex partners among the male and female youth populations are two important measurable HIV risk behaviors, however, they were known to be infrequent activities among the youth. While the sample size of the survey was adequate to estimate the prevalence of these behaviors among youth at baseline, it was impossible to achieve a sample size that would be large enough to identify statistically significant changes of 15% or less in these behaviors over time. Instead, the indicators selected for calculating the sample size in this Ugandan survey in order to measure trends over time were the following:

1. More than one sex partner in the past 12 months among men and women aged 15-49 years
2. Comprehensive correct knowledge about HIV/AIDS among men and women aged 15-49 years
3. Accepting attitudes towards people living with HIV or AIDS among men and women aged 15-49 years

Table C8-5 illustrates the sample sizes necessary to measure changes of various magnitudes in the prevalence of behaviors over time.

Table C8-5: Sample Sizes Necessary to Calculate Change from Baseline Values

Baseline prevalence	Sample size necessary to calculate change from baseline prevalence over time			
	5% change	10% change	15% change	20% change
10%	540	156	78	48
20%	860	231	108	64
30%	1083	280	128	73
40%	1206	305	136	76
50%	1231	305	133	73
60%	1157	280	119	64
70%	984	231	95	48
80%	712	156	59	27

Sample size assumes 95% alpha, 80% beta, no design effect and no non-response

Step 3: Determine the sampling methodology

A description of different sampling methodologies for surveys is included in Annex A. Before finalizing the sample size for your survey, determine which type of sampling methodology you will use. First, decide whether you are going to use a probability sampling method or a non-probability sampling method. If you choose a probability sampling method, there are three types of probability sampling to consider. A decision chart to help you decide when to use each sampling method is provided in Figure C8-2.

If you employ a cluster sampling methodology, you will have to inflate your sample size by a certain factor to account for the effect the survey design will have on the measurement of standard error, called *design effect*. Frequently, the design effect is not known at the outset of the survey and a standard factor of 2, or sometimes less, is applied. The more homogenous your population, the lower your potential design effect will be. Before determining the design effect for your sample size, you should review literature and reports of the design effects used in other cluster surveys done in your populations and regions relating to the specific indicators you wish to measure.

No complete household lists were available in Uganda for either the refugee or surrounding populations and the households were spread far apart. Therefore, households were selected for the survey using a cluster sampling methodology. Because a number of different ethnic groups were in the survey and there was a high potential of heterogeneity between respondents from different countries, a design effect of 2 was determined to be adequate to account for cluster sampling, and, thus, the sample was doubled in size.

Figure C8-2: **How to Decide Which Probability Sampling Method to Use**

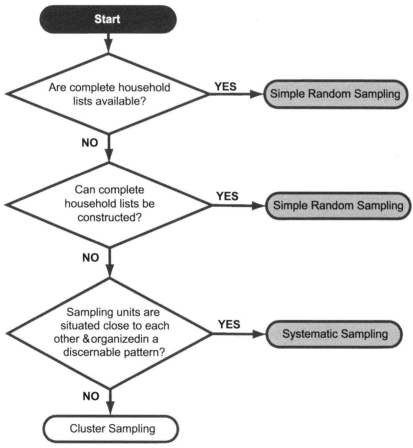

Source: Authors

Step 4: Calculate your sample size

To determine your sample size, you will need the following information:

- Are the results going to be used to measure trends across multiple survey rounds?
- The indicators of interest you want to measure
- The estimated baseline values of the indicators of interest
- The desired % change in behavior to be measured (for surveys measuring trends)
- The estimated non-response rate (including refusals and absences)
- The estimated design effect (for cluster surveys)
- The desired level of statistical significance
- The desired level of statistical power

The sample size calculation depends on whether you intend measuring indicator values once, in a one-off survey, or whether you intend to measure changes in trends over time, with repeated surveys.

Resources on sample size calculation for single surveys. There are a number of helpful on-line resources to assist you in calculating the sample size for a one-off survey. For more information, please refer to the following:

- Measuring and Interpreting Malnutrition and Mortality: A Manual, U.S. Centers for Disease Control and Prevention and the World Food Programme, 2005. http://www.unhcr.org/publ/PUBL/45f6abc92.pdf
- Food and Nutrition Technical Assistance: Sampling Guide, http://www.fantaproject.org/publications/sampling.shtml
- Measuring Mortality, Nutritional Status, and Food Security in Crisis Situations: The SMART Protocol, January 2005, http://www.smartindicators.org/SMART_Protocol_01-27-05.pdf
- Sample size calculator for cross-sectional surveys, freeware from Emory University, http://www.sph.emory.edu/~cdckms/Sample%20size%20for%20comparing%20two%20cross-sectional%20surveys.html
- SampleSX sample size calculator for cross-sectional surveys, freeware from Brixton Health, http://www.brixtonhealth.com/index.html. Note: This tool does not calculate sample sizes for surveys measuring changes over time.

Formula for sample size calculation for surveys that measure changes in trends over time:

$$n = D \frac{\left[\sqrt{2P(1-P)} Z_{1-\alpha} + \sqrt{P_1(1-P_1) + P_2(1-P_2)} Z_{1-\beta} \right]^2}{\Delta^2}$$

Where:

D = design effect;

P_1 = the estimated proportion at the time of the first survey;

P_2 = the proportion at some future date such that the quantity (P2 - P1) is the size of the magnitude of change it is desired to be able to detect;

P = (P1 + P2) / 2;

Δ^2 = $(P2 - P1)^2$;

$Z_1\alpha$ = the z-score corresponding to the probability with which it is desired to be able to conclude that an observed change of size (P2 - P1) would not have occurred by chance;

$Z_{1-\beta}$ = the z-score corresponding to the degree of confidence with which it is desired to be certain of detecting a change of size (P2 - P1) if one actually occurred; and

α = 0.05 ($Z_{1-\alpha}$ = 1.65)

β = 0.20 ($Z_{1-\beta}$ =0.84).

You do not need to know the mathematics behind selecting sample sizes in order to calculate them. For more information about sample size calculations, we suggest you either contact a local statistician or refer to this guideline:

- Behavioral Surveillance Surveys: Guidelines for Repeated Behavioral Surveys in Populations at Risk of HIV, Family Health International, 2000, http://www.fhi.org/en/HIVAIDS/pub/guide/bssguidelines.htm

8. Summary of Chapter 8 Knowledge and Skills

In this chapter, you learned about the range of data collection strategies and the usefulness of more structured strategies for comparing program interventions and outcomes. You learned all the important survey terms and terminology: sampling frame, sampling unit, and sampling methodologies.

You learned about the benefits of surveys and surveillance; specifically how they help to generate some of the impact and outcome-level data required for impact and outcome indicators in your M&E system, so that program efforts can be directed to where they are needed most. You learned about various types of surveys and surveillance as well as issues in planning, managing and carrying out surveys. You learned about technical process steps that are required to develop and implement a survey to provide data for your M&E system. Finally, you also learned about the steps involved in calculating a sample size.

9. Learning Activity

Component 8 is about surveys for your organization's program. You can either conduct your own surveys or collect data from existing surveys.

LEARNING ACTIVITY 1: IDENTIFY WHICH INDICATORS NEED SURVEYS AND WHICH INDICATORS NEED ROUTINE DATA

Complete the data source matrix for data sources needed for each of the indicators in the list below. Each indicator may need only one, or several data sources, for example, different sources for the numerator and denominator.

Learning Activity 1 Output

Indicator	Data source	Responsible agency	Frequency of collection
1. Percentage of young people aged 15 to 19 who are enrolled in private and public secondary schools			
2. Percentage of students who attend remedial mathematics classes during school holidays			
3. Percentage of students whose parents attend parent-teacher meetings			
4. Average scores in mathematics and science			
5. Percentage of parents who are positive about the quality of education			
6. Percentage of teachers who consult with their head of department at least once a month			

Chapter 8

LEARNING ACTIVITY 2:   DESIGN GOOD QUESTIONS

For each of the questions in the table below, identify the possible problem with the question and try and think of a way to improve it.

Learning Activity 2 Output

Question	Problem with the question	Improved question
1 Did you import or export any material in the past 12 months?		
2. Do you think other people would enjoy the course?		
3. What is the percentage increase in your information technology budget from 2007 to 2008?		
4. Please provide budget details for the past five years		
5. What do you think of the mobility policy?		
6. Do you regularly consult the company intranet?		
7. What type of technology is used for managing your website?		
8. Do you still have confidence in your top management?		
9. Most organizations review management plans every year. What do you believe is the correct time period?		
10. How would you rate your company's website? ☐ Not important ☐ A Little important ☐ Important ☐ Very Important		
What assets does your organization hold? ☐ Land ☐ Property ☐ Equipment ☐ Buildings ☐ Computers		
How do you learn about news in your organization? ☐ Intranet ☐ Corporate website ☐ Newsletter ☐ Events		

Annex A: Sampling Methodologies

Summarized by authors from the source: (FHI, 2000)

Sampling procedures fall into two broad classes: **probability methods** and **non-probability methods**.

In **probability sampling (also known as random sampling)**, every person in the sampling universe has a known (non-zero) probability of being selected for the sample. There are three sub-types of probability sampling: simple random sampling, systematic sampling, and cluster sampling. Probability sampling tends to be used when sample frames are available or can be developed. This method has two main advantages: (a) it yields survey results that are less likely to be affected by bias; and (b) statistical calculations can be performed on the survey results. The main disadvantage is that a sampling frame is necessary and it can take a long time to develop a sample frame if one does not exist because as a census of respondents is necessary. Probability sampling is the only method that will yield survey results that:

- Are systematic and replicable
- Can produce estimates with minimum bias
- Can measure trends over time

Non-probability sampling is a collective term for a variety of sampling approaches that are not based on the statistical principles that govern probability samples. Snowball sampling is an example of non-probability sampling. In a snowball sample, respondents nominate other respondents that meet a set of criteria (i.e., there is no sampling frame to begin with). Non-probability sampling is less expensive, easier to implement and takes less time. The major disadvantages are that there will be sampling bias, so statistical tests cannot be performed on the survey results, and it is more possible that future survey results will differ due to the difference in how the sample was obtained, rather than due to real changes in observed behavior (or other variables being surveyed).

A survey based on non-probability methods may be seen as less objective and its results may be given less credibility.

Annex B: Sample Table of Contents for a Survey

Foreword and Acknowledgements

List of Tables and Figures

Acronyms

Glossary of Terms

1 Introduction

    1.1   Introduction

    1.2   Background and rationale for the topic or topics being surveyed

    1.3   Objective of the survey

    1.4   Core survey indicators

2 Management of the Survey

    2.1   Survey Team Management Structures

    2.2   Survey Team Management Roles and Responsibilities

        2.3.1   Identification of Enumerators and Field Supervisors

        2.3.2   Project Manager

        2.3.3   Field Managers

        2.3.4   Field Supervisors

        2.3.5   Enumerators

    2.3   Overview of Survey Implementation Process and Timeline

    2.4   Quality Assurance

        2.4.1   Quality Assurance during Questionnaire Design

        2.4.2   Quality Assurance During Training and Field Implementation

    2.4.3   Quality Assurance During Database Management

    2.5   Capacity Enhancement

3 Survey Procedures for Start-up, Field Planning, Survey and Sampling Design

    3.1   Inception Report

    3.2   Sampling

        3.2.1   Population

        3.2.2   Sample Size

Chapter 8

Making Monitoring and Evaluation Systems Work

Source: Adapted from the Swaziland Protocol for the Swaziland Quality, Comprehensiveness and Relevance of Impact Mitigation Services Survey; Swaziland Government, 2009

Chapter 8

Chapter 9
Databases Useful to Monitoring and Evaluation Systems

Chapter Aim

The aim of this chapter is to enable you to know the basics of how to develop an electronic database to hold your entire organization's monitoring and evaluation data. This knowledge can help you to oversee a database development process.

Chapter Knowledge and Skills

By the end of this Chapter, you should be able to:

a) Explain to others the terminology and functions related to databases.

b) Recognize the various issues involved when choosing a database, and the process of developing a database.

c) Develop a national, sub-national, or sectoral database (this HowTo guide is for in-country technicians responsible for database design and implementation, or for managers interested in this field).

d) Manage a national, sub-national, or sectoral database development process (this HowTo guide is for managers of M&E systems at all levels).

Before You Begin…

Take a few minutes to read through the questions below. You may find it helpful to write down your answers. As you work through the chapter, compare your answers to the views of the authors.

- Is a database necessary for your organization?

- What are the challenges of using a database instead of simply keeping paper records?

- Does the entire M&E system need to be on a database for the M&E system to work?

- Do all program facilities require computers?

- How would a new database link with your organization's current database?

- What data should be contained within a database?

- What are some important factors to help ensure that the database design is successful?

Thinking about these questions can help you reflect on whether a database would help increase the efficiency of the M&E system, and improve access to data from various stakeholders. This chapter will teach you how to develop a database system for your organization and how to manage the development process from start to finish.

Note: This chapter provides an introduction and conceptual overview to electronic databases. It does not provide detailed technical guidance about database development which would require a specialist consultant or training.

Chapter 9

Component 9: Databases Useful to M&E Systems

1. Introduction

"Errors using inadequate data are much less than those using no data at all."
Charles Babbage (1792-1871)

Databases are part of the middle ring of the 12 Components of a functional M&E system, which deals with the collection, capturing, and verification of data. Databases are used to capture the data collected through routine monitoring (Chapter 7), surveys and surveillance (Chapter 8), and evaluation and research (Chapter 11).

How this chapter is organized: Chapter 9 begins with selected background information and definitions related to national and sub-national databases (Section 2). The desired result for this Chapter is covered in Section 3. The benefits of having databases as part of an M&E system are listed in Section 4. There are several implementation issues in database development and management. These range from technical issues such as what type of database software to use, to management issues such as adequate human capacity or too much reliance on technology. These issues, and more, are presented in Section 5.

The next sections are devoted to the HowTo Guides. One guide is for technicians on how to develop a national, sub national, or sectoral database (Section 6); and the other guide is for managers of M&E systems at all levels on how to manage a database development process (Section 7). The chapter closes with a summary of lessons and a practical exercise to reinforce what you have learned.

2. Background Information and Definitions

Database: An organized set of records usually in columns and tables. By this definition, a database does not need to be computerized. However, for the purpose of this chapter, we refer to electronic databases (on computers) for which the computer science definition of a database is relevant: A collection of data that has been organized so that a computer program can quickly select desired items (Business Link, 2007).

Relational database: A relational database is the most-common database form. In such a database, all data are not stored in the same table but in different related tables. In the example, the part of each record in Table C9-1 (the Customer ID) is repeated in Table C9-2 thus allowing information in Table C9-1 to be linked to

Table C9-2 through the repeated customer ID field:

Table C9-1:   Relational Database Table 1

Customer ID	Name	Address	City	State	Zip
1001	Mr. Smith	123 Lexington	Smithville	KY	91232
1002	Mrs. Jones	12 Davis Ave.	Smithville	KY	91232
1003	Mr. Axe	443 Grinder Ln.	Broadville	GA	81992

Table C9-2:   Relational Database Table 2

Account Number	Customer ID	Account Type	Date Opened	Balance
9987	1001	Checking	10/12/1989	4,000.00
9980	1001	Savings	10/12/1989	2,000.00
8811	1002	Savings	01/05/1992	1,000.00
4422	1003	Checking	12/01/1994	6,000.00
4433	1003	Savings	12/01/1994	9,000.00

Relational database design steps: The basic steps in developing a relational database are to:

- **Develop tables** to define the *locations* in which data will be stored. Do not store any data that are calculations.

- **Define relationships** between data in tables. This will ensure that the database can access all data.

- **Develop queries** to define how data will be extracted from the tables and how the data in the tables will be manipulated. Queries are also used to perform any calculations required.

- **Develop forms** to create ways in which data can be displayed on the screen in order to view existing data, capture new data, or edit existing data.

- **Develop reports** that are able to print data in a standardized way, using real-time data from the database.

DBMS: This computer program is used to manage and query a database. For the DBMS (software) to be used effectively, it needs to be installed onto hardware (computers) that are properly maintained. DBMS could be installed as a stand-alone software application on one computer or installed on a network of different computers that are linked via cables or the internet to a central server. If installed on a network of computers, data typed in one computer is immediately visible on the all the others in the network (Source: http://en.wikipedia.org/wiki/Database).

Database requirements: Requirements describe all the functions the database will perform.

Database specifications: Specifications detail how the database will perform the functions defined in the database requirements (Source: http://www.neindex.org/services-db.html New England INDEX, University of Massachusetts Medical School, accessed on 24 October 2007).

3. Results to Be Achieved When Implementing This Component

Long-term result:

Develop and maintain databases that enable stakeholders to access relevant data for policy formulation, program management, and improvement.

Short and medium-term results:

- Database requirements respond to the decision making and reporting needs of stakeholders.
- Well defined and managed database for collating, verifying, cleaning, analyzing and presenting program monitoring data from all levels and sectors.
- If applicable, linkages among different, relevant databases, to ensure consistency and avoid duplication.

For reflection 1:

Reflect on your organization for a moment. Does a database exist in your organization? If so, how does one access the data? Are there problems with the database? How do the problems affect you? Are you aware of the process by which the database was established and/or developed? How many of the short- and medium-term results listed are visible in your organization?

---

4. Benefits of Databases as Part of an M&E System

Some of the benefits of using databases as part of M&E systems are that these databases, if used correctly, can:

- Make data immediately available when it is needed and in the format required;
- Ensure that data are available in a format that facilitates analysis in a variety of ways without having to perform manual calculations;
- Be more efficient and accurate than a paper or manual filing and retrieval system;

- Enable cross-referencing between different data sets and comparison of data sets with each other;

- Enable processing of large quantities of data routinely, quickly, and accurately;

- Reduce the amount of time spent managing data by reducing data analysis processes;

- Turn disparate information into a valuable consolidated resource;

- Improve the quality, timeliness, and consistency of information;

- Enable spatial analysis performance and depiction of data on maps for easy comprehension by policy-makers.

5. Implementation Issues Regarding Databases

5.1. Do not rely only on technology to "provide all the answers"

An M&E system should, in most cases, function without a database. This does not mean that a database is not useful or important. A database can automate and make aspects of data management easier. However, a computerized database should not be the pivot around which the M&E system is designed. If for any reason the database stopped working (e.g., because of problems with the internet in the country), the M&E system should still be able to function as a simple, paper-based system. Databases are particularly useful for large, national M&E systems which usually contain and manage large amounts of data.

5.2. Government databases need to adhere to government IT policy

It is of paramount importance that a national government database development process follows the requirements and technical specifications of government. Therefore, one of the first steps in the database design process should be to meet with the IT section and identify any specific approval processes or protocols that have been mandated by government. If an IT policy exists, consult it before designing your database.

5.3. Database functionality and security

The database should be designed to store large data sets; be user-friendly; have good built-in data quality features; and link to other commonly used databases in the country so that it can easily import and export data. The database should also have sufficient levels of security to protect the data but ensure that the data is available to all relevant staff and external stakeholders, including the public.

Although database functionality and design is important, it is equally important to pay attention to how data enters and exits the database (i.e., the data flow to and from the database) and how data is used.

5.4. What data the database(s) should capture

Databases should all contain relevant data about the program, be it an individual or a large-scale national program. If it is a large-scale national program, it is likely that more than one database may need to be linked and that different data may be required at, for example, a district education office compared to the national education ministry headquarters (see Figure C9-1).

The database should capture more than just indicator values. This will enable managers to use the database as a management information system and not only as a warehouse to store periodic indicator values. For the database to be used as a management tool, it needs to capture data about the 12 Components of a functional M&E system. Table C9-3 illustrates a list of the kind of data the database could store on each of the 12 Components:

Figure C9-1:   Different Databases at a National and District Office Level That are Linked Together

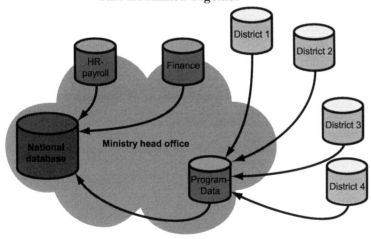

Source: Authors

Table C9-3:   Data About the M&E System in the Database

Component of a functional M&E system	Type of data that should be captured
1. Organizational structures with M&E	An up-to-date registration system/contact list of stakeholders
2. Human capacity for M&E	Capacity building efforts (e.g., training courses and participants)

Component of a functional M&E system	Type of data that should be captured
3. M&E partnerships	Contact list of partners
	Meeting attendance
	Meeting frequency
4. M&E plans	Data on all program indicators
5. Costed M&E work plans	Capture and track resource data
	Outcomes of development processes
6. M&E advocacy, communications & culture	M&E advocacy and communications efforts
7. Routine monitoring	Status of systems are known (examples of systems: routine medical and non-medical program data, education system attendance data, student achievement scores, etc.)
8. Periodic surveys	Status of all surveys and surveillance
	Latest survey and surveillance data (key cross tabs captured)
9. Databases useful for M&E systems	Functionality of the database itself
10. Supervision and data auditing	Capture details of supervision visits
11. Evaluation and research	Inventory of research and researchers
	Research dissemination efforts
12. Using data to improve results	Produce data for information products
	Provide web interface access for the general public
	Library for electronic documents for online data download

Source: Authors

5.5. What software should be used?

The choice of software would depend on the needs of the users. Different software packages are available on the market, including *off-the-shelf* databases that can be customized to meet specific requirements (*parameterized*) and some that require database design from scratch (RDBMSs). Many countries have opted to design their own databases. These range in levels of sophistication and functionality.

Examples of off-the-shelf databases used by the development community include UNDP's "DevInfo", an indicator database with a geographic mapping facility that is very useful for displaying data from a national M&E system (i.e., indicator values). The CDC's Epi Info database is designed to manage epidemiological data. UNAIDS' CRIS database manages and warehouses data about a national HIV response. There are many other database options available.

5.6. Spatial analysis software is useful as part of a database

The database data can be used for spatial analysis, in which data is referenced or linked to geographic coordinates (e.g., towns, provinces, districts, roads, rivers or countries). Global Information System (GIS) software is a toolbox: "An information system that is designed to work with data referenced by spatial or geographic coordinates. In other words, a GIS is both a database system with specific capabilities for spatially-referenced data, as well as a set of operations for working with the data" (Star & Estes, 1990, p. 2).

One output of GIS are color-coded and customized maps, like the examples in Figure C9-2. However, GIS software is expensive and requires specialist skills. If GIS skills or outputs are needed only occasionally, one option for an organization is to develop some introductory-level skills in GIS and then contract another agency with the necessary GIS skills and capacity (e.g., Central Statistical Office) to develop maps on their behalf. This would still require that the organization use its *introductory-level* skills in GIS to inform and guide its agreement with such an agency, be it private or public sector.

If this option were selected, the database would be linked to the GIS software and used as the basis for the development of data characteristics connected to any geographic point. Thus, any change in the database would be reflected automatically in any new spatial analysis or maps generated and printed.

Figure C9-2:   Examples of Maps Generated by GIS Software

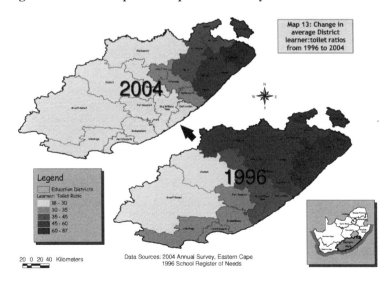

Figure C9-2: (Continued)

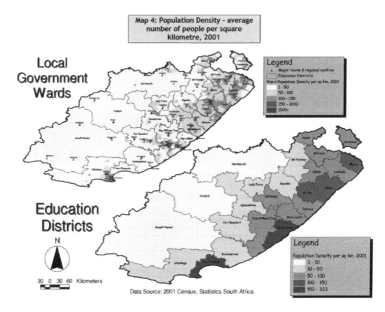

Source: Eastern Cape Department of Education: Review of Education Indicators, 1995, 2004, EduAction & Eastern Cape EMIS, 2005

Figure C9-2: (Continued)

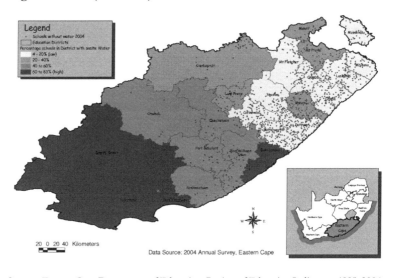

Source: Eastern Cape Department of Education: Review of Education Indicators, 1995, 2004, EduAction & Eastern Cape EMIS, 2005

Chapter 9

5.7. Linkage to other databases

Figure C9-3: Database Development Life Cycle

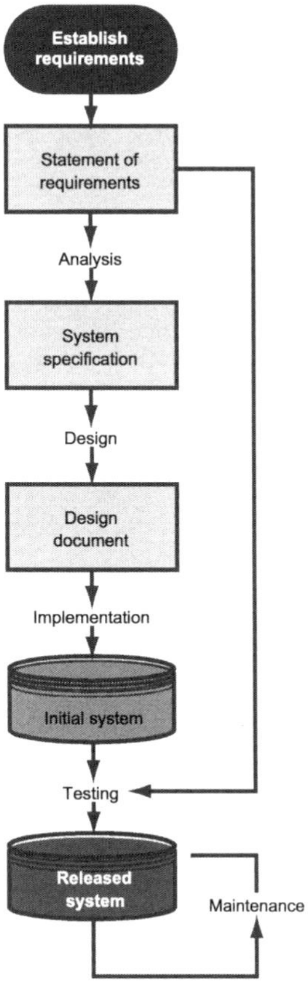

Databases exist at different levels and for different purposes (e.g., Ministry of Education, Ministry of Agriculture, Ministry of Finance, local government institutions, etc.) Linking these different databases may make it easier to export and transfer data between them (see Figure C9-1), but this is seldom easy in practice. If databases are not properly linked, data transfer becomes extremely difficult.

If or when a new national database is designed, it is critical to know what other databases exist, what their software platforms are, what level of data they collect, and how functional they are.

In some countries, databases for all routine data are created at the sub-national level, but may be impossible for others due to the lack of computers or skilled persons at that level. For this reason, a high technology option may not always be the best solution at all levels or in all sectors. For a national database to be functional, it is not necessary to install all components in all sectors and at all levels simultaneously. It is possible to design the database architecture and software, then implement the software incrementally, as different sectors and levels attain an acceptable measure of IT competency.

Source: Open University (accessed online on 12 Oct 2008 at http://openlearn.open.ac.uk/mod/resource/view.php?id=187268

5.8. Need for capacity building in database design and management to improve use of, and access to information

A certain level of technical understanding is needed in order to manage a database process and the team developing it. There is a widespread lack of skills in managing database development contracts, in database design, and in establishing back-up systems.

There is also a lack of professional capacity to convert technical database concepts and language into something that the layperson (including managers) can understand, interact with, and even comment on. This requires capacity building in software and database development processes, from basic computer operation to interaction with a database user interface.

Chapter 9

6. HowTo Guide C9-1: Developing a Database

Developing a database is a specialized field, requiring systems analysts and database designers. The purpose of this HowTo Guide is not to provide the technical training for a lay-person to become a database designer or systems analyst (which requires years of training). Instead, it provides an overview of the steps involved in designing databases and key outputs of each step so that technicians can understand what M&E system managers will require of them. There are different ways to describe the database development cycles. Figure C9-3 shows a common life cycle development process and the six steps illustrated in the figure are briefly described below.

Step 1:   Plan the database

After assembling a database development team, collect information to understand the problem that the database is trying to solve. Then, define the overall goals of the database. Based on these goals, database requirements are collected from a variety of stakeholders including non-technical, output-oriented statements of what is needed for the database to work.

Deliverable: Statements of database requirements.

Step 2:   Analyze information for the database

During this step, **database system specifications** are prepared. The purpose of the database system specification is to show the client how the database solution being proposed will address and provide all the functionality of the database specified in the database concept note, including what the database will do, and the proposed database architecture. The specification document defines how the database will address each of the needs defined in the statement of requirements, and includes user requirements (i.e., what will be stored; how it will be used; and

Table C9-4:   Specification for Designing the Database

User Interface requirements	Functional requirements
• Specify which data will be captured • Describe what user interfaces will be able to do • Describe what reports will look like • Search functionality (if required), and explain what the search function will be able to achieve	• Security • Back-up • Public interface • Platform • User levels • Application • Linkage with other applications • Hardware requirements

Source: Adapted from Rwanda MAP Database Design Document

what reports can be expected) and functional requirements (i.e., how these user requirements will be addressed in the database).

Deliverable: Database system specifications.

Step 3: Design the database

The database system specifications from Step 2 are used to design each technical component of the database and document them in a technical specifications document. This document records agreement on all technical specifications of the database (database design) and database processes (process design). During this step, the database developers need to show how the specifications will address the original database goals and develop a conceptual schema of how the database components will fit together. Specifications need to be approved, after which the DBMS is selected.

Deliverable: Database technical specifications document with a conceptual schema.

Step 4: Implement the database

Implementing the database entails the actual design of every aspect of the database and then installing it on computers where it is needed. This involves "a series of steps leading to an operational information system, that includes creating database definitions (such as tables, indexes, etc), developing applications, testing the system, developing operational procedures and documentation, training the users and populating the database."[1] Implementation may be staged, ensuring that each component of the database is functioning.

Deliverable: Actual database.

Step 5: Test the database

After the database is operational, it needs to be tested to ensure that it addresses each of the requirements defined in Step 2 of the development process. During this step, the database is installed on all necessary computers and linkages between the database components should also be tested.

Deliverable: Functioning database.

Chapter 9

---

[1] From "Computer Free Tips", accessed at http://www.computerfreetips.com/Datebase_tips/sql_server/Administration/h_add_data.html on 12 October 2008

Step 6: Maintain the database

Maintenance tasks are performed to ensure the ongoing operation of the database that include monitoring database functionality. Maintenance activities can be pro-active or reactive and may include preventive maintenance (such as backup services), corrective maintenance (such as the recovery of lost data), or adaptive maintenance (to meet new requirements. This includes assigning user access, regular monitoring, and periodic checking of functionality.

Deliverable: Continuously functioning database with backed-up data, adapted for new requirements over time.

7. HowTo Guide C9-2: Managing a Government Database Development Process

The steps described here explain how to manage a national, government-driven and operated database development process. The technical processes (e.g., what the database development team should do) are summarized in the HowTo Guide C9-1.

Step 1: Obtain government or organizational IT policies and investigate links with the IT department

Whatever database is developed, it should link to, and be aligned with, the information technology policies of the government. Find out if the government has any preferred database development processes, software, templates, or documents that are a mandatory requirement. Identify relevant policies and seek further information from those concerned before starting the development of the national or sub-national database.

Deliverable: Knowledge of government IT policies, preferred process, software, templates and/or documents.

Step 2: Develop a draft database concept note

The database concept note is not a technical database document. It is a short document explaining why a database is needed and what resources will be required to develop it. The purpose of the concept note is to motivate for the development of the database, to secure resources that fund the database planning costs (not including the database design costs), and to motivate for a project champion as part of the development process.

The concept note, therefore, needs to contain the following information:

- Background and Context
- Problem Statement: current data processes, current status of the M&E systems, etc.
- Database Vision and Objectives
- Benefits of the database
- Request for funds for database planning to cover the database planning specialist and two planning workshops with key stakeholders

Deliverable: Draft database concept note.

Step 3: Secure a project sponsor and present the project concept note to senior management

A project sponsor is a senior-level official who supports the database and will motivate its development at senior government level. This project sponsor will be important both for overall support, resource mobilization, and database implementation.

After presenting the draft concept note to the project sponsor, obtain his/her comments and make changes accordingly.

Deliverable: Identified project sponsor who has approved the project concept note.

Step 4: Present the draft concept note, together with the project sponsor, to gain political and managerial buy-in and support

During the presentation, make sure that senior management provides guidance on:

a) Approval for database planning to proceed;

b) Who should constitute the database technical review committee;

c) Resource availability for the database planning phases;

d) How funding for the eventual implementation will be secured; and

e) Related government initiatives of relevance or interest.

Deliverable: Notes from draft concept note presentation on various questions listed in Step 4.

Step 5: Nominate members of the technical review group and set up an initial meeting

The technical review group will be the principal interface with the database developers. The selection of its members is as important as the selection of the database developers and should include database development experts, expert users, and people who represent the interests of M&E stakeholders.

- It is suggested that at least one user is included in the technical review group. Make sure that the user has some database experience, in order for meaningful interaction during group discussions.
- Ask the project sponsor to attend the initial meeting and to express support for the process.
- Present the concept note to the technical review group and ask for their input for the TOR (terms of reference) of the database-planning specialist.

Deliverable: Technical Review Group members nominated; concept note presented to them.

Step 6: Nominate/appoint a database planning specialist

The database planning specialist will be responsible for supporting the M&E team in all aspects of planning the database development. This specialist can be a staff member, a consultant appointed for the purpose, or a person from another government unit (e.g., the IT unit), who is prepared to commit time to fulfill the database planning functions. The functions of the database planning specialist are to:

- Prepare an inventory of existing databases with routine and other data that may be useful as a source for the new program database from which to import data or as a resource to export data.
- Investigate the feasibility of developing a database and likely maintenance requirements.
- Determine, through key informant interviews and study of other country databases, the database requirements (i.e., what the users want from it).
- Assess hardware requirements for the proposed database.
- Develop Terms of Reference for the database developer or development team.
- Estimate the cost of the database development process.
- Write the motivation requesting funds for the database development process.

The database planning specialist should have a formal qualification in database development; should have worked in M&E, should be familiar with the program;

and should be able to translate user requirements into technical *database* language and terminology. The specialist, therefore, needs to be both a technician and conceptual thinker, with a good understanding of relevant M&E issues.

Deliverable: Identification and nomination of the database planning specialist.

Step 7: Develop an inventory of existing databases with links to the program database

Developing this inventory is important in order to ensure that the database does not duplicate data and that it links with all other relevant database processes and systems. Two types of links apply: databases to which the new program database link, so that data can be imported, and databases that need to link to the new program database to draw (extract/export) data to complement their databases. After preparation, submit the inventory to the technical review group for input and finalization.

Deliverable: Inventory of existing databases to avoid duplication of data.

Step 8: Determine user requirements

The user requirement process is useful for all involved. It is an opportunity to understand contributions to the M&E system and the whole system, and to suggest other ideas that may not have been considered. Interactive discussion generates new ideas and testing them usually results in improved design or flags ideas for future improvements. The requirement process is typically conducted in a series of workshops that enable a user requirement document listing to be drafted, reviewed, revised, and then finalized. This process may continue iteratively until everyone is satisfied that the design is acceptable.

Spending time in defining user requirements provides a fully-documented specification of exactly what the database is going to do and will ensure that the database analyst understands the needs well enough to provide an accurate development cost.

Deliverable: Statement of requirements.

Step 9: Develop database planning documents

Agree on the database development model that will be followed, if government has not prescribed one. Based on this model, develop the necessary database planning documents. These planning documents are the basis for development, testing, and approval of the system. Development would potentially be risky and lack focus without good planning documents. This is a critical stage and, if done correctly, will provide a solid foundation for success.

The database planning documents need to include a database project plan and terms of reference for the database developers.

Database project plan

This plan defines how the database design will be implemented, defines the roles of all stakeholders, provides a detailed cost breakdown, and describes funding sources for the database development. It should contain information about:

- Project scope and management
- Project costs (both for database development and hardware acquisition) and cost management
- Project quality management
- Project time management
- Project HR management
- Project procurement management
- Project communications management
- Project risk management
- Project integration management

Terms of reference (TOR) for the database developers

TOR for the database developers is another important document that defines what the database developer (individual service provider) or developers (company or organizational service provider) will do in the execution of their contract. The database technical specifications should be included in the TOR, as well as the database concept note. In the TOR, the development team should be allowed the opportunity to refine or finalize the database technical specifications. The TOR should specify the terms of the contract; the expected deliverables; the payment terms (amount and schedule); and qualification requirements of the database developer(s)

A database developer should hold primary degrees in computer science or Information Management Systems. In addition, depending on the technical specifications and complexity of the database, the developer may be required to have knowledge in application development (i.e., writing codes for data retrieval); database design and programming including SQL; stored procedures development; ColdFusion; intranet/internet based programming; HTML; and Javascript. Prospective developers must have a strong knowledge of Oracle and SQL server DBMS, and significant experience with document management-upload and tracking. Developers should have at least 10 years of work experience in companies or institutions where database development/documentation repository solutions have been implemented. They should ideally have strong writing and presentation skills. Database and computer language programming certification would be a strong recommendation, as would extensive work experience in the design of databases to capture district-level or program-related activities and interventions.

Completeness of documentation is critical for future maintenance and modification. For continuity and sustainability, consider developing in-house expertise or a long-term contract for development and maintenance.

Deliverables: Database project plan and database developers' Terms of Reference.

Step 10: Procure the services of a database developer

Once the Database Planning Specialist has developed all the documents and estimated the cost of the database development and hardware installation, submit the documents to the technical review group for input and approval.

Use the approved documents as a basis for resource mobilization for the full database development. Follow relevant government procurement procedures to appoint a developer. Ensure that the technical review team reviews the draft contract and that they are comfortable with the process. When conducting an evaluation of proposals received from various suppliers, do not take only costs into account. The following technical questions should also be considered during the bid evaluation process:

- How long has the developer been established?
- What are the specific costs associated with the project or program output (i.e., one-off purchase price; annual renewable license costs; charge per user, etc.)?
- What is the gross cost of technical support?
- Does the developer provide consultancy services after the database has been established and, if so, at what rates?
- Is the system scalable? If it is required to cope with a 200% increase in capacity, could the system grow automatically to deal with expansion?
- Can the supplier recommend any third-party developers that make use of their RDBMS?
- Is there an active independent user group?
- Can the supplier provide references from known businesses or agencies that use their software?

- Does the supplier offer training in the RDBMS and, if so, at what typical unit cost?

In designing the database, it is also critical to consider long-term maintenance and future modifications. This is a strong argument for using local expertize and considering the inclusion of future maintenance and modification in the terms of reference for the initial contract.

Deliverable: Database developer contract (including a clear statement of how local expertise will be used for continued maintenance and any future modifications).

Step 11: Manage the database development contract

Introduce the successful bidder to the technical review team. Agree on specific deliverables, completion deadlines and turnaround times for the technical review team to submit comments. During the execution of the contract, send deliverables for review to the technical review group and keep the project sponsor involved (e.g., provide final technical specifications; prototypes user manuals; database training materials; etc.). The technical review group should also be involved in all presentations, demonstrations, and other interactions with the database development team.

The purpose of database development materials is to support the facilitator undertaking the training and provide information to the database user on front-end database functionality. The training materials should contain the learning objectives, show screen-shots of all database processes, be easy and logical to understand and be customized for all levels of users. During every step of the development, consider the long-term implications required to keep the system functional, discuss them with the project sponsor and, as appropriate, brief management.

Deliverable: See HowTo Guide C9-1, Steps 1 to 6.

Step 12: Manage the procurement and installation of hardware needed for the new database

This step also requires TOR or purchase specifications to be developed for the hardware that is required for database installation. Ensure that the database development team sees and approves these specifications so that there are no compatibility problems at a later stage.

Deliverable: TOR or purchase specifications for the hardware required for database installation.

Step 13: Manage database maintenance

Ensure access to the various sites where the database is to be installed and also arrange the training of users and database administrator(s). Depending on how computer-literate the database users are, training may need to include database functionalities and basic computer literacy and use.

Deliverable: Arrangements made for installation and training at various sites.

For reflection 1:

Reflect on your organization for a moment. Does a database exist? If so, do you access the data through paper records or through a computerized database management system? Are you aware of the process by which the database was established and/or developed? How many of the listed short- and medium-term results are visible in your organization?

---

8. Summary of Chapter 9 Knowledge and Skills

In this chapter, you learned about how to develop a database system and manage the process by which the system was designed and implemented. You learned about the benefits of using a database system to improve access to data within and between organizations and stakeholders. You learned about implementation issues related to installation and maintenance of database systems. You learned about generalized steps for database development (though this process would be handled by a specialized group of system analysts and database designers). You learned about technical process steps that are required to manage the development process for the eventual goal of database installation and training at various sites.

9. Learning Activity

Component 9 is about the *electronic side* of M&E systems, the data that is stored electronically. Although it is generally assumed that only routine data and indicators need to be captured, there are, in fact, data about all 12 Components that need to be captured. For your organization, think of the M&E system data that could be captured in a database. Capture the information in this table. After completing the table, ask yourself if it is worthwhile capturing the data electronically in a database? Give a reason why or why not.

Component of a functional M&E system	Type of data that should be captured (and a reason why)
1. Organizational structures with M&E	
2. Human capacity for M&E	
3. M&E partnerships	
4. M&E plans	
5. Costed M&E work plans	
6. M&E advocacy, communications, and culture	
7. Routine monitoring	
8. Periodic surveys	
9. Databases useful for M&E systems	
10. Supervision and data auditing	
11. Evaluation and research	
12. Using information to improve results	

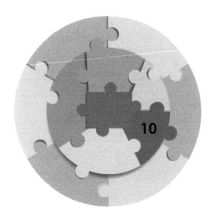

Chapter 10
Supportive Supervision and Data Auditing

Chapter Aim

The aim of this chapter is to enable you to improve the quality of data and build the capacity of staff involved in M&E by implementing supportive supervision and data auditing processes in your organization on a routine basis.

Chapter Knowledge and Skills

By the end of this Chapter, you should be able to:

a) Recognize the need for supportive supervision and data auditing as part of the M&E system.

b) Explain the difference between data auditing and supportive supervision.

c) Distinguish between M&E supervision and implementation supervision.

d) Identify all the levels in your organization where supportive supervision and data auditing should take place.

e) Develop guidelines for supportive supervision and data auditing.

f) Access global resources about supportive supervision and data auditing.

g) Prepare, plan for, undertake, and follow up after supportive supervision and/or data auditing processes.

Before You Begin...

Take a few minutes to read through the questions below. You may find it helpful to write down your answers. As you work through the chapter, compare your answers to the views of the authors.

- How is data auditing done, what steps are involved, and what are the outputs?
- Why is it called *supportive* supervision?
- Why undertake supervision and data auditing?
- What is the difference between supervision and data auditing?
- Does data auditing always need to be part of supervision?
- Why are data auditing and supportive supervision challenging?
- What is the difference between *M&E supervision* and *implementation supervision*?

These questions remind us that mechanisms are necessary to verify the quality and integrity of routine data that has been collected and captured. This chapter explores terminology relating to supportive supervision and data auditing and how one conducts *supportive* supervision that enables participants in the process to reflect, receive feedback, and deliver guidance that will improve implementation.

Component 10: Supportive Supervision and Data Auditing

1. Introduction

> *"Supervisors serve as the keepers of the faith and the mentors of the young. Theirs is a quiet profession that combines the discipline of science with the aesthetic creativity of art... It is a curious paradox that at their best they are the least visible."*
>
> Alonso, "The Quiet Profession"

The *raison d'être* for monitoring and evaluation is to use the data and information that M&E systems generate to improve decision making and thereby improve results. Many factors can influence these improvement processes, one being the credibility of the data. If decision makers have confidence in the quality of the data presented, they are much more likely to use the data.

Supportive supervision and data auditing is part of the middle ring of data collection, verification, and capture. It is a series of processes through which data is verified for the purpose of improving its quality.

How this chapter is organized: Chapter 10 begins with selected background information and definitions related to data auditing and supportive supervision, noting that data auditing may be done as part of M&E supportive supervision (Section 2). The desired result for this Chapter is presented in Section 3. The benefits of data auditing and supportive supervision within a national M&E system are outlined. These processes help to improve the credibility of the data, build program implementers' capacity for data capture, and encourage informed decision making based on data (Section 4). Implementation issues are presented (Section 5) followed by a HowTo Guide on Undertaking a Supportive Supervision Visit (Section 6). The chapter closes with a summary of lessons learned (Section 7) and a practical exercise to cement what you have learned in the chapter (Section 8).

2. Background Information and Definitions

a) **Data quality:** Data quality refers to the extent to which data adheres to the six dimensions of quality; accuracy, reliability, completeness, precision, timeliness and integrity (Table C7-3 provides detailed definitions of each of these dimensions) (USAID, 2007). When managing routine data, it is essential to consider issues of data quality throughout these six data management processes. Data quality is, therefore, not an additional data management process as one needs to consider how the six dimensions of data quality can be determined during each of the data management processes and to implement accordingly.

Table C10-1: Operational Definitions about Data Quality

Dimension of data quality	Operational definition
Validity	Valid data are considered correct: the data measure what they are intended to measure. Valid data minimizes error (e.g., recording or interviewer bias, transcription error, sampling error) to a point of being negligible.
Reliability	The data generated by a program's information system is based on protocols and procedures that do not change according to who is using the data and when or how often it is used. The data are reliable because they are measured and collected consistently.
Completeness	Completeness means that an information system from which the results are derived is appropriately inclusive and represents the complete list of eligible persons or units and not a fraction of the list.
Precision	This means that the data has sufficient detail. For example, an indicator requires the number of individuals who received HIV counseling & testing, and received their test results, by sex of the individual. An information system lacks precision if it is not designed to record the sex of the individual who received counseling & testing.
Timeliness	Data is timely when it is up-to-date (current), and when the information is available on time. Timeliness is affected by: (1) the rate at which the program's information system is updated; (2) the rate of change of actual program activities; and (3) when the information is actually used or required.
Integrity	Integrity is when data generated by a program's information system is protected from deliberate bias or manipulation for political or personal reasons.

Source: USAID, 2007

b) **Data Quality Assurance** entails a set of internal and external mechanisms and processes to ensure that data meets the six dimensions of quality defined in Table C10-1. Data quality assurance measures include planning for quality, controlling quality, and implementing remedial actions to improve quality. Supportive supervision and data auditing is only one of the processes associated with data quality assurance.

c) **Supervision** is defined as directing and overseeing the performance of others while transmitting skills, knowledge, and attitudes. It offers the opportunities to receive an account or record of work done; reflect on it; provide feedback and, where appropriate, provide guidance to improve implementation. Supervision is also part of the process of building capacity and transferring knowledge "the five steps in teaching an employee new skills are preparation, explanation, showing, observation and supervision" (Attributed to Bruce Barton, 1886-1967).

Supportive supervision: This specific approach to supervision is where (a) the focus is on learning and support, and not on *policing*; (b) the person or organization being supervised is part of the learning process; and (c) the person doing the supervision is part of the learning process – "Supervision has the dual purpose of supporting the continued learning and development of the coach, as well as giving a degree of protection to the person being coached." (Bluckert)

This chapter specifically addresses **supportive M&E supervision**, not implementation of the program supervision or service delivery. It is possible to combine supervision of M&E and implementation but their purpose should not be confused. M&E supervision verifies the quality and completeness of routine monitoring data management processes. (For example, a national M&E officer may go to the regions to find out how the M&E system is being implemented and managed at the regional level, whether data dissemination is being done, perceptions about M&E, and to help with M&E system challenges.)

d) **Data auditing** is the process of verifying the completeness and accuracy of one or more data management processes (see Chapter 7). In data auditing, one follows a specific set of steps to check the data in the M&E system against the data sources, verify the quality and accuracy of data sourcing, data collation, data analysis, data reporting, and data use. Data auditing can be done as part of M&E supervision.

As the term suggests, data auditing focuses specifically on the auditing of the process of data management and not on the auditing of the finances of the organization. Practically, data auditing often includes the processes of (i) field visits to the organizations that submitted the data (often using forms); (ii) checking the quality of raw data (the source data) kept by the reporting organizations by examining the daily records used to complete the output monitoring form for a specific reporting period; (iii) comparing the output monitoring form data against the raw data; and (iv) checking for internal consistency; and (e) ensuring that the sourcing of data was done accurately.

e) Internal and external data auditing: As clarified in the definition above, data quality is an internal process as much as it is an external process. Supportive M&E supervision and data auditing is one of the ways in which data quality can be assured. For example, the Global Fund et al. (2008) has developed both a data quality assessment tool (which is used by the funders themselves during an external process to assess data quality) and a routine data quality assessment tool (which organizations involved in implementation and, therefore, in routine data management use themselves on a more regular basis as a self assessment).

The Global Fund et al. describe the differences as follows:

The data quality assessment tool is designed for use by external audit teams while the routine data quality assessment tool is designed for more flexible use, notably by programs and projects:

Data quality assessment tool	Routine data quality assessment tool
• Assessment by funding agency	• Self-assessment by program
• Standard approach to implementation	• Flexible use by programs for monitoring and supervision or to prepare for an external audit
• Conducted by external audit team	
• Limited input into recommendations by programs	• Program makes and implements own action plan

Source: The Global Fund To Fight AIDS, TB and Malaria, et al., 2008: 1

3. Results to Be Achieved When Implementing This Component

Long-term result:

Data quality (data are valid, reliable, comprehensive, and timely) and the thoroughness of all six data management processes are externally verified on a periodic basis and actions implemented to address obstacles to production of high quality data.

Short- and medium-term results:

- Guidelines for supportive supervision are developed.
- Data auditing protocols are followed.
- Supportive supervision visits, including data assessments and feedback, take place.
- Data audit visits take place periodically.
- Supervision reports and data audit reports are produced.

For reflection 1:

Reflect on your organization for a moment. Is data monitored in any way and if so, how frequently does that monitoring take place? Does this monitoring include data auditing as described in the Background and Definitions section above? Have you ever been part of a supportive supervision process? Did you learn through the process? How many of the short- and medium-term results listed are visible in your organization?

4. Benefits of Supportive Supervision and Data Auditing as Part of an M&E System

Supportive supervision and data auditing are useful because:

1. **These processes help improve the credibility of the data** by improving program stakeholders' confidence that the data presented to them represent a true picture of the services delivered.

2. **These processes help build program implementers' capacity** in routine data collection and capture, and in using data to improve their own programs.

3. **These processes help to improve the use of information for decision making**, as more program implementers collect, capture, and learn how to use better quality data.

5. Implementation Issues in Supportive Supervision and Data Auditing

5.1. Supportive supervision and data auditing are integral parts of a routine monitoring system

When designing a routine monitoring system, supervision and data auditing procedures should also be designed. In this way, data management processes are linked with data auditing processes.

5.2. Adequate funding and skilled human resources for supportive supervision are needed

Appropriate funding should be allocated to these processes. The team of supervisors should be well versed in M&E and be able to respond to M&E questions and needs of implementers when supportive supervision is undertaken.

Chapter 10

For new, national routine monitoring and supportive supervision processes, human capacity may need to be built (see Chapter 2) and advocacy (see Chapter 6) may be needed to explain the purpose of supervision and data auditing visits.

5.3. Supervision should be supportive

Feedback should be given to the organization at the end of the supervision process and an improvement plan agreed on. This is all part of making supervision efforts supportive and avoiding a perception that supervision is a punitive or negative experience.

5.4. Data auditing focuses on all six data management processes

Data quality assurance processes such as supportive supervision and data auditing, among others, need to assess the design of the data management and reporting systems; check system implementation for design compliance at selected service delivery and intermediary reporting sites; trace and verify historical reporting on a limited number of indicators at a few sites; and communicate the audit findings and suggested improvements in a formal audit report. Five types of verification are needed (The Global Fund et al., 2006) at the implementer levels:

Verification 1: Observation at the place where data are sourced (data sourcing)

Verification 2: Documentation review (data collection and collation)

Verification 3: Trace and verification (data collation)

Verification 4: Cross-checking (data analysis)

Verification 5: Spot checks

5.5. Supervision and data auditing take place at all levels where data flow

Data auditing is not restricted to a national system. Every organization that collects data should have its own auditing and supervision procedures in place. At each level, where data is managed, the quality of these processes need to be investigated from time-to-time. An example of a two-level supervision and data auditing model is shown in Figure C10-1.

Making Monitoring and Evaluation Systems Work

Figure C10-1:   Supportive Supervision and Data Auditing at Two Levels

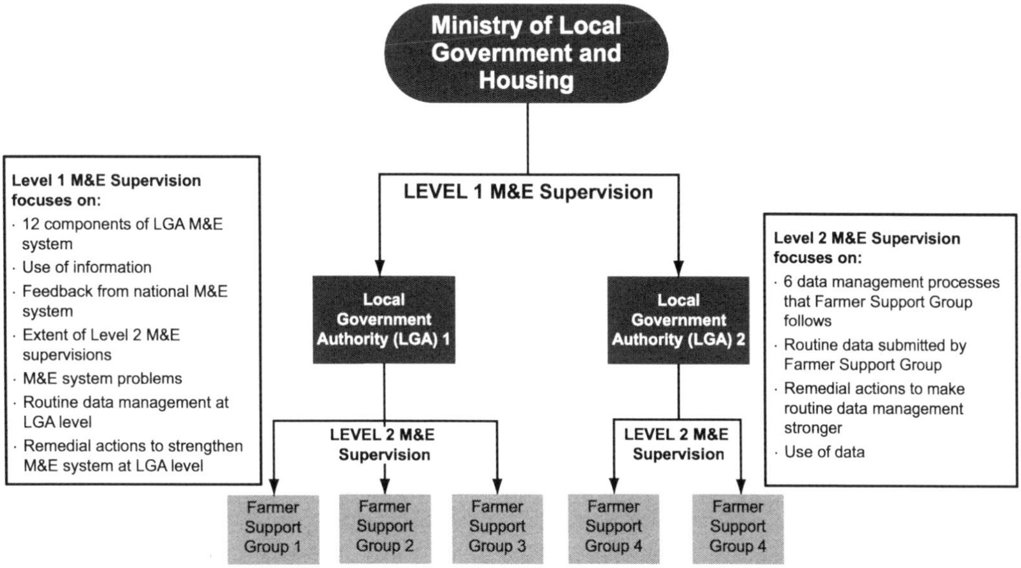

Source: Authors

5.6. Guidelines and protocols are needed to ensure the quality and uniformity of data auditing and supervision

Guidelines for supportive supervision: Standardized checklists and guidelines are useful tools for performing supportive supervision. These checklists will ensure that supervision is done routinely and that all intended purposes of the visit are fulfilled. It is useful if guidelines for supportive M&E supervision contain at least the following information:

•   **Ethical considerations and *principles of engagement*** for M&E supervision (respect, integrity, honesty, focus on support, and strengthening, etc.).

•   **Description of the stakeholders** involved in supervision (supervisors and the supervisees) and the supervision chain (clarification of who is supervised by whom, recognizing that there may be different levels of supervision (see Figure C10-1).

•   **Purpose of each type of M&E supervision:** In Figure C10-1, for example, the Level 1 M&E supervision will have a different focus than the Level 2 M&E supervision.

•   **Description of the process for each type of M&E supervision:** A detailed description of the process steps that supervisors and supervisees need to follow before, during, and after an M&E supervision visit.

- **Description of how supervisees will be selected:** The guidelines should describe how the supervisees will be selected and whether the supervisees have *right of refusal* (and in which circumstances).

- **Standard form** on which to record the M&E supervision visit proceedings, findings, and agreed action points. Such a standard form should be designed for each level of supervision, and should be specific to the purpose of that particular type of M&E supervision.

- **Agreed follow-up procedures:** A description of how the remedial actions, agreed to during the supervision process, will be executed.

- **Statement on the repercussions** of (a) refusing to participate in a supervision process, or (b) not implementing the agreed action points.

- **Overall statement about the links between M&E supervision, implementation supervision, and data and financial auditing:** Descriptions of how these processes will work together, who does what, whether (and in which circumstances) the processes may be combined and how this would work.

Data audit protocols: Data auditing can only take place if indicator protocols are in place. Protocols for data auditing should include the specific aspects to be audited so that the audit team is clear on what to do, depending on what the audit reveals. The Global Fund and its partners (2008) have, for example, developed data audit and quality tools that can be used by external teams or adapted by governments to measure data quality. Protocols for data auditing, whether be it internal or external data auditing, such as the data quality assessment tool and the routine data quality assessment tool developed by The Global Fund contain the following information:

- Principles and processes for data auditing
- Responsibilities for internal and external data auditing
- Detailed description of how the five verification processes will be carried out during both internal and external data auditing
- Format for capturing data quality audit results that include:
  - % verified reports that were available
  - % verified reports that were on time
  - % verified reports that were complete
  - Recommended actions for proceeding

6. HowTo Guide C10-1: Undertaking a Supportive M&E Supervision Visit

This HowTo Guide is structured slightly differently to the other HowTo Guides. It describes the processes before, during, and after undertaking a supportive M&E supervision visit.

Before the visit

Step 1:   Select organizations to be supervised

Select organizations for M&E supervision that:

*   Have requested support (e.g., through an *umbrella* or other large organization);

*   Have completed routine monitoring forms incorrectly (incomplete, late, or incorrect information) for more than one reporting period;

*   Have provided other valid reasons for requiring a supportive supervision visit;

*   Have not been visited in the last 18 months (unless there is no compelling reason for a follow-up visit); or

*   Provide a large proportion of program services in a specific area, or manage large funding amounts.

Deliverable: List of selected organizations to be supervised.

Step 2:   Develop a schedule and budget for supportive supervision visits

Submit for approval to the manager concerned, the list of organizations to be visited; reasons why these organizations were selected; the schedule of supportive supervision visits; and the budget to carry them out.

Deliverable: Schedule of supportive supervision visits to selected organizations with rationale for selection and projected budget.

Step 3:   Collect all relevant information about the organizations to be supervised

Decide on the reporting period for which monitoring data should be verified and obtain from the filing system a copy of the actual routine monitoring form that is to be verified. Do not choose a reporting period for verification that is prior to the data archive period specified in the routine monitoring guidelines.

Take the following items when undertaking supportive supervision visits:

- The file relating to the organization including all correspondence
- Copies of previous supervision visit report forms
- The name and contact details of the lead person responsible for the routine monitoring system, and the name and contact details of the head of the organization
- A list of periods for which the organization has submitted routine monitoring forms
- Copies of the routine monitoring guidelines
- Routine monitoring advocacy materials
- Minutes, handouts or other materials from the latest program planning and feedback workshop, and logistical details of the next workshop
- Copies of the letters informing the organization of the supportive supervision visits
- Routine monitoring form for the period for which data will be audited
- Examples of data use and reports from other organizations
- Routine monitoring supervision forms for any previous supervision visits
- Reporting forms for previous periods
- Blank routine monitoring supervision forms for this supervision visit

Deliverable: Relevant information for a specified reporting period.

Step 4: Set up the visit

Make appointments according to the schedule of supportive supervision visits. When making an appointment to visit an organization:

- Confirm the date of the appointment in writing at least 14 days before the visit is to take place;
- Inform the organization to be visited about the purpose, format, the three persons the supervisor would need to meet (head of organization; routine monitoring lead; and head of finance), and the duration (approximately three hours);
- Advise the organization of the expected outcomes and how they should prepare for the visit.

Deliverable: Appointment date for supervision visit confirmed with the organization to be visited.

During the visit
Step 5:   Undertake the visit

The aspects of supervision described here are based on a sample supervision form and visit process. Also look at the data quality audit assessment tool that the Global Fund has developed (both are in the ERL).

- **Introduction:** Meet the head of the organization and state the purpose of the visit. Check that the head of the organization received the letter in which s/he was informed of the visit. Complete the relevant part of the M&E supervision form.

- **Initiate meetings:** Formally confirm a request for a meeting with the routine monitoring lead person (pre-arranged with the organization for the supportive supervision visit). If a routine monitoring lead person has not been nominated or is not available, request a meeting with the person responsible for monitoring and evaluation, reporting and/or projects in the organization. Complete the relevant part of the M&E supervision form.

- **Follow-up on previous supervision visit:** Using the previous routine monitoring supervision form (if one took place), check with the routine monitoring lead person or organization's representative whether or not the remedial actions agreed to have been implemented/maintained. Complete the relevant part of the M&E supervision form. (Skip this step if it is the first routine monitoring supportive supervision visit to the organization.)

- **Organization's own system of monitoring and reporting of routine monitoring:** Ask the routine monitoring lead person (or other organization representative, see Step 2) about their own M&E systems and reporting of routine monitoring data, specifically about each of the six data management processes in place in their organization. Ask to see evidence, where needed, of the processes described by the supervisee.

- **Use of routine monitoring data:** Ask how the routine monitoring data has been used and note examples shown. Share examples of how other organizations have used the routine monitoring data and show how they can be adapted to improve the way that they plan and implement projects. Complete the relevant part of the M&E supervision form.

- **Routine monitoring data verification:** Verify the routine monitoring data for the reporting period, and use the routine monitoring form to carry out five types of verification (see Table C10-2).

Table C10-2: Aspects of Data Verification

Verification #1 **Observation**	If practically possible, observe the connection between the delivery of services/commodities and the completion of the source document that records that service delivery.
Verification #2 **Documentation Review**	Review availability and completeness of all source documents (records) for the selected reporting period.
Verification #3: **Trace and Verification**	Trace and verify reported numbers: (1) Re-count the reported numbers from available source documents; (2) Compare the verified numbers to the site reported number; (3) Identify reasons for any differences.
Verification #4: **Cross checks**	Crosscheck the verified report totals with other data sources (e.g., inventory records, laboratory reports, etc.), if they are available.
Verification #5: **Spot checks**	Perform spot checks to verify the actual delivery of services or commodities to the target populations, if feasible.

Source: Adapted by authors from Global Fund (2006)

- **Data archiving:** Check whether records have been archived appropriately (i.e., on computer; in files; in a drawer; etc.). Establish whether the records are in a safe place; are secure (if the records contain sensitive data); are filed in an orderly manner; and are easily accessible.

- Routine monitoring resource tracking: Request that the financial manager of the organization to join the meeting.

Deliverable: Supervision findings.

Step 6: Provide feedback to the organization that has been visited and whose data has been audited

- **Feedback and the way forward:** Meet with the routine monitoring lead person and head of the organization. Discuss the findings, agree on remedial actions, and ask the head of the organization to stamp and sign the M&E supervision form. The time frame, responsibility, and budget implications of each remedial action should be specified. When discussing them, ensure that proposed actions are realistic and within budget limitations.

- **End of visit:** Thank the organization and every individual met for their time. Invite them to the next M&E workshop or feedback session and inform them when and where it will take place.

Deliverable: Supervision report.

After the visit

Step 7:   Report back after the visit

On return to the office, finalize the M&E supervision form. Capture the contents of the completed supervision form on applicable databases for use at future supervisions visits. Send a copy of the completed form to the organization that was supervised. Make sure to follow up on remedial actions agreed on during the visit, within the agreed timeframes.

Deliverables: Finalized supervision forms, summary of the findings/ recommendations, input into applicable databases.

For reflection 2:

Reflect on your organization for a moment. Who supervises the monitoring of programs and data auditing in your organization? Do you feel that this supervision is *supportive* in the ways described in this chapter and HowTo guide? What changes would you recommend to improve the supervision and auditing processes in your organization to make them supportive? How do you handle supervision processes yourself?

---

7. Summary of Chapter 10 Knowledge and Skills

In this chapter, you learned about supportive supervision and data auditing. You learned that although data auditing is a separate process, there are benefits to including it in scheduled supportive M&E supervision visits. You learned about the usefulness of data auditing and supportive supervision in that these processes improve credibility of the data, build program implementers' capacity in routine data collection and capture, and improve the use of information for decision-making on all levels. You learned about various implementation issues, including when to design supportive supervision and data auditing procedures, allocation of funding and skilled personnel to conduct the supervision, importance of the supportive supervision process in the feedback loop, and the importance of guidelines and protocols to ensure the quality and uniformity of the procedures. You learned about the five types of verification needed in data auditing and you learned the technical process steps required to undertake a supportive supervision visit from beginning to end.

8. Learning Activities

Chapter 10 is about supervision and data auditing. Break up into two groups for the learning activity or, if you are doing this activity on your own, complete the tasks one after the other.

LEARNING ACTIVITY 1: IDENTIFY LOCATIONS FOR SUPPORTIVE SUPERVISION VISITS

In the routine data flow schematic that you developed in the Learning Activity for Chapter 7, identify all types of M&E supervision, the stakeholders involved, and the purpose of each type of M&E supervision. If you did not complete the Chapter 7 learning activity, use one of the example data flow schematics in Annex B of Chapter 7. Draw a supervision chain similar to the diagram you used in the Chapter 7 Learning Activity (also see Figure C10-1 for an example of a supervision chain).

LEARNING ACTIVITY 2: DESIGN A SUPPORTIVE SUPERVISION FORM

Design a form for reporting back on a supportive M&E supervision visit that has been undertaken.

LEARNING ACTIVITY 3: UNDERTAKE A SUPERVISION PROCESS

a)   What do you think happens during a supervision visit? Think through the process steps and if a colleague is available, try to act out the supportive supervision process in a role play.

b)   What do you think happens during a data auditing visit? Think through the process steps and if a colleague is available, try to role play the process.

c)   Based on your answers to the above two questions, what is the difference between a supervision visit and a data audit visit?

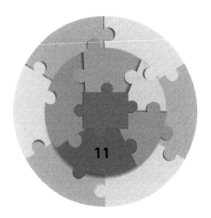

Chapter 11
Evaluation and Research

Chapter Aim

The aim of this chapter is to enable you to improve your program by doing better, more targeted evaluations and research when needed.

Chapter Knowledge and Skills

By the end of this Chapter, you should be able to:

a) Explain why evaluation is important and useful to help programs achieve results.

b) Be familiar with definitions of evaluation and research and the different types.

c) Develop a national evaluation and research strategy.

d) Ensure that HIV research and evaluations are done in an ethical way.

e) Develop and/or update a national evaluation and research agenda.

f) Manage and oversee a program evaluation.

Before You Begin...

Take a few minutes to read through the questions below. You may find it helpful to write down your answers. As you work through the chapter, see how your answers compare to those of the author.

- What are the differences between research, evaluation and surveys?

- How can I use evaluation and research results?

- How can I promote the use of evaluation and research data in my organization?

- How can research be coordinated in a country?

- Who approves research to be undertaken?

- What is ethical review and who does it?

- When do I need to submit my proposed evaluation or research for ethical review?

- Is it ethical to interview children? Are there rules to help ensure that they are treated fairly?

- Can information about a research participant be released without their knowledge?

- Where can I get more information about evaluation and research?

We often take for granted that the programs our organizations implement in communities are well researched and evaluated. However, evaluation and research are among the most neglected parts of any M&E system. This chapter explains how to plan, design and coordinate evaluation and research that will help us understand the *so what* questions (What difference has our program made in the long-term? What has our project achieved?) Answering these questions helps us all learn how to improve programs so they have greater impact.

Component 11: Evaluation and Research

1. Introduction

"The world has never taken on a more challenging task in the field of international health. It is imperative that as these major programs roll out, country by country, we put in place the mechanisms to measure, to study, to learn lessons, and to share those lessons widely."

Richard Feachem, Executive Director of the Global Fund to
Fight AIDS, Tuberculosis and Malaria 2003 to 2007 (2004)

The *fuel* of an M&E system is its data. The data that the M&E system requires to *run* are determined by the indicators and the research questions in the M&E plan (see Chapter 4: M&E plans). The different indicators (input indicators, output indicators, outcome indicators, and impact indicators) in the M&E system require three types of data sources: routine, periodic, and one-off, as Table C11-1 illustrates.

Table C11-1: Types of Data Sources for Different Types of Indicators

Indicator type	Data collection time frame	Types of data sources
Input/ Process	Continuously	Routine data sources such as statistics about education or other government services
		Routine data sources such as routine monitoring data about training materials developed for schools
Output	Quarterly, semi-annually, or annually	Routine data sources such as statistics about education or other government services
		Routine data sources such as routine monitoring data about teacher absenteeism or the number of visits by agriculture extension officers
		Periodic data sources such as exit interview surveys
Outcome	1 to 3 years	Periodic data sources such as population-based surveys
		One-off data sources such as special studies (research or evaluation)
Impact	2 to 5 years	Periodic data sources such as surveillance
		Periodic data sources such as population-based surveys
		One-off data sources such as special studies (research or evaluation)

Source: Adapted by authors from the Global Fund et al. (2006)

Chapter 11

Each of these three types of data sources are components of the middle ring (data collection, capture, and verification) of the 12 Components of a functional M&E system and are covered in this training course in the following chapters:

- Routine data sources (Chapter 7: Routine Data)

- Periodic data sources (Chapter 8: Periodic Surveys)

- One-off data sources (Chapter 11: Evaluation and Research – **this chapter**)

How this Chapter is organized: Chapter 11 begins with background information and definitions of research, operations research, and types of evaluation (Section 2). The desired chapter result and benefits of evaluation and research as part of a national M&E system are presented in Sections 3 and 4. Section 5 describes implementation issues related to evaluation and research, including ethical principles for evaluators and researchers. The next sections provide specific steps and guidance in four HowTo guides: Developing a national evaluation and research strategy (Section 6); Developing or updating a national evaluation and research agenda (Section 7); Ensuring that evaluations are conducted in an ethical way (Section 8); and Undertaking a program evaluation (Section 9). The Chapter closes with a summary of lessons learned and a practical exercise to cement what you have learned.

2. Background Information and Definitions

a) **Research:** Systematic investigation designed to develop or contribute to generalized knowledge; includes developing, testing, and evaluating the research.[1]

b) **Types of Research:** Research can be categorized in many different ways. For example by fundamental purpose, type of data and research method, level of understanding sought, type of research question, and way in which research results will be used.

    i. Research is either done for the *purpose* of building knowledge, driven by curiosity or scientific interest (**basic** research, or *pure* or fundamental research) or to solve practical problems and answer practical questions (**applied** research). Most scientists believe that a fundamental understanding of all branches of science is needed in order for progress to take place. In other words, basic research lays down the foundations for the applied science that follows. In health, basic science research includes clinical trials, testing new monitoring or diagnostic technologies and formative research around behavioral/social issues. Often important external research partners will be engaged in these activities, which should be included as part of the overall research agenda.

---

[1] There are different definitions and distinctions made between research and evaluation; the ones selected for this course are widely accepted, and give insight into a range of evaluation and research activities, approaches and uses.

ii. Research can also be distinguished by the general type of data approach: **quantitative** research collects, analyzes and uses numerical data while **qualitative** research data (explanations, descriptions, opinions, or other information expressed in words rather than numbers) is collected using focus group discussions, observation, key informants, or other qualitative data collection strategies. There are many computer software packages that help analyze qualitative data.

iii. Research can also be distinguished by whether *new data (primary data), or existing data (secondary data)* are collected and analyzed:

1. A common way to **collect new (primary) data is through a survey:** (see Chapter 8 for more details about surveys). The main features of a survey are: (a) use of standardized questionnaires and (b) selection of a representative, scientifically-valid, and statistically-valid sample of respondents to whom the standardized questionnaire is administered. "Surveys are used to ascertain beliefs, attitudes, opinions, behaviors, needs, abilities, social status, and other aspects of peoples' lives. Data are used to describe individuals, estimate population parameters, and discern relationships between what people think, how they act, and the circumstances in which they live" (Michigan State University: <http://research.chm. msu.edu/RO/rschtypes.htm>).

2. Analysis of **secondary data:** Secondary data analyses use data that have already been collected, that the researcher was not responsible for collecting, or were collected for a different purpose. Sometimes primary data collection is not necessary and available secondary data may be entirely appropriate and wholly adequate to draw conclusions and answer a research question. Secondary data analyses can be cheaper, less time-consuming, and more accurate than collecting primary data (Luz, 2006).

iv. Research questions differ in the *level* at which they seek to understand the topic as follows:

1. **Descriptive level:** A study designed primarily to describe what is going on or what exists. Public opinion polls that seek only to describe the proportion of people who hold various opinions are primarily descriptive in nature. For instance, if we want to know what percent of the population would vote for a Democrat or a Republican in the next U.S. presidential election, or want to know how well children perform on school achievement tests, we are simply interested in describing something.

2.   **Relational level:** A study designed to look at the relationships between two or more variables. A public opinion poll that compares the proportions of males and females who say they would vote for a Democratic or a Republican candidate in the next presidential election is studying the relationship between gender and voting preference.

3.   **Causal level:** A study designed to determine whether one or more variables (e.g., a program or treatment variable) causes or affects one or more outcome variables. A public opinion poll to determine whether a recent political advertising campaign changed voter preferences would be studying whether the campaign (cause) changed the proportion of voters who would vote Democratic or Republican (effect) (Trochim, 2006: <http://www.socialresearchmethods.net/kb/resques.php>).

v.   Research can be distinguished by the domain of study related to *ways in which research information will be used*:

1.   **Services Research:** Services research is a multi-disciplinary field that studies how social factors, financing systems, organizational structures and processes, technologies, and behaviors affect access to services, the quality and cost of providing the service (e.g., health care, education or agriculture support) and, ultimately, how it affects people's well-being. The main goal of services research is to identify the most effective ways to organize, manage, finance, and deliver high quality services. Its research domains are individuals, families, organizations, institutions, communities, and populations (Luz, 2006).

2.   **Policy Analysis:** Policy analysis refers to research on a fundamental social problem and its related public policies. Analysts are interested in the process by which policies are adopted as well as their effects and usually provide policymakers with briefings and pragmatic, action-oriented recommendations.

3.   **Operations Research (OR):** Also called program evaluation or evaluation research, the main objective of OR is to provide program managers with the required information to develop, improve, or scale-up programs. Operations Research focuses on whether the program design is right or optimally designed to achieve the desired results, whereas evaluation (see below) focuses on whether a change in results can be attributed to a program. OR can be thought of as a practical, systematic

process for identifying and solving program-related problems (The Global Fund and WHO M&E toolkit, 2006).

Examples of OR:	Main questions OR asks:
Adherence to treatment	Are our programs optimally structured to allow the highest possible adherence to therapy?
Equitable access to services	Are we reaching our target population?
Cost effectiveness analysis	Which of the compared program modalities delivers the most desired outcome/output for the least cost?
Different models of intervention	Which intervention model or design works best/ achieves the strongest results?

For more information about research methods and design, you can visit these two websites:

Research Knowledge Base: http://www.socialresearchmethods.net

Research Methods: http://allpsych.com/researchmethods

c) **Evaluation:** The OECD-DAC Working Party on Aid Evaluation defines evaluation as "the systematic and objective assessment of an on-going or completed project, program or policy, its design, implementation and results." The aim is to determine the relevance and fulfillment of objectives, development efficiency, effectiveness, impact and sustainability. An evaluation should provide information that is credible and useful and learn things that can improve the decisions made by implementers, policy-makers, and funders.

Evaluation also refers to the process of determining the worth or significance of an activity, policy, or program. It is an assessment that is as systematic and objective as possible, of a planned, on-going, or completed development intervention. The American Evaluation Association suggests that evaluation involves assessing the strengths and weaknesses of programs, policies, personnel, products, and organizations to improve their effectiveness. Rossi and Freeman (1993:5) define evaluation as "the systematic application of social research procedures for assessing the conceptualization, design, implementation, and utility of ... programs." Evaluations use experimental and quasi-experimental designs to gather evidence about the value of a program. Both quantitative and qualitative information collection strategies are commonly used.

d) **Types of evaluations:** Formative or process evaluations focus on the quality of program design and implementation, whereas outcome evaluations, economic evaluations and impact evaluations focus on the end-products of program implementation, as described in table C11-2 below.

Table C11-2: Types of Evaluation and Their Uses

Type of Evaluations	When to use	What it shows	Why it is useful
A: Formative Evaluation "Evaluability" Assessment Needs Assessment	• During the development of a new program • When an existing program is being modified or is being used in a new setting or with a new population	• Whether the proposed program elements are likely to be needed, understood, and accepted by the target population • The extent to which an evaluation is possible, given the goals and objectives of the evaluation and the program	• It allows modifications to be made to the plan before full implementation begins • Increases the likelihood that the program will succeed
B: Process Evaluation Routine Monitoring	• As soon as program implementation begins • During operation of an existing program	• How well the program is working • The extent to which the program is being implemented as designed • Whether the program is accessible and acceptable to its target population	• Provides early warning of any problems that may occur • Allows programs to monitor how well their program plans and activities are working
C: Outcome Evaluation Objectives-Based Evaluation	• After the program has made contact with at least one person or group in the target population	• The degree to which the program is having an effect on the target population's behavior	• Tells whether the program is being effective in meeting its objectives

Making Monitoring and Evaluation Systems Work

Type of Evaluations	When to use	What it shows	Why it is useful
D: Economic Evaluation Cost Analysis, Cost-Benefit Analysis, Cost-Effectiveness Evaluation, Cost-Utility Analysis	• At the planning stage, using cost estimates/projections • During operation of a program, using actual costs	• The resources that are being used in a program and their costs (direct and indirect) compared to outcomes	• Provides program managers and funders with a way to assess effects relative to costs
E: Impact Evaluation	• During the operation of an existing program at appropriate intervals • At the end of a program	• The degree to which the program meets its ultimate goal	• Provides evidence for use in policy, funding, and future programming decisions

Source: CDC, 2006

A: **Formative evaluation:** Designed to assess the strengths and weaknesses of program design, materials, or campaign strategies (for example) before implementation. It permits necessary revisions before the full effort is implemented. Its purpose is to increase the chance of program success before the activity starts.

Typical formative evaluation questions:	Information from a formative evaluation may include:
Is it necessary to focus on a certain sub-group or target population in our program response?	Target populations to focus on and their sizes
What intervention could work in this context (interventions that have proven effective in this context)?	Other projects that have been undertaken in the area or with the target populations

B: **Process evaluation:** Examination of procedures and tasks involved in implementing a program. This type of evaluation can also include examination of administrative and organizational aspects of the program. It fulfils an audit and monitoring function and looks at how well the program is working. It is, therefore, critical for quality improvement.

Typical process evaluation questions:	Information from a process evaluation may include:
Are the outreach workers working in the right place?	Geographic areas of implementation
Are program staff carrying out all the required steps?	Service coverage adequacy

C: **Outcome evaluation:** Used to obtain descriptive data on a project and to document short-term results. Task-focused results are those that describe the output of the activity (e.g., the number of public inquiries received as a result of a public service announcement). Short-term results describe the immediate effects on the target audience (e.g., percentage of the target audience showing increased awareness of the subject) and try to assess the actual causal link between interventions and desired outcomes.

Typical outcome evaluation questions:	Information from an outcome evaluation may include:
Is the intervention working?	Knowledge and attitude changes
Is it making the intended difference in outcomes such as changes in knowledge and behavior?	Expressed intentions of the target audience
To what degree did the desired/ planned change(s) occur?	Short-term or intermediate behavior shifts
	Extent of behavior change, policies initiated, or other institutional changes

D: **Economic Evaluation:** Economic evaluation looks at costs and funding associated with development interventions in order to assess value for money, i.e., how efficient are the interventions.

Typical economic evaluation questions:	Information from an economic evaluation may include:
Which intervention is the most cost effective?	Unit costs for implementation of interventions
What % of allocated funding reached beneficiaries and what costs were borne by beneficiaries?	Out-of-pocket expenses for beneficiaries to access services
How long did it take for funding to reach beneficiaries?	*Choke-point analysis* identifying bottlenecks in funding flows

E: **Impact evaluation:** Impact evaluation is the systematic identification of the long-term effects (positive or negative, intended or not) on individuals, households, institutions and the environment, caused by a given activity such as a program or project. Impact evaluation looks

Making Monitoring and Evaluation Systems Work

beyond the immediate results of policies, interventions, or services to identify longer-term as well as unintended program effects. When designing these studies, particular consideration is given to measuring changes that are directly related to the effects of an activity or program and not the result of other (external) influences on the target population that occur over time. Impact evaluation requires specially designed research protocols (frequently employing randomization of study populations), often original data collection, and the involvement of specifically trained researchers to implement the studies.

Typical impact evaluation questions:	Information from an impact evaluation may include:
Are our efforts affecting change on a population level?	Changes in morbidity and mortality in the target population, compared to a control group
Have target behaviors changed?	Changes in absenteeism/productivity/ achievement etc post- intervention compared with baseline measures
What effect (if any) did the policy/program have?	Long-term maintenance of desired behavior

e) **Distinguishing between Evaluation and Research:** Research and evaluation both systematically collect and analyze data and use the same scientific methods. The knowledge gained from an evaluation is often generalizable to other situations or countries which is also the hallmark of research. The distinction lies in the primary intent of the activity. The primary intent of research is to generate or contribute to generalizable knowledge. The primary intent of evaluation is to assess some aspect(s) of a particular program, policy or project, usually to generate information or knowledge for a specific (often practical) purpose, such as whether to continue, modify, scale up, or replicate the activities.

The reason it may matter whether an activity fits the definition of evaluation or of research is because different, usually more stringent, procedures (reviews and approvals) often apply to research. For example, research activities conducted by staff at the U.S. Centers for Disease Control (CDC) are subject to Federal regulation to ensure protection of human subjects. The CDC's criterion for research is whether it generates generalizable knowledge (explained as "new information that has relevance beyond the population or program from which it was collected, or information that is added to the scientific literature"): "When the purpose of an evaluation is to test a new, modified, or previously untested intervention, service, or program, to determine whether it is effective, the evaluation is research. The systematic comparison of standard or non-standard interventions in an experimental-type design is research. In these cases, the knowledge gained is applicable beyond the individual, specific program. Thus, the primary intent is to generate new knowledge or contribute to the knowledge in scientific literature. Further, it is intended to apply the knowledge to other sites or populations." On the other hand, an evaluation of an existing program — usually to provide useful information for managing it — is not classified as research." (CDC 1999) (Please refer to Annex A for an example, used by the CDC, to help them distinguish between research and evaluation, and therefore to decide whether or not ethical approval is needed.)

It is also worth pointing out that work labeled as *research* and work labeled as *program evaluation are* often funded from different sources, the former from research institutions, medical, or academic budgets, the latter often by program implementers or policy makers. Approval and financial support for the study might depend on whether it is consistent with the national research agenda or program evaluation strategy.

3. Results to Be Achieved When Implementing This Component

Long-term result:

Evaluation and research results are used to inform policy, programming, and intervention selection.

Short- and medium-term results:

- Inventory of completed and ongoing program evaluations and research studies.

- Inventory of evaluation and research capacity, including major research institutions and their areas of work.

- Program evaluation and research agenda.

- Ethical approval procedures and standards in place.

- Guidelines on evaluation and research standards and methods.

- Participation in a conference or forum to disseminate and discuss evaluation and research findings.

- Evidence of use of evaluation/research findings (e.g., research results referenced in planning documents).

For reflection 1:

Reflect on your organization and its programs. Are your programs based on evaluation and research? What types of evaluation or research (as listed in Section 2) have been conducted by your organization? What types of evaluation and research might be useful to undertake? How many of the short- and medium-term results listed here are visible in your organization?

4. Benefits of Evaluation and Research as Part of an M&E System

Evaluation provides information to answer questions related to program performance, and to understand critical areas of the program, for example: to identify the factors driving (or inhibiting) progress towards program targets; to test and assess the likely effectiveness of proposed program interventions; to improve interventions; to assess the impact of a program.

Evaluation and research help develop new strategies, programs and targets. Evaluating new approaches is very important to program development in any field. Developers of new programs need to conduct methodical evaluations of their efforts before making claims to potential users. Rigorous evaluation of longer-term program outcomes is a prerequisite to asserting that a model is effective.

Evaluation is useful for project management: Administrators are often most interested in keeping track of program activities and documenting the nature and extent of service delivery. The information they need may be called a *management information system*. An evaluation for project management may, for example, monitor routine program operations. It can provide program staff or administrators with information on such items as participant characteristics, program activities, allocation of staff resources, or program costs. Analyzing information of this type (process evaluation) can help program staff make short-term corrections ensuring, for example, that planned program activities are conducted in a timely manner and are reaching the intended people. This analysis can also help staff to plan future program direction and determine resource needs for the coming year.

Evaluation helps a program stay on track. Evaluation can help to ensure that project activities continue to reflect plans and goals. The data needed for this may be similar to (or a subset of) data for project management. This type of evaluation can help to strengthen service delivery and maintain the connection between program goals, objectives, and services.

Evaluation and research builds capacity of the organization and its staff. Evaluation and research builds knowledge in an organization and, in the process, the capacity of the organization to implement better programs or design more effective plans. Individuals learn by observing the importance of using data to drive decisions and improve their own skills. Skills and knowledge learned in evaluation or research of one program are often broadly applicable to other programs.

Evaluation and research can help improve project efficiency. Evaluation can help streamline service delivery or enhance coordination among various program components, lowering the cost of services. Increased efficiency can enable a program to serve more people, offer more services, or target services to those whose needs are greatest. Evaluation for program efficiency may focus on identifying the areas in which a program is most successful and expand them. It may identify weaknesses or duplication to make improvements, eliminate some services, or refer participants to services elsewhere. Evaluations of both program process and program outcomes are used to determine efficiency.

Evaluation helps to keep projects accountable. Users of the evaluation results interested in accountability are likely to come from outside the program operations. These might include, for example, funding agencies, elected officials, and other policymakers.

For reflection 2:

What is the capacity of your organization to do research and evaluation? What partners could you engage with to enhance the skills available to the team?

---

5. Implementation Issues Related to Evaluation and Research

This section does not aim to provide a comprehensive review of all implementation issues relating to evaluation and research. Volumes have been written and are available in the Electronic Resource Library (http://gametlibrary.worldbank.org). Rather, four critical issues relating to evaluation and research are discussed here; when to do research, developing TORs, ethical standards, and using research results.

5.1. The timing of evaluation and research design

Deciding when, how, and what type of research and evaluation to undertake all influence the required budget. This is but one of the reasons why the timing of evaluation and research design is critical. Too often the need for an evaluation is realized only after the project has been started when the whole budget has been allocated to other things. At this stage, it may be too late to have a randomized design or to identify a cohort and the opportunity to gather baseline data has been lost. Early consideration during the planning phase avoids compromise later and allows for better research and evaluation studies with stronger results.

5.2. Developing TORs for an evaluation

An evaluation is as good as the instructions given to the person carrying out the evaluation. Often, evaluations do not meet their desired goal (of influencing implementing, and planning) because the evaluation is carried out at the wrong time or the evaluation questions are not specific enough or matched to the answers needed by decision makers and programmers, or the evaluator is not given access to all necessary information.

Many problems can be avoided if an accurate Terms of Reference for the evaluation is developed. The Terms of Reference sets the scene for the entire evaluation and is the evaluator's starting point. It is also the tool that should be used to measure the quality of the evaluator's outputs. If the TOR is vague, unclear, unspecific, incomplete or outdated, the evaluation may not be successful or result in program improvement.

To assist in the process of developing TORs, Annex B contains a step-by-step guide to develop a good quality TOR for an evaluation.

5.3. Ethical standards in evaluation and research

What are ethics? Ethics for evaluation and research are "**norms for conduct** that distinguish between acceptable and unacceptable behavior" (Resnik, 2007:1) when conducting research or evaluations.

Why consider ethics? Following ethical standards in evaluation and research is beneficial for a number of reasons. First and foremost, ethics are intended to protect individuals involved in the research or evaluation (research subjects/ evaluation respondents) from harm. They also encourage researchers and evaluators to adhere to procedures to minimize/avoid error (and so promote research/evaluation towards achieving its intended goal), they promote trust and respect (and thus collaboration) among members of the same or different research/evaluation teams, help researchers and evaluators be accountable to the public, help garner public support for research and evaluations, and promote important norms and social values in society (AfrEA 2006, Resnik, 2007).

Which principles can my research/evaluation project follow to ensure that it is ethical? The Declaration of Helsinki, developed by the World Medical Association (WMA), is a set of ethical principles for the medical community regarding human experimentation. It is widely regarded as the cornerstone document of human research ethics (WMA 2000, Bošnjak 2001, Tyebkhan 2003). Several countries have also developed similar ethical standards. In 1979, for example, the U.S. National Commission for the Protection of Human participants of Biomedical and Behaviorial Research developed the "Belmont principles" for ethical research (Belmont Report, 1979). According to the Belmont principles, all research should have:

(a) **Respect for Persons:** Individuals should be treated as autonomous agents and persons with diminished autonomy are entitled to protection.

(b) **Beneficence:** Two general rules for ensuring that actions are beneficent: maximize possible benefits and minimize possible harm.

(c) **Justice:** In deciding who ought to receive the benefits of research and bear its burdens, one should be guided by one (or more) of the following concepts: to each person an equal share, to each person according to individual need, to each person according to individual effort, to each person according to societal contribution, and to each person according to merit.

In practice, the Belmont principles place a three-fold burden on researchers: they must obtain informed consent of research subjects, including communicating risks and benefits; assess and maximize benefits and minimize risks in study design; and select subjects with the principles of justice in mind.

Using the Belmont and other principles, Shamoo and Resnik (2003) suggested criteria for ethical behavior in research that applies, to a certain extent, to evaluations as well. Pimple (2002) suggested that ethical research meets three basic criteria: "It is true, fair, and wise?".

Table C11-3: Ethical Principles for Evaluation and Research: Criteria, Principles, and Explanations

Ethical principle	Explanation
A: Is it true?	
Honesty	Strive for honesty in all scientific communications. Honestly report data, results, methods and procedures, and publication status. Do not fabricate, falsify, or misrepresent data. Do not deceive colleagues, granting agencies, or the public.
Carefulness	Avoid careless errors and negligence; carefully and critically examine your own work and the work of your peers. Keep good records of research and evaluation activities, such as data collection, research/ evaluation design, and correspondence.
Competence	Maintain and improve your own professional competence and expertise through lifelong education and learning; take steps to promote competence in science as a whole.
Integrity	Keep your promises and agreements; act with sincerity; strive for consistency of thought and action.
Objectivity	Strive to avoid bias in research/evaluation design, data analysis and interpretation, peer review, personnel decisions, grant writing, expert testimony, and other aspects of research/evaluation where objectivity is expected or required. Avoid or minimize bias or self-deception. Disclose personal or financial interests that may affect research or evaluation.

Ethical principle	Explanation
B: Is it fair?	
Confidentiality	Protect confidential communications, such as papers or grants submitted for publication, personnel records, trade or military secrets, and patient records.
Human Subjects Protection	When conducting research on human subjects, minimize harm and risks, and maximize benefits; respect human dignity, privacy, and autonomy; take special precautions with vulnerable populations; and strive to distribute the benefits and burdens of research fairly.
Legality	Know and obey relevant laws and institutional and governmental policies.
Non-Discrimination	Avoid discrimination against colleagues or students on the basis of sex, race, ethnicity, or other factors that are not related to their scientific competence and integrity.
Openness	Share data, results, ideas, tools, resources. Be open to criticism and new ideas.
Respect for Colleagues	Respect your colleagues and treat them fairly.
Respect for Intellectual Property	Honor patents, copyrights, and other forms of intellectual property. Do not use unpublished data, methods, or results without permission. Give credit where credit is due. Give proper acknowledgement or credit for all contributions to research and evaluation. Never plagiarize.
C: Is it wise?	
Social Responsibility and Improved Decision Making	Strive to promote social good and prevent or mitigate social harms through research, evaluation, public education, and advocacy.
Responsible Mentoring	Help to educate, mentor, and advise team members or others you are mentoring as part of the evaluation or research process. Promote their welfare and allow them to make their own decisions.
Responsible Publication	Publish in order to advance knowledge and scholarship, not to advance your own career. Avoid wasteful and duplicative publication.

Source: Adapted by the authors from Pimple (2002), Shamoo and Resnik (2003), Resnik (2007)

NOTE: Although evaluations do not always have the same elaborate implementation procedures as research, the ethical principles described in Table C11-2 are still relevant. Even a community-based project can ensure that its evaluation is true, fair, and wise.

Chapter 11

Where/how can I access ethical standards for my country or project? One of the questions that may come to mind as you read this section is whether principles for ethical research and evaluation exist in your country. Many countries have developed national guidelines or codes of ethics for researchers, often through national laws, policies, or national ethical committees (for example, see Czech Republic, 2006). Some institutions have their own code of ethics (see, for example, FHI, 2001). Ask experienced researchers whether there is an ethical code specific to your institution and whether there is a national code and ethics committee.

Setting up a national ethics committee can be a laborious process but one that international research partners are likely to support enthusiastically. It need not be overly complex or have a wide technical base among its members but it must have legitimacy from civil society and, importantly, from the highest levels of government.

The absence of an ethical code or standards should not deter research and evaluation from being ethical. You can, for example, insist that all your team members complete the Research Ethics Training Curriculum (see http://www. fhi.org/training/en/RETC/) or you could make sure that ethical procedures are built into the TOR of the evaluation or research. Other useful resources may be found on the website of the Office for Human Subjects Research at the National Institutes of Health in the United States. Research projects carried out with U.S. federal funding have to register with this office. Visit http://ohsr.od.nih.gov/ guidelines/index.html for more information.

Please note that the list of resources for ethical standards in research and evaluation is meant as a *starting point* for a country or project to consider. More information about ethics can be found in the GAMET M&E Resource Library at http://gametlibrary.worldbank.org .

5.4. Using evaluation and research results

For evaluation and research results to be used and to influence decisions that are made about programs, people who make decisions need to internalize new knowledge (they need to learn). This requires a rigorous dissemination strategy and concerted efforts to *translate* or explain research results so they can be used. Research translation and use requires persons with writing skills to be able to convert technical documents into non-technical language and forums need to be developed to share these documents. There also must be willingness from managers of the program, at all levels, to learn and apply the findings.

Annex C contains a conceptual framework for getting results into policy and practice (GRIPP), as well as an example from Swaziland where a conceptual framework was used to plan how the research results would be used early on, as part of the planning for the studies.

6. HowTo Guide C11-1: Develop a National Evaluation and Research Strategy

Step 1: Find a *custodian* of the National Evaluation and Research Strategy

The first step is to discuss and agree on where the National Evaluation and Research Strategy will be housed. The *custodian* of the strategy will need to champion the strategy and its implementation.

The best place to house a research and evaluation strategy depends on a number of country-level factors. **Technical factors** include the nature of the strategy (is it a strategy for one sector, such as agriculture which may be housed in the relevant ministry, or a national strategy for all sectors in the country) and the range of institutions involved in research and evaluation (e.g., whether the country has a national research council, university-based research institutes, or a national medical research council). **Political factors** would include the readiness of institutions to be the custodian of such a strategy. By readiness, we mean the enthusiasm, commitment, and motivation of the leadership of institutions to take on and be involved in research and evaluation.

Step 2: Obtain political and senior management buy-in

Management needs to lead the process of developing a national evaluation and research strategy and support efforts to use the findings. In advocating the adoption of a national evaluation and research strategy, the custodian (see Step 1) could work with academic institutions, use the results of an assessment to show challenges with program research in the country, and refer to the results of countries that have successfully implemented such strategies.

The custodian may also highlight the benefits of a national evaluation and research strategy that include better availability of data; more effective programs; better use of existing research funding; and better protection of human rights through the assurance that all research will be done according to ethical guidelines. Should management approve the concept, the technical team should ask management for specific guidance on:

- Funding availability to conduct a research assessment and develop a strategy.
- Nominees for the technical advisory group to oversee the research assessment and the evaluation and research strategy development.
- Authority for approving the research assessment and the steps that would be followed to develop an evaluation and research strategy.
- Funding to implement the strategy, including the possible appointment of a research officer.

Deliverable: Concept note on development of a national evaluation and research strategy.

Step 3: Assemble a technical advisory group for the research and evaluation assessment

A technical advisory group should represent the stakeholders involved in evaluation and research in the country and may include the National Research Council, academic and research institutions, other research committees, in-country ethical review boards, the appropriate government officials, and representatives of other key relevant stakeholders.

In many countries, important stakeholders will include representatives of foreign academic institutions with a history/interest in research in the country. These are usually a significant resource for capacity development, technical support, and funding for research. Local representatives of some international development organizations should also be included such as development partners like relevant UN agencies and technical partners, and national and international NGOs involved in evaluation and research.

Deliverable: List of members for a technical advisory group. (These members should represent stakeholders involved in research relevant to the organization and/or its programs.)

Step 4: Conduct a research and evaluation assessment

First, review the information and knowledge available to the technical advisory group:

- Is there an inventory of program research and program researchers and evaluators?
- Have these research studies been peer reviewed and published?
- Is there a research council? If yes, what work does it do and how functional is it?
- Are there formally adopted standards for evaluation and research in the country?
- Is there a prioritized evaluation and research agenda for the country?
- Is there a process for ethical approval for research? If yes, how does it work?
- How have evaluation and research results been disseminated?
- Who has the mandate (based on policies, laws, and regulations) for coordinating evaluation and research?

- Is the mandate at a national level, is it multi-sectoral, or within one or more specific sectors?
- What plans for evaluation and research exist?
- What funding sources for evaluation and research are available?
- How can evaluation and research capacity be built?
- Is there in-country capacity to offer training and mentoring in evaluation and research?

If the group does not have answers to these questions, a formal research and evaluation assessment is needed. The assessment could focus on:

- Developing an inventory of research & evaluations and researchers and evaluators (studies undertaken, peer review mechanisms and how/if the study results were published).
- Finding out whether a national research council exists and is functional.
- Collecting information about previous efforts to coordinate research among tertiary institutions and efforts to coordinate evaluation efforts.
- Finding out about the existence of research conferences and other avenues to disseminate the results of evaluation and research.
- Identifying the appropriate steps to develop an evaluation and research strategy and agenda.
- Conceptualizing options for the governance of evaluation and research in the country.

NOTE: A formal assessment such as the one described above, is optional. If a country has sufficient information about research and evaluation available, then a formal assessment is not needed.

Deliverable: Research and evaluation assessment results; knowledge on which to build the development of a strategy.

Step 5: Finalize the steps for developing the evaluation and research strategy with the technical advisory group

The research assessment will determine the steps to be followed to develop a research strategy in the country. Discuss these steps with the research advisory group and agree on the structure that will approve this strategy.

Deliverable: Steps for designing a research strategy.

Chapter 11

Step 6: Assemble a peer review group for the evaluation and research strategy

It should be made clear which group will be responsible for overseeing the research strategy development and approving it. This may be a challenge if the evaluation and research covers more than one sector.

Deliverable: Peer review group formed.

Step 7: Secure resources and technical support for developing the evaluation and research strategy

Appropriate budgets and work plans need to be developed, approved, and resources mobilized.

Deliverables: A costed work plan and funding for the process secured.

Step 8: Develop the evaluation and research strategy

The development steps will depend on what is agreed by the advisory group in Step 4. The M&E Electronic Resource Library contains an example TOR for developing a research strategy and an example of a completed research strategy (http://gametlibrary.worldbank.org).

The contents of the strategy should include at least the following:

- The types of evaluation and research governed by the strategy.
- Applicable laws and regulations.
- Ethical guidelines and principles for all program research in the country.
- Minimum requirements for coordinating evaluation and research.
- Minimum requirements for approving evaluation and research.
- Ethical review processes (where human subjects are involved).
- Minimum requirements for peer review of evaluation and research.
- Minimum requirements for disseminating findings at the national, sub-national, and sector levels.
- Processes for developing and updating the evaluation and research strategy.
- Processes for maintaining an up-to-date evaluation and research inventory.
- Recommendations on minimum funding requirements for program evaluation and research.
- Linkages between research institutions.

- Mechanisms to minimize duplication of evaluation and research, particularly at project and sub-national levels.

Deliverable: Evaluation and research strategy.

Step 9: Approve the evaluation and research strategy

The agency responsible for coordinating a particular program may be the most suitable agency to coordinate implementation of the program evaluation and research strategy. Whether the agency has this mandate needs to be determined. The research assessment is the ideal means to clarify this mandate.

Deliverable: Approval of the evaluation and research strategy (by the agency responsible for the coordination of its implementation).

Step 10: Disseminate the strategy widely

The evaluation and research strategy needs to be disseminated to stakeholders that archive, plan, fund, undertake, and use program evaluation and research results, including:

- University libraries
- Government archives
- National and international research institutions
- Local and regional universities
- Development partners
- Program implementers
- Civil society umbrella organizations

Deliverables: Dissemination of strategy to defined stakeholders (including posting on an appropriate website).

7. HowTo Guide C11-2: Develop or Update a National Evaluation and Research Agenda

This process is often undertaken together with the development of an evaluation and research strategy (see HowTo Guide C11-1). However, the steps have been detailed separately as a country may elect to develop an agenda first, or may already have an evaluation and research strategy.

Step 1: Develop an inventory of program evaluation and research that has been undertaken

- This step can be done jointly with Step 2 of developing an evaluation and research strategy if an inventory does not already exist. This detailed list of all research and evaluations will help during later steps.

- If an inventory already exists, confirm how regularly it is updated. If it is regularly updated, then further updates should not be necessary.

- If an inventory exists but has not been updated, updating it would be a priority before the new research agenda can be developed.

- Articles and reports can be obtained from academic journals, researchers, and websites. (www.google.scholar.com is a good tool for searching the web.)

Deliverable: An up-to-date inventory of program evaluations and research found online and from other sources.

Step 2: Group and sort studies that have been undertaken to identify key themes

Research could logically be grouped by sub-population; geographic area; type of program service being evaluated/researched; or a combination of these. Having a standard way to catalog items in the inventory will make it easier to group evaluations/research and identify major themes.

Deliverable: All items grouped and sorted (using agreed categories) within the inventory catalog.

Step 3: Consider the latest evidence about programs being implemented

Consider factors driving or inhibiting progress toward program targets, the latest program review, latest M&E system assessment, and latest policy and consensus statements by relevant technical agencies.

- What information is known and not known?

- What has already been researched but not yet well communicated?

- What is not well known, has not yet been researched, and is important for achieving program targets? (This will constitute the research agenda.)

Deliverable: Knowledge of, and consideration of, current/latest research and evidence to inform the process.

Step 4: Frame the important unanswered evaluation and research questions

Based on the gaps identified in Step 3, the important unanswered evaluation/research questions should be framed in a careful way. These questions are the basis for an evaluation/research agenda. The ERL contains more information about how to develop evaluation/research questions.

Deliverable: Framed important evaluation/research questions that have yet to be answered.

Step 5: Publish the agenda

The evaluation and research agenda needs to be disseminated to stakeholders that archive, plan, fund, undertake, and use research results, including:

- University libraries
- Government archives
- National and international research institutions
- Local and regional universities
- Development partners
- Program implementers
- Civil society umbrella organizations

Deliverable: Dissemination of published evaluation and research agenda to identified stakeholders.

Step 6: Undertake evaluations and research

Following approval of the agenda, undertaking research and evaluation will entail:

a) Formalizing (and institutionalizing, if necessary) the structure that has been mandated to coordinate program evaluation and research.

b) Planning and estimating the cost of implementing the strategy and including these costs in the relevant national work plans.

c) Mobilizing resources for evaluation and research.

d) Establishing a mechanism to electronically maintain and update the evaluation and research inventory.

Chapter 11

Mobilizing resources for evaluation and research is often a major hurdle. These strategies can help:

a)   Ensuring that new projects have a dedicated budget for evaluation and research.

b)   Including evaluation and research as a component in applications for development partner support.

c)   Working closely with international organizations traditionally engaged in research to develop a common agenda and work plan.

d)   Lobbying within the ministry for an increased allocation of national resources for evaluation and research (e.g., to a national research body or as a component of department funding).

e)   Making it part of someone's job to review international sources of research funding on a regular basis and to keep apprised of research priorities and calls for proposals that may be relevant to the country or project.

Building capacity for research and evaluation: One of the main hurdles to research and evaluation is the lack of capacity and experience in undertaking good quality research and evaluation.   There are a number of mechanisms to develop this capacity and experience including but not limited to:

a)   Scholarships, in partnership with international academic/research institutions, to allow a number of young researchers to undertake postgraduate study abroad.

b)   Developing a clear career path and mechanism for continued support for country researchers.

c)   Developing or expanding an evaluation and research training curriculum in as part of undergraduate courses.

Deliverable: Evaluation and research studies carried out and programs improved as a result of studies that are used to inform decision making.

For reflection 3:

What are some of the challenges you foresee in following these steps for developing a national evaluation and research strategy and/or agenda? What support can you identify that might help you to address some of these challenges?

Chapter 11

8. HowTo Guide C11-3: Undertake a Program Evaluation

Program evaluations are usually undertaken to determine one or more of the following (McNamara, 1997):

- Reactions and feelings (feelings are often poor indicators that your service has lasting impact)
- Learning (changes in attitudes, perceptions, or knowledge)
- Changes in skills or behaviors
- Effectiveness (improved performance or outcomes because of changes in behavior)

There are a number of evaluation guides that explain in detail how to undertake a program evaluation. A basic guide to program evaluations can be found at: http://www.managementhelp.org/evaluatn/fnl_eval.htm

The following three resources may be very useful when planning a Program Evaluation:

a) **Program Evaluation Planning Checklist:** This checklist, in Annex D of this chapter, provides a series of checks and questions that, when answered, helps to crystallize the purpose and type of evaluation and data collection techniques.

b) **Tool for designing a TOR for an Evaluation:** Once the basics of an evaluation have been planned, the next step is to write a Terms of Reference. The guide in Annex B of the chapter provides you with a step-by-step logical process for developing good quality TOR for a program evaluation.

c) **Criteria for Good Evaluations:** The African Evaluation Association has developed criteria for good evaluations, a useful benchmark against which to assess if: (i) a TOR is well-defined; (ii) an evaluation is well-designed; or (iii) an already-completed evaluation has been carried out well. The criteria are built on the following four principles:

- **Utility principle:** The information produced and the results expected and provided should be useful so that the evaluation can have an impact. Its stakeholders, especially those who will be able to use the results, should be identified. The clarity, format, and dissemination of the report should promote and contribute to knowledge building and to the credibility of the evaluator and evaluation team.

- **Feasibility:** Realism, cautiousness, and efficiency, which encompass the need to have practical procedures, political viability, costing done effectively.

- **Respect for ethics:** Respect legal and ethical rules, including the need to have formal agreements to conduct the evaluation, respect

Chapter 11

stakeholder rights, and be transparent and impartial when conducting the evaluation.

- **Precision and quality:** The methodology should be relevant and appropriate for the goal and subject matter of the evaluation and should include, context analysis, defined goals, traced information sources, reliable information, thorough and accurate qualitative and quantitative analyses, relevant conclusions and realistic recommendations that are based on consensus among the research team. (AfrEA, 2006)

The criteria for good evaluations, linked to each of these four principles, are summarized in the African Evaluation Guidelines, which may be found in Annex E.

9. Summary of Chapter 11 Knowledge and Skills

In this chapter, you learned about various types of evaluation and research and how to distinguish between the two. You learned that evaluation and research often are the most ignored aspects of the M&E system. They enable you to identify the needs of your organization, its programs, and the community, which are key to achieving strong program outcomes and impact. You learned that evaluation and research lead to important learning that may be useful to many others in addition to your organization and area of research. You learned principles to help you, as a researcher or evaluator, discern whether research or evaluation is ethical. You learned theory and steps for designing, developing, and implementing a national evaluation and research strategy and agenda. You also learned where to find guidance on how to undertake a program evaluation and resources to help you plan and undertake a successful program evaluation.

10. Learning Activities

LEARNING ACTIVITY 1: ETHICAL RESEARCH AND EVALUATION BEHAVIOR OR NOT?

Read through the ethical principles listed in Table C11-3 in Section 5.2. Then complete the table below by reading each statement (which describes something a hypothetical evaluator or researcher has done). Decide whether each was ethical (Column 2), and list the ethical principle that was either adhered to or not (Column 3). The first three have been completed as examples:

Making Monitoring and Evaluation Systems Work

Statement	Ethical? YES or NO	Ethical principle at stake
Publishing the same paper in two different journals without telling the editors.	NO	Openness
Discussing with colleagues data from a paper that he/she is reviewing for a journal.	NO	Integrity
As a co-author, informing a journal that the lead author has included a colleague as an author on a paper in return for a favor even though the colleague did not make a serious contribution to the paper.	YES	Respect for colleagues
Trimming outliers from a data set without discussing the reasons in a paper.		
Presenting all evaluation results, even negative ones that may impact on the country's ability to secure further funding.		
Drug manufacturers paying doctors to test a new drug by prescribing it to patients.		
Agreeing to conduct a peer review of an author's work who you know has been caught plagiarizing in the past.		
Using different statistical techniques to present evaluation results in different ways.		
Presenting only the most favorable facts in the situation analysis (formative evaluation) during a project's grant application and ignoring the factors which would make the proposal seem less favorable.		
Conducting a review of the literature as an introduction to the evaluation that fails to acknowledge the contributions of other people in the field or relevant, earlier work.		
Withholding treatment from a control group of a study (e.g., treatment for syphilis), even though the treatment (penicillin) is widely used.		
Conducting a trial to assess the efficacy of a new and expensive cancer medication not yet available in your country by comparing a treatment group, with a control group that receives a placebo.		

Source: Authors

LEARNING ACTIVITY 2: CASE STUDIES FOR ETHICAL RESEARCH CONDUCT

Read the four case studies below [case studies from FHI (2001) and Resnik (2007)]. In each case, think about and answer the questions that follow the particular case study:

CASE STUDY A: An urban church-run health center is a popular alternative for many people who complain about the poor services and lack of confidentiality in the public-run clinics. As a researcher investigating the effects of a new post-test HIV counseling and case management program, the church health center seems like a perfect site. The well-trained staff members of the health center are interested and have past experience implementing similar research with other diseases. The center is already the preferred HIV-testing site in the city. Upon further discussions with the health center staff, you learn that they are not willing to distribute condoms to post-test clients, even those who test positive for HIV. Although your study does not require condoms to be distributed, you are alarmed that the center would refuse to distribute condoms to HIV-positive clients, thus putting their partners at risk of HIV.

Questions about Case Study A:

1. Should you continue to include this health center in your study?

2. Are there effective alternatives to providing condoms to infected participants?

3. The trial does not depend upon the provision of condoms and could still be conducted. Do you have a moral obligation to the participants?

CASE STUDY B: Dr. T has just discovered a mathematical error in a paper that has been accepted for publication in a journal. The error does not affect the overall results of his research, but it is potentially misleading. The journal has just gone to press, so it is too late to catch the error before it appears in print. In order to avoid embarrassment, Dr. T decides to ignore the error.

Questions for Case Study B:

1. What ethical principle is at stake here?

2. What would you do in this situation?

3. How will what Dr. T has done affect his reputation?

---

[2] **Spermicides** are agents used to kill spermatozoa (male sperm) and mostly have been used as a form of contraception for use by women. Already available without prescription in many countries, spermicides have been studied to assess whether they could prevent HIV.

CASE STUDY C: Nonoxyl-9 (N-9), a widely used spermicide[2], has been on the market for 50 years with an excellent safety record for its intended use (as a contraceptive). The product has been found to be effective in laboratory studies against a number of important pathogens for which it was not originally intended, including HIV. Numerous clinical trials with N-9 are being conducted to show effectiveness in preventing infection by the new pathogens, some of which lead to death. At a large international conference, a researcher presents preliminary analysis of interim data results from a randomized phase III trial comparing N-9 to a similar product. The results show that the group of women using the test product had a higher incidence rate of HIV infection than the group using the comparison product. There is a general call from the media, international health and leading U.S. health organizations to halt all ongoing and planned clinical trials using N-9, and inform all women in these trials that they may be at increased risk of contracting the deadly infection. You are currently conducting a study to test N-9. However, your participant population is very different from the population enrolled in the trial that produced the results.

Questions about Case Study C (Select appropriate answer for each of the two questions below):

1. Would you continue your research study?

    (a) No, there is no justification for putting women at risk.

    (b) Proceed with ongoing research.

    (c) Proceed with planned and ongoing research but increase safety surveillance.

2. Should women who are enrolled in your research be informed of the data announced at the international conference?

    (a) Yes; they deserve to know.

    (b) No; it would create unnecessary fear and confusion.

CASE STUDY D: Dr. S is a post-doctoral student in computer science working on some programs that eliminate computer viruses. Two other graduate students are working with her on the project, which is directed by a senior researcher. Dr. S has just received an email from a research team that is working on a similar project at another university. The other team would like Dr. S to share some preliminary data and designs related to the project. Dr. S has not applied for a patent on this research although she has discussed possible patents with her supervisor.

Questions about Case Study D:

1. What would you advise Dr. S to do?

2. Which ethical principles are at stake?

3. How can she make a sound decision?

Chapter 11

Evaluation and Research

389

LEARNING ACTIVITY 3: GOOD QUALITY EVALUATION?

Read the criteria for a good quality evaluation in Annex E, then read Case Study E and answer the questions:

> **CASE STUDY E:** In 2004, one year after project implementation, baseline information about the project was collected using qualitative data and a survey questionnaire. In 2007, when the midterm review of the project indicated that there was insufficient data, another evaluation was undertaken by the project team, using a different survey questionnaire (the previous one had not been saved and new data was required). The survey showed that the project, which was meant to increase enrolment of young girls, was resulting in lower enrolment. Since different methods were used to collect the baseline and interim data, the project team did not share the results with the rest of the country or with the government, agreeing among themselves that the two evaluations *did not compare apples with apples.*

Questions about Case Study E:

1. Was the evaluation undertaken in an ethical manner?

2. Was it a good quality evaluation?

3. If you had the chance to advise the team on how to improve the evaluation, what would your advice be to the team?

Annex A: Example Criteria for Needing Ethics Committee Approval

Activities funded by the U.S. CDC or in which CDC staff are involved, only need to be submitted to the Ethics Committee [known as the Institutional Review Board (IRB)] if they meet the definition of research, as well as two additional criteria: (1) The research involves human subjects, and (2) does not meet the Review Board criteria for exemption. A decision about whether or not an activity requires Review Board approval is illustrated in Figure C11-1.

Figure C11-1: Deciding Whether or Not an Activity Needs Ethics Committee Approval – A Public Health Example

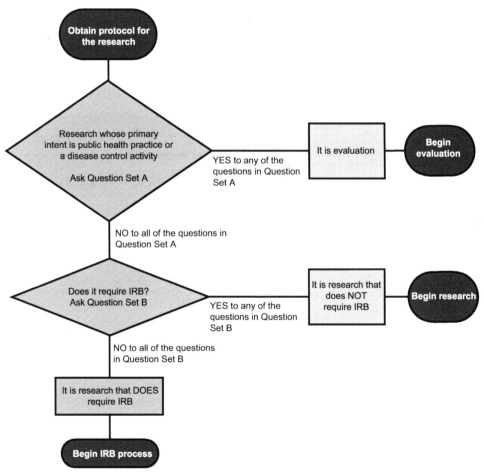

Source: Authors, using text from CDC (1999)

Question Set A: Primary intent is a public health practice or a disease control activity.

- Epidemic/endemic disease control activity; data directly relates to disease control needs
- Routine **disease surveillance** activity; data used for disease control program or policy purposes
- **Program evaluation** activity; data is used primarily for that purpose
- **Post-marketing surveillance** of efficacy and/or adverse effects of a new regimen, drug or device
- **Activity is purely administrative** (e.g., purchase orders or contracts for services or equipment) and not related to research

Question Set B: Activity is research but does NOT involve identifiable human subjects.

- Activity is research involving collection/analysis of data about health facilities or other organizations or units that are not individual persons **or**
- Activity is research involving data and/or specimens from deceased persons **or**
- Activity is research using unlinked anonymous data or specimens. **All** (1-4) of the following are required:
    1. No contact with human subjects is involved for the proposed activity;
    2. Data or specimens are/were collected for another purpose;
    3. No extra data/specimens are/were collected for **this** purpose;
    4. Identifying information either was not obtained **or** has been removed so that data cannot be linked or re-linked with identifiable human subjects.

Annex B: Tool for Developing a TOR for an Evaluation

Template for
HIV Prevention Evaluation Terms of Reference
Quick Reference Guide[1]

Template for HIV Prevention Evaluation ToR – Sections

A Why do the evaluation?
1 Evaluation topic
2 Background and rationale
3 Evaluation objective
4 Users of the evaluation

B What are we evaluating?
5 Evaluation questions
6 Target group(s)
7 Prevention interventions
8 Prevention indicators

C How are we evaluating?
9 Evaluation design
10 Data sources and procedures
11 Data analysis procedures

D How will the evaluation be managed?
12 Evaluation activities and schedule
13 Evaluation team members and level of effort
14 Administrative and logistical support
15 Budget

An evaluation is a 'systematic and objective assessment of an on-going or completed project, programme or policy, its design, implementation and results. The aim is to determine the relevance and fulfilment of objectives, development efficiency, effectiveness, impact and sustainability. An evaluation should provide information that is credible and useful, enabling the incorporation of lessons learned into the decision–making process of both recipients and donors'. [2]

Evaluations are useful because they help managers to improve programmes, identify lessons learned and inform decisions about future funding. An HIV prevention evaluation, therefore, helps decision makers understand the efficiency and effectiveness of programmes to prevent the transmission of HIV.

A high quality evaluation starts with a terms of reference (ToR) that clearly defines all aspects of the evaluation. This user-friendly guide helps staff of civil society organisations (CSOs) [3] commissioning process and outcome evaluations, and develop good prevention evaluation ToRs. The guide does not focus on impact evaluations, since they are not usually commissioned by CSOs, but rather by national authorities. Users are not necessarily evaluation specialists, but managers of evaluations.

This template does not have to be followed strictly and certain sections of the ToR could be changed, combined or not included, depending on the situation.

For a full example of a ToR for HIV prevention evaluation please go to http://gametlibrary.worldbank.org.

[1] This quick reference guide was abstracted from the MERG document *Developing terms of reference for prevention evaluation*. www.worldbank.org/aids. Please refer to this document for further guidance.
[2] *Glossary of key terms in evaluation and results-based management* by the OECD, 2002, accessible on http://www.oecd.org/dataoecd/29/21/2754804.pdf.
[3] Civil society organisations (CSOs) is used as an umbrella term to include non-governmental organisations (NGOs), community-based organisations (CBOs), and faith-based organisations (FBOs).

DEVELOPED BY:

www.aidsalliance.org

WORLD BANK GROUP
www.worldbank.org/aids

1

Chapter 11

Abbreviations

BCC	Behavioral change communication
CSO	Civil society organisation
HCT	HIV counselling and testing
IDU	Injecting drug user
MARPs	Most-at-risk populations
MSM	Men who have sex with men
NAC	National AIDS Commission
MOH	Ministry of Health
SW	Sex worker
ToR	Terms of reference

Key terms

Data analysis

Qualitative analysis involves analysing qualitative data (text, pictures or visual observations) to draw conclusions about, for example, people's feelings or perceptions.

Quantitative analysis uses quantitative data (numbers or percentages) for analysing trends (changes in values over time) and summarising the data. Types of quantitative analysis include:

- **Descriptive statistics** – the mean, mode and median – to describe the data. Statistical tests can show how significant the observed changes are.

- **Cost analysis** monitors the amount and percentage of expenditures by category.

- **Cost-effectiveness analysis** compares results and costs of different prevention approaches; the approach with the lowest cost per unit result is the most efficient.

Evaluation types

Process evaluation focuses on program implementation and uses largely qualitative methods to describe program activities and perceptions, especially during the developmental stages and early implementation of a program. It may also include some quantitative approaches, such as surveys about client satisfaction and perceptions about needs and services.

Outcome evaluation is concerned with determining if, and by how much, program activities or services achieved their intended outcomes. Outcome evaluation attempts to attribute observed change to the intervention tested, describe the extent or scope of program outcomes, and indicate what might happen in the absence of the program. It is methodologically rigorous and requires a comparative element in design, such as a control or comparison group.

Impact evaluation looks at the rise and fall of disease incidence and prevalence as a function of AIDS programs. The effects (impact) on entire populations can seldom be attributed to a single program or even several programs, therefore, evaluations of impact on populations usually entail a rigorous evaluation design that includes the combined effects of a number of programs for at-risk populations. For this reason, as well as comparatively high costs, impact evaluations are not usually commissioned by CSOs, but rather by national authorities. [*]

Evaluation design

An **experimental design** results from randomly selected control groups at the individual or cluster/community level which are then compared to the target groups of prevention programmes.

For **quasi-experimental design** a non-random *comparison group* is required (it could be generic, for example, from a national survey) or a *time series design* (when multiple observations of the same individuals or communities are carried out over time).

Non-experimental design does not require comparison or control groups; the target groups of prevention programmes are examined at the beginning and end of project to observe and analyse changes; the least cost, least robust design.

Results chain

A **results chain,** or theory of change, describes assumptions about how activities contribute to achieving results, e.g. if pregnant women are tested and counselled and positive women are treated, then mother-to-child transmission will be reduced.

Inputs	Activities	Outputs	Outcomes	Impacts

In the results chain, resources (inputs) are processed into goods and services (outputs). These result in knowledge and behaviour change, improvements in access to and utilisation of services (outcomes), which, in turn, eventually produce changes in the socio-demographic or epidemiological profile of a population (impact).

The causal links of the results chain

* Please note that impact evaluations are not usually commissioned by CSOs, thus they are not a focus of this guide.

Chapter 11

Making Monitoring and Evaluation Systems Work

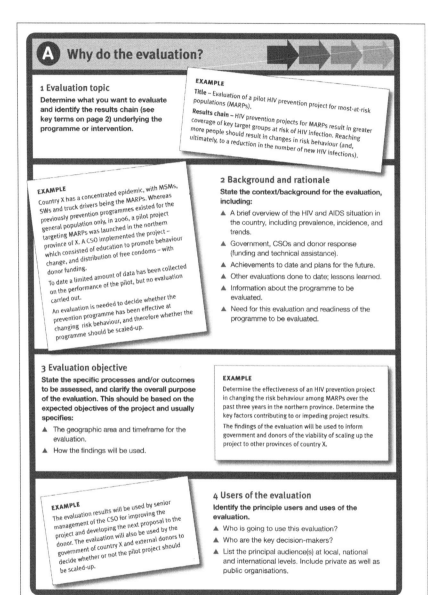

A Why do the evaluation?

1 Evaluation topic

Determine what you want to evaluate and identify the results chain (see key terms on page 2) underlying the programme or intervention.

EXAMPLE

Title – Evaluation of a pilot HIV prevention project for most-at-risk populations (MARPs).

Results chain – HIV prevention projects for MARPs result in greater coverage of key target groups at risk of HIV infection. Reaching more people should result in changes in risk behaviour (and, ultimately, to a reduction in the number of new HIV infections).

EXAMPLE

Country X has a concentrated epidemic, with MSMs, SWs and truck drivers being the MARPs. Whereas previously prevention programmes existed for the general population only, in 2006, a pilot project targeting MARPs was launched in the northern province of X. A CSO implemented the project – which consisted of education to promote behaviour change, and distribution of free condoms – with donor funding.

To date a limited amount of data has been collected on the performance of the pilot, but no evaluation carried out.

An evaluation is needed to decide whether the prevention programme has been effective at changing risk behaviour, and therefore whether the programme should be scaled-up.

2 Background and rationale

State the context/background for the evaluation, including:

▲ A brief overview of the HIV and AIDS situation in the country, including prevalence, incidence, and trends.

▲ Government, CSOs and donor response (funding and technical assistance).

▲ Achievements to date and plans for the future.

▲ Other evaluations done to date; lessons learned.

▲ Information about the programme to be evaluated.

▲ Need for this evaluation and readiness of the programme to be evaluated.

3 Evaluation objective

State the specific processes and/or outcomes to be assessed, and clarify the overall purpose of the evaluation. This should be based on the expected objectives of the project and usually specifies:

▲ The geographic area and timeframe for the evaluation.

▲ How the findings will be used.

EXAMPLE

Determine the effectiveness of an HIV prevention project in changing the risk behaviour among MARPs over the past three years in the northern province. Determine the key factors contributing to or impeding project results.

The findings of the evaluation will be used to inform government and donors of the viability of scaling up the project to other provinces of country X.

EXAMPLE

The evaluation results will be used by senior management of the CSO for improving the project and developing the next proposal to the donor. The evaluation will also be used by the government of country X and external donors to decide whether or not the pilot project should be scaled-up.

4 Users of the evaluation

Identify the principle users and uses of the evaluation.

▲ Who is going to use this evaluation?

▲ Who are the key decision-makers?

▲ List the principal audience(s) at local, national and international levels. Include private as well as public organisations.

3

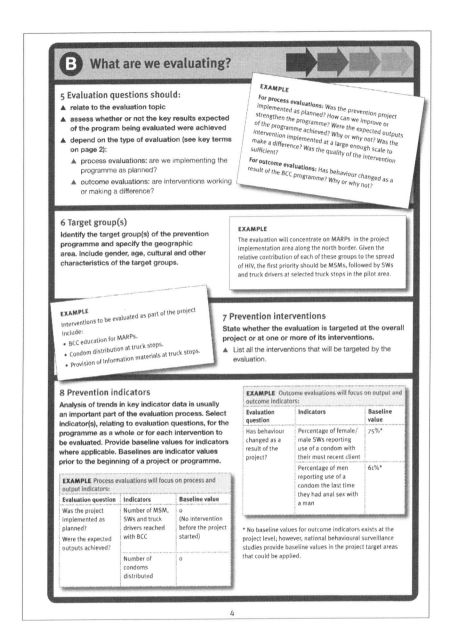

B What are we evaluating?

5 Evaluation questions should:

▲ relate to the evaluation topic

▲ assess whether or not the key results expected of the program being evaluated were achieved

▲ depend on the type of evaluation (see key terms on page 2):

  ▲ process evaluations: are we implementing the programme as planned?

  ▲ outcome evaluations: are interventions working or making a difference?

EXAMPLE

For process evaluations: Was the prevention project implemented as planned? How can we improve or strengthen the programme? Were the expected outputs of the programme achieved? Why or why not? Was the intervention implemented at a large enough scale to make a difference? Was the quality of the intervention sufficient?

For outcome evaluations: Has behaviour changed as a result of the BCC programme? Why or why not?

6 Target group(s)

Identify the target group(s) of the prevention programme and specify the geographic area. Include gender, age, cultural and other characteristics of the target groups.

EXAMPLE

The evaluation will concentrate on MARPs in the project implementation area along the north border. Given the relative contribution of each of these groups to the spread of HIV, the first priority should be MSMs, followed by SWs and truck drivers at selected truck stops in the pilot area.

EXAMPLE

Interventions to be evaluated as part of the project include:

• BCC education for MARPs.

• Condom distribution at truck stops.

• Provision of Information materials at truck stops.

7 Prevention interventions

State whether the evaluation is targeted at the overall project or at one or more of its interventions.

▲ List all the interventions that will be targeted by the evaluation.

8 Prevention indicators

Analysis of trends in key indicator data is usually an important part of the evaluation process. Select indicator(s), relating to evaluation questions, for the programme as a whole or for each intervention to be evaluated. Provide baseline values for indicators where applicable. Baselines are indicator values prior to the beginning of a project or programme.

EXAMPLE Outcome evaluations will focus on output and outcome indicators:

Evaluation question	Indicators	Baseline value
Has behaviour changed as a result of the project?	Percentage of female/ male SWs reporting use of a condom with their most recent client	75%*
	Percentage of men reporting use of a condom the last time they had anal sex with a man	61%*

* No baseline values for outcome indicators exists at the project level; however, national behavioural surveillance studies provide baseline values in the project target areas that could be applied.

EXAMPLE Process evaluations will focus on process and output indicators:

Evaluation question	Indicators	Baseline value
Was the project implemented as planned? Were the expected outputs achieved?	Number of MSM, SWs and truck drivers reached with BCC	0 (No intervention before the project started)
	Number of condoms distributed	0

4

How are we evaluating?

Steps 9 – 11 might be part of the ToR, or can be determined by the implementers of the evaluation at a later stage. It is also possible to combine them into one step.

9 Evaluation design

This can be experimental, quasi-experimental or non-experimental (see key terms on page 2). As experimental design is costly and difficult to implement, quasi or non-experimental designs are usually used by NGOs for process or outcome evaluations.

EXAMPLE OF A NON-EXPERIMENTAL DESIGN

Outcome data is gathered from a sample of MARPs in the northern province and compared over time to baseline data obtained in 2006 in order to establish association between participation in the pilot project and less risky behavior. Factors that might have affected behavior patterns other than participation in the project are also taken into account.

EXAMPLE OF A QUASI-EXPERIMENTAL DESIGN

The southern province of country X, with no prevention interventions targeted at MARPs, will be identified as a comparison group for the evaluation. Comparing behaviour data for southern and northern provinces will indicate whether the pilot project (as opposed to other interventions such as national radio campaigns implemented in both provinces) led to any changes in behaviours. Other factors, apart from the intervention under consideration, that might have affected behaviour patterns in one geographical area but not in the other are also taken into consideration when interpreting the results.

10 Data sources and procedures

Evaluations usually include secondary and primary data sources.

Primary data sources (new data to be collected) include:	Secondary (pre-existing) data sources include:
▲ Direct observations ▲ Interviews and focus groups ▲ Tests (e.g. blood tests) ▲ Inventories ▲ Self-administered questionnaires	▲ Performance monitoring data ▲ Project or programme strategic plans, logframe, reports, M&E plans ▲ Recent evaluations and surveys (e.g. demographic and health surveys, behavioural surveillance data, etc.) ▲ Special reports (e.g. human development, HIV sector report)

EXAMPLE

The following data sources will be used:

A desk review of all relevant documents.

A structured survey of MSMs, SWs and truck drivers; a sample of approximately 500 respondents will be used to collect data on key indicators.

A qualitative client satisfaction survey of approximately 100 representatives of MARPs who were reached by BCC activities within the programme.

EXAMPLE

Quantitative analysis will be used to determine changes in indicator values, comparing baseline data from 2006 with data obtained as a result of the evaluation. A mixture of quantitative and qualitative analysis will be used to process data obtained from the client satisfaction survey. Joint analysis of these results will be carried out to derive conclusions about the effectiveness of the prevention project under study.

11 Data analysis procedures

Qualitative and quantitative analysis are the two main analytical procedures (see key terms on page 2):

▲ **Qualitative analysis** involves analysing qualitative data (text, pictures or visual observations) to draw conclusions about, for example, people's feelings or perceptions.

▲ **Quantitative analysis** uses quantitative data (numbers or percentages) for analysing trends (changes in values over time) and summarising the data.

5

Chapter 11

How will the evaluation be managed?

12 Evaluation activities and schedule

These are usually developed as a bar chart.

▲ Include the **activities** start and end dates, personnel requirements and level of effort.

▲ Highlight the key **deliverables** of the evaluation (with delivery dates), i.e. workplan, evaluation protocol, initial briefing, final debriefing, summary of key findings, conclusions and recommendations, first and final draft of the report.

EXAMPLE Timetable chart (bar chart)

Activity	Month 1	Month 2	Month 3	Month 4
Preparation				
Team planning				
Fieldwork				
Milestone data entry & coding				
Data analysis and review				
Report preparation				
Debriefing; revisions				
Finalise report				

The key deliverables for this evaluation include: a workplan and evaluation protocol (to be provided by the end of month 1), a draft report (end of month 3) and a final report (end of month 4).

EXAMPLE
The evaluation will be carried out by an international team of experts.

The evaluation team will consist of a team leader/HIV specialist, a BCC specialist, a sociologist, interviewers and data entry clerks (not all full-time).

It is expected that the team leader will spend 20 working days on this evaluation, the BCC specialist 5 days, the sociologist 5 days, interviewers 30 days (e.g. 3 people working 10 days each) and data entry clerks a total of 30 days.

13 Evaluation team members and level of effort

The evaluation can be conducted internally (by the organisation itself) or externally (tendered) by another organisation. In either case the ToR would specify the skills requirements and number of work days needed for each activity (if not determined in the evaluation schedule) and should include:

▲ The roles and responsibilities of the staff involved.

▲ The estimated number of days for each team member.

14 Administrative and logistical support

Spell out who will provide what kind of administrative and logistical support, i.e:

▲ Local transportation

▲ Hotel arrangements

▲ Office space and equipment

▲ Printing and photocopying

▲ Interpreters and translators

▲ Report production

▲ Report dissemination

▲ International transportation

EXAMPLE
The CSO will provide local transportation, office space, and equipment and report dissemination. The implementers of the evaluation should provide for international transportation, interpreters and translators, and report production.

15 Budget

The budget must reflect all activities and their costs. Both monetary and in-kind contributions are usually indicated.

EXAMPLE Estimated cost for this evaluation is $17,450. The total cost breaks down into the following categories:

Cost category	Units	Unit cost	In-kind cont.	Total cost
Team leader	20 days	$300 per person/day		$6,000
BCC specialist	5 days	$200 per person/day		$1,000
Sociologist	5 days	$200 per person/day		$1,000
Interviewers x 3	10 days/person	$40 per person/day		$1,200
Data entry clerks x 2	15 days/person	$40 per person/day		$1,200
Sub-total personnel				$10,400
Overheads (@25%)				$2,600
Local transport			$100 (CSO)	$100
International transport	3 flights	$600/flight		$1,800
Office supplies			$50 (CSO)	$50
Accommodation for 3 people	10 (total days of fieldwork)	$100 per day		$1,000
Report printing	1,000 reports	$0.50/report		$500
Translator	10 days	$100/day		$1,000
Total				$17,450

6

Annex C: Conceptual Framework to Help Plan and Get Research into Policy and Practice (GRIPP)

The conceptual framework may be applied both prospectively and retrospectively.

- Prospectively, it may be used in the planning stages by donors, researchers, or program managers, to assess, and potentially influence factors that may enhance research use.

- Retrospectively, the framework may be useful for analyzing case studies (both *success stories* and *failures*), in order to document and learn from experience.

The conceptual framework (CF) is applicable across a range of research domains (e.g., basic, clinical, epidemiological, social sciences, or operations research), with varied research questions, stakeholders, communication strategies, and use goals. Although the CF may be applied within the scope of a particular research initiative, it should locate the research within the context of a broader body of pre-existing and accumulating research evidence. In some cases, use of research may be measured by its contribution to a developing theoretical base or its influence in stimulating further areas for investigation.

The CF may be useful for highlighting where further attention to certain factors may be critical, but it does not necessarily follow that these factors lie within the responsibility or influence of the researcher. In this respect, the CF may be a useful tool for engaging the perspectives and participation of multiple stakeholders, including donors, government, advocacy groups, policy makers, and program managers. The following section describes the main components of the Conceptual Framework for Research Use.

A. Factors

There are a range of factors to consider which may impact on research utilization. They are divided into 4 broad categories in the first column of the conceptual framework (see below).

1. Research process:

These factors relate to the research process itself, and are divided into 3 phases:

- **Pre-research:** factors primarily relevant to the research planning stage

- **Research:** factors relating to the conduct of the research

- **Post-research:** factors of importance in the post-research period

These phases are not always distinct/separable and it is helpful to consider them as part of a continuum.

2. **Stakeholder involvement:**

There may be a diverse range of stakeholders who need to be engaged in order to strengthen research use and they may vary according to the type of research (basic research, operations research, etc.). Stakeholders include both potentially supportive and dissenting groups and the nature and extent of their involvement may vary throughout the phases described above.

3. **Communication:**

These factors relate to activities that communicate and disseminate research findings to relevant target groups.

4. **Macro Contextual factors:**

Although many of the above factors are, to some extent, within the influence of researchers, there are a range of contextual factors which may impact on research use, but are generally beyond the control of researchers.

B. **Utilization and Scale-up Activities**

These factors (represented as an **arrow** bridging the gap between research process and research application) refer to activities that may play an influential role in the use of research findings. In the absence of explicit planning, resource allocation, and modifications (e.g., adaptation from pilot phase to scale-up), the ultimate application of research findings may be limited.

C. **Application**

The last column documents the extent of research use through its potential applications at 5 levels: research, advocacy, policy, programs, and practice. The contribution of a particular piece of research to each of these levels will vary, as will the directionality of influence (e.g., research influencing policy and, hence, programs or the reverse).

Source: The information in this Annex comes from Annex A of Nath, 2007

On the next page, you will find an example of how this framework was applied to one secondary analysis (synthesis) project in Swaziland.

Applying the Conceptual Framework of Research Use to the HIV Epidemiological Synthesis Project in Swaziland

FACTORS	Pre-research	Research	Post-research	Scale-up activities	Application/ utilization
					Evidence Base
Research Process	• HIV prevention not providing desired results • New infections and current targeting of prevention not sufficiently understood to align prevention where new infections occur • Multi-country study to "Know your epidemic" and "Know your response" by UNAIDS and the World Bank • Local study team supported by the World Bank team members and UNAIDS local & regional technical support teams	• Synthesis with 4 components • Application of best current incidence model • Comprehensive epidemiological review to triangulate model data • Data collection on policy context and strategic information regarding prevention, and provision of prevention services by implementers, jointly analyzed with information from the National AIDS Spending Assessments • Capacity building of local study team through *hands-on* workshops and coaching	• Synthesis report with clear structure and language • Report giving evidence-based policy and program implications • Timely dissemination of findings to inform National HIV Strategic plan and new HIV projects • Potential need to re-define prevention agenda, primary targets, messages and approaches	• National HIV Strategic plan and new HIV project based on study findings • Incidence model re-run every time relevant new data sets become available • Local capacity to conduct the study • Technical assistance from UNAIDS and World Bank available in future	• Two countries in multi-country study with similar drivers of the epidemic (Lesotho, Mozambique) • Identification of data gaps on drivers of the epidemic **Advocacy** • Policy & program implications awaited (stakeholders, media) • High-level Government represented in study's Policy Team • Use of results by advocacy groups • Media personnel trained to provide quality reporting on HIV

FACTORS	Pre-research	Research	Post-research	Scale-up activities	Application/utilization
					Policy
Stakeholder Involvement	• Key stakeholders (planners, policy-makers, technical partners) participate in inception seminar and technical planning workshop to give input into study design and implementation • Steering committee & high-level policy committee to oversee study implementation & research • Stakeholders consulted on data collection tools and literature base for study • Training workshops on incidence modeling, data triangulation, synthesis writing, and how to get research into policy and practice • Government and stakeholders presented with preliminary findings to maximize input and ownership • Champions/advocates in Ministry of Health and National AIDS Commission			• National HIV Strategic plan and new HIV project based on study findings • Incidence model re-run every time relevant new data sets become available • Local capacity to conduct the study • Technical assistance from UNAIDS and World Bank available in future	• National HIV Strategic Plan development awaiting the study findings • National policies (gender, poverty alleviation, etc) to be reviewed • Commitment of resources: Development partners mobilized to work jointly

FACTORS	Pre-research	Research	Post-research	Scale-up activities	Application/utilization
Communication	• Clear communication lines established (National AIDS Commission, World Bank, UNAIDS) • Research objectives and implementation communicated to stakeholders through workshops and key documents (inception report, implementation calendar) • Results to be packaged in different formats: Full synthesis report, brochure, policy note • Discussion with media, HIV portfolio committee, department heads, Regional AIDS Committees • 37% of study budget allocated to dissemination (planning/validation/dissemination workshops $10,000; Discussion $10,000; Printing of synthesis report $8,000)			• National HIV Strategic plan and new HIV project based on study findings • Incidence model re-run every time relevant new data sets become available	**Programs** • National AIDS Commission to give strategic objectives & direction to prevention implementers (is this mechanism in place?) • Targeting to become evidence based
Macro Contextual Factors	• Recent survey data and census data (population stagnant or possibly shrinking) call for more drastic action to prevent further HIV infections • Traditional power structures, privileges and dependencies not amenable to rapid changes • Country has strong M&E system and some research data but service delivery not evidence-based • Classified as middle income country, therefore, not eligible for certain donor support/initiatives			• Local capacity to conduct the study • Technical assistance from UNAIDS and WB available in future	**Practice** • Message, targeting and approach to be reviewed in light of the study findings

Annex D: Program Evaluation Planning Checklist

1. **Name of Organization**...
    ....

2. **Name of Program being**
    considered for evaluation...
    ....
    ....

3. **Purpose of Evaluation? (Tick all that apply)**
    What do you want to be able to decide as a result of the evaluation?

    ☐   Better plan a project or intervention (i.e., formative evaluation)

    ☐   Provide information to clarify program goals, processes and outcomes
        for management planning (i.e., formative evaluation)

    ☐   Understand, verify, or increase impact of products or services on
        customers/clients (i.e., outcome evaluation)

    ☐   Improve delivery mechanisms so they are more efficient and less costly
        (i.e., process evaluation)

    ☐   Verify that we're doing what we think we're doing (i.e., process
        evaluation)

    ☐   Program intervention comparisons to decide which should be retained
        (i.e., economic evaluation)

    ☐   Fully examine and describe effective programs for duplication
        elsewhere
        (i.e., impact evaluation)

    ☐   Understand all the program's intended and unintended results/
        successes achieved (i.e., impact evaluation)

    ☐   Other reason(s)

4. **Audience(s) for the Evaluation?**

    ☐   Funders/Investors

    ☐   Board members

    ☐   Management

☐ Staff/employees

☐ Beneficiaries of programs (clients/customers)

☐ Community leaders, politicians and other leaders

☐ Scientific community

☐ General public

☐ Other(s) (specify)..
....
....

5. **What Kind of Information is Needed?**

What kind of information is needed to make the decision you need to make and/or enlighten your intended audiences, for example, information to understand:

☐ Background information about the situation needed before an intervention is planned or executed

☐ The process for product or service delivery (its inputs, activities and outputs)

☐ The customers/clients who use the product or service

☐ Strengths and weaknesses of the product or service

☐ Benefits to customers/clients (outcomes and impacts)

☐ Cost-benefit or other aspect of the financing of the intervention

☐ How the product or service failed and why

☐ Lessons learned for future improvement

☐ Comparison of different types of implementation

☐ Other type(s) of information? (specify)...
....

6. **Type of Evaluation?**

Based on the purpose of the evaluation and the kinds of information needed, what type of evaluation is being planned?

☐ Formative Evaluation

☐ Process Evaluation

☐ Outcome Evaluation

☐ Economic Evaluation

☐ Impact Evaluation

7. **Who or Where Should Information Be Collected From?**

☐ Staff/employees

☐ Clients/customers

☐ Program documentation

☐ Funders/Investors

☐ Other(s) (specify)..
....
....

8. **How Can Information Be Collected in Reasonable and Realistic Fashion?**

☐ Questionnaires

☐ Interviews

☐ Documentation

☐ Observing clients/customers

☐ Observing staff/employees

☐ Conducting focus groups among (describe typical focus group members)..
....
....
....
....
....

☐ Other(s) (specify)...
....

9. **When Is the Information Needed?**...
    ....
    ....
    ....
    ....
    ....
    ....
    ....

10. **What Resources Are Available to Collect the Information?**......................
    ....
    ....
    ....
    ....

After having thought about your evaluation using the Program Evaluation
checklist provided here, develop a Terms of Reference for the Evaluation (see
Annex B of this Chapter for more information regarding how to design a TOR).
After designing the TOR for the Program Evaluation, check the quality of the
evaluation by assessing the TOR against the evaluation criteria set out in
Annex E.

Evaluation Checklist adapted from : http://www.managementhelp.org/evaluatn/
chklist.htm

Annex E: Guidelines for Conducting Evaluation
Guidelines for Evaluation in Africa: 2006 Edition

Published by African Evaluation Association (AfrEA)
(Reproduced with permission from the African Evaluation Association)

Preamble

The guidelines for evaluation are ethical principles and quality criteria. They are a set of rules and requirements that are necessary to all stakeholders and applicable throughout the evaluation process. These principles show a shared system of values among all evaluation stakeholders in Africa. The evaluation standards help enhance independence and impartiality in the conduct of evaluation. They ensure transparency and a participative methodology and create conditions of ownership of evaluation and its results. Also, they aim to standardize methods and upgrade the trustworthiness and usefulness of evaluation. This second edition of the evaluation guidelines aggregates the various works of stakeholders in the field of evaluation in Africa. It is also in tune with the major trends and good practices in evaluation worldwide. The new edition of guidelines on evaluation takes into account both the universal standards and promotes requirements justified by the state of evaluation in Africa. It supervises the process and products and embraces all sectors and timeframes of the evaluation project. These standards target all types of evaluation. They are adaptable and incorporate a pluralist dimension. They help provide integrity to evaluation stakeholders and make the evaluation processes reliable while improving the professionalism of the evaluation in Africa.

They include 34 rules divided into 4 major principles:

1. **Utility principle:** for produced information and expected and provided results.

2. **Feasibility:** for realism, cautiousness and efficiency.

3. **Precision and quality:** for a relevant methodology related to the goal and the subject matter of the evaluation.

4. **Respect of ethics:** respect of legal and ethical rules.

1. Utility principle: The utility guidelines are intended to ensure that an evaluation will serve the information needs of intended users and be owned by stakeholders.

   U1. **Evaluation Impact.** Evaluations should be planned, conducted, reported and disseminated in a manner and within a timeframe that empowers stakeholders, creates ownership and increases the chances that the findings will be used for effective development.

U2. **Stakeholder Identification.** Persons and organizations involved in or affected by the evaluation (with special attention to community participants and vulnerable groups) should be identified and included in the evaluation process in a participatory manner, so that their needs can be addressed and so that the evaluation findings are utilizable and owned by stakeholders, to the extent this is useful, feasible and allowed.

U3. **Credibility of the Evaluator.** The persons conducting the evaluation should be independent and trustworthy. They should have cultural sensitivity, appropriate communication skills and proven competence in evaluation methodology, so that the evaluation process and findings achieve maximum credibility and acceptance. When unsure of competencies evaluators should seek to work in teams to ensure complementary skills and knowledge for credibility of results.

U4. **Credibility of the Evaluation Team.** Evaluation teams should be constituted to include proven competence in evaluation methodology and in the specialist area(s) under review, as well as cultural competence.

U5. **Information Scope and Selection.** Data and information collected should be broadly selected to address pertinent questions and be responsive to the needs and interests of stakeholders, with special attention to vulnerable groups.

U6. **Values Identification**. The rationale, perspectives and methodology used to interpret the findings should be carefully described so that the bases for value judgments are clear. Multiple interpretations of findings should be transparently reflected, provided that these interpretations respond to stakeholders' concerns and needs for utilization purposes.

U7. **Report Clarity.** Evaluation reports should clearly and concisely describe what is being evaluated and its context, the purpose, methodology, evidence and findings so that essential information is provided and easily understood.

U8: **Reporting Format.** The reporting format should be adapted to suit diverse stakeholder needs and increase the chance of use.

U9: **Report Dissemination.** Significant interim findings and evaluation reports should be disseminated to stakeholders, to the extent that this is useful, feasible and allowed. Comments and feedback of stakeholders on interim findings should be taken into consideration prior to the production of the final report.

U10. **Contribution to Knowledge Building.** Evaluations should be reported and disseminated to contribute to a body of knowledge that can be accessed and utilized by a wider audience. Evaluators should negotiate issues of authorship, publication and copyright with commissioners of evaluation so that results/findings will be utilized by a wider audience, to the extent that this is feasible and allowed.

2. Feasibility principle: The feasibility principle is designed to ensure that evaluation is useful, participative, realistic and efficient.

    F1. **Practical procedures.** Evaluations methodologies should be practical and appropriate to help data collection if necessary.

    F2. **Political viability.** Evaluation should be planned and conducted in a participative manner in order to achieve total involvement of all stakeholders. It should be prepared and conducted on the basis of scientific principles of neutrality and strictness to avoid disputes conducive to negative impact on processes and findings as well as on implementation and recommendations.

    F3. **Cost effectiveness.** The efficiency principle should be respected throughout the evaluation process so that the resources engaged are justified with regard to the data and findings achieved. Those responsible for evaluation and all the other evaluation stakeholders should always lock in budget, human and organizational resources in an optimal way and according to evaluation targets.

3. Precision and quality principles: This principle aims to ensure that evaluation has resulted in technically relevant data, demonstrating efficiency of project, program and policies to be evaluated.

    A1. **Program documents.** Any project, program or policy (PPP) subject to an evaluation should be sufficiently documented. A communication process should be adopted that targets various stakeholders.

    A2. **Context analysis.** The context in which the PPP evolves should be examined in detail including social, political, cultural and environmental aspects. Gender should also be highlighted.

    A3. **Described goals and procedures.** Evaluation goals and procedures should be clearly followed. They are defined in full details and refer to evaluation criteria that are commonly accepted (relevance, effectiveness, efficiency, viability, impact) to evaluate them.

    A4. **Tracing information sources.** The information sources utilized in evaluation should be described in full detail to ensure reliability without any breach to anonymity and/or cultural and personal sensitivity of informants.

A5. **Valid information.** Data collection procedures and sampling should be selected, developed and implemented to make sure that information produced is valid and adequate.

> A5b. **Representative information.** Data collection procedures should be selected, developed and implemented to ensure that information produced is representative of the diversity.

A6. **Reliable information.** Data collection procedures should be selected, developed and implemented to ensure that data obtained is reliable.

A7. **Systematic information.** The data collected, processed and reported with regard to an evaluation should be systematically reviewed, and any mistake should be reported and corrected as best as possible.

A8. **Analysis of quantitative data.** In an evaluation, the quantitative data should be properly and systematically analyzed so that various questions on evaluation, including expected results, are conclusive.

A9. **Analysis of qualitative data.** When one is engaged in an evaluation, qualitative data should be properly and systematically analyzed to ensure that various questions on evaluation, including expected results, are conclusive.

A10. **Relevant conclusions.** The conclusions of an evaluation should result from methods and analysis so that stakeholders can appreciate them in full objectivity.

> A10b. **Realistic recommendations reached by consensus.** The recommendations of an evaluation should be validated by stakeholders, be feasible and linked to expected results.

A11. **Impartiality of the report.** The evaluation report should be written so that it does not reflect the subjectivity of those involved in its design, to ensure that it is not biased. It is important that the report actually reflect the findings of the evaluation.

A12. **Meta-evaluation.** The evaluation itself should be formally and systematically evaluated with respect to guidelines to ensure that it is appropriately carried out; this will allow stakeholders to evaluate its strengths and weaknesses.

Chapter 11

4. **Principle of respect and ethics:** These principles safeguard the respect of legal and ethical rules as well as the well being of stakeholders involved in the evaluation or affected by its findings.

P1. **Goal and scope of the evaluation.** The evaluation should be designed to efficiently meet the needs of all target stakeholders.

P2. **Range and quality.** The evaluation should be comprehensive and satisfactory. It should identify and analyze strengths and weaknesses of the evaluated project, program or policy. Its objective is to make useful recommendations in order to strengthen the positive components of a program and propose how to tackle occurring difficulties.

P3. **Formal agreements.** Objectives, methodologies, responsibilities, duration and ownership of the evaluation should be negotiated and formalized within a liability charter that can be revised. Particular attention should focus on implied and informal aspects of the commitment made by involved parties.

P4. **Stakeholders' rights.** The evaluation should be designed and conducted in compliance with rights and moral and physical integrity of stakeholders and their community. Respect of privacy of personal data collected should be observed.

P5. **Human relations.** Evaluators should respect the dignity and the human value in their interaction with people involved in the evaluation in such a way these people do not feel threatened, or are harmed physically, or culturally, or in their religious beliefs.

P6. **Disclosure of conclusions.** The findings of the evaluation should be owned by stakeholders and the limits of the methodologies used should be precise. Recommendations resulting from this ownership will be designed with stakeholders. Privacy should be maintained during the whole process to avoid any attempt to intimidate executing agencies or evaluators.

P7. **Disputes over interests.** These disputes should be settled in an objective manner so that they do not jeopardize the evaluation process and results.

P8. **Transparency.** The evaluator should apply the principles of effectiveness and transparency in every management action linked to the project and in the conduct of the evaluation.

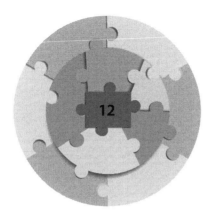

Chapter 12
Using Information to Improve Results

Chapter Aim

The aim of this chapter is to show how you can use information to improve
the results your organization achieves. We aim to teach strategies that
increase the extent to which information from the M&E system is used to
inform decisions that improve results.

Chapter Knowledge and Skills

By the end of this Chapter, you should be able to:

a) Explain to others all the concepts relating to data, information, how
   decisions are made, how data are analyzed and displayed.

b) Analyze and synthesize routine survey research and evaluation data
   generated by the M&E system.

c) Put together dynamic reports (information products), including effective
   displays of information that help managers and decision makers take action.

d) Implement innovative and diverse strategies to maximize use of the
   information.

Before You Begin...

Take a few minutes to read through the questions below. You may find it helpful to write down your answers. As you work through the chapter, compare your answers to the views of the authors.

- What challenges or problems does your organization face at the moment?
- Why are you doing this course on the 12 Components of a functional M&E system?
- What influences the decisions your organization makes and the services it provides?
- Why does your organization have an M&E system?
- What information does your organization's M&E system generate?
- Who makes decisions about strategies, programs, and work plans in your organization?
- Do strategies, programs, or plans change as a result of the information collected through the M&E system?
- Can you recall one time when a program design was improved or implementation activities changed as a result of data reviewed from the M&E reports?
- Has an unpopular decision ever been made in your organization? What motivated the decision?
- Do decision makers you work with ask for information? Why and when do they want the information? What do they use it for?
- What does it mean to use *information to improve results*?
- What factors have prevented or encouraged you to use information that has been presented to you?
- Is information studied and examined before decisions are made about strategies or programs, or new plans are developed?
- Do the decision makers in your organization consciously consider how, when, and by whom the information generated by the M&E system will be used when deciding which information to collect?

The central and most important purpose of an M&E system is to help your organization achieve its mission: to improve strategies that outline the results that your organization wants to achieve; to improve work plans and budgets for the activities designed to achieve the results; and to improve the way in which the activities are implemented. This chapter will *unpack* concepts about how to improve results by using information, explain some proven strategies to improve how information is used as part of the decision making process, and provide examples of how information can be, or has been, used.

Component 12: Using Information to Improve Results

1. Introduction

"Researchers have found that the better informed members are about the problem they are required to solve, as well as the positive and negative qualities of available choices, the better able they are to reach a high-quality decision."

Hirokawa, 1996

Why is the *Using information to improve results* component represented in the middle of the 12 Component graphic red? Monitoring and evaluation systems provide information to help organizations solve the problems and challenges they face in their work and to achieve the results they aim for. The heart of an M&E system, the *bull's eye* (and, therefore, in the middle and red in the 12 Components graphic), is using the information the M&E system generates when making decisions about strategies, programs, plans, budgets, resource allocation, staffing, and implementation.

Not all information is used for its intended purpose. The extent to which information is used depends on many factors: the willingness, ability, and ways in which decision makers make decisions; the nature of the information (information could be inaccurate, incomplete, or irrelevant for decisions that need to be made); how information is presented; the culture in the organization (which could motivate employees to embrace, be ambivalent towards, or discourage use of information); group dynamics (i.e., if a committee has to reach a consensus decision); and the nature of the decision that needs to be made (information that suggests the need for a complete turnaround in strategy or implementation is more likely to be rejected).

In this chapter, we show you how to improve the extent to which information from your M&E system is used to help your organization achieve its results.

How this Chapter is organized: Section 2 defines key concepts relating to data, information, the data management cycle, and how decisions are made. The long-term result of using information for decision making is presented in Section 3; and the benefits of using information to improve results are presented in Section 4. Section 5 describes strategies to improve the extent to which information is used to improve results. The HowTo Guides in this chapter describe (a) how to analyze quantitative data, (b) how to analyze qualitative data, and (c) how to improve the visual presentation of data (Sections 6, 7, and 8). The chapter closes with a summary of all the lessons (Section 9), and some practical learning activities to reinforce what you should have learned in the chapter (Section 10).

2. Background Information and Definitions

How do we know that information is used when decisions are made? When decision makers demand the information. One can increase the likelihood of them demanding information by putting in place incentives or motivations for them to base their decisions on information. The following definitions provide some additional context and background information.

Policy evaluation: Getting the right policy to address a national problem requires evidence-based decision making. There is substantial overlap between the methods and strategies used in policy studies and M&E. Policy evaluations may be prospective or retrospective. Prospective policy evaluations involve a comparative analysis of future scenarios given policy alternatives whereas retrospective policy evaluations involve a process of examining the consequences or a particular policy (Mathison, Encyclopedia of Evaluation 2005).

Strategic planning: Strategic planning involves activities that are concerned specifically with determining in advance, the human and physical resources required to achieve a goal. The process includes identifying alternatives, analyzing each one, and selecting the best ones (Mintzberg 1994). To know which goals to reach and which activities will best contribute to those goals, information is needed. Having information will help one to accurately identify the goals that are needed to address the key challenges or problems that need to be addressed.

Quantitative and qualitative data: Observations about persons, things, and events are central to answering questions about government programs and policies. Groups of observations are called data, which may be qualitative (words or text) or quantitative (numbers). Data are raw, un-summarized and un-analyzed facts (Wikipedia, 2007). Different types of quantitative data exist: nominal, ordinal, interval or ratio data (see Annex A for explanations and examples of each of these types of data). Qualitative data can also be in different forms: written texts (e.g., diaries); verbal accounts (e.g., voice recordings); and visual forms (e.g., photos and video).

- A quantitative way to report cruising altitude during a flight would be "we have reached our cruising altitude of 35,000 feet."

- A qualitative way to report cruising altitude would be to say "we are flying higher than any bird and even above some clouds".

Information and information products: Data are of little use to decision-makers if they contain far too much detail. For data to be useful during decision making, they need to be converted into information that can be analyzed, synthesized, interpreted, and presented in a useful way. Information is data that have been processed into a meaningful form (Wikipedia, 2007). Information is usually captured in some kind of information product such as a report, brochure, policy brief, or PowerPoint® presentation.

Data analysis: Data analysis involves manipulating (qualitative or quantitative) data by summarizing, performing calculations, comparing, and using other data analysis methods to better describe, understand, and see relationships between data over time. Data analysis, like data itself, may be qualitative or quantitative. Qualitative data analysis techniques are inductive and involve categorizing or interpreting text, the spoken word or visuals. They include matrix analysis, where data is put into a matrix, and content coding in which narrative text is analyzed by searching for recurring themes. Quantitative data analysis is deductive and involves statistical analysis to manipulate, summarize, and interpret data. It can involve comparing observations from different periods to see trends over time.

> **Analysis** = the art of finding 3 errors in a thousand rows
>
> **Insight** = the art of knowing which 3 statistics are relevant
>
> Adapted from: Kaushik, 2006

- Descriptive statistics give a *picture* of the data using measures of central tendency (average/mean, median and mode) and measures of variability about the average (range and standard deviation).

- Inferential statistics are the outcomes of statistical tests that help make deductions from the data, in order to test hypotheses and relate the findings of the sample to the population.

Analyzing data is not enough: analysts need to understand the needs of the decision maker and interrogate their analyses. They need to interpret the data to gain insights and to explain what the data mean or imply.

Knowledge: Knowledge is the information that a person already has and new information he/she assimilates. Knowledge is the capacity to use information, which requires learning and experience. Foskett (1982) said that "knowledge is what I know, information is what we know." In other words, knowledge is what happens when an individual has internalized information, has learned through it, and is able to apply it to a specific situation. Learning and adapting are very important in our fast changing environment and as Alvin Toffler has pointed out, "the illiterate of the twenty first century will not be those who cannot read and write, but those who cannot learn, unlearn, and re-learn."

Reporting and dissemination: Reporting involves documenting evidence in a written format and dissemination is sharing reports with others. During data analysis, data are transformed into useful information and then "dissemination activities ensure that the right information reaches the right users at the right time" (USAID, undated: 2).

Information use: Information is used when decision makers and stakeholders explicitly consider information provided to them in policymaking, program planning and management, or service provision. The final decision or actions may not be based on that information alone but its use is a part of the process of decision-making (MEASURE Evaluation and USAID, undated).

Using data to solve problems: How do all these concepts *work together* when there is a problem to be solved? Figure C12-1 shows how one sources, collates, collects, and analyzes data in order to create information. The information is then internalized (by the organization and individuals involved in reporting) and reported (to other individuals and organizations), often in the form of information products. The extent to which information products are disseminated and the extent to which information is internalized, impacts on the extent to which new knowledge is generated (by the individuals reporting or others) and, therefore, the extent to which these individuals use this new knowledge to make better decisions.

Figure C12-1: Using Data to Solve Problems

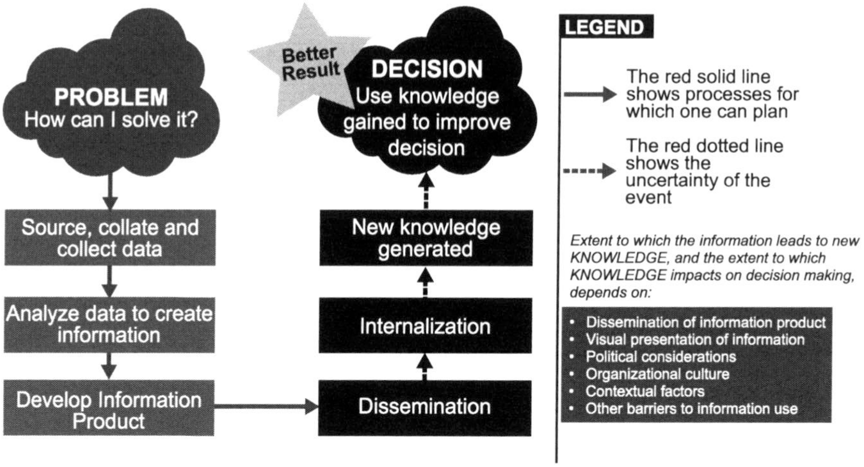

Source: Authors, with assistance from De Beyer

For reflection 1:

Are decisions in your organization based on rational choices among options and their expected consequences, or on rules or *gut feelings,* or preferences of the decision maker? Is decision making in your organization a consistent, clear process or one characterized by ambiguity and inconsistency? Is decision making in your organization significant primarily for its outcomes or for the individual and social meaning it creates and sustains? Are the outcomes of decision processes in your organization attributable mostly to the actions of individuals or to the combined influence of interacting individuals, organizations, and information? (Adapted from March, 1994)

How are decisions made in organizations? Decisions in organizations are not made mechanically. They involve problems (identified using information), solutions (where information describes the possible consequences), and stakeholders (Borun, 2000), all of which can be influenced by political and non-technical factors (non-information-driven decisions) (Amason, 1991).

How decision making **should** work and how it **actually** works, can differ dramatically. In theory, in an ideal decision making situation, one would first classify and define the problem and then specify possible answers (define alternatives, consequences, and preferences). Armed with this knowledge, one would then decide which of the alternatives and consequences are best. Finally, one would build implementation actions into the decision, and test the validity and effectiveness of the decision against the actual course of events (Drucker et al., 2005). In practice, though, decision making in organizations is often inconsistent and ambiguous and is influenced more by behavior and organizational culture (individual behaviors and possible reactions to the decision, the organizational culture, the opinion of the highest-paid person, international or national standards, or practices from other countries) than a pure rational process:

> "Students of decision making in the real world suggest that (in a real decision making process) not all alternatives are known, not all consequences are considered, and not all preferences are evoked at the same time. Instead of considering all alternatives, decision makers typically appear to consider only a few and to look at them sequentially, rather than simultaneously. Decision makers do not consider all consequences of their alternatives. They focus on some and ignore others. Instead of having a complete, consistent set of preferences, decision makers seem to have incomplete and inconsistent goals, not all of which are considered at the same time. Instead of calculating the "best possible action," they search for an option that is "just good enough" (March, 1994:9).

> "Decision makers ...often do not recognize a 'problem' until they have a solution" (March and Romelaer, 1976).

How can decision making improve in organizations? Decision makers face serious limitations that impede their ability to make good decisions: limitations of attention, memory, comprehension, and communication (March, 1991). Bazerman (2008) suggested that decision making can be improved by using decision analysis tools, acquiring expertise, de-biasing decision makers' judgment, taking an outsider's view and understanding the biases in others. **All of these improvement strategies require information.** Depending on the stage of implementation, different stakeholders face different problems and therefore need to make different decisions using different types of information (Table C12-1).

It seems simple and straightforward: collect data, analyze and use information to improve the decisions made in your organization about how best to achieve the results your organization is striving for. In reality, it is complex. Using information has become *fashionable* (many organizations and activities are said to be evidence-based), but sometimes actual use of information is more symbolic than scientific (Feldman et al. 1981).

Most organizations gather much more information than they use, yet continue to ask for more. This seems to be because "information has become a signal and a symbol of competence in decision making. Gathering and presenting information symbolizes (and demonstrates) the ability and legitimacy of decision makers. A good decision maker is one who makes decisions properly, exhibits expertise, and uses generally accepted information. The competition for reputations among decision makers stimulates an overproduction of information" (March and Romelaer 1976). Decision-related information is, however, rarely *innocent.* Most information can easily be misrepresented or unconsciously biased (March 1991) and there is, therefore, not only a political component to decision making but also a political component to information itself.

Table C12-1: Types Of Information Required Depends on the Stage of Implementation

Stage of a new policy or program	Typical type of problem	Decisions being made	Stakeholders involved in decisions	Type of information they need
1. **Problem identification and recognition**	Understand the baseline situation Understand the likely impacts of different policy options	Priority-setting, Advocacy, Target-setting, and Policy Determination	Public officials, civil society, opinion leaders	Situation analysis, routine/surveillance data, survey, policy evaluation, readiness assessment
2. **Selection of the solution**	Assess likely Impact of different options Assess alternative solutions	Selecting intervention Operational planning Program budgets	Public policy officials, service providers, beneficiaries	Literature review, secondary analysis of existing data, (including cost-effectiveness), special studies, operational and formative research, and research synthesis

Stage of a new policy or program	Typical type of problem	Decisions being made	Stakeholders involved in decisions	Type of information they need
3. Implementation and routine monitoring	Progress not as planned Quality not as planned Inadequate or wasted resources How can implementation be improved	Maintain operational plan and continue funding budget Mid-course adjustments	Service providers and program managers, civil society	Process monitoring and evaluation, quality assessments, outputs monitoring
4. Closure	Uncertainty of the program's impact What lessons have we learned Should the program be repeated	Scale up program Discontinue and test alternative intervention	Public officials, civil society, opinion leaders	Outcome evaluation studies, surveys, routine sources and surveillance

Source: Adapted from Table 1 on p11 of the DDIU conceptual framework, MEASURE Evaluation, undated

It is challenging to collect the right kind and right amount of data, present it in an objective way, and make entirely objective decisions.

Reasons why information is not always used when making decisions to improve your organization's results: One reason why data may not be used is the perception that the data are collected for someone else's purposes (Levesque et al., 1996). Other reasons are:

- **Timing:** Decisions often have to be made quickly and managers rely on their instincts or years of experience, rather than waiting to review pertinent information that could inform the decision.

- **Conflicting government policies:** For example, policies to safeguard climate change may constrain the government's economic growth policies and conflict with powerful interests.

- **Political ideology and public opinion:** A decision may follow the political ideology of the majority party or public opinion in the country, for example, to increase (or decrease) welfare payments, irrespective of the likely economic and social impact, or to uphold or abolish the death penalty irrespective of cost and effect on crime.

- **Dispute over the data, measures of impact, data collection methods, or data analysis tools.** Disputed data or information are less likely to be used for decision making.

- **Unclear measurement or analysis tools, or measurement tools that have not yet been agreed on:** Such uncertainty may reduce the credibility of information presented.

- **Challenges with data storage and analysis:** Thoughtful analysis of data can entail a great deal of labor if data are stored or compiled in ways that frustrate flexible analysis (Wayman 2005:298).

If data are not used, it sends a powerful message to those who collected them that data are not important. This, in turn, will influence stakeholders' motivation to continue reporting data.

How do we know when information has been used to make decisions to improve your organization's results? Most decision makers, when asked, will affirm that they use information. How do we verify that information has been used? Although it is difficult to quantify or measure information use objectively, evidence of information use can be tracked by qualitative means:

- Mid-term corrections of a program design or its implementation are made based upon new data reported.

- Funds are redirected to high performing programs away from poorly performing ones.

- Poorly performing programs are identified and improved, well-performing programs are recognized.

- Accurate reference to the latest available information in reports.

- Dissemination of reports and visual evidence of these in program implementers' offices.

- Implementers ask for further information on M&E reports.

- The strategic plan identifies solutions to noted problems in the country or organization.

- Implementers refer to reports and information when discussing matters relating to the behaviors or situations they seek to change.

3. Results to Be Achieved When Implementing This Component

Long-term result: Analyze data generated by the M&E system and disseminate information to key decision makers to support use of the data for policy, planning and programming

Short- and medium-term results:

- Analysis of information needs and information users

- Standard formats for reporting and tabulations

- Timetable for reporting

- Information products tailored to different audiences

- Evidence of information use (e.g., program improvement decisions based on information, programs have improved, etc.)

For reflection 2:

Reflect on your organization and the ways decisions are made. Are data collected and then converted to information that is useful and used? How are data managed in your organization? Is this done routinely or sporadically? How many of the short- and medium-term results listed above are visible in your organization?

---

4. Benefits Information to Improve Results

4.1. Using information will help your organization or sector solve the problems it is trying to address

Problems can be identified and understood better if data and information are available about the problem. This enables one to determine the root causes of problems or challenges that the organization or country faces and to estimate the effect of implementing various solutions. The Ministry of Transport, for example, can use a combination of data sources to identify high-crash locations and evaluate possible solutions (SEMCOG, 2008). Knowing the locations where large volumes of crashes occur provides planners with a framework for making objective and sound decisions and will help build support for the solutions they propose. The same data can be used to evaluate the success of solutions and to propose further improvements.

Dr. John Snow made use of data in a classic way that paved the way for modern epidemiology. In 1865, a terrible cholera epidemic broke out in a small area of London. Helped by a local clergyman, (Reverend Henry Whitehead), Snow discovered that everyone who had died drank the water from a particular and very popular water pump. This provided strong evidence for his hypothesis that cholera was caused by contaminated water and he was able to deduce from the pattern of deaths that the particular water pump must be the source (see Figure C12-2).

(The pump is circled. Dark bars indicate where the people who died from cholera in the first week of the epidemic had lived.)

At the time, Snow was almost alone in suspecting that cholera was a water-borne disease, while everyone else believed that cholera was spread by bad air. Snow appealed to local decision makers and the handle was removed so the pump could not be used. Although skeptical of Snow's interpretation of the data he had collected, they were desperate to end the epidemic, which had killed about 500 people in a week.

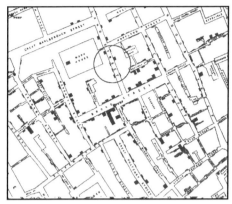

Figure C12-2: Map by Dr. John Snow

However, as in many cases, valid and verifiable data were not enough. People refused to accept that the water pump was the source of the cholera outbreak. Water from that pump looked better than water from other (uncontaminated) pumps. After the epidemic subsided, the water pump handle was replaced. Despite the evidence, Snow's theory about how cholera was spread was unpalatable and it was some years before people were persuaded by the data compiled and mapped by Snow and other investigators.

Champions of data, the information deduced from the data, and the implications for action are key to ensuring that data are used to guide action. Usually there are one or more people who believe that available information from an M&E system can assist with a particular problem. Seeking out these decision makers and showing them how valid data can help solve a problem is an important step towards getting data used.

4.2. Using information creates a joint and shared understanding of problems, and builds unity of action

Information, if presented clearly and objectively, provides a common basis for creating a joint and shared vision. Looking at an objective set of information allows common conclusions to be drawn (or at least differences in opinions understood and discussed). Using information helps stakeholders to sit on the same side of the table, each envisioning how he/she could contribute towards addressing the problem.

Commenting on what happened when her school started to compile data and extract information to inform contentious decisions, the school head said: "The biggest change is that our school went from a group of individual teachers to a community." (Ailen Dickey, Principal and Data Coach, Wildflower Elementary School, Colorado Springs, Colorado)

4.3. Using information can help ensure that policies and solutions are relevant

By describing the current situation as well as the effects of past policies, information helps to determine cause and effect. *Implementing policy A should address problem B.* Information is, therefore, essential to help formulate good policies, instead of choosing policies simply because other countries have chosen them or because international guidelines stipulate that they should be in place. In the John Snow example above, his investigations and the data that he compiled, interpreted, and presented, established the basis for modern public health approaches. If he had not collected data to test his hypothesis about how cholera spread, or presented his data in a less compelling way, or drawn the wrong conclusions, London's viability and England's history might have been quite different.

4.4. Using information will help your organization or sector improve its programs and make better use of available funds (and thus help your organization manage to results)

Once a problem is known, your organization or sector can define how it will address the problem and what results the organization wants to achieve. Information helps track progress toward results and, therefore, helps when making decisions about which policies and implementation strategies work best, as Figure C12-3 illustrates. It can also help allocate funding to more cost-effective and efficient solutions. With good information, a stock control system, for example, responds to actual supply levels and stock shortages and is not based on perceived demand.

An education researcher notes that "Many studies …have shown that the thoughtful use of student data positively correlates with a range of measures of student achievement. Research on school improvement and school effectiveness has suggested that data use is central to the school improvement process" (Wayman 2005: 297).

Figure C12-3: The Policy, Program, and Organizational Improvement Process

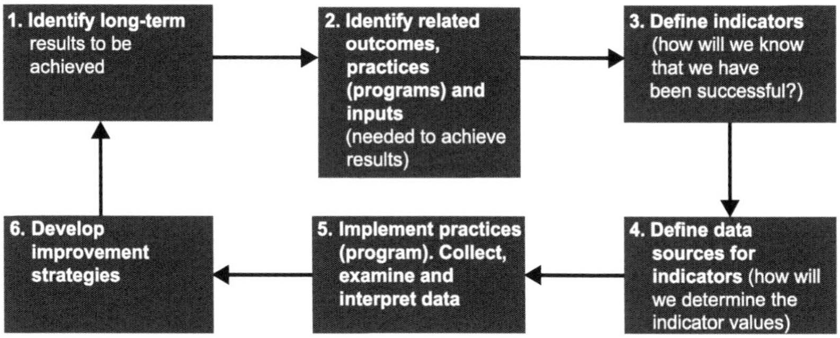

Adapted from: Levesque et al, 1996

4.5. Using information can help to build public support for the programs and services provided by your organization or a sector

Being able to access data to check on progress helps build credibility and allows stakeholders to engage jointly with a new program or policy. The U.S. Government, for example, recently signed into law a U.S. Recovery Bill to provide an economic stimulus costing U.S. $787 billion. To build public support for the measures contained in the Bill and to instill a sense of accountability, spending under the stimulus package will be publicly available on a website (www.recovery.gov). The World Bank has a public information policy that determines which documents can be made available on its website and the Global Fund to Fight AIDS, Tuberculosis, and Malaria publishes detailed information on its grants on its website.

For reflection 3:

Have you been part of any improvements in your organization? Was information used to decide on the improvements? How was information used and what were the direct benefits of using information? Are there any other ways that your organization could use data in the future?

5. Strategies to Promote the Use of Information to Improve Results

To improve the extent to which your organization embraces and uses data, focus on the problems that the organization or sector faces and how they can be addressed. It is also necessary to create supportive leadership and an information-embracing organizational culture. People need to understand the *business* of the organization and understand the information disseminated. In addition, standard data management processes need to be implemented as part of a performance management system and quality assured during all steps of M&E and data management. Good information products report and present information in a way that is relevant to the target end-users and audiences. Standardized information product formats enable users to know what to expect and to become familiar with the data.

5.1. Focus on the problems facing the organization or sector and how they can be addressed

By focusing on the problems that the organization or sector faces, the demand for information becomes stronger and more visible, as people begin to realize that the information helps them to; (a) understand the problem; (b) define possible solutions; (c) know which solutions worked best; and, hence, (d) make good decisions. It also helps programs focus on program improvement and opportunities for collaboration.

Why program improvement? Focusing on program improvement helps to identify strengths and weaknesses and generates discussion about causes and appropriate improvement strategies. Ultimately, a performance management system produces evidence about whether strategies are working or not.

Why opportunities for collaboration? Organizations are often made up of different groups, each with members who know different things and hold different opinions about what they know. When members of groups share the information they have, the group has access to a larger pool of information than any one member has, potentially enabling them to make better decisions (Dennis, 1996). Communication with staff and stakeholders about the data are also important opportunities to collaborate and increase understanding and interpretation of the evidence to improve the results.

For example, before developing a new education sector policy, ministries of education would want to understand the current education situation in the country, including the gross and net enrollment rates at different ages. These data, combined with drop out rates, pass rates, and qualitative feedback from parent-teacher associations about challenges in the education system, provide a situation analysis of the education system, which informs new education policies.

5.2. Create supportive leadership and an information-embracing organizational culture

Leadership is necessary for a supportive data climate. Armstrong and Anthes (2001) and Massell (2001) found that strong leadership and a supportive culture were characteristics of the schools in their studies that used data the most (Wayman, 2005:303), and Dean and Sharfman (1996) found that political behavior in organizations and *the odds at stake*, greatly influenced the nature of decisions taken.

Leadership can also support a positive organizational culture that embraces information use. Organizational culture has proven to be a stronger driving force behind decisions than performance management processes. An organization's culture may need to change in order to improve the extent to which information is used. It is essential to take into account the culture when considering how to present information and when making decisions (Naor et al, 2008). Organizational attitudes to information use need to be strategic, flexible, and customer-oriented. Organizations need to start to view information differently, as Table C12-2 suggests.

Table C12-2: How Organizational Culture Needs to Change to Embrace
Information Use

Less emphasis on...	More emphasis on...
External accountability	Internal and collective responsibility
Premature data-driven decision making	Ongoing data-driven dialogue and decision making
Data use as the specialty of a few	Widespread data use and literacy
Data as carrot and stick	Data as feedback for continuous improvement
Data to sort	Data to serve

Adapted from: http://usingdata.terc.edu/about/UDOnlineArtifacts/DCGuide.pdf on December 23, 2008

Acknowledging that a supportive organizational culture is needed for information use to be valued, an information-embracing organization has the following characteristics:

- It recognizes that decision making is not a robotic process where decisions are made purely on the basis of information. Influencing decisions, therefore, requires more than preparing information products. Decision making is not simply evidence-based but is evidence-informed. (The term *evidence-based decisions* implies that decisions are made only, purely, and immediately after data have been presented whereas the term *evidence-informed decisions*, on the other hand, recognizes that there are other factors and considerations that influence decisions.) A good decision, therefore, requires not only data but also a focus on managing the other processes and factors that influence decision making. A good decision making process:

- Accepts that it is essential that leaders set an example in using and demanding information as part of the decision making process;

- Acknowledges that there needs to be rewards in place in an organization for the use of information, in order to motivate all employees; and

- Recognizes and celebrates achievement of verifiable results so that others are encouraged to do the same.

5.3. Professional development to better understand the business of the organization and information disseminated

For organizations to have an information-embracing culture, professional development is needed (Wayman, 2005). Operational staff need to be numerically and statistically literate, and statistical/M&E staff need to understand how the organization and its programs operate. Operational staff need to learn about data interpretation, analysis tools and presentation so that they can better interpret the information that they receive, whereas M&E/data staff need to learn about the organization's operations so that they can provide relevant data to address the questions and issues that decision makers face.

"Respondents commented that they spent a great deal of time gathering data but do not have the time or talent to do anything with this information. Even if libraries gather the right measures for their purposes, developing the requisite skills to analyze, interpret, present and use the data are separate challenges" (Covey, 2002:3).

5.4. Implement standard data management processes as part of a performance management system

What is a performance management system? Its ultimate goal is program improvement and it centers around well-defined data management processes for defining what needs to be done (based on the problem at hand), measuring success using relevant indicators, analyzing the data collected, improving programs and controlling program implementation (including supervision). Indicators are statistics that *indicate* or signal something about the performance of, for example, a district, school, or a program. Indicators describe crucial outcomes, processes, and inputs, and typically appear as averages, percentages, or rates. In a good performance management system, relationships among the outcome, process, and input statistics have a clear causal logic, and stakeholders can monitor these statistics on an ongoing basis (Wayman, 2005).

Another reason for having a clear performance management system in place is that data will only be used if people can get them easily. Putting in place a system that will **ensure that information is accessible when it is needed** will increase the extent to which it is used. O'Reilly (1982) found that the frequency of use of available information was a function of its accessibility.

A performance management system should also identify who is responsible for action within an organization. Government is almost always vitally important or the ultimate decision maker. Government stakeholders are more likely to use data when they have been involved in its collection and analysis, and, therefore, know the context within which the data were obtained and analyzed, and accept responsibility and *ownership* of the data (UNAIDS, 2003; McCoy, Ngari and Krumpe, 2005).

5.5. Quality assurance during all steps of M&E design and data management

Producing good quality data improves the credibility of the information and good quality information is more likely to be used (Dennis, 1996). Quality assurance is needed at all steps of M&E system design and data management (i.e., source, collection, collation, analysis, reporting, and use), from when indicators are developed to when information is presented and discussed. Supervision and data auditing are specifically included as a component (Component 9) of an M&E system to ensure that there is deliberate effort to improve data quality. It is also important to highlight in the information products how supervision and data auditing were done, as this is relevant to the interpretation of data.

Quality assurance also involves interpreting the information to better understand whether changes are statistically significant and relevant to the desired results, and what the information tells us about the results we want to achieve.

Part of the interpretation process includes validating information using other information sources by means of synthesis or "triangulation" of data. Results that can be validated with complementary information give a stronger basis for action.

"Data have no meaning. Meaning is imposed through interpretation. Frames of reference—the way we see the world—influence the meaning we derive from data. Effective data users become aware of and critically examine their frames of reference and assumptions. Conversely, data themselves can also be catalysts for questioning assumptions and changing practices based on new ways of thinking" (Love et al 2007/08).

5.6. Defining and targeting different end-users

End-users have different information needs and it is important to understand them. An information product may be translated into different languages for some stakeholders and summarized or simplified for others. Designing an information product for a specific target audience will ensure its relevance and facilitate its accessibility and use.

5.7. Reporting and presenting information in a way that is relevant to target audience

"Decision makers look for information, but they see what they want to see" (March, 1994). It is important to report and present data in a format that makes it easy for decision makers to make the best possible decisions (decisions that are objective and likely to have the greatest positive effect).

Dennis (1996) conducted an experiment where different group members received different (but not conflicting) data about a task to be completed which they needed to combine to identify an optimal decision. Verbally interacting groups exchanged only a small portion of the available information and made poor decisions as a result. Groups that used written communication tools to work together shared more information indicating that written information is essential.

A: Reporting data from an M&E system

In reporting information, data can be communicated in different ways and using different language styles. The example below (from UNAIDS, 2000) shows how important it is to choose a language style appropriate for the report target audience.

Language Style 1. HIV incidence in 15—19 year old age cohort is high and prevalence among 19-year-old women is 33%.

Language Style 2. New HIV infections are common among those in their late teens; a third of 19-year old women are HIV positive.

Language Style 3. Hundreds of teenagers get infected every week. If there are 60 girls in your daughter's class, then around 20 of them will have HIV by the time they graduate.

B: Presenting information (displaying information)

The way in which data are presented directly affects how they are understood and interpreted and consequently the decisions that are made as a result of the data. Edward Tufte (2000: p. 3 and p. 31) summarizes it well:

"An essential analytical task in making decisions based on evidence is to understand how things work – mechanisms, trade-offs, process and dynamics, cause and effect. That is, intervention-thinking and policy-thinking demand causality thinking. Making decisions based on evidence requires the appropriate display of that evidence.

Good displays of data (information) help to reveal knowledge relevant to understanding mechanisms, process and dynamics, cause and effect. That is, displays of statistical data (information) should directly serve the analytical task at hand. For this to happen, we need to have an endless commitment to finding, telling and showing the truth."

Visual representations of data include tables, graphs, and other graphical displays (Figure C12-4). Irrespective of the type, all visual representation should follow a logical design that corresponds with scientific reasoning.

Figure C12-4: Types of Visual Representations of Information

A: Table

Ministry	Funding allocated for 2009	Funding spent in 2009 (3 quarters)	Balance remaining	Priorities
Ministry of Education	400 000	370 000	30 000	School buses
Ministry of Health	200 000	50 000	150 000	New hospital
Ministry of Transport	300 000	100 000	200 000	Rehabilitation of roads

B: Graph

Budgeted funding and actual expenditure in 2009 for Ministries of Education Health and Transport

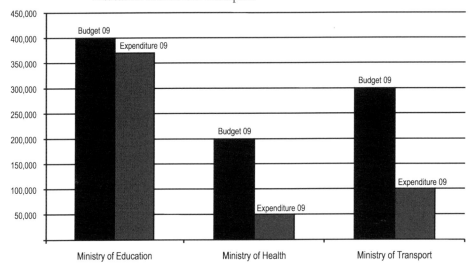

C: Other graphical display

The size of the picture is indicative of the amount of funding available in each Ministry's budget.

Clear and precise display of information aids clear and precise thinking. Howto Guide 12-3.1 provides details and examples that illustrate some principles for clear and precise information display (Tufte, 1997, 2001):

- Documenting the sources and characteristics of the data
- Insistently enforcing appropriate data comparisons
- Demonstrating mechanisms of cause and effect
- Recognizing the inherently multivariate nature of analytical problems
- Inspecting and evaluating alternative explanations
- Avoid distorting what the data have to say
- Represent many numbers in a small space
- Make large data sets coherent

Ministerial priorities in relation to funding available

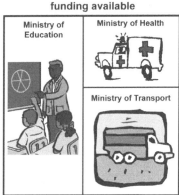

- Encourage the eye to compare different pieces of data
- Reveal the data at several levels of detail

5.8. Standardized information product formats

Displaying data in a standardized way has the benefits of showing trends over time and increasing users' familiarity with the presentation format. The better the users understand how the information is presented, the more they can focus on interpreting the information.

Before preparing information products, it is important to define what the final products will look like and to have clear dissemination channels. Spend time doing analysis before coming to conclusions and doing the writing. (UNAIDS, 2003; McCoy, Ngari and Krumpe, 2005). The same information may need to be presented in different ways to different stakeholders, at different points in time.

In the M&E plan, the organization should commit to providing stakeholders with regular and structured feedback and deliver relevant, summarized, and analyzed information.

The M&E plan should, ideally, define information product templates that clearly show the contents and use of each information product. There should be a data tabulation plan for each type of standardized information product including those that report on surveys and surveillance, as well as those that report routine data. The M&E plan should also define how information products will be disseminated. An information product dissemination matrix is a useful table to include in the M&E plan.

Table C12-3: Example of an Information Product Dissemination Matrix

		INFORMATION PRODUCTS	
		Information product 1	Information product 2
STAKEHOLDERS	Stakeholder 1	Workshop	E-mail
	Stakeholder 2	E-mail	Post
	Stakeholder 3	Post	Workshop
	Stakeholder 4	Workshop	Parliament briefing
	Stakeholder 5	Workshop	Workshop
	Stakeholder 6	Post	E-mail
	Stakeholder 7	E-mail	Cabinet briefing

Source: Authors

When developing a dissemination matrix, do not only consider stakeholders directly involved in the program but also those who may be interested in the program results. One way to reach the general public is to disseminate well-digested (i.e., summarized and simple) information on good ideas or practices to the mass media (e.g., newspapers, TV, radio) (UNAIDS, 2003; McCoy, Ngari and Krumpe, 2005).

Standard information products should be disseminated as part of quarterly, bi-annual, or annual review, so that data are used for decision making during reviews and the results feed into the preparation of annual work plans (UNAIDS, 2003; McCoy, Ngari and Krumpe, 2005).

In summary, Information-Embracing Organizations:

- Focus on the outcomes or results that they want to achieve
- Reward analysis, interrogation, and insights
- Tell the truth when displaying data
- Measure success in achieving results against performance targets
- Use a well defined and standardized process that people know about, anticipate, and welcome

Adapted from Kaushik (2006)

For reflection 4:

"Data used to be secret. Now everyone uses data." Is this statement true of your organization? If yes, which information use strategies have you implemented to ensure that information is used as part of the decision making processes in your organization? If no, are there any strategies that you could implement that would help improve the extent to which information is used in your organization?

6. HowTo Guide 12-1: How to Analyze Quantitative Data

"Statistics, like veal pies, are good if you know the person that made them, and are sure of the ingredients."
Lawrence Lowell, 1909.

In analyzing quantitative data, there are two main types of statistical analysis, descriptive and inferential.

- **Descriptive Statistics:** The most common type of statistical analysis is descriptive, in which findings and data are summarized. Graphs, tables or single number statistical measures can be used. There are two basic questions that descriptive statistics answer:

    1. **To what extent are the data points similar?** This is described using measures of central tendency: the mean (average), median and mode.

    2. **To what extent do the data points vary?** This is described using measures of variability: range, standard deviation, variation, coefficient of variation, quantiles, and inter-quartile range.

See this website for a primer on all descriptive statistics: http://allpsych.com/stats/index.html.

- **Inferential Statistics:** Inferential statistics use statistical tests and formulae to draw broader conclusions from the data, test hypotheses, and relate the findings from the sample to the population from which the sample is drawn. These powerful techniques may be able demonstrate if a change has occurred as a result of a program, by comparing groups and discovering relationships.

In this HowTo Guide, we describe how to analyze data using descriptive statistics and summarize the key steps in analyzing data using inferential statistics.

A: Process of Analyzing Data Using Descriptive Statistics

Step 1: Make copies of your data and store the master data away. Use the copy for making edits, cutting and pasting.

Step 2: Tabulate the information, i.e., count/add up ratings, rankings, yes's, no's for each question.

Step 3: Determine how the data are distributed. To do this, draw a histogram to show the distribution of the data.

Step 4: Decide which measure of central tendency to use by inspecting the distribution of the data. The most appropriate measure depends on (a) whether data is "**symmetric**" or "**skewed**;" and (b) whether data clusters around one ("**unimodal**") or more values ("**multimodal**").

Figure C12-5 summarizes how data can be distributed.

- If data are symmetric, the mean, median, and mode will be approximately the same.

- If data are multimodal, report the mean, median and/or mode for each subgroup.

- If data are skewed, report the median.

Figure C12-5: Different ways in Which Data Are distributed

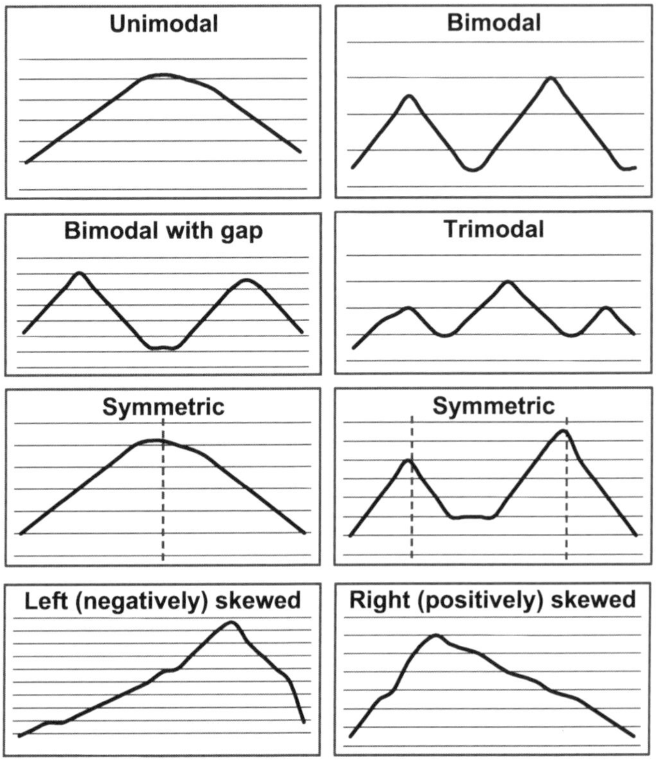

Source: Wild and Seber (2000. pg. 59). Modified by authors

Step 5:   Calculate the appropriate measures of central tendency (mean, mode or median, as applicable)

Step 6:   Calculate the measures of variability (range and standard deviation)

Step 7:   Present data in tables and graphs, using the tips provided in HowTo Guide 12.3.

B: Example of Process for Analyzing Data Using Inferential Statistics

Using inferential statistics, you can estimate the population mean using the sample mean test the hypothesis that the sample is representative of the entire population by running statistical tests, and draw conclusions and make decisions concerning the population based on sample results.

For more information about how to perform the calculations related to inferential statistics, please visit this website that provides a full online summary to inferential statistics: http://allpsych.com/stats/index.html.

7. HowTo Guide 12-2: How to Analyze Qualitative Data

Qualitative information includes respondents' verbal answers in interviews, focus groups, or written commentary on questionnaires. Relatively small amounts of data can be analyzed manually, although if the data are in electronic format, even basic software packages can save time. There are also many specialized and sophisticated computer programs for analyzing qualitative data which follow these same basic principles.

Step 1: Read through all the qualitative data (e.g., transcripts of interviews or notes from focus group discussions).

Step 2: Identify categories or themes in the qualitative data, e.g., concerns, suggestions, strengths, weaknesses, similar experiences, program inputs, recommendations, outputs, outcome indicators, etc.

Step 3: Give a name to each category or theme, e.g., concerns about climate change, suggestions to improve the economic situation, reasons why current HIV programs fail, etc.

Step 4: Attempt to identify patterns, or associations and causal relationships in the themes, e.g., all people who attended programs in the evening had similar concerns, most people came from the same geographic area, most people were in the same salary range, respondents experienced x, y, and z processes or events during the program, etc.

Step 5: Keep all qualitative data for several years after completion in case it is needed for future reference.

This qualitative analysis process can also be done more formally using **qualitative content coding**, which is "a research method for the subjective interpretation of the content of text data through the systematic classification process of coding and identifying themes or patterns" (Hsieh and Shannon, 2005:1278). In summary, it involves:

Step 1: Arrange the data for qualitative content analysis (it is usually most convenient to have everything in electronic format).

Step 2: Decide on the unit of analysis (e.g., households, communities, or individuals).

Step 3: Read through the data: identify patterns in the data (similar responses, raising similar issues, or describing similar situations) and use these patterns to develop categories (e.g., if household is chosen as the unit of analysis, develop categories of household responses. For a focus group discussion about the impact of the economic crisis, the categories (based on what respondents have said) may be; no impact to HIV; impact in the form of more domestic duties; impact in the form of more domestic responsibilities, or impact in the form of less money available for entertainment and impact in the form of watching more home movies.

Step 4: Develop a coding scheme. Give each category a separate code, e.g., a different shape (e.g., triangle or square), or different colors as illustrated in the example below.

Category	Coding	
No impact	Red circle	●
Impact in the form of more domestic duties	Blue triangle	▲
Impact in the form of more domestic responsibilities	Yellow circle	●
Impact in the form of less money available for entertainment	Green triangle	▲
Impact in the form of watching more home movies	Purple circle	●

Step 5: Test the coding scheme on sample text by reading through the text, underlying when text associated with a specific category is mentioned and visually displaying a code in the text when a specific category is mentioned.

Step 6: Code all text.

Step 7: Assess coding consistency by checking whether the coding matches all the concepts referred to in the data and whether the codes are clearly understood (i.e., whether two persons would code the same text in the same way).

Step 8: Draw conclusions from the coded data. Based on our example, such conclusions may include the types of impacts caused by the economic crisis and the types of impacts most frequently felt by households (keeping in mind that the unit of analysis is *households* – see Step 2).

Step 9: Report the conclusions taking into account the categories and the main research question.

For a more detailed account of how qualitative content analysis works go to: http://ils.unc.edu/~yanz/Content_analysis.pdf) For an example of qualitative content analysis see Annex B.

8. HowTo Guide 12-3: How to Improve the Visual Presentation of Data

Below is some practical advice and illustrations to keep in mind when designing tables, graphs, and other graphical displays (ideas from Tufte, 2001, and authors' own experience).

A: Designing tables

Tables are good for presenting exact numerical values and preferable to graphics for small data sets. Tables also work well when you want to display localized comparisons or when you want to compare data sets (see Figure C12-6). Tables should convey information to the reader. If the table does not tell you anything new when you develop it, then it most likely will convey little information to the reader.

- Present statistics according to groups under investigation where appropriate. Keep tables clear and concise.

- Note statistical testing where appropriate.

- Consider whether rounding off data will make it easier to interpret.

	Number of beds	Private wards	Intensive care unit
Hospital 1	100		✓
Hospital 2	340	✓	✓
Hospital 3	230		✓
Hospital 4	270	✓	✓
Hospital 5	280	✓	
Hospital 6	120		

Figure C12-6: Table That Compares the Characteristics of Different Hospitals

B: Designing graphs and graphical displays

" …as long as we are unable to put our arguments into figures, the voice of our science, although occasionally it may help to dispel gross errors, will never be heard by practical men." (J.A. Shumpeter 1933, The common sense of econometrics. Econometrica 1:5-12)

- Graphics should stimulate thinking and highlight patterns in the data that may not be immediately obvious by displaying the data in a table format or describing it narratively. Use a graphic if it shows the patterns that you think are important in the data more clearly than the table.

- Ensure the graphic has a descriptive heading

- Label the components of your graphic such as the axes, add a legend, and make sure that data can be easily read from the graphic.

- Indicate data source(s).

- Use a graphic that clearly shows what the data indicate by using appropriate labels and color to sort the data, add labels, use color.

- Maximize the *data-to-ink* ratio. Do not waste ink by adding unnecessary dimensions or shapes or too much text. The simple, 2 dimensional graph at the top of Figure C12-7 is much clearer than the three-dimensional graph (with the same data) at the bottom.

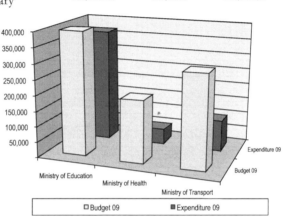

- Minimize chart or graphic *junk* or clutter that may

Figure C12-7:   Illustration of Data-to-Ink Ratio in a Graph

look nice but conveys no information. In the child growth chart in Figure C12-8, the pictures of children playing add color and visual appeal but they are distracting and unhelpful, partly because they are so much bigger than the actual data.

- Never cut the y-axis of a graph (see Figure C12-9). The data in the two figures below are exactly the same, with one difference: the first graph has a y-axis that starts at zero whereas the second graph starts at 15000. Cutting off the y-axis makes

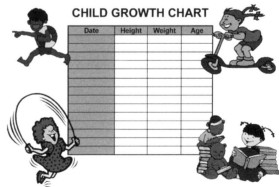

Figure C12-8:   Illustration of Distracting Effect of Chart Junk or Clutter

Making Monitoring and Evaluation Systems Work

the increases in funding for the Ministry of Education seem much bigger (second graph).

Funding Allocations for Ministry of Education from 2000 to 2007

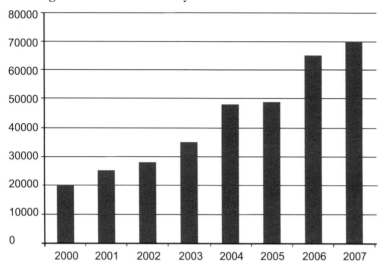

Figure C12-9: Illustration of the Effect of Cutting the y-Axis of a Graph

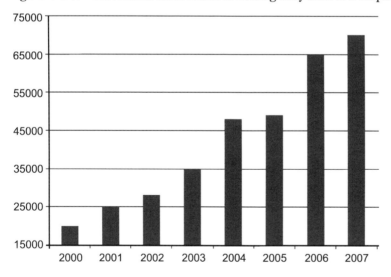

Figure C12-9: (continued)

Ensure that the proportions in your display are not misleading or confusing (Figure C12-10).

Figure C12-10: Illustration of Misleading Proportions in Graphical Displays

Changes in the price of a barrel of crude oil over time

Displayed as a three-dimensional series of barrels, with the size of the barrel relative to the price per barrel of crude oil.

Adapted from: Tufte, 2001

The same data display in a bar chart

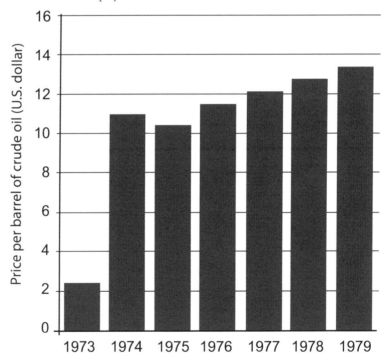

Note how the graphic distorts the increases in the price of a barrel of oil. It makes the latest increases seem much bigger, which is not actually the case.

- Follow the *Golden Rectangle* principle for most graphs: graphs look better if the width is longer than the height. The graphs in Figure C12-11 illustrate the *Golden Rectangle* principle. The graphs on the left shows the ideal shape (a rectangle that is wider than it is high) and the graph on the right shows that it is better to have the "cause" on the x-axis (horizontal axis) and the effect (impact, or outcome, or result) on the y-axis (vertical axis).

Figure C12-11: The "Golden Rectangle" Principle of Graph Design

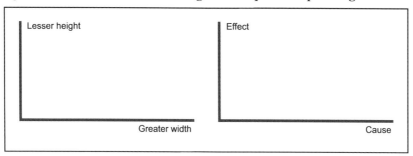

Source: Tufte, 2001

- Do not deliberately mislead people with data that distort the truth. The impression created by the graph in Figure C12-12 is that expenditure has dramatically decreased in the past 3 years in all three ministries. Upon closer inspection, it is clear that the data for 2009 are only for half of the year (see red circle) and that it is a distortion of the trend to compare this with the data for the other three full years.

Figure C12-12: Do Not Deliberately Distort the Data

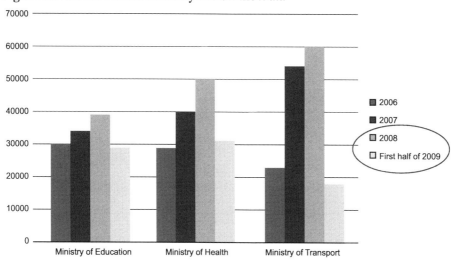

Use the right type of graph to portray your message (See Figure C12-13).

Figure C12-13: When to Use Various Kinds of Graphics

Type of graph	Good example
Pie charts: Show percentages or proportional share • Useful for displaying categorical data/nominal data. • Useful for epidemiological studies and behavioral studies. • Readily shows the breakdown into groups so that one can easily see the distribution of the data by group.	Children in schools Primary 6 489 381 Secondary 3 691 132 Intermediate 1 808 380 This data in the table can be better displayed in a pie chart which shows the proportion of children at each level of the education system. 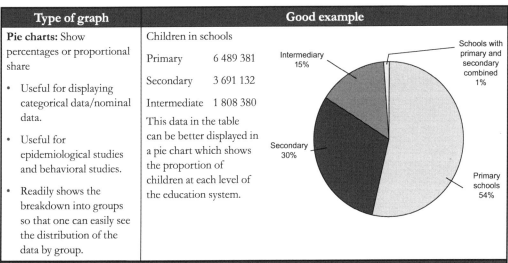

Bad example
Two pie charts are not good for displaying trends over time. It is difficult to compare the sizes of the pie slices (which are also relative and not absolute as they are show percentages and not numbers). The bar graph shows the trend much more clearly.

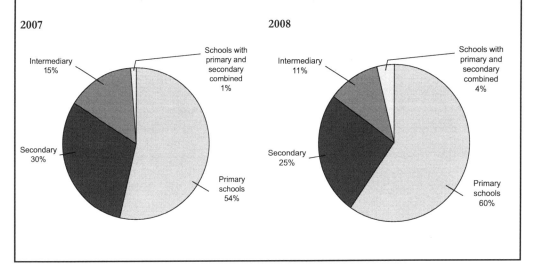

Figure C12-13: (Continued)

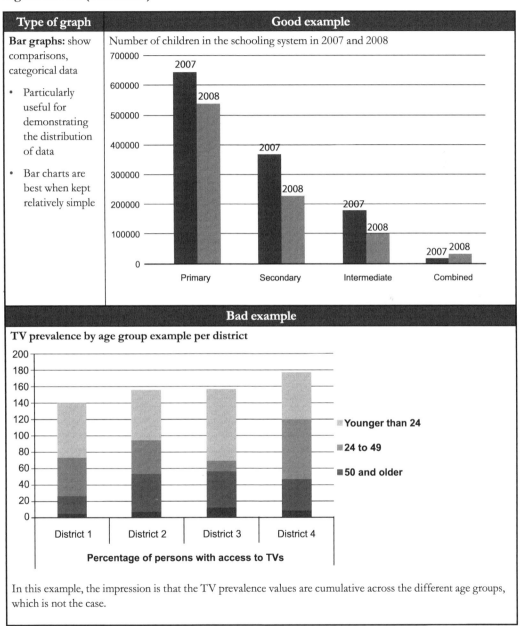

Type of graph	Good example
Bar graphs: show comparisons, categorical data • Particularly useful for demonstrating the distribution of data • Bar charts are best when kept relatively simple	Number of children in the schooling system in 2007 and 2008

Bad example

TV prevalence by age group example per district

Percentage of persons with access to TVs

In this example, the impression is that the TV prevalence values are cumulative across the different age groups, which is not the case.

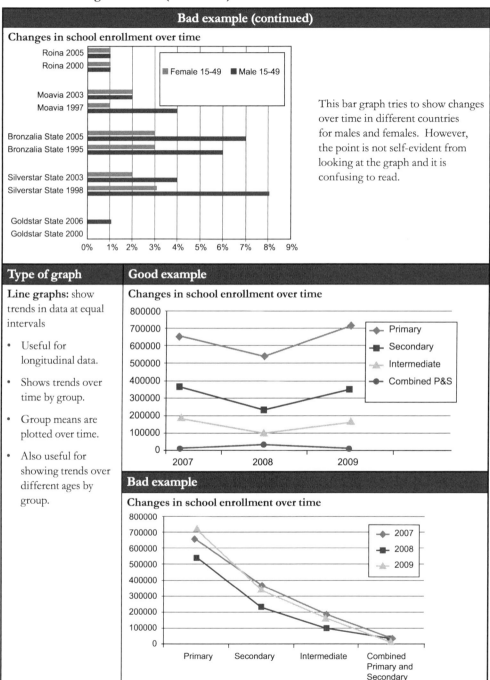

Bad example (continued)

Changes in school enrollment over time

This bar graph tries to show changes over time in different countries for males and females. However, the point is not self-evident from looking at the graph and it is confusing to read.

Type of graph	Good example
Line graphs: show trends in data at equal intervals • Useful for longitudinal data. • Shows trends over time by group. • Group means are plotted over time. • Also useful for showing trends over different ages by group.	Changes in school enrollment over time

Bad example

Changes in school enrollment over time

Figure C12-13: (Continued)

Type of graph	
Histograms: This is a special kind of bar chart that shows the frequency of an event occurring. It is used in graphical representation of frequency distributions of ordinal or interval data. • Data are grouped to better demonstrate distribution.	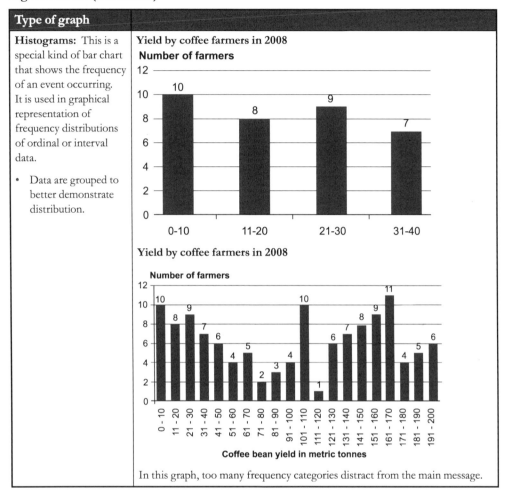 **Yield by coffee farmers in 2008** In this graph, too many frequency categories distract from the main message.

Figure C12-13: (Continued)

Type of graph	Good example
Scatter plots: illustrate relationship among data points • Used for univariate analysis • Useful for investigating the association between two parameters. • Can be used to show association between two parameters or lack of an association between two parameters. • It is useful to examine scatter plots before fitting regression models, to get a sense of the *shape* of the regression line that best fits the data.	**Learner to educator ratio and class average exam results** 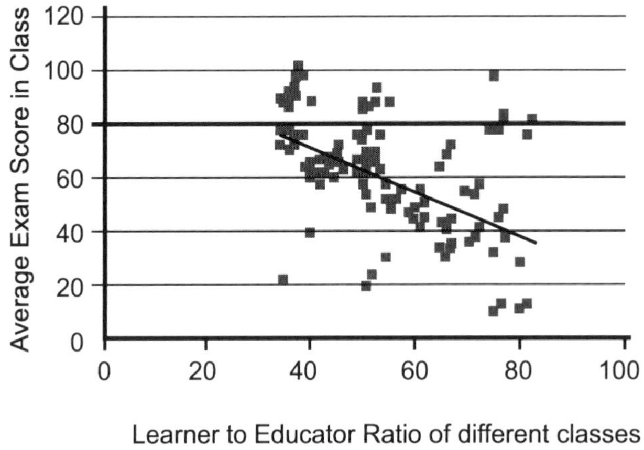

Bad example

New HIV infections (incidence) and levels of comprehensive knowledge about HIV

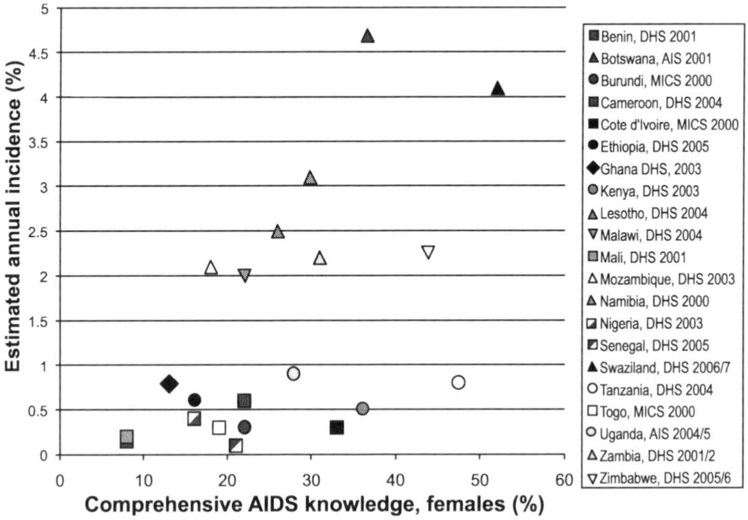

Every circle or triangle represents a different country. It difficult to see whether there is any pattern because one is distracted by the different shapes and colours and the legend

The following summary of friendly and unfriendly graphs or graphical displays provides a useful checklist for you to use when designing your own graphs:

Table C12-4: Characteristics of Friendly and Unfriendly Graphs or Graphical Displays

Friendly graph or graphical display	Unfriendly graph or graphical display
Words are spelled out, mysterious and elaborate encoding avoided	Abbreviations abound, requiring the viewer to sort through text to decode abbreviations
Words run from the left to right, the usual direction for reading occidental languages	Words run vertically, particularly along the y-axis; words run in several different directions
Little messages help explain facts	Graphic is cryptic, requires repeated references to scattered text to understand
Elaborately encoded shadings, cross hatching, and colors are avoided; instead, labels are placed on the graphic itself, and no legend is required	Obscure coding requires going back and forth between the graphic and the legend
Graphic attracts viewer, provokes curiosity	Graphic is repellent, filled with uninformative clutter
Colors, if used, are chosen so that the color blind can read them (5% - 10% of the population; most color deficient persons can distinguish blue from other colours)	Design is insensitive to color-deficient viewers; red and green are used for essential contrasts
Type is clear, precise, modern	Type is cluttered and overbearing, or small, and difficult to read
Type is "Sentence case" using both upper and lower case	Words are ALL IN UPPER CASE

Source: Tufte, 2001

9. Summary of Chapter 12 Knowledge and Skills

In this chapter, you learned about the different concepts related to data, information, knowledge, data analysis, reporting, and data display. You learned about how organizations make decisions and that although information is not the only factor, it is an important aspect that influences how decisions are made.

You learned how information informs policy decisions, planning, and program impact and, therefore, can help to improve the results that your organization can achieve. Good information enables better understanding of the problem which leads to program improvement.

You learned about the barriers to using information when making decisions, the benefits of doing so, and about strategies to promote information use. You learned how to analyze quantitative and qualitative data and how to improve the visual information display.

10. Learning Activities

LEARNING ACTIVITY 1:   DECISION MAKING CASE STUDY

Read the case study below and then answer these two questions:

a)   What are the five main challenges facing decision makers in trying to reach consensus on future airport expansion in the UK?

b)   What steps would you suggest to improve the situation and lead to consensus?

CASE STUDY

Wed May 21, 2008 — A report jointly undertaken by the Sustainable Development Commission (SDC) and the Institute for Public Policy Research (IPPR) concludes that there is such considerable dispute about the environmental, economic, and social impact of air transport that a three-year moratorium should take place on any proposed airport expansion until further research and consultation has been carried out.

The report, entitled *Breaking the Holding Pattern*, finds that available data on the benefits and impacts of aviation is "widely disputed" and inadequate for reliable decision making on the future of UK air travel. It also warns that decisions about the future of air transport must not pre-empt crucial UK and international policy decisions addressing aviation's climate impacts.

It argues there is widespread controversy over key data on air travel in the UK, including the benefits to the UK economy, its contribution to climate change, noise and air pollution, and the potential for technology to reduce aviation's environmental impacts. "The high levels of conflict around the effects of aviation are bad for government, industry and citizens, creating rising distrust and undermining policy decisions," the report claims.

The findings come after a year-long series of workshops and meetings with representatives from national and local government, the aviation industry, academics, NGOs and citizen groups. The three main areas of disagreements are:

- **Lack of agreed measures for assessing the benefits and impacts of aviation:** Although widely credited with bringing economic benefits through trade and tourism, controversy remains over:
  - the benefits of inbound tourism versus the losses from outbound domestic tourism and the impact of tourism on developing countries;
  - job and wealth creation from aviation; actual levels of inward investment and the opportunity cost to other modes of transport; and
  - the quantifiable impact of aviation on health and well-being, particularly from noise and local air pollution.
- **Lack of established data on the climate impacts of aviation and lack of clarity over the role of technology:** Significant scientific uncertainties remain over the contribution of aviation to climate change; and the potential for technology to make significant reductions in aviation's climate impacts; how soon improvements can be made; and whether other measures must be taken in the interim.
- **A lack of policy coherence across government:** Clashing government priorities across different departments and agencies — including promoting economic growth, meeting future travel needs, protecting the environment, addressing climate change and ensuring the health and well-being of communities are contributing to a lack of coherence.

The report warns that decisions about UK aviation policy must not pre-empt and undermine crucial UK and international policies addressing aviation's climate impacts such as the UK Climate Change Bill, the UK Aviation Duty Consultation, the EU Emissions Trading Scheme (ETS), and the post-2012 Bali Roadmap.

However, the report also claims "broad support" amongst stakeholders for "the inclusion of aviation and maritime emissions in a post-2012 climate change agreement, and the renegotiation of the Chicago Convention and associated bilateral agreements that currently restrict fuel tax."

Story from http://www.greenaironline.com/news.php?viewStory=180

LEARNING ACTIVITY 2: INTERPRET AND IMPROVE THE GRAPHICAL DISPLAY OF DATA

View the two *data and graph sets* provided below as well as the third graphical display. For each set, (a) write down how you interpret the data and the questions that you would have for the program team, and (b) suggest and illustrate how the graphical display of data may be improved.

Data and Graph Set 1:

Percentage of People With Waterborne Diseases And Percentage of People with Running Water at Their Homes in Six Districts in Goldstar State from 2004 To 2007

	People with waterborne diseases – 2004		People with waterborne diseases – 2007		Houses with treated running water on the premises – 2004	Houses with treated running water on the premises – 2007	Houses with treated running water on the premises — national target by 2010
	Men	Women	Men	Women			
District 1	45%	56%	34%	31%	12%	32%	50%
District 2	23%	12%	27%	29%	34%	36%	60%
District 3	25%	67%	23%	54%	45%	53%	45%
District 4	21%	43%	21%	56%	67%	69%	70%
District 5	34%	21%	25%	19%	19%	38%	80%
District 6	21%	39%	19%	39%	51%	51%	60%

Men and Women in 2004 with Waterborne Diseases

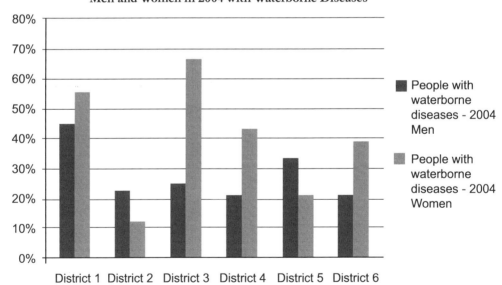

Men and Women in 2007 with Waterborne Diseases

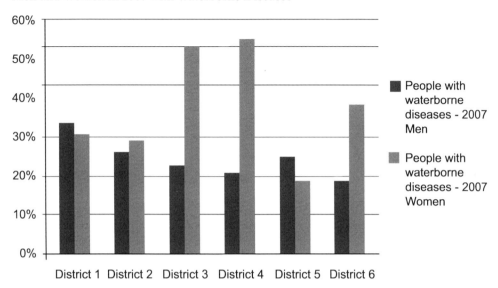

Houses with Treated Running Water on the Premises - 2004

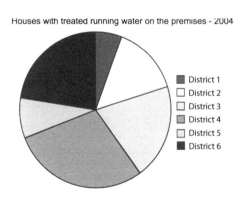

Houses with Treated Running Water on the Premises - 2007

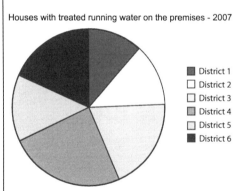

Data and Graph Set 2: Economics of tobacco control in South Africa

Data and Graph Set 2: Economics of Tobacco Control in South Africa

Year	Price	Consumption	Income	% Excise	Year	Price	Consumption	Income	% Excise
1970	R100	R100	R100	45.70	1984	R73	R144	R121	34.62
1971	R103	R100	R108	40.37	1985	R69	R140	R114	31.19
1972	R100	R102	R112	43.32	1986	R68	R140	R108	28.29
1973	R97	R109	R111	41.80	1987	R64	R147	R110	26.11
1974	R92	R115	R115	41.27	1988	R63	R151	R114	27.15
1975	R92	R120	R117	46.48	1989	R64	R148	R115	23.61
1976	R93	R125	R112	46.54	1990	R66	R151	R114	21.90
1977	R92	R114	R115	41.26	1991	R70	R165	R112	23.85
1978	R89	R116	R109	38.55	1992	R71	R135	R113	21.70
1979	R84	R125	R113	38.65	1993	R73	R119	R113	20.05
1980	R77	R135	R122	39.86	1994	R72	R119	R113	27.57
1981	R71	R142	R117	48.13	1995	R81	R105	R112	23.78
1982	R75	R147	R116	38.26	1996	R85	R95	R116	32.00
1983	R73	R143	R116	39.06	1997	R90	R90	R116	52.00

Source: Adebian, undated

Graph 2: Economics of Tobacco Control in South Africa

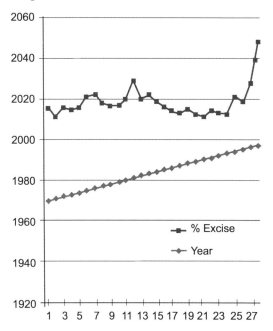

Graph 3: How HIV was Initiated in Different Parts of South Asia, East Asia, and the Pacific

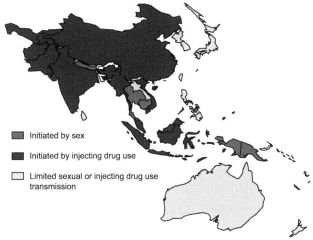

Source: Cited by Wilson, 2004

LEARNING ACTIVITY 3: MAKING REAL-TIME DECISIONS USING DATA

Goldstar State is in the process of reviewing its annual government budget to find ways in which to save costs. The Ministry of Health has to incur cost savings of 10% and it has identified that it can do so if it could rectify problems in hospital allocations of staff and hospital budgets. The data are provided in the table below.

As a planning team in the Ministry of Health, you are asked to propose a solution to rectify the issues at hospitals using the policy recommendations and the data provided below.

Policy recommendations

>> No more than 10 patients per doctor

>> One nurse for every 6 patients

Other factors and costs

>> Every reassignment costs G10,000 (once-off cost)

>> Every doctor costs G25,000 a month

>> Every nurse costs G8,000 a month

>> Cost per patient per day = G2,500

>> Total hospital cost is the cost of the doctors, nurses, and patients

Data About All Hospitals in Goldstar State

	Number of hospital beds	Number of doctors at hospital	Number of nurses at hospital	Average number of patients per hospital per month	Average number of days in hospital per patient	Monthly budget per hospital	Monthly actual expenditure per hospital	Monthly savings or (loss)
Hospital 1	200	19	40	34	3	G 1,000,000	G 1,050,000	G (50,000)
Hospital 2	220	24	45	119	2	G 1,309,800	G 1,555,000	G (245,200)
Hospital 3	250	26	34	63	4	G 1,453,200	G 1,552,000	G (98,800)
Hospital 4	200	29	33	40	5	G 1,560,000	G 1,489,000	G 71,000
Hospital 5	210	34	35	54	3	G 1,398,200	G 1,535,000	G (136,800)
Hospital 6	370	39	65	157	2	G 2,284,000	G 2,280,000	G 4,000
Hospital 7	50	4	10	10	2	G 257,800	G 230,000	G 27,800
Hospital 8	210	9	38	54	3	G 335,000	G 934,000	G (599,000)
Hospital 9	215	30	36	80	1.5	G 1,328,000	G 1,338,000	G (10,000)
Hospital 10	340	34	51	43	3.5	G 1,456,000	G 1,634,250	G (178,250)
Hospital 11	400	32	56	43	4	G 1,467,800	G 1,678,000	G (210,200)
Hospital 12	100	12	16	16	6	G 295,000	G 668,000	G (373,000)
Hospital 13	210	18	32	103	2	G 898,000	G 1,221,000	G (323,000)
Hospital 14	120	23	21	46	3	G 987,000	G 1,088,000	G (101,000)
Hospital 15	400	34	56	126	3	G 2,301,000	G 2,243,000	G 58,000
Hospital 16	210	20	32	69	3	G 1,346,700	G 1,273,500	G 73,200
Hospital 17	370	24	49	219	2	G 1,891,000	G 2,087,000	G (196,000)
Hospital 18	45	1	12	2	5	G 296,980	G 146,000	G 150,980
Hospital 19	320	30	54	129	2	G 1,429,800	G 1,827,000	G (397,200)
Hospital 20	20	4	6	6	3	G 359,000	G 193,000	G 166,000
TOTAL	4460	446	721	1413		G 23,654,280	26,021,750	G (2,367,470)

Monthly shortfall: 10%

LEARNING ACTIVITY 4: USING ROUTINE MONITORING DATA TO IMPROVE PROGRAM IMPLEMENTATION

There are five questions below. Each question displays routine data that have been collected, cleaned, and captured about program implementation in Goldstar State and that are now ready for use by a program manager [G = Golden (the currency of Goldstar State)].

QUESTION 4.1: **How can the data in this table be used to report progress?**

YEAR 1 - QUARTER 1						
Activity description	Indicator	Quantity planned	Quantity reached for the quarter	Budget planned for this quarter	Actual expenditure this quarter	Progress
Train road safety educators	Number of trained and active road safety educators	23	30	G 300,000	G 460,560	
Conduct workplace road safety prevention program	Number of persons reached	300	276	G 800,000	G 800,000	
Support vulnerable households with food parcels	Number of households supported	100	120	G 600,000	G 450,000	
Support orphans with school fees	Number of orphans supported	20	0	G 550,000	G 10,000	

QUESTION 4.2: How can the data in the six tables below be used to report trends over time? Explain in words and draw a graph to illustrate your point.

YEAR 1 – ANNUAL TOTALS						
Activity description	Indicator	Quantity planned	Quantity reached for the year	Budget planned for this year	Actual expenditure this year	Progress
Train road safety educators	Number of trained and active road safety educators	23	30	G 300,000	G 460,560	Completed
Conduct workplace road safety prevention program	Number of persons reached	300	276	G 800,000	G 800,000	Completed

YEAR 2 – WORK PLAN									
Activity description	Indicator	Planned				Budget			
		Q1	Q2	Q3	Q4	Q1	Q2	Q3	Q4
Train road safety educators	Number of trained and active road safety educators	10	20	30	20	G 100,000	G 150,000	G 200,000	G 150,000
Conduct workplace road safety prevention program	Number of persons reached	100	80	55	200	G 100,000	G 200,000	G 300,000	G 50,000
Support orphans with school fees	Number of orphans supported	100	30	60	400	G 300,000	G 20,000	G 40,000	G 700,000

YEAR 2 - QUARTER 1 REPORT					
Activity description	Indicator	Quantity planned for the quarter	Quantity reached for the quarter	Budget planned for this quarter	Actual Expenditure this quarter
Train road safety educators	Number of trained and active road safety educators		8	G	G 80,000
Conduct workplace road safety prevention program	Number of persons reached		105	G	G 165,000
Support orphans with school fees	Number of orphans supported		80	G	G 300,000

YEAR 2 - QUARTER 2 REPORT					
Activity description	Indicator	Quantity planned for the quarter	Quantity reached for the quarter	Budget planned for this quarter	Actual Expenditure this quarter
Train road safety educators	Number of trained and active road safety educators		20	G	G 80,000
Conduct workplace road safety prevention program	Number of persons reached		105	G	G 200,103
Support orphans	Number of orphans supported		24	G	G 56,000

YEAR 2 - QUARTER 3 REPORT					
Activity description	Indicator	Quantity planned for the quarter	Quantity reached for the quarter	Budget planned for this quarter	Actual Expenditure this quarter
Train road safety educators	Number of trained and active road safety educators		34	G	G 198.000
Conduct workplace road safety prevention program	Number of persons reached		50	G	G 305.000
Support orphans	Number of orphans supported		54	G	G 400.000

YEAR 2 - QUARTER 4 REPORT					
Activity description	Indicator	Quantity planned for the quarter	Quantity reached for the quarter	Budget planned for this quarter	Actual Expenditure this quarter
Train road safety educators	Number of trained and active road safety educators		18	G	G 230,000
Conduct workplace road safety prevention program	Number of persons reached		202	G	G 50,000
Support orphans	Number of orphans supported		456	G	G 994,000

QUESTION 4.3: Using data from Question 4.2 and the additional data below, explain how data can be used to mobilize resources. You can also use graphs to illustrate your points.

Number of orphans in Goldstar: 2 000

Number of vulnerable households: 4 000

QUESTION 4.4: How can data from the following four tables be used to compare different organizations? Explain in words and use a graph to illustrate your points

SAFE-ROADS-ARE-US ORGANIZATION

Activity description	Indicator	Quantity planned for the quarter	Quantity reached for the quarter	Budget planned for this quarter	Actual expenditure this quarter
Train road safety educators	Number of trained and active road safety educators	8	8	G 76,000	G 80,000
Conduct workplace road safety prevention program	Number of persons reached	105	105	G 170,000	G 165,000
Support orphans with school fees	Number of orphans supported	76	80	G 69,000	G 300,000

SALAMANDER ORGANIZATION

Activity description	Indicator	Quantity planned for the quarter	Quantity reached for the quarter	Budget planned for this quarter	Actual expenditure this quarter
Train road safety educators	Number of trained and active road safety educators	60	20	G 400,000	G 80,000
Support orphans with school fees	Number of orphans supported	55	24	G 300,000	G 56,000

KELELE SQUARE ASSOCIATION OF TAXI DRIVERS

Activity description	Indicator	Quantity planned for the quarter	Quantity reached for the quarter	Budget planned for this quarter	Actual expenditure this quarter
Train road safety educators	Number of trained and active road safety educators	40	34	G 250,000	G 198,000
Conduct workplace road safety prevention program	Number of persons reached	48	50	G 408,000	G 305,000

SHANGANI SUPPORT SINGERS					
Activity description	Indicator	Quantity planned for the quarter	Quantity reached for the quarter	Budget planned for this quarter	Actual expenditure this quarter
Train road safety educators	Number of trained and active road safety educators	9	18	G 165,000	G 230,000
Conduct workplace road safety prevention program	Number of persons reached	100	202	G 54,000	G 50,000
Support orphans with school fees	Number of orphans supported	205	456	G 43,000	G 994,000

QUESTION 4.5: How can data from the weekly report forms of the four road safety educators (below) be used to identify training needs?

JABU'S WEEKLY REPORT

Number of hours worked: 34

Number of peer education sessions: 64

Number of road safety booklets distributed: 32

THEMBISILE'S WEEKLY REPORT

Number of hours worked: ALL DAY

Number of peer education sessions: MANY

Number of road safety booklets distributed: NOT

NHLENGIWE'S WEEKLY REPORT

Number of hours worked: 12

Number of peer education sessions: 2

Number of road safety booklets distributed: 500

HALIMA'S WEEKLY REPORT

Number of hours worked: 40

Number of peer education sessions: 20

Number of road safety booklets distributed: 20

QUESTION 4.6: Read the road safety peer education guidelines below. With these peer education guidelines in place, how could data from the weekly report forms of the four peer educators in question 4.5 be used to improve the quality of the facilitators' efforts?

Peer education guidelines:

- Do not immediately rush into talking about road safety (or other programs), ask some general questions first to make the person feel comfortable

- A peer education session should last one hour

- Road safety materials should always be distributed at road safety peer education sessions, to make sure that a person has a reference, if they want more information later, or, perhaps want to share what they have learned with a friend

Annex A: Types of Quantitative Data: Explanations and Examples

Type	Explanation	Example
Nominal	Have no inherent order but it is possible to assign numbers to the categories of a nominal variable (but are no "less than" or "greater than" relations between the categories)	Gender, marital status, race, religious affiliation, political party affiliation, college major, birthplace, geographical location in a country represented by that country's international telephone access code, or the make or model of a car
Ordinal (or ranked)	The numbers assigned to objects represent the rank order (1st, 2nd, 3rd etc.) of the entities measured, but the intervals between numbers are not meaningful	Examples include the Mohs scale of mineral hardness; the results of a horse race, which say only which horses arrived first, second, third, etc., but no time intervals; attitudes like preference, conservatism, or prejudice; and social class
Interval	Same as ordinal except that, in addition, equal differences between measurements represent equivalent intervals but there is NO meaningful **zero** value	Year date in many calendars and temperature in Celsius or Fahrenheit scale
Ratio	Same as interval and, **in addition,** the zero value is meaningful; so the ratio between any two measurements is meaningful	Mass, length, energy, temperature measured in kelvin, age, length of residence in a given place, number of organizations belonged to, number of church attendances in a particular time

Source: www.uky.edu/CommInfoStudies/JAT/Telecommunications/300/Descriptive_statistics.ppt

Level	Can define...	Example data set	Example calculations
Nominal	Mode	Yes, yes, no, no, yes, no, yes, no, yes, yes, yes,	Mode — response that appears most frequently = 'yes'
Ordinal	Median	1, 9, 12, 3, 10, 7, 8, 8, 9, 2, 5, 10, 11	Median = 50th percentile Organize from high to low 1 2 3 5 7 8 8 9 9 10 10 11 Middle value = 8
Interval	Mean, standard deviation	Temperatures in one week (in Fahrenheit) 40, 35, 35, 37, 55, 32, 60	Calculate mean: 294/7 = 42

465

Annex B: Example of a Write-up of Qualitative Data Analysis

Summary of Three Ones challenges and M&E system challenges: ASAP participants

Methods

Data was collected from 16 M&E course participants using emailed open ended questionnaires. The purpose of the questionnaire was to ascertain views on M&E systems building before the course started and in the process design a more focused M&E course. One of the respondents mentioned that her/his work does not include particular direct M&E work. Data, focusing on the last two questions (number 3 and 4), was then analyzed using qualitative content analysis.[1] Such analysis allows for similarities and differences between respondents to be analyzed rather than highlighting individual specific issues and circumstances. As such, the process evaluation entailed by this analysis provided an *overview* and is used to identify salient themes that emerge from the data. The data is presented below, initially answering the key questions (number 3 and 4) that appear in the two topic areas.

Most challenging M&E assignment

The majority of the respondents tried to describe additional challenges related to HIV/AIDS M&E environment and culture, as well as different or general challenges, like engaging stakeholders and data quality/collection problems in terms of developing strategies and programs. Few respondents addressed particular challenging M&E assignments, although those assignments were usually mentioned to explain wider problems or challenges related to an existing operational M&E environment. Only one respondent mentioned cultural drives and stigma as a challenge with regards to planning and implementing M&E activities in HIV/AIDS.

More detailed break down of answers to the questions exposed a number of different weaknesses or challenges that emerged in the responses around *the most challenging M&E assignment*. The challenges range from compiling reports and developing national frameworks, the lack of economic and human resources, through to the lack of support from the government. Particular tasks that were mentioned related to international training courses (as a trainer presenting a national experiences and lessons learned to the other M&E course participants; 2 respondents), compiling UNGASS reports and developing a national framework (5 respondents), and establishing a national M&E unit

---

[1] Flick (1998) An Introduction to Qualitative Research. Sage Publications: London

(1 respondent). However, it appears the majority of responses were centered around a lack of quality data, working with multiple stakeholders involved in the M&E at different levels, and developing an enabling M&E environment in general.

The main challenges mentioned related to involving multiple stakeholders and partners in the M&E work. A number of participants (6) reported that it was challenging to get stakeholders involved in the M&E process and build consensus among various players. Some respondents felt that it was challenging to build common understanding of what needs to be monitored and what indicators should be used:

"The drafting of the M&E Framework on Children Affected by HIV and AIDS. It was challenging in the sense that multiple stakeholders had a different understanding of what needs to be monitored, the national indicators suitable for the Action Plan, and the timeframes for achieving the objectives of the Action Plan. In the end it was very difficult for me to meaningfully work in such an environment, and the assignment was never completed."

"To harmonize the M&E perspectives from several players (more than 40), to build a consistent M&E system for the Global Fund programs… this included training, advocacy, negotiation skills and an open mind for learning from the others."

Two respondents mentioned challenges with cooperating and aligning international partners to a national M&E system. The other respondents also mention specifically a challenge with implementing the Three Ones due to "the fact that some UN Agencies insisted on a national health driven response versus a multidisciplinary response, mainstreaming HIV into the PRS." It was also felt that decentralized structure of data collection fragmented the data collection, resulting in a lack of coordination:

"Challenge is also to get all stakeholders involved, to develop understanding of the relevance of these M&E guidelines and develop a sustainable M&E environment: During UNGASS reporting we could get everybody on board, and data were coming from everywhere, but it also shows how fragmented the data collection is without a clear coordination/analysis/action point."

Another strong thematic area identified as an M&E challenge was related to data quality, data gaps and existing resources. Number of the participants (4) mentioned that lack of data or poor data quality is the biggest challenge with regards to the M&E work in the field of HIV/AIDS. Existing data was described as "poor" and "unreliable."

"Absence/inadequate/poor quality of M&E data for some programs."

"Challenge was to follow the M&E guidelines of the UNGASS indicators, given the specific conditions and available resources in the country. This demands flexibility and creativity but is difficult if simultaneously you want to hold on to the standards set."

"I was carrying out baseline survey and I had difficulties finding data because the country hasn't got data on HIV/AIDS."

There was a feeling among some participants that the problems with regards to data quality derives from data collection and reporting which are not strong and sound enough to produce quality data:

"Poor data reporting system/timeliness of report lead to lack of database for some components."

Two respondents felt that lack of planning and coordination makes evidence based programming difficult.

"As we still do not have one M&E plan and one strong Coordinating body, it is a big challenge to translate information into action: into effective programs that have 'evidence based' impact on the HIV epidemic."

The lack of sufficient economic resources and also a high turn around or lack of the qualified and sufficient human resources was suggested as one of the contributing factors of poor data quality.

"M&E is everybody's responsibility, but shortage of personnel is severely affecting on M&E of programs as majority of them are multi-task officers."

Another challenge mentioned with regards to the funding was related to cost and also to a difficulty of having access to financial or expenditure information, due to the reluctance of donors and implementers to share the information.

"Separating what expenditure is put on HIV and AIDS from other activities is challenging in a situation of mainstreamed/integrated HIV and AIDS activities and promoted mainstreaming policy. Not even in Health sector is it easy to attribute expenditures more accurately to all HIV and AIDS or related interventions in a health facility setting."

On the other hand, one of the respondents reported that actually the economic resources were sufficient but the lack of political support made establishing the M&E unit difficult.

"Establishment of a national M&E Unit... Support for the National M&E Unit is budgeted in the current GF grant; however, due to lack of commitment from the government, it was not yet officially established..."

Greatest challenges for the Three Ones in the next 3 years

Most of the responses in this section (four) appear to be complementary or overlap with question three of *the most challenging M&E task.*

Some respondents felt that to build an operational enabling environment (staffing, secure funding, the M&E culture, stakeholder engagement) in order to have a functioning M&E system in place will be the biggest challenge within the current environment. The majority of responses revolved around the lack of stakeholder and donor interest in the three ones. However, the respondents also mentioned more macro-level challenges such as food crises and lack of political commitment which may have an affect on developing and implementing *the three ones.* However, it appears that respondents were more in agreement about challenges regarding question four and the answers seem to focus on four key areas:

1. **Lack of involvement/interest/understanding from stakeholders and donors with regard to *three ones*.**

   "To increase the participation level of national implementers to the elaboration process of the National strategic plan and the national M&E plan"

   "…the main challenge is to implement this plan in the several layers of government, e.g. in the most affected states and municipalities"

   "To increase the alignment level of international implementers to the national strategic plan and the national M&E plan"

   "Commitment of counter parts in results based management"

   "Lack of commitment on the part of the governments"

   "Difficulties in coordination of various donor- and state-funded efforts at the country levels"

2. **Secure sufficient resources**

   "Could work better if joint funding is made to support three ones as long as there are transparent arrangements and stakeholder owned response management, and not an autocratic NAC that commands actions instead of strategic interpretation of roles"

   "To have national plans costed"

3. **Secure national, international and global support for HIV/AIDS and keep HIV/AIDS on the political agenda**

   "To keep AIDS on the political agenda"

   "Unsure whether governments of developing nations will be able to sustain and meet their commitments to the fight against HIV/AIDS given the current challenges from spiraling food prices"

   "Lack of agreement between donor and international agencies at the global level"

   "To sustain the national response, after Global Fund and other donor's contribution and support"

   "Poor Leaderships in NACs greatly undermining it [HIV/AIDS M&E) and this may continue with general state of bad governance in many countries and may continue in the near future"

   "Development partners/Donors should be seen to promote three ones and not undermining it for it to work"

   "Donor fatigue"

4. **To build or sustain a national M&E system**

   "[Challenge is] to have a national M & E framework in place"

   "To build an "M&E culture" and practicing M&E of National Strategic and Multisectoral Plans on the basis of the effectiveness and efficiency of the national response"

   "To institutionalize high quality and timeliness M&E systems"

   "Build the national response structure and let it work!: mobilize national and international resources to select the required human resources (right person at the right place), develop adequate communication procedures between all partners, develop adequate monitoring and evaluation structures and mechanisms, and build a truly national comprehensive coherent response, that is efficient and effective in achieving the goals and objectives."

References

Abedian, I. undated. *Economics of Tobacco Control in South Africa*, PowerPoint presentation made at the School of Economics, University of Cape Town, South Africa

African Evaluation Association (AfREA). 2006. *Guidelines for Evaluation in Africa-edition 2006*. Published by African Evaluation Association (AfrEA).

Ainsworth, M., Beyer, C. & Soucat, A. 2003. *AIDS and public policy: The challenges of 'Success' in Thailand*. Health Policy 64: 13-37

American Heart Foundation. 2008. *Types of Research*, accessed on 13 October 2008 at http://www.americanheart.org/presenter.jhtml?identifier=218

Antonacopoulou, E. 1999. *Individuals' Responses to Change: The Relationship Between Learning and Knowledge, in Creativity and Innovation Management*, Volume 8, Number 2, June 1999 , pp. 130-139(10)

Atherton, J.S. 2005. *Learning and Teaching: Experiential Learning*. Accessed online on 21 November 2008 at http://www.learningandteaching.info/learning/experience.htm

Australian National Health and Medical Research Council, 2007. *National statement on ethical conduct in human research*. Canberra, Australia: Australian Government. ISBN Print: 1864962690

Bazerman, M.H. 2008. *Judgment in managerial decision making* (7th Ed.). Wiley publishers. ISBN-10: 0471684309

Belmont Report. 1979. *Ethical Principles and Guidelines for the protection of human subjects of research*. The National Commission for the Protection of Human Subjects of Biomedical and Behavioral

Binnendijk, A. 1999, "*Results-based management*," Prepared for the International Conference on Evaluation Capacity Development, Beijing, China.

Borum, F. 2000. 2000 *Honorary member: Laudatio* by Finn Borum, Accessed online on 1 March 2009 at http://www.egosnet.org/jart/prj3/egosnet/main.jart?rel=en&content-id=1227251866223&reserve-mode=active

Bošnjak, S. 2001. *The Declaration of Helsinki The cornerstone of research ethics*. Archive of Oncology. 2001; 9(3):179-84. 2

Boyle, R., and D. Lemaire, eds. 1999, *Building Effective Evaluation Capacity*. Transaction Books, New Brunswick, N.J.

Byrne, G. undated. *Integrating Impact Assessment Data into Decision-Making - Dealing with Socioeconomics Surrounding Biotechnology in the Canadian Federal Government.* IDRC. Accessed online on 28 February 2009 at http://www.idrc.ca/en/ev-30727-201-1-DO_TOPIC.html

Business Link. 2007. *Benefits of databases.* Accessed online on 24 October 2007 at www.businesslink.gov.uk/bdotg/action/layer?topicId=1075422967

Centres for Disease Control and Prevention (CDC). 1999. *Guidelines for defining public health research and public health non-research.* Revised October 4, 1999. Accessed on 15 October 2007 at http://www.cdc.gov/od/science/regs/hrpp/researchDefinition.htm

Centres for Disease Control and Prevention (CDC). 2006. *Types of Evaluations.* Accessed online on 3 March 2008 at http://www.cdc.gov/STD/program/progeval/ApC-PGprogeval.htm

Centers for Disease Control and Prevention (CDC). 2007. *HIV/AIDS statistics and surveillance.* Accessed on 20 October 2007 at http://www.cdc.gov/hiv/topics/surveillance/

Coffman, J. 2007. *What's different about Evaluating Advocacy and Policy Change? The Evaluation Exchange: A Periodical on Emerging Strategies in Evaluation.* Harvard Family Research Project, Harvard Graduate School of Education. 8(1), Spring 2007. Accessed online at http://www.hfrp.org/var/hfrp/storage/original/application/6bdf92c3d7e970e7270588109e23b678.pdf on 3 October 2008

Constella Futures. Not dated. Essential Advocacy Project. *Implementation: Developing Advocacy Action Plans*

Covey, D.T. 2002. *Usage and Usability Assessment: Library Practices and Concerns.* Washington DC. Digital Library Federation and Council on Library and Information Resources.

Cradler, C., Beuthel, B., and Vance, E. 2008. *Data-Driven Decision-Making and Electronic Learning Assessment Resources* (ELAR). California Department of Education. Accessed online on 28 February 2009 at http://www.clrn.org/elar/dddm.cfm

Czech Republic. 2006. *Code of Ethics for Researchers of the Academy of Sciences of the Czech Republic.* Accessed online on 24 December 2008 at http://www.cas.cz/en/code_of_ethics.php

Dean, J.W., and Sharfman, M.P. 1996. *Does Decision Process Matter? A Study of Strategic Decision-Making Effectiveness,* in The Academy of Management Journal, Vol. 39, No. 2 (Apr., 1996), pp. 368-396. Accessible at http://www.jstor.org/stable/256784

Dennis, A.R. 1996. *Information Exchange and Use in Group Decision Making: You Can Lead a Group to Information, but You Can't Make It Think*, in MIS Quarterly, December 1996. Management information Systems Research Center, University of Minnesota.

Drucker, P.F., Hammond, J., Keeney, R., Raiffa, H., and Hayashi, A.M. 2001. *Harvard Business Review on Decision Making*. Harvard Business School Press: Massachuchets. ISBN-10: 1578515572

Errkola, T. 2007. *Personal communication*s (Contact mgorgens@worldbank.org).

Evaluation, no. 33. Jossey – Bass, San Francisco, California.

Family Health International FHI. 2000. *Behavioral Surveillance Surveys: Guidelines for Repeated Behavioral Surveys in Populations at Risk of HIV*, Family Health International, 2000, http://www.fhi.org/en/HIVAIDS/pub/guide/bssguidelines.htm

Family Health International FHI. 2001. *Research Ethics Training Curriculum*. Accessed online on 10 February 2009 at http://www.fhi.org/training/en/RETC/

Family Health International FHI. 2001. *Research Training Curriculum*. Accessed online on 5 October 2008 at http://www.fhi.org/en/RH/Training/trainmat/ethicscurr/RETCCREn/index.htm

Family Health International – FHI. 2002. *Human capacity development for an effective response to HIV/AIDS: The community response report*. Addis Ababa, Ethiopia.

Feldman, M.S., and March, J.G. 1981. *Information in Organizations as Signal and Symbol*, in Administrative Science Quarterly Volume 26 (1981). pp 171 - 186

Ferber, R., Sheatsley, P., Turner, A., Waksberg, J. 1980. *What is a Survey?* Accessed online on 5 Oct 2008 at http://client.norc.org/whatisasurvey/downloads/pamphlet_1980.pdf

Flinders University. 2007. Flinders University/Southern Adelaide Health Service. *Ethical guidelines for social and behavioural research*. Adelaide, South Australia: Flinders University

Foskett, A.C. 1982. *The subject approach to information*, Linnet Books, The Shoe String Press, Inc., Hamden, CT, 1982, p1.

Furubo, J., Rist, R., and R. Sandahl, eds. 2002, *International Atlas of Evaluation*. Transaction Books, New Brunswick, N.J.

Goold, M., and Campbell, A. 2002a. *Designing effective organizations: How to create structured networks*. Jossey-Bass, 2002.

Goold, M., and Campbell, A. 2002b. *Do you have a well designed organization?* Harvard Business Review, March, pp. 117-124.

Goold, M., and Campbell, A. 2002c. *Nine tests of organization, design, directions.* The Ashridge Journal, Summer.

Görgens-Albino, M., and Victor-Ahuchogu, J. 2008. *Planning for, measuring and achieving HIV results: A handbook for task team leaders of World Bank lending operations with HIV components.* Washington D.C: The World Bank.

Governance. Smith, M.F. 1989, *Evaluability Assessment: A Practical Approach.* Kluwer Academic Publishers, Boston, Mass. United Way, 1996, *Measuring Program Outcomes: A Practical Approach.* Alexandria, Virginia.

Government of the Kingdom of Swaziland, UNAIDS and The World Bank. 2008. *Inception Report for the Analysis of HIV Prevention Response and Modes of Transmission Study.* Swaziland National Emergency Response Council on HIV and AIDS (NERCHA): Mbabane.

Government of Republic of Namibia (GRN). 2008. *Guidelines for managing the System for Programme Monitoring of HIV, TB and Malaria data.* GRN: Windhoek.

Greenair. 2008. UK Government's environment adviser says disputed data undermines aviation policy decision-making. Accessed online on 27 February 2009 at http://www.greenaironline.com/news.php?viewStory=180

Guerrero, P. "Comparative Insights from Colombia, China, and Indonesia," in Boyle, R. and D. Lemaire, eds., *Building Effective Evaluation Capacity.* Transaction Books, New Brunswick, N.J.

Hiller, S. 2002. *'But what does it mean?' Using statistical data for Decision Making in Academic Libraries.* Statistics in Practice – Measuring and Managing pp 10 - 23.

Hirokawa, R. Y., and Poole, M. S. 1996. *Communication and Group Decision Making.* SAGE: United States of America. ISBN 076190462X

Holzer, M. 1999, *"Public Performance Evaluation and Improvement,"* Prepared for the International Conference on Evaluation Capacity Development, Beijing, China.

Hopkins, T. J. 1994. *Handbook on capacity assessment methodologies: An analytical review.* UNDP. Accessed online on 2 April 2007 at www.pogar.org/publications/other/undp/governance/capmet94e.pdf.

Horton, R. 2006. *The Lancet,* Vol. 368: pp. 716-718.

IEG. 2007. Russian federation: Health reform pilot project. Project performance assessment report. World Bank, Washington, D.C., March 27. Bartol, K. M.; Martin, D. C.; Tein, M. H., and Matthews, G. W. 2001. *Management: a Pacific Rim focus.* 3rd Edition. Roseville, NSW: McGraw-Hill Book Company.

Irani, K. 2007. *Type of organizational structures.* Accessed online on 10/06/2008 at: www.buzzle.com/articles/type-of-organizational-structures.html

Kaushik, A. 2006. *Occam's Razor*, published online on 23 October 2006 at http://www.kaushik.net/avinash/2006/10/seven-steps-to-creating-a-data-driven-decision-...02/27/2009

Kemerer, V. (ed.), Swaziland National AIDS Programme, Swaziland; Ministry of Health and Social Welfare, Swaziland; The National Emergency Response Council on HIV and AIDS, Swaziland; United States Agency for International Development, Southern Africa Regional HIV/AIDS Program; and MEASURE Evaluation (2007). Training workshop: Basic monitoring and evaluation concepts, data quality, and data analysis and use. Chapel Hill, NC: MEASURE Evaluation.

Kenneth Lafferty Hess Family Charitable Foundation. 2008. *Designing a Survey.* Accessed online on 5 October 2008 at http://www.sciencebuddies.org/science-fair-projects/project_ideas/Soc_survey.shtml

Ketz de Vries, M.F.R. 2001. *The leadership mystique: A user's manual for the human enterprise.* London: Prentice Hall, Financial Times.

Kiernan, N.E. (2001). *Steps for Writing Program Objectives*: Tipsheet #10, University Park, PA: Penn State Cooperative Extension. Accessed on 2 October 2008 from http://www.extension.psu.edu/evaluation/pdf/TS10.pdf

Leung, W.C. 2001a. *How to conduct a survey.* StudentBMJ 2001;9:143-5. (May.) Accessed online at http://student.bmj.com/back_issues/0501/education/143.html on 5 October 2008

Leung, W.C. 2001b. *How to design a questionnaire.* Accessed online on 5 October 2008 at student.bmj.com/back_issues/0601/education/187.html

Levesque, K., Bradby, D., and Rossi, K. 1996. *Using Data for Programme Improvement: How Do We Encourage Schools To Do It?* In Centerfocus, Number 12.May 1996. National Center for Research in Vocational Education. University of California at Berkeley. Accessed online on 25 February 2009 at http://vocserve.berkeley.edu/centerfocus/CF12.html

Love, N., Stiles, K. E, Mundry, S. E., and DiRanna, K. 2007/08. *A Data Coach's Guide to Improving Learning For All Students - Unleashing the Power of Collaborative Inquiry.* Hands On! Winter 2007/2008, volume 30, number 2. Accessed online at: http://usingdata.terc.edu/attachments/DCGuide.pdf on April 3,

2009. Lamptey P.R., Zeitz P., and Larivee C. 2001. *Strategies for an expanded and comprehensive response (ECR) to a national HIV/AIDS epidemic.* Family Health International – FHI. Accessed online on 2 October 2007 at www. fhi org/NR/rdonlyres/e3vplv5peej6b3a4hj2j6cs4a4dgru4ccifai577sbmf7 v3xl4pcozryre76t7aocb3rd6gwbohr6h/ECRenglishwithChapter9.pdf.

MacDonald, R. 2001. *'Avoiding biases'*, in Student BMJ Volume 9 144 May 2001

Mackay, K. 1999, *"Evaluation Capacity Development: A Diagnostic Guide and Action Framework,"* The World Bank, Washington, D.C.

Mackay, K. 2007. *How to use monitoring and evaluation to build better government.* The World Bank: Washington DC.

March, J. G. 1991. *How decisions happen in organizations, in Human-Computer Interaction* Volume 6, Issue 2 (June 1991), pp 95-117. L. Erlbaum Associates Inc. Hillsdale, NJ, USA. ISSN:0737-0024

March, J. G. (1994). *A Primer on Decision Making: How Decisions Happen.* Simon and Schuster: USA.
ISBN 0029200350

March, J. G., and Romelaer, P. J. (1976). *Position and presence in the drift of decisions.* In J.G. March & J. P. Olsen (Eds.), Ambiguig and choice in organizations (pp. 25 1-276). Bergen, Norway: Universitetsforlaget.

Mayne, J. 1997, *"Accountability for Program Performance: A Key to Effective Performance Monitoring and Reporting,"* in Mayne, J. and E. Zapico – Goni, eds. Monitoring Performance in the Public Sector. Transaction Books, New Brunswick, N.J.

Mayne, J. and E. Zapic – Goni, eds. 1997, *Monitoring Performance in the Public Sector.* Transaction Books, New Brunswick, N.J.

McCoy, K. L., Ngari, P. N., Krumpe, E. E. 2005. *Building monitoring, evaluation and reporting systems for HIV/AIDS programs.* Washington D.C: PACT.

McNamara, C. 1997. *Basic Guide to Program Evaluation.* Accessed online at 5 October 2008 at http://www.managementhelp.org/evaluatn/fnl_eval. htm#anchor1587540

MEASURE Evaluation. 2008. *Routine Data Quality Assessment Tool (RDQA): Guidelines for Implementation.* Accessed online on 30 May 2009 at

MEASURE Evaluation. 2008. *Routine Data Quality Assessment Tool* (RDQA): Guidelines for Implementation. Accessed online on 30 May 2009 at http:// www.cpc.unc.edu/measure/tools/monitoring-evaluation-systems/data-quality-assurance-tools/RDQA%20Guidelines-Draft%207.30.08.pdf

MEASURE Evaluation, USAID. Undated. Data demand and information use in the health sector (DDIU): Conceptual framework. North Carolina: University of North Carolina.

Michigan State University: <http://research.chm.msu.edu/RO/rschtypes.htm>

Moock, J.L. Not dated. *How we invest in capacity building*. Rockefeller Foundation. New York: United States of America.

Naor, M., Goldstein, S. M., Linderman, K. W., Schroeder, R.G. 2008. *The Role of Culture as Driver of Quality Management and Performance: Infrastructure Versus Core Quality Practices, in Decision Sciences*. Volume 34 Issue 4, Pages 671 – 702

Nath, S. 2007. Final Report: *Getting Research into Policy and Practice GRIPP*. JSI Europe. USAID: Washington DC

Nzima, M. 2007. *Personal communications*. (Contact mgorgens@worldbank.org).

OECD. 2003. DAC Guidelines and Reference Series: *Harmonising donor practices for effective aid delivery*. Paris, France: OECD.

OECD. 2006. DAC Evaluation Series: *Guidance for managing joint evaluations*. Paris, France: OECD.

O'Reilly, C. A. 1982. *Variations in Decision Makers' Use of Information Sources: The Impact of Quality and Accessibility of Information,* in Academy of Management Journal Volume 24 Nr 4. pp 756 – 771.

Osborne, D., and Gaebler, T. 1992. *Reinventing government*. Boston: Addison-Wesley Publishing.

Pimple, K. D. 2002. "*Six domains of research ethics: A heuristic framework for the responsible conduct of research*." Science and Engineering Ethics 8:191-205 Kusek, J.Z. and R.C. Rist, 2001, "*Making M&E Matter – Get the Foundation Right*," Evaluation Insights, Vol. 2, no. 2.

PowerPoint presentation accessed online at www.futuresgroup.com/fg/resources/E.1-Advocacy-Action-Plans-and-ME.ppt on 3 Oct 2008.

Research. April 18, 1979. National Institutes of Health, USA

Resnik, D.B. 2007. *What is Ethics in Research & Why is It Important?,* National Institute of Environmental Health Sciences. Accessed online on 24 December 2008 at http://www.niehs.nih.gov/research/resources/bioethics/whatis.cfm

Rossi, P. H., and Freeman, H.E. 1993. *Evaluation: A systematic approach*. Newbury Park, Calif. Sage Publications. ISBN 0803944586.

Rist, R.C. 2000, *"Evaluation Capacity Development in the People's Republic of China: Trends and Prospects,"* in Malik, K. and C. Roth, eds., Evaluation Capacity Development in Asia. United Nations Development Program Evaluation Office, New York, New York.

Robbins, S., and Decenzo, D. 2004. *Fundamentals of Management.* New Jersey: Prentice-Hall.)

Robbins, S.P., and Decenzo, D.A. 2001. *Fundamentals of management: Essential concepts and applications.* Third edition. Upper Saddle River, N. J.: Prentice-Hall.

Rugg, D., Carael, M., Boerma, T., and Novak, J. 2004. *Global advances in monitoring and evaluation of HIV/AIDS: From AIDS case reporting to programme improvement.* In: *Global advances in HIV/AIDS monitoring and evaluation*, Rugg D, Peersman G, Carael M (Eds), *New Directions in Evaluation*, Nr 103, Fall 2004, p1-11.

Rugg, D., Peersman, G., and Carael, M. (eds). 2004. *Global advances in HIV/AIDS monitoring and evaluation: New directions in evaluation*, Nr 103, Fall 2004, pp. 1-11.

Schreuner, F. 2004. *What is a survey?* American Statistical Association

Shamoo, A., and Resnik, D. 2003. *Responsible Conduct of Research* (New York: Oxford University Press).

Shannon, A. 1998. *Advocating for Adolescent Reproductive Health in Sub-Saharan Africa.* Washington, DC: Advocates for Youth, 1998. Accessed online on 3 October 2008 at http://www.advocatesforyouth.org/PUBLICATIONS/advocate/chapter9.htm

Sharp, C. 2001, *Strategic Evaluation: Performance Measurement in the Service of Effective*

Southeast Michigan Council Of Governments (SEMCOG). 2008. *Using Data for Better Decision-Making.* Accessed online on 22 February 2009 at http://tsp.trb.org/assets/BP18_SEMCOG.pdf

Star, L., and Estes, J.E. 1990: *Geographic information systems: an introduction. Englewood Cliffs,* NJ: Prentice-Hall.

Swaziland Government (2009). *Swaziland Protocol for the Swaziland Quality, Comprehensiveness and Relevance of Impact Mitigation Services Survey.* Swaziland Government: Mbabane.

Tanzania Commission for AIDS (TACAIDS). 2007. *Guidelines for the Tanzania Output Monitoring System for HIV/AIDS.* Dar Es Salaam: Government of Tanzania.

The Global Fund to Fight AIDS, TB and Malaria. 2006. Data Quality Audit Tool Briefing Paper. The Global Fund: Geneva.

The Global Fund to Fight AIDS, TB and Malaria, WHO, UNAIDS, OGAC, PEPFAR, USAID, WHO, UNAIDS

The Global Fund to Fight AIDS, TB and Malaria; WHO; World Bank; UNICEF; UNAIDS; USAID; HHS/CDC; MEASURE Evaluation and Family Health International. 2006. Monitoring and Evaluation Toolkit HIV/AIDS, Tuberculosis and Malaria. WHO and Global Fund, Geneva, January 2006 (2nd ed.). http://www.theglobalfund.org/pdf/guidelines/pp_me_toolkit_en_lowres.pdf

The World Bank. 2000. *"Thailand's response to AIDS: Building on success, confronting the future."* Thailand Social Monitor V. World Bank, Bangkok. McCoy, KL., Ngari, PN., and Krumpe, EE. 2005. *Building monitoring, evaluation and reporting systems for HIV/AIDS programs.* PACT: Washington DC.

The World Bank. 2005. *The LogFrame handbook: A logical framework approach to project cycle management.* The World Bank: Washington DC.

The Global Fund to Fight AIDS, TB and Malaria; WHO; World Bank; UNICEF; UNAIDS; USAID; HHS/CDC; *MEASURE Evaluation and Family Health International. 2006. Monitoring and Evaluation Toolkit HIV/AIDS, Tuberculosis and Malaria.* WHO and Global Fund, Geneva, January 2006 (2nd ed.). http://www.theglobalfund.org/pdf/guidelines/pp_me_toolkit_en_lowres.pdf

Trochim, W.K. 2008. *Types of Research.* http://www.socialresearchmethods.net/kb/resques.php

Tyebkhan, G. 2003 *DECLARATION OF HELSINKI: the ethical cornerstone of human clinical research.* Indian J Dermatol Venereol Leprol. 2003 May-Jun;69(3):245-7.

UK Department of Health. 2001. *Governance arrangements for NHS Research Ethics Committees.* Accessed online on 3 November 2007 at http://www.doh.gov.uk/research

UNAIDS. 2003. *HIV Monitoring and evaluation training chapters.* Geneva: UNAIDS.

UNAIDS (Joint United Nations Programme on AIDS) and the MERG (global HIV Monitoring and Evaluation Reference Group). 2009. *Indicator standards: Operational guidelines.* UNAIDS: Geneva.

UNAIDS/Monitoring and Evaluation Reference Group (MERG). April 2008. *Organizing framework for a functional national HIV monitoring and evaluation system.* Geneva: UNAIDS.

UNAIDS, WHO. 2000. *Second-generation surveillance for HIV: The next decade.* Geneva, Switzerland: World Health Organisation. Accessed electronically on 23 October 2007 at http://www.who.int/emc

UNDP. 1997. *General guidelines for capacity assessment and development to support the development and implementation of national programme frameworks (NPF). UNDP. September 1994.* Accessed online on 30 March 2007 at www.pogar.org/publications/other/undp/governance/genguid97e.pdf.

U.S. Agency for International Development (USAID). 2007. *Data Quality Assurance Tool for Program-Level Indicators.* USAID: Washington DC. USAID. Accessed online on 30 May 2009 at http://www.pepfar.gov/documents/organization/79628.pdf

USAID. Undated. *Contraceptive security: Ready Lessons 5 – Using data for decision-making.* USAID: Washington DC.

Vercic, D. *Messages and Channels,* part of a World Bank Distance Learning Training Course. Available on the World Bank Learning Management System at "Communicating Reform -The Missing Link: A Distance-Learning Course for the Central Asia Region"

Wayman, J. C. 2005. *Involving Teachers in Data-Driven Decision Making: Using Computer Data Systems to Support Teacher Inquiry and Reflection,* in Journal Of Education For Students Placed At Risk, 10(3), 295–308

Weiss, H. 2007. *From the Editor's Desk. The Evaluation Exchange: A Periodical on Emerging Strategies in Evaluation.* Harvard Family Research Project, Harvard Graduate School of Education. 8(1), Spring 2007. Accessed online at http://www.hfrp.org/var/hfrp/storage/original/application/6bdf92c3d7e970e7270588109e23b678.pdf on 3 October 2008

Wholey, J.S. 1987, "*Evaluability Assessment: Developing Program Theory,*" in Bickman, l., ed., *Using Program Theory in Evaluation.*" New Directions for Program

Wikipedia. 2006. 'Evaluation' accessed at www.evaluationwiki.org/index.php/Evaluation_Definition (3Oct 2006)

Wikipedia. 2007. Searched for 'database management system', on 3 October 2007, and accessed at http://en.wikipedia.org/wiki/Database

Wilson, D. 2004. *World Bank contribution to Building National HIV/AIDS Monitoring and Evaluation Capacity in Africa: Going Beyond Indicator Development and Conceptual Training,* in Rugg, D., Peersman, G. and G. & M. Carael (eds). "Global Advances in Global HIV/AIDS Monitoring and Evaluation" New Directions in Evaluation, 103, UNAIDS, Fall 2004.

World Medical Association 2000. *DECLARATION OF HELSINKI - Ethical Principles for Medical Research Involving Human Subjects.* Accessed online on 2 April 2009 at http://www.wma.net/e/policy/pdf/17c.pdf

The following Resources were accessed online:

http://www.cpc.unc.edu/measure/tools/monitoring-evaluation-systems/data-quality-assurance-tools/RDQA%20Guidelines-Draft%207.30.08.pdf

www.uky.edu/CommInfoStudies/JAT/Telecommunications/300/Descriptive_statistics.ppt

home.business.utah.edu/bebrpsp/URPL5010/Lectures/10_DescriptiveStatistics.pdf

www.stat.psu.edu/~lsimon/stat250/fa99/slides/location/location.ppt

www.stat.nus.edu.sg/~stayapvb/lec2.ppt

www.pauldickman.com/teaching/game/descriptive_statistics.pdf

http://ils.unc.edu/~yanz/Content%20analysis.pdf

Index

Boxes, figures, and tables are indicated with b, f, and t following the page number.

A

accountability
  advocacy and, 229
  decentralization of government
    and, 6
  evaluation for, 372
  M&E unit location and, 64
  in partnerships, 129
  public support and, 426
  results-based M&E systems and, 3
activity-based costing (ABC) method, 208,
  210, 214
advocacy, communication, and culture, 19,
  225–46
  background, 227–28
  benefits of, 229–30
  definitions, 227–28
  developing and implementing plan for,
    237–42
    budget considerations, 241
    communication channels for,
      239–40, 246
    communication message agreement
      for, 239
    communications materials and
      monitoring plans for, 240–41
    organization of advocates for, 242
    resource mobilization, 242
    target audiences and allies for, 238
    understanding desired results,
      237–38, 238*t*
  examples for, 244–45
  implementation issues, 230–33
    communication channels, 232–33, 246
    leading efforts in, 230–31
    recipients, 230, 231–32
    techniques, implementation, and
      monitoring in, 233
  knowledge and skills, 225, 242–43
  learning activities for, 243
  organizational culture for, 233–36
    identifying M&E resistors, 235
    managing for results in, 234
    strategies for influencing, 235–36, 236*t*
  overview, 227
  results for this component, 228–29
  routine monitoring and, 257, 270–71
African Evaluation Association, 385
African Evaluation Guidelines, 386,
  408–12
AIDS. *See* HIV M&E functions
air travel and aviation, 450–51
alignment of organizations. See
  organizational structure and
  alignment
allocation of resources, 42
American Evaluation Association, 365
American University of Cairo, 37–38*b*
analysis of data. *See* data analysis
Answer Book for learning activities, 22
Anthes, K., 427
archiving of data, 356
Armstrong, J., 427
assembly-line approach to tasks, 71–72
assessment issues
  See also evaluation and research
  in communication efforts, 240–41
  in costed work plans, 200
  in evaluation and research, 378–79
  in grouping M&E functions, 71
  human capacity and, 92–93, 94*f*, 95,
    100–106, 111–20
  in M&E plans, 159–61, 165–66
  readiness, 4, 35–36, 37*b*, 39, 41–42
attendance registers, 282–84
auditing. *See* supportive supervision and
  data auditing
authority, organizational, 62, 70, 148
aviation and air travel, 450–51
Aviation Duty Consultation (UK), 451

B

Bali Roadmap, 451
baseline values, 5, 39, 162, 309
Bazerman, M.H., 419

bean counting, 251
behavioral surveillance, 291–92
"Belmont principles" for ethical research, 373–74
benchmarks, 148, 385
biases in surveys, 292, 294, 301–2*t*, 306
Binnendijk, A., 32
biological surveillance, 291–92
brainstorming activities, 134, 162, 203–4, 211, 239, 240
Breaking the Holding Pattern (Sustainable Development Commission & Institute for Public Policy Research), 450
brochures, 232, 243, 244
budget considerations
  in advocacy and communication, 231, 241
  assessments and, 160, 377
  in costed work plans, 201–2, 203, 206
  in evaluation and research, 372, 384
  information usage and, 425
  for supportive supervision, 349–50, 353
  with surveys, 297–98, 303, 309
Building monitoring, evaluation and reporting systems for HIV/AIDS programs (McCoy et al.), 179
buy-in of management
  in costed work plans, 201, 202
  databases and, 335
  in human capacity development, 103, 105, 109
  in M&E plans, 164
   in Egypt, 37*b*
  for National Evaluation and Research Strategy, 377
  in routing monitoring systems, 265
  in structure and organizational alignment, 69–70

C

Cabinet Information Decision Support Center (Egypt), 38*b*
capacity building
  See also human capacity
  for communication and advocacy, 231
  in database design and management, 331
  in evaluation and research, 371, 384

in M&E plans, 163–64, 167
  poverty reduction and, 94
  in routine monitoring, 258, 270, 349
carrots and sticks, 243
CCA (conventional cost accounting), 209, 210
census-type data, 250–51, 259, 294, 303
Centers for Disease Control and Prevention, U.S. (CDC), 329, 369–70, 391
Central Agency for Public Mobilization and Statistics (Egypt), 38*b*
cervical cancer screening, 304
chains of command, 73
champions (M&E advocates)
  communication channels and, 232
  of data and information, 424
  identification of, 69–70, 78, 235
  in M&E systems, 41, 44, 228
  of National Evaluation and Research Strategy, 377
  for national work plan, 202
change-management, 70, 76–77
channels of communication. *See* communication channels
chart junk, 440, 440*f*
Chicago Convention, 451
children. *See* orphans and vulnerable children
China, People's Republic of, M&E implementation in, 40–41
cholera, 423–24, 424*f*
civil society
  communication materials for, 243
  evaluation and research strategy and, 381, 383
  M&E plans and, 148
  national ethics committees and, 376
  partnerships and, 128, 131, 132, 132*t*
  registration of organizations, 258
  routine data and, 251
Climate Change Bill (UK), 451
coding schemes, 438
Coffman, J., 241
ColdFusion, 338
collection of data. *See* data collection
communication channels, 232–33, 239–40, 240*t*, 246
communication for M&E. *See* advocacy,

communication, and culture
communication messages, 239, 239*t*, 246
competencies for M&E, 103–4, 121–22
computer literacy, 341
Concept Note and Project Plan, 102, 103, 104–5
concept notes for database, 334–35
conferences and professional meetings, 96
confidentiality of survey respondents, 297
confounding variables, 305
consensus building, 204–5, 303
consent of participants, 297, 374
consultancy arrangements, 66–67, 67*f*
continuing education, 96–97
conventional cost accounting (CCA), 209, 210
corruption, 36–37, 42
costed work plans, 19, 195–223
  See also plans for M&E
  background, 197–99
  benefits of, 199–201
  definitions, 197–99
  format for, 219
  implementation issues, 201–2
  knowledge and skills, 195, 217
  learning activities for, 217–18, 220–23
  multi-year, multi-sectoral, and multi-level, 209–15
    brainstorming for, 211
    methodology selection, 209–11
    practical tips for, 214
    resource mobilization and assignment, 213–15
    unit cost table development, 211–12
  national M&E work plan, 166, 202–8
    advocacy for, 202
    brainstorming activities for, 203–4
    budgets in, 203
    consensus building for, 204–5
    M&E TWG involvement in, 203, 205–6
    practical tips for, 206–8
    reviewing and updating work plan, 206–8
    stakeholders' involvement in, 203
  overview, 197
  results for this component, 199
  system management and, 215–16
cost issues. *See* budget considerations

counter-reformers, 69–70, 78, 235
CRIS database, 329
cross-functional flow chart, 278, 280
culture. *See* advocacy, communication, and culture; organizational culture
curricula development, 45–53, 97, 98, 105, 384

D

data analysis, 434–36, 437–38, 465, 466–69
data archiving, 356
data auditing. *See* supportive supervision and data auditing
databases, 20, 321–42
  background, 323–25, 324*t*
  benefits of, 325–26
  coordinating agency, 263
  definitions, 323–25
  development guide for, 331*f*, 332*t*, 332–34
  government development process, 334–41
    developer services for, 339–40
    development contract and hardware, 340
    inventories, user requirements, and planning documents, 337–39
    IT policies and draft concept note development, 334–35
    maintenance issues, 341
    project sponsors, 335
    technical review group and planning specialist nominations, 336–37
  in human capacity development tracking, 99–100, 108
  implementation issues, 326–31
    data collection, 327*f*, 327–28, 327–28*t*
    functionality and security, 326–27
    IT policy, 326
    linkages and capacity building, 331, 331f
    software, 328–30
  knowledge and skills, 321, 341
  learning activity for, 342
  overview, 323
  results from this component, 325
  for routine monitoring, 267, 270, 271
data collection

databases and, 327*f*, 327–28, 327–28*t*
in data management process, 252
for human capacity development, 104
for joint missions/trips, 137–38
for M&E plans, 158, 166
in partnerships, 133
for routine monitoring, 276–81
for routing monitoring, 256–59, 259*f*,
267–68
for supportive supervision visits, 353–54
surveys and, 303, 305–6, 363
data dividends, 257–58
data entry, 306
data flow schematics, 276–81
data management charts, 278–79, 281
data management processes, 252–54, 268,
272, 285–86, 350, 429
data presentation. *See* visual presentation
of data
data quality, 160, 253, 253–54*t*, 272–73,
345–48, 346*t*
Data Quality Assurance tool, 160
data sets, dummy, 258
data source matrices, 183–84, 314
data-to-ink ratios, 440, 440*f*
data verification, 355, 356*t*
DBMS computer program, 324, 338
Dean, J.W., 427
debriefing, 139, 306
decentralization of governments, 6
decision making
case study on, 450–51
evaluative information for, 5, 39–40
for improving organizations, 419–22,
420–21*t*
organizational culture and, 428
real-time, 456–57
in supportive supervision and data
auditing, 349
decision trees, 182, 295*f*
Declaration of Helsinki, 373
Dennis, A.R., 430
Department for International
Development, 64
dependent variables, 304
descriptive statistics, 435–36, 436*f*
design effect, 310–11
design issues
for databases, 331, 333

in human capacity development, 104
in routing monitoring, 265–71
in structure and organizational
alignment, 68–77
with surveys, 301–2
developing countries, 40–43
DevInfo database, 328–29
directorates in organizational structure,
79–80
diseases
See also HIV M&E functions
cervical cancer screening, 304
cholera, 423–24, 424*f*
surveillance, 291–92, 392
dissemination matrices, 185, 186, 433*t*,
433–34
distance-learning, 96–97
distortion of truth in graphical materials,
443*f*
divisional structures, 60–61
double-reporting systems, 230
dummy data sets, 258

E

Education Act, 229
education sector, 152
efficiency, increase in, 371–72
Egypt, M&E systems in, 37–38*b*, 41
Electronic Resource Library (ERL)
evaluation and research in, 372, 376,
380, 383
human capacity development in, 95, 104,
108
language and writing styles in, 158
partnerships and, 131
resource mobilization in, 214
SWOT analysis in, 133
Emissions Trading Scheme (EU), 451
end-users, 430
Epi Info database, 329
ERL. *See* Electronic Resource Library
ethical issues
in evaluation and research, 373–76,
374–75*t*, 385–89, 391–92, 408, 412
in supportive supervision, 351
with surveys, 296–97, 303
European Union, 36
evaluation and research, 20–21, 359–412

in-service training. *See* on-the-job training

Institute for Public Policy Research, 450

institutional analysis, 111

Institutional Review Board (CDC), 391

International Monetary Fund, 34

IT (information technology) policies, 326, 334

J

Javascript, 338

job descriptions, 63, 74–75, 103, 216

joint missions/trips, 127, 129, 137–40

Joint United Nations Programme on AIDS (UNAIDS), 7, 157, 160, 191, 329

junk in charts, 440, 440f

K

Ketz De Vries, M.F.R., 76

knowledge networks, 96

Krumpe, E.E., 179

Kusek, Jody Zall, 4, 30, 31, 234

L

Labor Ministry, 296

language choice and writing styles, 158, 245, 270, 300, 376, 430–31

Leung, W.C., 304

line structures, 59–60

Local Government Authorities (LGAs), 126, 201, 230, 232, 257, 270

logical frameworks, 147, 153, 169–75

M

Mackay, K., 160

mainstreaming, 240

Malaysia, M&E experience in, 37*b*

management buy-in. *See* buy-in of management

management information systems, 371

management processes. *See* data management processes

managing for results, 9, 129–30, 151–52, 233–34

mandates, organizational, 62, 70, 148

M&E. *See* monitoring and evaluation

M&E TWG. *See* Technical Working Group

Massell, D., 427

mathematical modeling, 209

matrix structures, 61

  See also data source matrices; dissemination matrices; information product matrices

McCoy, K.L., 179

Medium-Term Expenditure Framework, 201

mentorship, 258

milestones in work plans, 206

missions. *See* joint missions/trips

mobilization of resources. *See* resource mobilization

modeling, mathematical, 209

modular training courses, 96–97

monitoring and evaluation (M&E)

  advocacy, communication, and culture for, 225–46

  costed work plans for, 195–223

  databases for, 321–42

  definition of, 2

  evaluation and research and, 359–412

  human capacity for, 89–122

  organizational structure and alignment of, 57–87

  partnerships for, 123–41

  plans for, 143–94

  results improvement for, 413–69

  routine monitoring for, 247–86

  supportive supervision and data auditing for, 343–58

  surveys for, 287–319

  toolkit for, 12–23, 13–17*t*

monitoring-without-indicators, 265

Most Significant Changes methodology, 265

N

National Commission for the Protection of Human Participants of Biomedical and Behavioral Research (U.S.), 373

National Council for Women (Egypt), 37*b*

National Evaluation and Research Strategy,

for communication and advocacy, 231
in data management process, 253
in evaluation and research, 409
joint missions/trips and, 139–40
in M&E systems, 5, 32, 40
for results improvement, 417, 430–33
in routine monitoring, 257–58
for supportive supervision visits, 356–57
for surveys, 306–7
workshops for, 264
research and evaluation. *See* evaluation and
research
Research Ethics Training Curriculum, 376
resistors of M&E system. *See* counter-
reformers
Resnik, D., 374
resource allocation, 42
resource gaps, 213–14
resource mobilization
for advocacy work, 242
costed work plans and, 200–201, 202,
213–15
for database development, 339
for evaluation and research, 380, 383–84
M&E plans and, 163, 167
responsibility, organizational, 62, 63,
148–49, 205, 208
results chains, 154, 154*f*, 156, 238*t*
results frameworks, 147, 153, 169–75
results improvement, 21, 413–69
background, 416–22, 418*f*
benefits of, 423–26, 425*f*
definitions, 416–22
knowledge and skills, 413, 449–50
learning activities for, 450–64
decision making case study, 450–51
graphical display of data, 451–55
program implementation, 458–64
real-time decision making, 456–57
overview, 415
qualitative data analysis, 437–38, 466–69
quantitative data analysis, 434–36, 465
results for this component, 422–23
routine monitoring for, 458–64
strategies to promote, 426–34
addressing problems, 426–27
data management processes and
quality assurance, 429–30
end-users in, 430

professional development, 428–29
reporting and presenting information,
430–33
standardized information product
formats, 433–34
supportive leadership and
organizational culture, 427–28,
428*t*
visual presentation of data, 431–32*f*,
431–33, 439–49, 440–49*f*, 451–55
rights of refusal, 352
Rist, Ray C., 4, 30, 31, 234
Rossi, P.H., 365
routine monitoring, 20, 247–86
background, 250–54, 252*t*
benefits of, 255–56, 256*t*, 291
definitions, 250–54, 252*t*
designing new system for, 265–71
buy-in for, 265
data collection and data flow for,
267–68, 276–81
data identification, 267
data management process, 268, 272,
285–86
guidelines for, 268–70, 269–70*t*
implementation preparation for,
270–71
inventory for, 266–67, 274–75
launching system, 271
M&E TWG involvement in, 266
forms for, 282–84
implementation issues, 256–65, 270–71
capacity building, 258
data collection for, 256–59, 259*f*
linking agencies' systems, 263–64
planning process linkage, 260–63
qualitative and quantitative data, 265
reporting rates, 257–58
sample surveys and, 264
supply and demand, 259
knowledge and skills, 247, 271
learning activities for, 272–73, 458–64
overview, 249–50
results from this component, 254–55
supportive supervision and data auditing
and, 349–50, 354–55